A Royal Passion

Also by Katie Whitaker

Mad Madge: Margaret Cavendish, Duchess of Newcastle,
Royalist, Writer and Romantic

KATIE WHITAKER

A ROYAL PASSION

THE TURBULENT MARRIAGE OF
CHARLES I AND HENRIETTA MARIA

Weidenfeld & Nicolson

LONDON

First published in Great Britain in 2010
by Weidenfeld & Nicolson

1 3 5 7 9 10 8 6 4 2

© Katie Whitaker 2010

A CIP catalogue record for this book
is available from the British Library.

ISBN: 978 0 297 86019 8

Typeset by Input Data Services Ltd,
Bridgwater, Somerset

Printed in Great Britain by
CPI Mackays, Chatham, Kent

The Orion Publishing Group's policy is to use papers that are natural,
renewable and recyclable and made from wood grown in sustainable
forests. The logging and manufacturing processes are expected to conform
to environmental regulations of the country of origin.

Weidenfeld & Nicolson

Orion Publishing Group Ltd
Orion House
5 Upper Saint Martin's Lane
London, WC2H 9EA

An Hachette UK Company

www.orionbooks.co.uk

For Elizabeth and Alexander

And in memory of
Vicki Harris
1967–2008

CONTENTS

LIST OF ILLUSTRATIONS

1. Charles and Henrietta departing for the chase, by Daniel Mytens. The Royal Collection © 2008, Her Majesty Queen Elizabeth II. Photographer: A. C. Cooper.
2. The Duke of Buckingham and his family, after Gerrit van Honthorst. © National Portrait Gallery, London.
3. Charles I and Henrietta Maria with their two eldest children, Prince Charles and Princess Mary, by Sir Anthony Van Dyck. The Royal Collection © 2008, Her Majesty Queen Elizabeth II. Photographer: A. C. Cooper.
4. Charles I with M. de St Antoine, by Sir Anthony Van Dyck. The Royal Collection © 2008, Her Majesty Queen Elizabeth II. Photographer: EZM.
5. Henrietta Maria, by Sir Anthony Van Dyck. The Royal Collection © 2008, Her Majesty Queen Elizabeth II. Photographer: A. C. Cooper
6. A view of Greenwich, c.1632, by Adriaen van Stalbemt. The Royal Collection © 2008, Her Majesty Queen Elizabeth II.
7. Charles I and Henrietta Maria dining in public, by Gerrit Houckgeest. The Royal Collection © 2008, Her Majesty Queen Elizabeth II. Photographer: SC.

8. Lucy, Countess of Carlisle, by Pierre Lombart, after Sir Anthony Van Dyck. © National Portrait Gallery, London.

9. The five eldest children of Charles I, by Sir Anthony Van Dyck. The Royal Collection © 2008, Her Majesty Queen Elizabeth II. Photographer: EZM.

10. William Laud, after Sir Anthony Van Dyck. © National Portrait Gallery, London.

11. Thomas Wentworth, 1st Earl of Strafford, after Sir Anthony Van Dyck. © National Portrait Gallery, London.

12. Marie de' Medici, after Sir Anthony Van Dyck. Reproduced by kind permission of the Syndics of Cambridge University Library. (*Icones Principum, virorum doctorum* ... (Antwerp, 1646): shelf-mark LE.32.19).

13. Charles I at his trial, by Edward Bower. The Royal Collection © 2008, Her Majesty Queen Elizabeth II. Photographer: SC.

14. The trial of King Charles I. Reproduced by kind permission of the Syndics of Cambridge University Library. (John Nalson, *A True Copy of the Journal of the High Court of Justice* ... (London, 1684: shelfmark R.8.40)

15. The execution of King Charles I, after unknown artist. © National Portrait Gallery, London.

16. Henrietta Maria, by William Faithorne. © National Portrait Gallery, London.

ACKNOWLEDGEMENTS

I wish wholeheartedly to thank my literary agents on both sides of the Atlantic, Peter Robinson and George Lucas, who helped the book take shape in its early stages, and my editors Bea Hemming and Maria Guarnaschelli, whose contributions were invaluable in the final stages of the process.

In the intervening years I have been truly grateful for the able research assistance of Eric Langley, Stewart and Becky Mottram, Chris Richardson, Jill Ramshaw and Vicki Harris. I would also like to thank the staff of the British Library, the Public Record Office, Cambridge University Library, Leeds University Library, The Royal Collection, The National Portrait Gallery, and my local branch of the North Yorkshire Libraries Service, who were all most helpful.

My husband, Weem, has been unstinting throughout in help and encouragement, and the boundless energies of my children, Elizabeth and Alexander, have provided most welcome distractions.

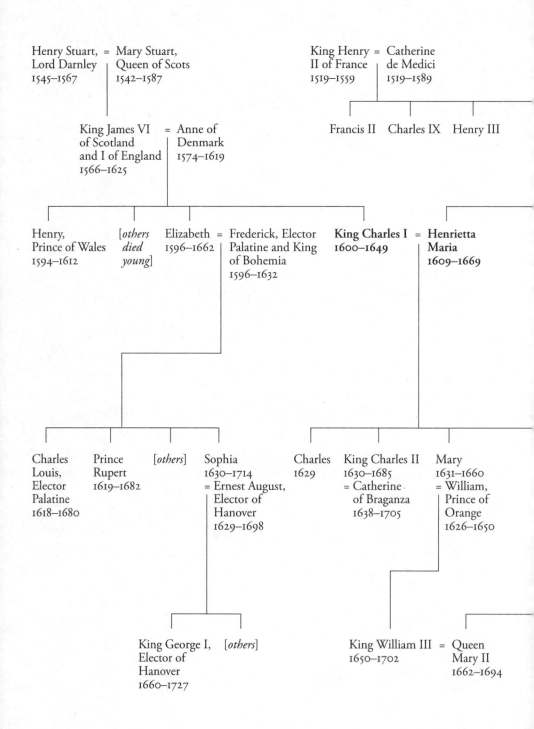

Henry Stuart, = Mary Stuart,
Lord Darnley | Queen of Scots
1545–1567 | 1542–1587

King Henry = Catherine
II of France | de Medici
1519–1559 | 1519–1589

King James VI = Anne of
of Scotland | Denmark
and I of England | 1574–1619
1566–1625

Francis II   Charles IX   Henry III

Henry,
Prince of Wales
1594–1612

[*others
died
young*]

Elizabeth = Frederick, Elector
1596–1662 | Palatine and King
of Bohemia
1596–1632

King Charles I = **Henrietta
1600–1649 | Maria
1609–1669**

Charles
Louis,
Elector
Palatine
1618–1680

Prince
Rupert
1619–1682

[*others*]

Sophia
1630–1714
= Ernest August,
Elector of
Hanover
1629–1698

Charles
1629

King Charles II
1630–1685
= Catherine
of Braganza
1638–1705

Mary
1631–1660
= William,
Prince of
Orange
1626–1650

King George I, [*others*]
Elector of
Hanover
1660–1727

King William III = Queen
1650–1702 | Mary II
1662–1694

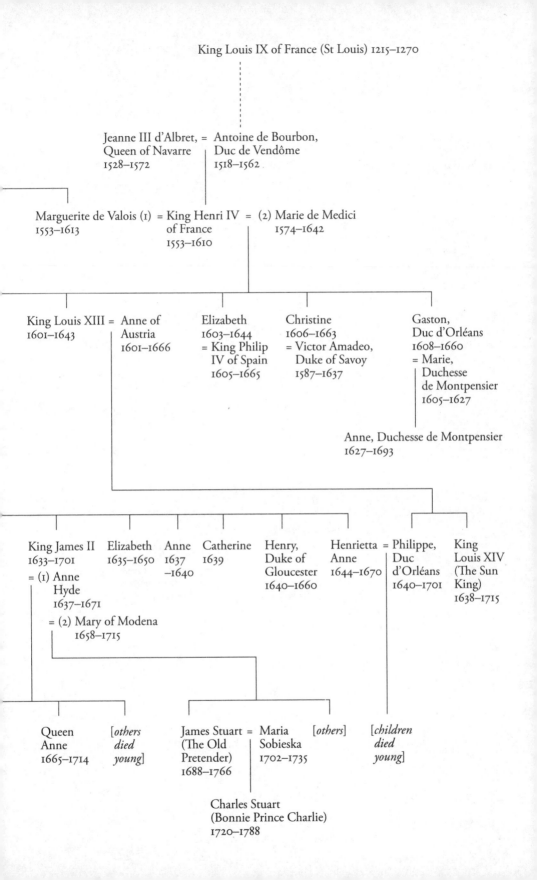

King Louis IX of France (St Louis) 1215–1270

Jeanne III d'Albret, = Antoine de Bourbon,
Queen of Navarre | Duc de Vendôme
1528–1572 | 1518–1562

Marguerite de Valois (1) = King Henri IV = (2) Marie de Medici
1553–1613 | of France | 1574–1642
| 1553–1610

King Louis XIII = Anne of
1601–1643 | Austria
| 1601–1666

Elizabeth
1603–1644
= King Philip
IV of Spain
1605–1665

Christine
1606–1663
= Victor Amadeo,
Duke of Savoy
1587–1637

Gaston,
Duc d'Orléans
1608–1660
= Marie,
| Duchesse
| de Montpensier
| 1605–1627

Anne, Duchesse de Montpensier
1627–1693

King James II
1633–1701
= (1) Anne
Hyde
1637–1671
= (2) Mary of Modena
1658–1715

Elizabeth
1635–1650

Anne
1637
–1640

Catherine
1639

Henry,
Duke of
Gloucester
1640–1660

Henrietta =
Anne
1644–1670

Philippe,
Duc
d'Orléans
1640–1701

King
Louis XIV
(The Sun
King)
1638–1715

Queen
Anne
1665–1714

[others
died
young]

James Stuart =
(The Old
Pretender)
1688–1766

Maria
Sobieska
1702–1735

[others]

[children
died
young]

Charles Stuart
(Bonnie Prince Charlie)
1720–1788

FOREWORD

Where does a book come from? What drives a writer to seize on an idea and see it through to its completion, perhaps many years later? For me the inspiration came from a collection of letters penned more than 350 years ago, but so intimate and impassioned that they drew me at once into their writers' world. For five years in the mid-seventeenth century, while thousands died in Britain's civil wars and a new political order took shape on the ruins of royal power, King Charles I and his beloved wife, Henrietta Maria, kept up a correspondence in spite of all difficulties and dangers. Every day or two a new letter crossed the sea between England and the Continent, full of plans, hopes, fears and confessions, and the undying devotion each felt for the other, which alone made all else bearable. 'Thy love preserves my life,' Charles told his wife, and Henrietta responded in kind: 'I shall never have my health till I see you again,' 'I cannot be happy.' In these letters I found a passion and loyalty that was irresistible, even as the terrible strains of war were testing their relationship to the limit.

I was moved, but also surprised. The characters I saw here were worlds away from the Charles and Henrietta passed down to us by centuries of historical tradition. The old story tells of a cold, haughty king, shy, weak and irresolute, and of a queen who metamorphosed from a frivolous teenage bride into a termagant who domineered ruthlessly over her husband and children. Instead I saw a woman of tremendous courage, energy and political insight, determined to protect those she loved. And Charles came to life as a man with a mission, who believed unreservedly in the justice of his cause and would never abandon his political and religious principles 'whatever it cost me'. This faith and his unshakeable love for his wife were the twin stars guiding his course, although their conflicting demands sometimes tore him almost in two.

The freshness and immediacy of the couple's letters and the drama of their situation made me determined to look further – for other original sources that would allow me, somehow, to get under their skins and see what made them tick. Who were these people who seemed so different from their traditional images? What bound them together so powerfully? Soon I realised that no normal birth-to-death biography of either of the royal pair could go to the heart of their characters; they were too intimately involved with each other. My quest, I realised, was for a joint biography – a portrait of the passionate royal marriage that lay at the heart of mid-seventeenth century Britain's descent into civil war.

On my way I amassed a huge array of primary sources. Charles and Henrietta's own letters, memoirs and speeches were vital, of course, but so too were the reports of foreign ambassadors stationed in London, and especially the secret missives of the Pope's diplomatic agent, who was welcomed at Henrietta's court in defiance of English Puritan public opinion. British government state papers, the private diaries and letters of the couple's friends and enemies, the literary outpourings of their courtiers, political tracts, international treaties, clergymen's sermons, doctors' prescription books, portraits and prints, financial accounts and inventories all played their part.

Among these I found manuscripts that had barely been looked at by historians in the centuries since they were first written: papers that revealed astonishing, undiscovered stories that went far beyond the sketchy summaries, misrepresentations and bowdlerisings passed on by the occasional Victorian scholar who had been here before me. Here I read of the pioneering use of forceps in the delivery of Henrietta's first, premature baby. In glowing colours I saw the happy affection of the royal couple among their children at Richmond Palace, and the pleasure of their eldest son when Henrietta took him to mass contrary to her husband's orders. In another case, a handful of French manuscripts in the British Library were sufficient to explode the entire myth of Henrietta as a selfish, tantrum-prone teenager – a story created for his own ends by Henrietta's Grand Chamberlain, the Comte de Tillières, and repeated by historians ever since. Having once seen the unreliability of Tillières's memoirs, I turned to other sources instead, piecing together a new account of the couple's first, explosive year together.

In published sources, too, there were new discoveries to be made: for instance, an illustration in an obscure seventeenth-century book of court poems, showing Charles and Henrietta's third child, James, the eager sportsman, out on the tennis court dressed in specialised tennis kit, a costume that historians knew existed but for which they thought no visual evidence survived. I was particularly eager to recover the freshness and reality of the couple's lives, and make the events of history feel immediate and contingent, like our own experience of everyday life. To achieve this I paid scrupulous attention to the dates of the events I followed, often on a day-by-day basis – a method that showed up telling details of their marriage even among old familiar sources like the Calendars of State Papers and the reports of the Historical Manuscripts Commission. Here, revealed for the first time, was Henrietta retreating into lute lessons just as war was escalating between England and France in 1626. Here too, surprisingly, was the fact that Charles and Henrietta's supposed great reconciliation after two tense years of marriage – a reconciliation portrayed by numerous earlier biographers – was in fact only by post: the couple were seventy miles apart at the time and had not seen each other for weeks.

These and many other discoveries combined to build up the rich fabric of Charles and Henrietta's life together and brought the pair alive as fascinating, complex individuals, far from the conventional caricatures reproduced by centuries of Protestant historians who were only too ready to follow the hostile assessments of the couple's enemies.

The story is certainly one that deserves telling afresh. This was a marriage of huge historical importance. Charles was the last medieval king in Britain – a man imbued with all the ideals of chivalry, who believed he was appointed by God to rule. His government and his marriage sparked off a revolution that turned his kingdom into the first modern republic, grounded in new ideals of liberty, equality and citizens' rights. In Britain this new political order existed only briefly, but the world had been changed for ever. Kings could now be held accountable to their people; deposing a monarch for political principles was no longer unthinkable; republicanism and democracy had entered the European stream of ideas and would not go away. In the coming centuries the democratic principles of Charles and Henrietta's opponents would fire further wars of liberation, from the American War of Independence and the French Revolution to the Soviet Revolution and beyond. And in Britain itself, though other monarchs returned to the throne, they would never again be absolute; they knew now that they were there only by the will of the people.

However, the real fascination of Charles and Henrietta's marriage lies not in its effect on later ages, but in the story itself: a drama of epic proportions. Theirs was one of the greatest and most unlikely romances of history: the tale of a mismatched couple who entered on their arranged marriage in innocence and hope, only to be bitterly disappointed, yet who at last fell passionately in love in defiance of all the forces pushing them apart. By 1630, five years into their marriage, the pair seemed set to live happily ever after, like characters in a fairy tale. And yet the greatest twist was still to come. As Parliament attacked the whole basis of their rule, the false calm of Charles and Henrietta's lives was shattered and their story becomes a dark political thriller, set in a chilling world of deception, plots and machinations, of coups and counter-coups, violence and death. The outcome at last was war, pitting the King against his own subjects. Here we enter the realm of true tragedy, with the principal players' destinies driven by their own character flaws and idiosyncracies, which they themselves never managed to see.

Woven throughout is a story of love: a love that fuelled the couple's desperate attempts to win back the idyllic life they had forged together; a love that drove the King to precipitate civil war to save his wife; a love that motivated them in their labours through many vicissitudes of fortune, yet brought them in the end to isolation, downfall and destruction. It was a love that shaped the course of British and world history, a love that was, as one observer of the time put it, 'beyond expression'.

PROLOGUE

Winter 1649

A round noon on 9 February 1649, Queen Henrietta Maria sat down to dinner in the Palace of the Louvre. Here, in her ground-floor apartments looking out over the River Seine, she was just a few rooms away from the bedchamber where she had been born almost forty years before.[1] As a girl of fifteen, seated on a throne in another nearby state chamber, Henrietta had received her first love letter from the English prince she was to marry. Everything about her then had been French: her exquisitely tailored silk dress, her hair in tiny curls, her witty conversation, her whole outlook on the world. But now, after twenty-three years of marriage, Paris was merely 'a sad place of exile'.[2] Her love for her husband and her children – three sons and three daughters still survived of the nine babies she had borne – tied her to England, as did a real affection for the country and its people. Visitors to the Louvre were regaled with praises of the land she had been forced to leave. For ten or twelve years, they heard, she had been 'the happiest princess in the world'.[3] Her husband, King Charles I – 'mon cher cœur', 'my dear heart' – was the best of men: 'good, just, wise', 'a king, a husband and a friend' all in one. The love between them was 'the admiration of all Europe'.[4] In those years, the continental

1

mainland had been torn apart by the 'fury ... miseries and desolation' of the Thirty Years War. Britain alone had flourished 'in entire peace and universal plenty':

> Tourneys, masques, theatres better become
> Our halcyon days. What though the German drum
> Bellow for freedom and revenge? The noise
> Concerns not us, nor should divert our joys.[5]

Now all that was past. In the south wing of the Louvre, Henrietta inhabited some of the most splendid rooms in France. Rebuilt by a succession of her ancestors in the previous century, this section of the palace was in lavish Renaissance style, with classical columns and statues, and ranks of huge rectangular windows allowing the light to flood through. Inside, the walls were smothered in paintings, tapestries and mirrors; the ceilings were elaborately moulded in plaster and richly painted. The furniture was of the finest; Henrietta's state bed was upholstered in silks and velvets, embroidered with gold and silver. Yet none of this was hers. She had no personal mementoes: the jewels she had brought from England were gone; her family portraits had been left on the palace walls at home. Everything here came from charity alone, lent by her brother's widow, the French Queen Regent, Anne of Austria, who had moved Henrietta into the vacant palace four years earlier.

At the time she had fled to France not just for her own safety, but for her husband's too. 'As your affairs stand, they would be in danger if you come to help me, and I know that your affection would make you risk everything for that,' she wrote to him from her sickbed in Exeter, doubled up with 'cruel pains' and struggling to breathe. With a parliamentarian army advancing to besiege her, she fled westwards into Cornwall. 'Adieu, my dear heart,' she wrote from Truro. 'If the wind is favourable, I shall set off tomorrow ... I am hazarding my life, that I may not incommode your affairs ... If I die, believe that you will lose a person who has never been other than entirely yours, and who by her affection has deserved that you should not forget her.'[6] As she crossed the Channel under fire from a fleet of parliamentarian warships, Henrietta's sole fear was of capture and imprisonment. The captain, she ordered, was 'to set light to the powder-magazine' and blow up the ship if he saw she could not escape. It was one of those moments of wartime heroism that her followers celebrated, the Queen 'one moment saved, another moment almost taken, ... relying only on God and her unshakeable courage'.[7]

In November 1644 she had entered Paris in triumph, sharing a gilded carriage with the French Queen Regent and six-year-old King Louis XIV. The King's guards rode before them; the French nobility followed in their coaches. Trumpets blared, church bells rang, bright hangings adorned the streets. At the Louvre dignitaries galore made flattering speeches.

However, Henrietta's visitors were shocked at the sight of the pale shadow they encountered. Madame de Motteville, a French lady-in-waiting who now became Henrietta's frequent companion, gives the clearest portrait of her, 'much disfigured by the greatness of her illness and her misfortunes', 'so pierced with her sorrows, that she wept almost all the time'. The heavenly queen painted by Van Dyck in former years – a glorious brunette, elegant and poised – was all but gone. Just a few traces remained: 'beautiful eyes, a good complexion and a well-made nose'. The dominant impression was of a woman, 'thin and small', who stooped a little, 'and her mouth, which was not naturally beautiful, had become large in the emaciation of her face'.[8] That was the sympathetic version. To less partial observers Henrietta seemed positively ugly: a 'little woman with long lean arms, crooked shoulders, and teeth protruding from her mouth like guns from a fort', as her niece Sophia put it.[9] Yet this impression did not last long. Henrietta's charm was irresistible. 'She had an infinity of wit, that sparkling wit which pleases beholders,' Madame de Motteville recalled. 'She was agreeable in society, courteous, pleasant and easy to get on with; living without the slightest ceremony amongst those who had the honour of being near her. Her temperament was inclined towards mirth; and among her tears, if something amusing occurred to her, she would somehow stop crying to entertain the company.' All in all 'she made herself loved by everyone'. Even the young Sophia was won round after a few minutes' conversation and 'from that time forward I considered her quite handsome'.[10]

Briefly that winter Henrietta seemed a queen once more, with 'numerous ladies in waiting, maids of honour, carriages, guards and footmen'. But within months this great French court had gone, for Henrietta would not pay them. Instead she sent almost all her government stipend to her husband, keeping for herself only what 'seemed absolutely necessary for her subsistence'. By 1648 she was nearing destitution. The French royal family, in conflict with the Paris Parliament, had stopped her stipend. One by one Henrietta sold her fine clothes, her furniture and the last of her jewels, just 'to be able to subsist a few days longer'.[11] She could no longer pay the few English courtiers who continued in her service, so they too were dressed in old, worn clothes, without jewels, struggling to survive on credit that the Parisian tradesmen were unwilling to give. As violence escalated on the streets of Paris that winter, the French royal family fled to the castle at St-Germain-en-Laye, ten miles to the west, while their army laid siege to the city. Left behind at the Louvre, Henrietta saw 'a lasting civil war' approaching, much like the English one she had left behind. Paris was completely cut off. Already people were going hungry, 'for the price of all things doubles and trebles upon us'.[12]

Yet still Henrietta's little band of courtiers kept up the proprieties. The British court before the war had been the most ceremonious in Europe and now, at that midday meal on Friday 9 February 1649, Henrietta was served with full royal etiquette. Her table was covered with an oriental carpet with a white cloth laid over it. A large salt cellar and a platter of new-baked bread stood in the centre. On a side table were basins and ewers for the Queen to wash her hands. When Henrietta was seated, one of her chaplains – a Capuchin in a plain brown habit – said grace in Latin. Then a procession of gentlemen entered, with swords at their sides and lace collars round their necks, each bearing a platter of meat or fish. On bended knee, the sewer (or server) at their head set every dish down on Henrietta's table, where her carver bowed, then cut some meat from each. The first pieces were tasted by the courtiers who had carried them in. Then Henrietta might eat, while her cupbearer stood by a sideboard of glasses and decanters, ready to present her wine, on bended knee, whenever she wanted to drink.

The rules were strict. No one was to come too close to the Queen, nor turn their backs towards her; if they had to walk away from her, they did it backwards. And no one sat down with Henrietta, since no one there equalled her rank. Instead her English ladies and gentlemen stood in a semicircle behind her chair. Meanwhile the Queen must eat with the greatest delicacy. She was to cut her bread, not break it with her hands. She must take salt from the salt cellar using her knife, wiped clean on a piece of bread, not on her napkin. She must try some of every dish, and wipe her mouth on her napkin before drinking. When finished, she must clean her cutlery on a piece of bread and set it down on the table, not in her dish. Then, after another Latin grace, she would wash her hands in a fresh basin of water.[13]

Today, however, Henrietta was hardly eating. She had slept badly, as was becoming her habit. She kept up a brave face by day, 'yet,' her ladies noted, 'her nights are more sad than usual'. The emerging French Civil War, so similar to her recent experience, doubtless weighed on her spirits, as did the utter destitution facing her. But these anxieties were light, she said, compared to her desperate worries for her husband, who faced a far 'greater calamity'.[14]

Since Henrietta's arrival in Paris, King Charles I had lost his war with Parliament. For two years now he had been a prisoner, cut off from those he loved, striving vainly either to negotiate an agreement with his captors or escape to join his wife in France. Occasionally Henrietta's letters got through to him, carried by loyal supporters who risked imprisonment and even torture if discovered. Once it was 'a handsome lady, and wondrous bold' who slipped a letter behind the hangings in his apartments, where his guards discovered it, but Parliament could make nothing of the cipher in which it was written. Another time a former royalist army officer, disguised as a peasant, stood with a fishing rod on a narrow bridge and passed up Henrietta's letter as the King crossed over. Caught by Charles's guards and questioned vigorously, he revealed what he knew: most importantly, that Henrietta urged her husband 'to accept any terms' his enemies offered and save himself, even if it meant she could never return to England.[15] Charles found great comfort in these letters, seeing his wife's 'sympathy with me in my afflictions': true proof 'that she loves me, not my fortunes'. Though driven away 'by my own subjects', she was still present in 'my own heart'.[16]

In all other respects he was unutterably alone. True, he was treated with full royal ceremony, just as before the war, but none of his former followers or friends was allowed access to him. Instead, his guards and servants were new men, 'appointed by parliament'.[17] Hardest to bear was the religious repression.[18] Charles was devoted to the grand religious ceremonies that he and his archbishop, William Laud, had enforced during his years of glory. For him, these were 'nearest to the practice of the Apostles', the only true way to approach God.[19] He detested Puritans, with their rejection of ceremony and use of extempore prayers. Their religious freedom was merely a cover for rebellion, he believed. And of all the Puritan sects, he particularly loathed Presbyterianism, as being utterly 'incompatible with monarchy'. He had learnt this principle from his father, King James, who had hated the preachings forced on him as the young King of Scotland. 'Scotch Presbytery', James had famously declared, 'agreeth as well with monarchy as God and the Devil.' And now Charles himself had 'too dearly bought the certain knowledge of it'.[20]

Back in the 1630s Charles had deprived English Puritans of their ministers. Now the tables were turned. All his requests for Anglican clergymen to 'perform the usual offices about his person' were refused; Presbyterian chaplains only were provided for him and his attendants.[21] Sometimes Charles engaged these men in debate. In years gone by he had delighted in tying his wife's Roman Catholic priests in knots, with his ruthless logic and profound knowledge of the Bible and the Church Fathers. Now he allowed his Presbyterian companions to be 'very earnest' in their opinions while replying himself with jokes, very 'pleasant and merry', finding some entertainment and relief from the solitude of his captivity, and often having the best of the encounter.[22]

But he would never conform to their religious practice. At mealtimes these chaplains stood ready to say grace, but Charles would not hear them. Instead, standing under his cloth-of-state, he prayed by himself, before sitting down to eat. Every Sunday he absented himself from their chapel ceremonies. Alone in his bedchamber, having ordered that no one enter 'until he called', he occupied himself in 'private devotion'. Even on weekdays he spent several hours every day 'in reading and other pious exercises'.

He had become, he said, 'my own chaplain'.[23] He wrote his own prayers, confessed his sins to God and begged forgiveness for three lapses in particular: once when he had 'suffered innocent blood to be shed by a false pretended way of justice'; again when he had 'permitted a wrong way of Thy worship to be set up in Scotland'; and again when he had 'injured the Bishops in England'. 'O Lord,' Charles prayed, 'I have no excuse to make, no hope left, but in the multitude of Thy mercies.' Reflecting on the events of recent years, Charles set pen to paper, seeking meaning in all that had happened to him. This was his consolation now: that everything had been God's will, a judgement on him for his sins, to which he must humbly submit in hopes of forgiveness.[24]

It was this religious faith in combination with his political beliefs that gave Charles his inner strength. He would abandon neither 'for any extremity or misery that may befall me'. In the last resort, he was sure, the British nations could not manage without him: the parliamentarians would 'ask so much and use it so ill' that finally the people would be 'glad to relodge the power they had taken from the Crown'.[25] So Charles remained 'patient and cheerful' throughout his troubles.[26] It was a matter of pride: he was 'above complaints or bewailings', he said. '*Dum spiro spero*' was his motto now: 'While I breathe I hope'.[27]

For a time he had his children's company. 'Do you know me, child?' he asked the seven-year-old Henry, whom he had last seen five years previously when the boy had been left behind as Charles and Henrietta fled from London in 1642. 'I am your father, child; and it is not one of the least of my misfortunes that I have brought you and your brothers and sisters into the world to share my miseries.'[28] Through the summer of 1647, Charles often saw Henry, Elizabeth and the thirteen-year-old James, who all remained in England, prisoners like himself. He was full of forebodings, instructing them carefully 'how to behave themselves, if the worst should befall him', when their eldest brother, Charles Prince of Wales, would be their king, to whom they must show 'unshaken . . . affection and duty'. To little Henry, Charles was especially insistent. He was 'never to be persuaded or threatened out of . . . the [Anglican] Church', and he must never be made a puppet king by his parliamentary keepers 'whilst either of his elder brothers lived'. This Charles repeated every time they met, 'with all the earnestness and passion he could express'.[29]

Charles found great solace in his children. Sometimes they dined together, with James in the place of honour on the King's right hand. 'His majesty is very fond of him, and loving to all the children; he bears the young lady often in his arms,' the news-sheets reported. At other times Charles expressed 'much joy' in his offspring, watching them 'running and playing' in the garden.[30] However, all too soon Charles was a close prisoner once more, as his opponents grew ever more extreme. The King 'was so great a dissembler, and so false a man, that he was not to be trusted', Oliver Cromwell declared. Parliament resolved to negotiate no longer, but to work instead 'towards the settlement of the kingdom without having further recourse to the King'. In Paris, Henrietta begged the Queen Regent for aid 'with her tears' but to no avail.[31] Hope revived only in the summer of 1648, with a flurry of royalist uprisings. Eagerly Henrietta sold the last of her jewels, giving the money to her eighteen-year-old son, Charles Prince of Wales, who left Paris to take command of the main English war fleet, which had mutinied in favour of the King. Under the combined threat of English, Scottish and Irish forces, Parliament agreed to reopen talks. Their armies were soon victorious and Prince Charles's fleet retreated to Holland. At Newport on the Isle of Wight, the talks continued nonetheless.

Everything depended on Charles's decisions now. He could expect no further military support, Henrietta wrote: France was too disturbed by its own internal divisions. And so, she implored, he must 'embrace all such counsels and consultations that may tend to the peace and tranquillity of his three kingdoms'.[32] By October, Charles was offering greater concessions than ever before. He would abolish bishops and allow Presbyterianism for three years. He would give Parliament control of the nation's armed forces for twenty years, and the government of Ireland would be settled in whatever way Parliament preferred. 'Censure us not for having parted with too much of our own right,' he begged his eldest son and heir. Although it was a great price, it aimed at a great gain: 'security to us, peace to our people'. Later, another Parliament 'would remember how useful a King's power is to a people's liberty'.[33] However, Charles was full of regrets, wishing there was only himself to consider. Then, like Job, 'I would willingly have rather chosen misery than sin.' Once he wept: 'the biggest drops that I ever saw fall from an eye', his secretary noted, though Charles turned his head away, 'loth to be discerned', and quickly recovered himself.[34]

But his offer to Parliament came too late. Even as it was being carried to London, where many MPs favoured accepting it, the army took matters into its own hands, saying that the King – 'that man of blood' – had caused the Civil War. Now he must be tried for high treason, to 'account for that blood he had shed, and mischief he had done to his utmost, against the Lord's cause and people in these poor nations'.[35] At dawn on 1 December 1648, soldiers pushed their way into Charles's bedchamber and carried him off to the bleak coastal fortress of Hurst Castle. The following day the main body of the army marched into London. When Parliament resumed four days later, soldiers stood at the entrance to the Commons, turning away MPs who favoured negotiating with the King. Just eighty or so Members remained in the 'Rump Parliament', as it came to be called: all of them army sympathisers who voted that Charles's offer was 'highly dishonourable to the Parliament, and destructive to the peace of the kingdom'.[36] On 15 December the army's Council of Officers ordered the King to be brought to Windsor Castle, ready for his trial.

In Paris, Henrietta was 'struck to the heart with amazement and confusion when she heard the news'.[37] Shivering in her apartments at the Louvre, for she could no longer afford firewood and it was so cold she would not allow her daughter Henrietta Anne out of bed, the Queen wrote swift letters to Parliament and to the army's general, Lord Fairfax, asking for a safe conduct to come to 'see the king my lord'. She wrote secretly to Charles too, promising to 'use her utmost power ... by all ways imaginable to help him', wishing even 'that she might die for him, without whom she cannot, nor will not live'. Then began the desperate wait for a reply, knowing that 'so little of what I desire succeeds'.[38]

It was at this point that the French royal family fled from Paris. Their army outside the walls stopped all letters coming in 'by the ordinary way of the post'. Not until the middle of January was there news from England, and even then there was no reply to Henrietta's letters.[39] In fact, their recipients had refused to open them, as they came from a person whom Parliament had voted 'guilty of high treason'.[40] Instead of giving her the assurances she hoped for, Henrietta learnt, the House of Commons had voted to put the King on trial.

Yet still there seemed room for hope. In Holland, Prince Charles told the Dutch government of the 'great and imminent danger' threatening his father and persuaded them to send an ambassador 'to save at least his life'. The Prince wrote to the English Parliament too: if they killed their king, he threatened, it would 'be resented by all the princes and states of the world'.[41] Meanwhile Henrietta got a messenger through to St-Germain, where the French court promised to send an ambassador 'with the object of staying the execution'. Forty thousand troops might also go 'for the relief of innocence'. In England itself there was only limited support for the King's trial, even among parliamentarians; of the 135 commissioners appointed to preside over the trial, only 52 were present when the court met.[42]

At the beginning of February 1649, Henrietta heard that Charles had been condemned and brought out for execution, but had been rescued by the common people. Some of the Queen's companions suspected this story was concocted by Henry Lord Jermyn, Henrietta's most intimate confidant, hoping thus to prepare her gradually for the blow he expected would soon come. Henrietta never guessed, briefly believing the tale. When she found it to be untrue she 'wept many tears', before seeking consolation in the hope that the English people would yet save her husband.[43]

At last she could bear the agonies of suspense no longer. It was still impossible for her to leave Paris – the parliament's guards on the gates would not permit 'any person of quality ... to stir out of the city'[44] – but one of her gentlemen could get through to St-Germain to hear the latest news from England. Seated at dinner on Friday 9 February, the day after he had left, the Queen anxiously expected him. Behind her, the courtiers in their accustomed semicircle struggled to maintain a semblance of normality. Many of them knew that Henrietta's messenger had already returned, with news that her chaplain, Father Cyprien de Gamache, remembered 'made me shudder all over'. But no one could bear to tell her yet. For a whole hour they delayed the terrible moment, labouring to keep up a 'variety of conversation ... on indifferent matters', although Henrietta was not really listening. Her mind was with her husband, and with the messenger who, she thought, ought to have come back by now. Finally she cut across her courtiers' uneasy talk to complain 'of his being so long in bringing her an answer'.

At this, Henry Lord Jermyn began very gently to break the news. The messenger was 'faithful and prompt' in her commands, he said; certainly he would have returned sooner 'if the news had been favourable'.

Henrietta did not miss the hint. 'What is it then?' she asked. 'I perceive plainly that you know.'

Still Jermyn could not say the words. As Henrietta pressed him to tell, he circled round and round with 'several evasions and many ambiguous expressions', hoping to prepare the Queen 'by little and little for the fatal intelligence'. At last he told her everything.[45]

On Friday 19 January the prisoner-king had returned to London for the first time since he had fled seven years previously. Next day his trial opened in Westminster Hall: the largest room in England, 300 feet long, spanned by a vast arched ceiling of dark oak beams. Here, eight years earlier, Charles had watched Parliament try his most trusted minister, the Earl of Strafford, for high treason. Now the King himself was conducted under heavy guard to the high-sided wooden box assigned to the accused. In front of him the court's president sat on a high-backed chair, with the rest of the commissioners on tiered benches behind him. Not one rose to his feet or took off his hat, as etiquette demanded. Rather Charles was supposed to remove his own hat, out of 'respect to the court', which of course he would never do.

Instead he looked sternly at the commissioners: sixty-eight were present that day, 'members of the House of Commons, officers of the army, and citizens of London': all 'high-flown Parliament-men'.[46] Charles cast his eyes too over the wealthy and privileged audience in the galleries above them, before he sat down on the crimson velvet chair in his box. Then he was up again to stare round behind him, where soldiers separated him from the 'multitude of spectators' who filled the space to the great arched doorway at the hall's further end.[47]

When he was seated once more, his charge was read aloud: that he, being King with only 'a limited power' to rule 'according to the laws of the land', yet 'out of a wicked design to erect ... an unlimited and tyrannical power ... and to overthrow the rights and liberties of the people' had 'traitorously and maliciously levied war against the present Parliament and the people therein represented'. He was 'the occasioner, author and continuer of the said unnatural, cruel and bloody wars', and so was personally 'guilty of all the treasons, murders, rapines, burnings, spoils, desolations, damages, and mischiefs, to this nation, acted and committed in the said wars'.[48] Now he must answer: guilty or not guilty.

Charles refused to do so. 'By what lawful authority I am seated here?' he demanded. 'Remember, I am your King, your lawful King ... think well upon it, before you go further from one sin to a greater ... I have a trust committed to me by God ... I will not betray it to answer to a new unlawful authority.'

All that day he stood firm and the next too. The courtroom bristled with hostility: 'Justice, justice,' the soldiers shouted, with a 'hideous cry'. The president overrode the King repeatedly: 'Sir, I must interrupt you ... you appear as a prisoner ... you are to give a punctual and direct answer ... you are not to dispute our authority ... you stand in contempt of the Court ... you ought not to interrupt while the Court is speaking to you. This point is not to be debated by you, neither will the Court permit you to do it.'[49]

Still Charles kept his cool. Dressed all in black, with the great Garter star shining on his long black cloak and his hat firmly on his head, he spoke without anger or hesitation. His lifelong stammer was gone in this moment of resolution: 'For the charge, I value it not a rush; it is the liberty of the people of England that I stand for. For me to acknowledge a new court that I never heard of before, I that am your King ... indeed I do not know how to do it ... there's no law for it, to make your King your prisoner.' At last the court would hear no more. It was not for Charles 'to dispute the jurisdiction of the supreme and highest authority of England', its president told him. Charles's failure to answer the charge was recorded and he was taken away.[50]

For three more days the court met in private, while Charles waited at St James's Palace. All the old ceremonies of kingship were gone now. His food was brought in by soldiers, with no tasting, nor cup given on bended knee – a proceeding so 'uncouth' to Charles that he now ate alone.

On 27 January, the court summoned Charles once more. 'Justice', 'Execution', the crowd shouted.[51] The King made a last attempt to propose negotiations with Parliament, but the court would not hear him; they were already 'resolved to proceed to sentence and to judgment', the President said. The clerk read aloud from his parchment: 'that he, the said Charles Stuart, as a tyrant, traitor, murderer, and public enemy to the good people of this nation shall be put to death by severing of his head from his body'.

'Will you hear me a word, Sir?' the King asked.

'Sir, you are not to be heard after the sentence,' the president returned.

'No, Sir?'

'No, Sir; by your favour, Sir.' Then, turning from the King, 'Guard, withdraw your prisoner.'

'I may speak after sentence. By your favour, Sir, I may speak after sentence, ever. By your favour – hold. The sentence, Sir, – I say, Sir, I do –' Already Charles was being hustled out by the soldiers. 'I am not suffered for to speak. Expect what justice other people will have,' he ended, as the soldiers renewed their shouts of 'Justice, justice', laughing and blowing their tobacco smoke over Charles, 'a thing very distasteful unto him'. 'Poor Soldiers, for a piece of money they would do so for their commanders,' some heard him say.[52]

Back at St James's Palace, Charles knew he had only a short time to prepare for death. At last he had the Commons' permission to summon an Anglican clergyman, and he chose William Juxon, Bishop of London. During the 1630s Juxon had served him as a bishop and as Lord Treasurer, in charge of the nation's finances. He had managed not to alienate Charles's parliamentarian opponents, for even they admired his 'meek spirit', noting how, in his 'mighty place and power', he had always shown 'an equal moderation and humility'.[53] During the Civil War years, while other bishops were prosecuted, imprisoned, or even executed, Juxon had lived quietly as a country vicar. In moments of need Charles had always turned to him, seeking his advice in his negotiations with Parliament. What the King respected even more than Juxon's 'solid and steady judgement' was his outstanding 'sincerity and integrity'. For, like Charles himself, Juxon was a man of conscience who believed that one's sense of right and wrong should be put before every other consideration whatever.

Back in 1641, as Charles agonised over Parliament's Bill declaring the Earl of Strafford guilty of high treason, Juxon alone advised against approving it, for Charles knew Strafford was innocent. Yet at last his other advisers had persuaded the King 'to choose rather what was safe than what seemed just; preferring the outward peace of my kingdoms with men, before that inward exactness of conscience before God'. So Strafford had died and, ever since, Charles had regretted this 'act of so sinful frailty'. From that moment he had determined 'to prefer ... the peace of my conscience before the preservation of my kingdoms'. Juxon had become his most 'esteemed and favoured' clergyman.[54]

Now, on Sunday 28 January, Charles welcomed Juxon 'very openfacedly and cheerfully'. As the bishop began expressing sympathy, Charles interrupted him. 'Leave off this, my Lord, we have not time for it. Let us think of our great work, and prepare to meet that great God to whom ere long I am to give an account of myself.' All through that evening and most of the next day the two remained alone together, 'in prayer and other pious exercises of devotion'. 'My time is short and precious,' Charles said, ordering that no visitors be admitted. Even his nephew, the Elector Palatine, was turned away, departing 'full of sorrow'.[55] Only a messenger from Prince Charles was admitted, bearing the Prince's 'sorrowing letter', asking for news and begging his father's blessing, which the King answered at once. On Monday, Juxon preached in Charles's chapel; although God's judgements might be delayed, he said, they would come in the end to all men. Then he gave Charles communion.[56]

There were only two other people the King still wanted to see: Elizabeth and Henry, who still remained in Parliament's custody after helping their brother James to escape. Now, with the Commons' permission, they came to 'take their sad farewell of the King their father'. The thirteen-year-old Elizabeth burst into tears at once, followed by her eight-year-old brother, who knelt beside her to beg their father's blessing. Raising them up, Charles kissed them and sat them on his knees while he spoke of the duty they owed to their mother and to Prince Charles, who would succeed him as king.[57] They must not grieve for him, Charles said, for 'it would be a glorious death that he should die, it being for the laws and liberties of this land, and for maintaining the true Protestant religion'. Afterwards, he was sure, God would restore his eldest son to the throne, and they would all be happier than if he had lived. In the meantime, he had already forgiven his enemies, and his children must do likewise.

Charles asked Elizabeth to deliver his last message to Henrietta: 'that his thoughts had never strayed from her, and that his love should be the same to the last'. To Henry he reiterated his old commands. 'Sweetheart ... they will cut off my head, and perhaps make thee a king; but mark what I say, you must not be a king, so long as your brothers, Charles and James, do live.'

'I will be torn in pieces first,' the boy replied.[58]

Then Charles gave them the last of his jewels, all except the few he still wore on his person. At last they said their farewells, the King kissing them in tears and 'praying God Almighty to bless them'. Elizabeth too wept bitterly, while Charles stood at a window to hide his grief. As his bedchamber door opened to let the children out, he came back quickly and kissed and blessed them once more. Then Charles returned 'immediately to prayer'. After Juxon left late that evening, he still continued 'reading and praying', preparing for his last day on earth.[59]

He slept for only about four hours. Around 5 a.m. on Tuesday 30 January 1649 he opened the curtains of his bed and called to Thomas Herbert, the only one of his parliamentarian servants that Charles had become close to, and the only one still left to help him now. Herbert was a congenial spirit: cultivated and well read, a courtier before he fought for Parliament in the Civil War. Gradually he had fallen under the spell of the tragic, lonely King; the memoir he later wrote provides a touching portrait of Charles's last years of 'solitude and sufferings'.[60] 'I will get up,' Charles said to him now, 'having a great work to do this day.' Herbert helped him into his clothes: a blue satin waistcoat and a lavish lace collar over two embroidered white linen shirts. 'Let me have a shirt on more than ordinary,' Charles told him: 'the season is so sharp as probably may make me shake, which some observers will imagine proceeds from fear. I would have no such imputation. I fear not death! . . . I bless my God I am prepared.'

Herbert combed the King's shoulder-length brown hair, then handed him his two watches, one gold and one silver, which Charles always wound himself. Around the King's neck went the broad sky-blue ribbon he habitually wore, with its oval pendant of the Order of the Garter: a figure of St George slaying the dragon, carved in onyx, surrounded with '21 fair diamonds'.[61] On the pendant's back, twenty-one matching diamonds ringed a miniature portrait of Henrietta, 'set in a case of gold, the lid neatly enamelled with goldsmiths work'. Below the King's left knee Herbert fastened the dark-blue velvet Garter ribbon with its motto, *Honi soit qui mal y pense*, embroidered in 412 diamonds, and in one ear Charles hung a large pearl-drop earring. A black hat and mittens and his black cloak, emblazoned with its bright silver Garter star, were placed ready for the cold walk to Whitehall.[62]

It was still dark when Bishop Juxon arrived. As the sun rose he performed the Anglican service of morning prayer. Then Charles continued 'in prayer and meditation', 'ready to resign himself into the hands of Christ Jesus'.[63] Around 10 a.m. guards conducted him out to St James's Park, where several hundred infantrymen stood in two parallel ranks right across the Park, their colours flying and drums beating loudly. Between them Charles walked amidst his guard of halberdiers, with Juxon on the King's right side and Thomas Herbert following after.

Mounting a wooden stairway between classical columns, Charles entered Whitehall Palace, his home before the Civil War. The windows here looked out over the tiltyard where, twenty-three years earlier, he had jousted to celebrate Henrietta's first arrival in England. Crossing the bridge over King Street, he passed on through another long gallery to his own bedchamber, hung round with portraits of his closest family and friends. Here he remained with Juxon and Herbert for over three hours while the House of Commons rushed to pass a final piece of legislation before he died: an 'Act for prohibiting the proclaiming of any person or persons to be King of England or Ireland, without consent of Parliament'.[64] Meanwhile Charles prayed and took communion. He ate a little – a few mouthfuls of bread and a small glass of claret wine, to keep up his strength – and he chose a white satin skullcap to wear on the scaffold.

Shortly before 2 p.m., the colonel of his guards came to call him. Juxon and Herbert knelt weeping, and Charles gave them each his hand to kiss. 'Go,' he told the colonel, 'I will follow.' And so he set off through the Palace once more, with his halberdiers, until they reached the Banqueting House. Here, in 1625, he had ratified his marriage treaty, then kissed his new wife 'in the presence of the whole people'.[65] Now Charles passed quickly along the room and out through a hole broken in the wall, onto the black-draped scaffold where his life would be ended.

The executioner's new-sharpened axe rested on the wooden block where Charles would lay his head. Beside it stood the headsman and his assistant, masked and wearing false beards to conceal their identity. In the street below, several hundred soldiers were packed around the scaffold's foot: infantrymen with iron helmets and ten-foot foot pikes held upright at their sides. Beyond them pressed 'the multitudes of people that came to be spectators', men, women and children, stretching to the Palace's great gateway on Charles's left, to the tiltyard wall in front of him, and far up the street on his right towards Charing Cross.[66] Among them was the future diarist, Samuel Pepys, now a fifteen-year-old schoolboy, playing truant to witness the death of the tyrant he hated. If he preached a sermon on the King, Pepys bragged to his friends later that day, he would take as his subject the Biblical text, 'The memory of the wicked shall rot.'[67] Beyond the crowd hundreds more troops were stationed in the street, both in the direction of Westminster and towards Charing Cross.

Once around the platform Charles walked, examining everything. Near the block, heavy iron staples had been driven into the floor, with ropes and pulleys attached, to restrain him if necessary. Charles merely smiled when he saw them, 'without being any way daunted'.[68] Then he began the speech he had prepared. Again, as at his trial, he spoke fluently, without a stammer, and without any written text, 'save only a few heads in a little scrip of paper'.[69] The crowd was too far off to hear a word, as were, he thought, perhaps even the infantrymen below the scaffold. He therefore spoke only to the handful of men who stood on the platform with him: soldiers from his guard and a few secretaries or newsmen taking notes, as well as Bishop Juxon.

Charles protested his innocence, 'for all the world knows that I never did begin a war with the two Houses of Parliament'; they had first encroached on his political privileges, not he on theirs. Yet it was right he should die: with this 'unjust sentence' God was punishing him for the injustice he had committed in allowing the Earl of Strafford's execution, eight years earlier. Charles had already 'forgiven all the world, and even those in particular that have been the chief causes of my death'. Yet they were following 'an ill way'. 'Believe it,' he advised the men in front of him, 'you will never do right, nor God will never prosper you, until you give God his due, the King his due (that is, my successors) and the people their due.'

Here Charles broke off, noticing that one of his hearers was touching the executioner's axe. 'Hurt not the axe,' he said: 'that may hurt me.' He wanted no painful, undignified death, hacked repeatedly with a blunt weapon. Then he picked up his thread once more. 'For the people,' he said, 'truly I desire their liberty and freedom as much as anybody.' Yet they were mistaken if they thought liberty came by 'having share in government'. Rather, their happiness came from fair laws, 'by which their life and their goods may be most their own'. It was for this political principle that Charles was going to die: 'the martyr of the people'.

There Charles would have ended, but Juxon intervened, reminding him to make a public statement of his faith. 'I thank you very heartily, my Lord, for that,' Charles replied, 'I had almost forgotten it.' Then turning back to his little audience, he said, 'Sirs, ... I declare before you all that I die a Christian, according to the profession of the Church of England, as I found it left me by my father. And this honest man I think will witness it,' he added, pointing to Juxon. 'I have a good cause, and I have a gracious God; I will say no more.'

Then he addressed his executioner: 'I shall say but very short prayers, and when I thrust out my hands——.' Charles could not bear to say what followed. He took off his hat and handed it to Bishop Juxon, receiving in return his satin skullcap, which he put on his head himself. 'Does my hair trouble you?' he asked the executioner, who said he should put it all under his cap. 'I go from a corruptible, to an incorruptible crown; where no disturbance can be, no disturbance in the world,' Charles said to Juxon. Then 'Is my hair well?' he asked the executioner again.

He took off his cloak and handed it to the bishop, then lifted the Garter pendant with its portrait of Henrietta from around his neck. 'Remember,' the King said as he handed it to Juxon. After removing his doublet with its fine lace collar, he put his cloak back on. 'You must set it fast,' he said to the executioner, looking at the block.

'It is fast, Sir.'

'It might have been a little higher,' Charles complained, hating to bow so low in front of his enemies.

'It can be no higher, Sir,' came the reply.

'When I put out my hands this way,' Charles instructed once more, holding his arms out wide, 'then—.'

For a few moments he stood and prayed 'with hands and eyes lift[ed] up'. Then he knelt down and put his neck on the block. 'Stay for the sign,' Charles commanded again, as the executioner tucked his hair under his cap again. Then, 'after a very little pause', Charles stretched out his arms. The swinging axe separated his head from his body at a single blow.[70]

As the head rolled and blood spurted from the severed neck, there came one vast, spontaneous groan from the crowd, 'such a groan by thousands then present as I never heard before, and desire I may never hear again,' the Puritan minister, Philip Henry, remembered years later. The executioner lifted the dripping head high for everyone to see, and at this signal the waiting troops began to march 'to disperse and scatter the people'. 'I had much ado amongst the rest to escape home without hurt,' Philip Henry recalled.[71] The whole drama up there on the scaffold had been played out in no more than a quarter of an hour. 'Sic transit gloria mundi,' gloated the parliamentarian news-sheets: thus passes the glory of the world.[72]

PART ONE

Love's Triumph

I

Strangers

On the afternoon of Sunday 12 December 1624 the British court gathered in the long panelled gallery of St John's College, Cambridge. On the throne at the head of the room sat King James I – a bulky figure in clothes thickly padded against the assassin's dagger. Though only fifty-eight, James already saw himself as 'an old king' and his looks confirmed his words. Large, tired eyes were deeply sunken in his long, creased face. His hair and wispy beard were flecked with white. Now, as so often, he was stiff with pain from gout, which swelled the joints of his feet, knees, elbows and hands.[1]

Beside him stood his twenty-four-year-old son, Charles Prince of Wales, bareheaded in honour of his father. Courtiers and nobles massed beneath them, summoned for a ceremony of 'the utmost splendour'. The French king's ambassador had just arrived in England, accompanied by a train of some eighty people. Now they entered for their first royal audience, bringing the 'great treaty' that Louis XIII had signed in Paris in November, which James was now to ratify.[2]

Few people knew exactly what the treaty contained; many of its terms would be hated by the English public, and the many months of negotiations had been conducted in the utmost secrecy. So, once the elaborate greetings demanded by royal etiquette were completed, the ambassador retired for a private session with the King, the Prince, and their two most trusted courtiers. Here, after last-minute discussions, Prince Charles signed the treaty and its associated documents, while James, his hands too swollen with gout to hold a quill, watched his own signature being stamped on the pages by his secretary of state. Finally, it was agreed. The English prince was to marry the last available French princess, Henrietta Maria, the youngest sister of King Louis XIII.[3]

For twenty years James had been planning such a marriage. When he had inherited the English throne in 1603 he had become the first ever monarch of a united England, Scotland and Ireland, and James was hugely proud of his new kingdom: 'Great Britain', as he called it. A marriage alliance to one of Europe's two Catholic superpowers – the Hapsburgs of Spain or the Bourbons of France – would prove to the world the true greatness of the King and his new realm. It would also be a chance to play an important part in the great game of international diplomacy. Acting out his preferred role as King Solomon the wise, the peacemaker, James would use his own family's marriages to reconcile Protestant and Catholic Europe, achieving his long-held ambition for the union and 'peace of Christendom'.[4]

In 1605 negotiations had begun, aimed at securing the Spanish Infanta for Charles's elder brother, Prince Henry. By 1612, as Spain demanded that Henry convert to Catholicism as a condition of marriage, James's hopes had switched to France. Royal marriages were primarily political tools and the English princes had been brought up to acquiesce. 'My part ... is to be in love with any of them,' Henry commented on his father's shifting choice of royal princesses.[5] That same year Henry died, aged just eighteen, leaving Charles to fulfil their father's matrimonial ambitions. By 1619 James was again determined on a Spanish marriage and for the next four years he ignored repeated French proposals that Charles marry Henrietta Maria. It was Charles himself, and his dearest friend, George Villiers, Duke of Buckingham, who chose the French marriage and then put James into 'a state of siege', depriving him of all pro-Spanish company so that he would be 'practically compelled to depend upon their wishes'.[6] All through the summer of 1624 the King had resisted, while Charles and Buckingham outmanoeuvred him. In November, when the treaty terms were agreed by the English ambassadors in Paris, James had finally been forced to comply.

The King had been angry then and he was still sulking now. Later that day, when his court celebrated the treaty with a 'magnificent feast', James declared himself too ill to attend and remained in bed, 'extremely melancholy'.[7] His place at the head of the table was taken by Prince Charles, who was served with all the ceremony normally reserved for the King. Then, with the musicians playing, the company stood up to dance, all men together since there were no ladies present. James had little interest in women. His real attachments in life were all to men – especially those with 'handsome persons and ... fine clothes'[8] – and the courtiers dancing tonight clearly reflected the King's tastes. Gorgeously dressed in rich, bright-coloured doublets, smothered in jewels, with fancy lace at their necks and wrists, and high-heeled shoes on their feet, they wore tight silk stockings that showed off their legs right up to the thigh.

Dancing with the rest, the newly engaged Prince of Wales was the reason for all this jollity, yet he was an inconspicuous figure. Charles was a slight young man, just five feet four inches tall. Preferring to appear 'sober ... clean and neat' rather than 'gaudy and riotous', he habitually wore dark colours and dressed 'absolutely without jewels, more modestly than any gentleman soever'.[9] Tonight, as always, he was far outshone by the Duke of Buckingham, the King's long-reigning favourite. Buckingham was the most dazzling man at court: tall, handsome, stunningly dressed, an exquisite dancer, poised, confident, a delightful conversationalist and a master of conspicuous con-sumption. Though he had started out as almost nobody – the younger son of a minor gentry family – Buckingham was now the most powerful man in the kingdom, his 'entire engrossing of the Prince's favour, as well as the King's', enabling him to do whatever he wanted in matters of government.[10] Charles had probably never noticed, but the French marriage had originally been Buckingham's idea, not his.

*

Charles had always lived in the shade of a more glamorous older rival. Born on 19 November 1600, the Prince had been a sickly child who was not expected to live to adulthood. His legs grew crooked and even by the age of four he could not walk well. He began to speak only as he approached his third birthday, with a stammer that lasted the rest of his life. It was his dashing brother Prince Henry – six years Charles's senior, handsome, athletic, clever and strong-willed – who won the hearts of the people, though neither he nor Charles could gain their father's affection. Lonely and insecure, Charles clung to his older paragon brother. 'Sweet, sweet brother,' he wrote to Henry, 'I will give any thing that I have to you; both my horse, and my books, and my pieces [guns], and my crossbows, or any thing that you would have. Good brother love me, and I shall ever love and serve you.'[11]

Charles copied Henry in everything. He dressed like him. He followed him into the new continental fashion for collecting antique medals, books, paintings and objets d'art. He shared his passion for manly sports: hunting, fencing, and shooting with crossbows, muskets and cannons. Especially he loved to ride with his brother in the artful displays of the joust and the manège. Exercising constantly, Charles gradually grew fit and strong. By his twenties he was recognised as one of the most accomplished horsemen of the age.

By then, however, he had also lost his beloved brother. In November 1612, two weeks before Charles's twelfth birthday, Henry died of typhoid and Charles was thrust into all the responsibilities of the heir to the throne. Dressed in black, he led his brother's funeral procession through the streets of London as chief mourner. The following February he conducted his sixteen-year-old sister Elizabeth to her wedding to the handsome young German Protestant hero, Frederick, Elector Palatine.* Three years later – in an investiture ceremony that was kept low-key to save money and avoid arousing painful memories of Prince Henry – Charles formally succeeded his brother as Prince of Wales.

As he entered his late teens Charles spent much more time with his

---

* Ruler of the Palatinate, now part of western Germany.

father, joining him in state functions and in the hunting expeditions they both loved. It was only out in the field that Charles won real approval from the King, who often said that in this he was 'a true and worthy son'. Nevertheless the two remained emotionally distant. Charles was 'excessively afraid of his father', whose hot temper often exploded in fits of ferocious foul language and even physical violence; James was always more attached to the personable young men he took up as court favourites.[12] The last and greatest of these arrived in London in 1614, aged twenty-one. George Villiers was the handsomest man in the kingdom, everyone agreed, and his experience at the French court had given him a polish and wit that immediately charmed the King. Soon the newcomer was appointed King's cupbearer, then gentleman of the bedchamber, whose duties required him to sleep in James's chamber at night.

Whatever occurred there in private can never be known, but certainly the two men kissed and flirted shamelessly in public. 'My sweet Steenie,' the King nicknamed his new favourite, because of his resemblance to the angelic beauty of St Stephen. Steenie was his 'only sweet child', his 'sweet child and wife', and James was 'his sweet boy's dear dad'.[13] In return Steenie played up to the older man with a mixture of cheeky presumption and grovelling self-abasement. He was, he repeatedly assured the King, 'Your Majesty's most humble slave and dog'. Yet the dog was rapidly becoming the master. Spoilt by the King like a favourite son, Steenie was showered in money, lands and honours: 'never any man in any age ... rose in so short a time to so much greatness of honour, fame and fortune, upon no other advantage ... than ... the beauty and gracefulness and becomingness of his person.'[14] He advanced to the best positions at court: Master of the King's Horse, then Master of the Wardrobe, Lord Warden of the Cinque Ports and Lord High Admiral of England. From gentleman to knight, baron, viscount, and then Earl and Marquess of Buckingham: he had soon outstripped most of the ancient English nobility in riches and titles. By 1616 he owned estates giving him an income of £80,000 per year – roughly £2 million in modern money. Buckingham was 'without a rival' and he used his power to advance his impoverished relations to wealth and influence, much to the other courtiers' annoyance.[15]

At first Charles resented the new favourite and there were some bitter quarrels – over a jewel of Buckingham's that disappeared; and over a match of tennis, when Buckingham told the Prince to 'kiss his arse' and threatened 'to strike him'.[16] Charles could never win these battles, for James always took his favourite's side – scolding his teenage son to the point of tears on one occasion, boxing his ears on another. Soon the Prince learnt to play second fiddle. He cultivated insignificance, moving around the court 'like a planet in its sphere, so naturally and quietly that one does not remark it'. He was reserved, even sullen, keeping his opinions to himself and rushing to agree with whatever his father or Buckingham said. Indeed, he behaved more 'as if the favourite were prince and himself less than a favourite'. Observers were shocked, taking the view that Charles was either very cowardly or very clever so to flatter a man he must actually hate.[17]

In fact, Charles grew to like his father's favourite. Realising the King could not live for ever, Buckingham began to cast his charm over 'Baby Charles', as both he and James called the heir to the throne.[18] Ever adaptable, Steenie treated the serious, shy young Prince with none of the mingled insolence and sycophancy that so delighted James. There was respect and affection in his tone – 'my dear young Master', he called him. And Charles, lonely and insecure, eagerly accepted the proffered intimacy. 'Steenie, there is none that knows me so well as yourself,' he told his new companion.[19]

To Charles, Buckingham became 'like a brother' – a leader, role model and much needed friend. He provided a buffer in the difficult relationship between father and son, pacifying the King when Charles angered him, flattering and cajoling James into doing what his 'Baby' asked. By 1621 an intense relationship had developed. Charles was 'yours more than can be expressed', he assured Buckingham.[20] The two were together all the time. Discarding the constraints of royal ceremony, Buckingham provided an easy camaraderie that Charles never otherwise experienced. Steenie came and went freely when others were denied access. He wore his hat in the Prince's presence; he sat with his feet up; he appeared only half dressed. In his role of older brother, he drew Charles out into public life. Together the two young men gadded about town, often making a foursome with Buckingham's wife and the Duchess of Lennox, who was 'much courted and respected by the Prince'.[21] And together, during James's increasing periods of illness, the pair worked to put royal policy through Parliament. Encouraged by Buckingham, Charles threw himself into this new business with energy and enthusiasm. He regularly attended the House of Lords where he spoke confidently, despite his stammer, and for the first time he began to gain public popularity.

With Buckingham, Charles also discussed the long-vexed question of his marriage plans. James had for years been locked in inconclusive negotiations with Spain, but now there was a new urgency. On the Continent the religious conflict had broken out that would be known as the Thirty Years War. In November 1619, Charles's sister, Elizabeth, and her husband Frederick had been crowned King and Queen of Bohemia, but within a year they had lost everything. Their home territory of the Palatinate was invaded by the Spanish, and the couple were forced to flee to Protestant Holland. Although James and Charles both vowed to help, the royal government was in no position to offer either forces or money.

Charles and Buckingham eventually abandoned their original plans for a European land war and began, like James, to hope that the Prince's marriage could secure foreign aid for Elizabeth. As Charles hated the never-ending stalemate of the Spanish marriage talks, he and Buckingham hatched a plan. 'How gallant and how brave a thing it would be', they thought, for the Prince to travel secretly with Buckingham to Spain and court the Infanta in person. By their presence the pair would speed on the marriage negotiations and persuade the Spanish to restore the Palatinate to Charles's sister and brother-in-law. Then Charles, like his grandfather and father before him, would bear his bride triumphantly home with him.[22]

James, when Charles on his knees told him their plan, hated the idea. Their absence in Spain 'would break his heart', he said. In his opinion Charles risked becoming a hostage, forced to accept whatever terms the Spanish dictated before he could return home. 'I am undone!

I shall lose Baby Charles,' James cried. However, the King was no match for the combined forces of his son and favourite. If he could not go to Spain, Charles said, he would never marry at all. If James denied this small request, Buckingham threatened, he could lose his son's love.[23]

And so, in February 1623, Charles dashed off on his great romantic adventure, riding incognito across Europe to save his sister and to woo the teenage princess with whom he soon pronounced himself 'deeply in love'. In Madrid he watched the Infanta 'as a cat does a mouse',[24] throwing himself repeatedly in her path. He jumped a high orchard wall to talk to her when she was out gathering flowers. 'No one loved a lady more ardently than he did the Infanta,' Charles professed: 'distance and other obstacles would never lessen it.'[25] In vain: the Infanta declared she would rather enter a nunnery than marry a Protestant infidel. In the six months Charles spent in Spain, he was never allowed time with her alone. And far from the Spanish yielding to his charms, Charles found them insisting on ever more stringent terms in the marriage negotiations.

Most problematic were Spain's demands for the toleration of Britain's Roman Catholics. Since the reign of Queen Elizabeth I this hated and feared religious minority had suffered severe persecution. Catholics were barred from public office; they could neither inherit nor purchase property; their children could be taken away for Protestant upbringing; their church ceremonies were illegal and they were fined for every Sunday that they did not attend an Anglican service. Furthermore, their priests were liable to the death penalty.[26] Though harsh, these laws were only intermittently enforced. Now Spain required that they must never be imposed again, and that James and Charles must swear to allow Catholics public freedom of worship in perpetuity.

Charles was staggered. Such a treaty would be hugely unpopular in England; Parliament would never agree to repeal the anti-Catholic penal laws. But the Spanish refused to compromise, and Charles was eager to marry. That summer he and James signed the treaty, which promised the Prince's marriage to the Infanta and toleration for British Catholics but contained no word of Spain aiding the Elector Palatine, nor the Infanta's large dowry, without which, James said, 'both my Baby and I are bankrupts for ever'.[27] Far from improving matters, Charles's journey to Spain had resulted in total British capitulation.

Yet still Spain delayed, demanding now that Catholic toleration must be put into effect in Britain before the wedding could take place – which would delay the marriage by a year at least. Charles and Buckingham lost all patience, believing that not only had the Spanish 'negotiated with cunning and fraud, and their object was the acquisition of the Palatinate', but that they even intended to trap Charles in an unconsummated marriage, thereby depriving Britain of royal heirs.[28] Though Charles 'dissimulated to a great extent and said nothing' to his hosts, both he and Buckingham were thoroughly 'offended and disgusted ... with Spanish perfidy and deceit'. In October they returned to England, determined instead to arrange a French marriage for the Prince.[29]

By February 1624, the Prince and the Duke – as Buckingham had now become by James's favour – were once again set on a British military campaign on the Continent, to defeat the Spanish and recover the Palatinate. First they needed to secure parliamentary funding. Sidestepping the King's opposition, they presented their case direct to Parliament. Attending every day, Charles spoke 'so bravely and judiciously' and 'with such prudence' that he gained 'universal applause'. Expressing their disgust with the Spanish, he and Buckingham delighted the anti-Catholic, anti-Spanish MPs, who rushed to do what was asked of them.[30] Within weeks Parliament demanded that the King 'must abandon all dealings with Spain both upon the marriage and the Palatinate'; only then would they grant any financial subsidies. James was furious and left London for the country, 'cursing and swearing'.[31] Finally, in desperate need of parliamentary money himself, he had to comply. In April he told the Spanish he must abandon the marriage, and that same month Parliament voted to pay the largest subsidy ever for military preparations. It came with a new demand: James and Charles must swear that, in the French marriage now being planned, there would be no toleration of English Roman Catholics, such as the Spanish had required. Readily both King and

Prince gave their word. Charles in particular, still bitter at the Catholic duplicity he had met in Spain, spoke to Parliament 'very strongly on the subject', promising 'he would abandon all thought of a marriage with France if they claimed what was granted to the Spaniards'.[32]

His new quarry was also Catholic: the fourteen-year-old princess, Henrietta Maria, youngest child of Henri IV and Marie de' Medici, and sister to King Louis XIII. An English ambassador had already arrived in Paris to sound out Louis XIII's court. Henry Rich, Lord Kensington was ideally qualified for the job: handsome, winning, witty, a fluent French speaker, every inch the courtier. He went everywhere, saw everyone and was soon sending enthusiastic reports back to England. The French were eager for a military alliance with Britain, he said, for they feared 'the power and usurpation of the Spaniards' who now encircled their borders from the Netherlands down through Germany to northern Italy and Spain itself.[33] Soon Lord Kensington was joined by a more senior diplomat, James Hay, Earl of Carlisle – another 'very fine gentleman and a most accomplished courtier' – empowered to discuss detailed terms with the French.[34]

All that summer and on through the autumn, intense negotiations continued across Europe. In Paris, Carlisle and Kensington met 'day and night' with the French king's ministers, thrashing out what the treaty would do for British Catholics and 'for the restoring of the Palatinate'. Meanwhile in Rome a French envoy pressed the Pope to grant the dispensation needed for Henrietta Maria to marry a Protestant. In England, the French ambassador was 'in perpetual movement and ... agitation', meeting regularly with the Duke of Buckingham and, when he could, the King.[35] James, however, still privately hoping for a Spanish match, now 'detested business ... more than ever'. All summer he was away in the country, where he spent 'all his days hunting except Sundays'. When the French ambassador finally caught up with him, he found the King only 'dealt seriously with him about hunting and such trifles, but trifled with him about the main business'.[36]

Throughout England the marriage was 'opposed by infinite passions'. People feared Catholic oppression in general, and the French in particular. It was expected that, once Parliament met again, it would 'break this match even more than the Spanish one'. Yet, driven on by Charles and Buckingham, the talks continued in the greatest secrecy. Always the question of religion was the great 'old stumbling block'.[37] In July the French offered to accept a mere private letter from James promising Catholic toleration. In August there was a crisis when Louis's new chief minister, Cardinal Richelieu, demanded that toleration again be put into the treaty itself. Charles raged at 'so scurvy a trick'. If it were not for his respect for Henrietta Maria, he 'would not care a fart' for the French, he ranted. 'If they insist upon these new grounds, let them go hang themselves, rather than treat with them any more.'[38]

All involved expected the match would be broken off, but Richelieu needed the British alliance, so he offered concessions. James and Charles could promise Catholic toleration in an *Escrit Secret*, separate from the treaty itself. By means of this 'Secret Writing', the toleration might be hidden from British Protestants, who need never know how the King and Prince had violated their anti-Catholic promises to Parliament that spring. Yet the French still flatly refused to sign any military alliance in aid of the Palatinate. Their king would simply give his word, they offered. Indignant, James refused to allow the marriage on such terms, but when he suggested reopening talks with the Spanish, Charles defied him. He 'would never match with Spain', he said.[39] Bullied by his son and outfaced by the French, James finally backed down. Angrily he ordered his ambassadors to sign whatever the French demanded and 'terminate the matter in any event'. Then he withdrew from the business, refusing to see anyone 'on the pretext of suffering from the gout'.[40]

Hurriedly, Louis and his ministers signed the treaty before James could change his mind, and Paris erupted with 'every sign of joy' – 'bonfires, illuminations, fireworks', a cannonade at the Arsenal and a grand ball in the Louvre. London too was ablaze with light, glowing 'in every part' with the bonfires ordered by the government. At the Tower they fired the guns while organs played in the city's churches and their bells rang out.[41] Charles was elated. Although the treaty contained no mention of the Palatinate, the French were effusive in their verbal promises, swearing they would do 'ten times more than we expect ... and they will never abandon us in that action'. Soon, he hoped, there might be a pan-European alliance against Spain, with the Italians and Germans too joining 'to overthrow that colossus'.[42]

At the end of November, Charles sat down to write his first ever letter to the girl he was now engaged to marry. Whilst he had never met Henrietta Maria, he had seen her once – fleetingly, from 'afar off, and in a dark room' – when he and Buckingham had stopped in Paris on their way to Spain in 1623.[43] Disguised in wigs, the pair had visited the French court where, Charles reported to his father, they saw 'nineteen fair dancing ladies' rehearsing for a masque. Among them was Henrietta, acting the part of Iris, handmaiden to Juno, queen of the gods. At the time the tiny performing princess, only just into her teens and small for her age, had made no impression on Charles. It was Juno herself – the plump blonde Queen, Anne of Austria, wife of Louis XIII and sister to the Spanish Infanta – who had struck Charles as the most beautiful woman present, inspiring him with a still greater desire to reach Spain and court her sister.[44]

Now, however, all that had changed. Since February, Charles had been swamped by praises of Henrietta Maria, sent back by Lord Kensington. As he was 'wooing ambassador',[45] it was Kensington's job to stir the royal pair into love and he had performed this romantic role with enthusiasm. Henrietta was 'the most admirable sweet creature in this world', he enthused to Charles. 'Both my eyes and judgement never considered a person of that wonderful loveliness.' 'More wit, good nature, honour and discretion were never seen.'[46] Henrietta danced 'as well as ever I saw any creature', he raved. No 'man or woman in France or in the world sings so admirably as she. Sir, it is beyond imagination; that is all that I can say of it.'[47]

It was hardly surprising then that Charles was now 'passionately in love with this paragon'.[48] Yet, bound by the rules of etiquette, Charles had not dared to write to Henrietta until the treaty was concluded. Only now, he told her, could he finally express 'the impatience with which my soul has been tormented during my long wait for the happy accord of this treaty'. Wound up to fever pitch by the overblown accounts of his ambassador, Charles was building romantic castles in the air. The fame of Henrietta's virtues 'blazed out everywhere', he assured her. Even his own memories of watching the dance rehearsals in Paris had swelled until now he thought it his 'crowning happiness' to have seen her great beauty then. Charles's letter has a tortured quality, a sense of repressed emotions that escape awkwardly onto the page. So far he had managed just a single, long, complicated sentence. Then he despaired, ending with: 'I cannot express in writing the passion of my soul.'[49]

A week later Thomas Carey, Charles's most trusted gentleman of the bedchamber, entered the great gateway of the Louvre in Paris, accompanied by the two English ambassadors. Across the courtyard, lit by torches through the dark winter evening, they entered the apartments of Henrietta's mother, Marie de' Medici. Three paces in front of her the Englishmen stopped and bowed deeply. Approaching closer, they went down on one knee and carried the hem of her dress to their lips. Then Marie, giving each one her hand to kiss, raised them up and the ambassadors introduced Carey, who formally begged permission to take Charles's love letter to her daughter.

As 'Madame de France', the senior remaining royal daughter, Henrietta had her own grand suite of rooms in the Louvre. Here, seated on a throne in her grand salon, Henrietta received Carey and the ambassadors. She was still small for her age – a slender brunette whose pale oval face was squarely framed by tiny tight curls that took hours to prepare. With a careful curtsy she took Carey's two letters – one from James, as well as the love letter from Charles – saying that she 'thanked the King of Great Britain for the honour of his notice, and Monsieur the Prince of Wales for the testimony he gave her of his affection'. Then she hurried through the palace, carrying the two letters, still unopened, to her mother's apartments.[50]

Marie de' Medici had always been a strict authority figure in Henrietta's life. Proud, majestic, addicted to the grandeur and trappings of monarchy, Marie was a woman of 'a commanding and high spirit', well able to 'cause herself to be obeyed'.[51] Even her closest associates admitted her coldness and lack of feeling, which extended to her own children. It was their father who was the affectionate parent, playing with the princes and princesses, kissing them, teasing them, sitting them on his knee at meals. By his orders the royal children were brought up at the country chateau of St-Germain-en-Laye with their half-brothers and sisters, Henri's children by his mistresses. Five legitimate and five illegitimate children made up what was fondly called the *troupeau*, the little flock of St-Germain. They ate together, studied together, played together indoors and out. Especially they loved to stage little entertainments for their parents and the courtiers: ballets or comedies with elaborate costumes and sets. As a toddler Henrietta was already joining in with a will, dressing up, singing, dancing and running about with the others. Her years in the *troupeau* had a defining effect on her character and she grew up highly sociable, lively, witty, loving informal companionship and a country life of retirement, but also every inch the princess, well schooled in all the ceremony of seventeenth-century royalty.[52]

In 1610, when Henrietta Maria was only six months old, her father King Henri IV was assassinated by a Catholic fanatic. To his youngest daughter he became a heroic figure, 'Henri le Grand' – King Henry the Great – as the French were already calling the man who had ended thirty years of religious civil wars and given France unity, religious tolerance and prosperity. In later life Henrietta would be proud of such a father, collecting his wise sayings and proposing his statecraft for her husband to imitate.[53] Now it was her mother who ruled France as Queen Regent, with absolute political power during Louis XIII's minority. Occupied in state affairs, she was a distant figure in her children's lives, visiting St-Germain only rarely. Her main role was to lay down rules for their household and be the ultimate figure of discipline, ordering beatings for misbehaving or boys or sending little notes and presents to children who were good. It was Madame de Montglat, the governess in charge of the whole *troupeau*, who provided the day-to-day maternal presence in the children's lives. 'Mamangat', they called her affectionately – Mother Monglat – and even in adulthood they continued to write her letters under this affectionate nickname. Mamangat's daughter Jeanne became a close friend, called 'Mamie' by the royal children – short for *mon amie*.

As the years passed, the flock at St-Germain diminished. On his accession to the throne in 1610, the eight-year-old King, Louis XIII, departed for the Louvre where he joined his mother in state functions but was still regularly birched for disobedience. Five years later Henrietta's eldest sister Elizabeth, aged just thirteen, parted from her family in tears, leaving France for ever to marry the future King Philip IV of Spain. In return, the fourteen-year-old Spanish Infanta, Anne of Austria, married Henrietta's brother Louis. In 1619, the twelve-year-old Christine left too, to marry the future ruler of the Duchy of Savoy.

By now Louis XIII was king in reality as well as name, having seized power from his mother in a bloody palace coup. While the young king watched from a window, his royal guards murdered Marie's favourite adviser, Concino Concini, who had accompanied her from Florence at the time of her marriage. Concini's wife, Marie's companion from childhood, was arrested and later burnt as a witch. Marie herself was sent under arrest to the castle of Blois, 100 miles south of Paris.

For three years Marie de' Medici remained in the political wilderness, until in 1620 there was a public reconciliation between mother and son, and she returned to Paris, where she lived magnificently once again. Over the following years the young Henrietta Maria was often in Paris, and from her mother especially she acquired all the cultivated and expensive tastes of continental monarchy: for music and the theatre, architecture, garden design, paintings and objets d'art, as well as precious stones, a particular love of Marie's. By 1624, driven on by her 'passion . . . to make her daughter a queen', Marie had become the principal force behind plans for Henrietta's British marriage.[54]

Henrietta had always known she would have an arranged marriage, chosen by her relations 'for her honour and advancement, and likewise for the advantage of . . . [the French] crown and kingdom'. Now, under orders from Marie, her courtiers eagerly pointed out the advantages of marrying the British prince. She would be a great queen one day, no mere duchess like her sister Christine, and she would rule over three kingdoms: England, Scotland and Ireland. In the meantime, she would have the grandest household any Princess of Wales had ever had, as the French were carefully ensuring in their negotiations. Life in England would be full of delights: as a keen horsewoman, Henrietta would find real companionship there, for the English ladies loved riding far more than the French.[55]

As for Charles, he was 'the most complete young prince and person in the world': 'a wonder', a man of 'infinite merit'.[56] All the court ladies had seen his handsome portrait, which Lord Kensington wore around his neck, and their admiring comments soon stirred up Henrietta's 'passionate desiring' to see the picture for herself. However, it was not yet proper for the Princess to show an interest in her suitor. So, while the other ladies tantalised her, repeatedly opening the portrait's case and examining it closely, Henrietta remained apart, daring only to cast glances from 'afar off'. Unable to bear the suspense, she sent secretly to Kensington, asking to borrow the portrait. Retiring into her cabinet, 'blushing in the instant at her own guiltiness', she kept the picture in her hands for a whole hour before returning it, with 'many praises of your person', the ambassador reported to Charles.[57]

By now Henrietta was thoroughly sold on the marriage. Good news of the negotiations brought 'blushing modest sweet joy' to her looks. But more often, as the talks seemed to founder, she suffered from melancholy and sleepless nights. 'My God, why is there no news from England?' she demanded.[58] In May, with Charles's Spanish match officially broken off, she was publicly acknowledged as the British prince's 'mistress' – 'a title she is not a little proud of'. At last she could openly send to Lord Kensington, saying she 'desired infinitely' to borrow Charles's portrait.[59]

All through the summer Kensington spent hours at a time with Henrietta at the Louvre, enthusing about her future life in England. With Marie de' Medici's permission he relayed formal little lovers' speeches from Charles, professing the Prince's 'passionate service' and his admiration for 'as well the beauties of her mind as her person', which Henrietta 'received with all the joy that can be both by countenance and language expressed'. Curtsying low, she replied, trembling, 'that she was extremely obliged to his Highness' and looked forward to 'meriting the place she had in his good graces'.[60] By the autumn Henrietta was proudly calling herself 'bride of the Prince of England'. 'Impatient of all delay', she pestered her mother and brother to complete the treaty. The day she heard it was finally settled was 'the happiest day that ever she had', she told her brother Gaston, Duc d'Orléans.[61]

Yet Henrietta was also long schooled in hiding her feelings in public. None of this passion showed in December 1624, when she arrived in Marie de' Medici's apartments and surrendered to her mother the two unopened letters from England. Marie broke the seals and read them through, professing herself delighted: they were 'filled with so many courtesies that nothing could be added'.[62] Only then was Henrietta allowed to read the letters herself. The one from Charles was the first love letter she had ever received, and after reading it she tucked it away inside the bosom of her dress, against her heart – a sure sign of her love. As the year drew to a close, Henrietta composed a short reply to Charles, in courtesies that soon became as convoluted as the Prince's own. Even if she was not truly worthy of all 'these testimonies of your affection', she promised, still she would try to prove that she was not ungrateful: 'I am and will always be, Monsieur, your very humble and very affectionate servant,' she ended.[63]

The British court was impatient for Henrietta's arrival, not daring to reconvene Parliament before the marriage was performed. Once she arrived, James and Buckingham were sure, Henrietta would charm everyone with her 'graces and virtues', preventing 'the exorbitant ... motions that might otherwise be made in the House of Parliament'. However, January passed and still Henrietta remained in Paris, while the French and British squabbled over Catholic toleration – James agreeing only to sign promises of 'favour' to his Catholic subjects, while the French demanded 'liberty'.[64] The Pope's dispensation for the marriage had already arrived in Paris but was being held by the papal nuncio, until the treaty had been changed to include new demands from His Holiness. When the French reopened negotiations, the English were outraged at 'the infidelity of these base perfidious

Monsieurs'. As people began to talk of the marriage being broken off, Marie de' Medici was in a state of 'distraction and passion', weeping whenever her daughter was mentioned.[65] Everyone assured Henrietta that there was no danger to 'the main business', 'yet she fears all is not right, though she knows not what is amiss', reported Lord Kensington. Her ladies 'never saw so great a perplexity as they find to be in her'.[66]

Henrietta's sole consolation lay in Charles's 'most welcome' little love letters, which flowed across the Channel 'to revive and comfort her, in ... her fears'. Charles was 'eternally' hers, he promised; he would 'be always happy to hazard his life to do you service'.[67] There were gifts too, including a collection of jewels of 'very great price and remarkable beauty'. 'Do me the honour of accepting this little present,' Charles implored, 'although it be very unworthy of you.'[68] Henrietta professed herself overcome, unable to express 'how much I cherish the honour of your friendship'. Hearing the English court was planning a tournament, she sent the Prince her colours to wear 'in the noise and breach of lances' – leaving James and Charles 'infinitely satisfied ... with ... the demonstrations of her affection upon that occasion'.[69]

Nevertheless James still angrily refused to renegotiate the treaty 'in the smallest degree'. At last, in March, King Louis XIII saved the match by decreeing that if the Pope did not issue the dispensation within thirty days, the wedding would go ahead without it. Charles was delighted. 'At this time I think of nothing else but of hastening by all means the day on which I shall have the honour of kissing your hands,' he assured Henrietta.[70] In fact other matters were already preoccupying him. King James was ill with a recurring fever. After eleven sharp attacks, the last of them 'very serious and accompanied by fainting', the King was growing weak, his mind wrapped up in 'a whirl of a thousand fears'. On Sunday 27 March he died of 'a violent dysentery ... the very bed exuding the excrement'.[71]

That same day, Charles was proclaimed 'King of Great Britain, France, and Ireland, [and] Defender of the Faith'.[72] Some people noticed disturbing omens – thunder boomed 'presently upon the proclamation, and 'twas a cold season' – but it was a time of hope for most. Charles was 'the new sun', whose 'wise government' would take the country into a popular war against Spain, and mourning for the old king was 'swallowed up in joy of so hopeful a successor'.[73] Charles spent his first week as king grieving privately in his bedchamber. Only then did he make his first public appearance, attending a sermon in the royal chapel at Whitehall, dressed in a black cloak that reached to his ankles.

His subjects approved of Charles's seriousness. In his father's louche court, with its drunkenness and sexual impropriety, Charles had been a misfit – 'sober, grave, sweet ... without any evil inclinations'. Now he promised his subjects 'constancy in religion, sincerity in action and that he will not have recourse to subterfuges in his dealings'.[74] At once he began to reform the royal household, aiming to remove not only the debauchery he abhorred but also the casual etiquette of his father's court. A king should 'be approached with respect and reverence', he believed; there must be 'state and order in his court'.[75] Whilst the new style suited Charles's reserved character, in years to come it would often make him seem arrogant, high-handed and supercilious, out of touch with the ordinary world around him.

Determined to be an 'active, resolute' king, Charles spent April energetically involved in the war preparations that he and Buckingham had long desired. He issued orders to hasten on the 'great fleet ... of above one hundred sail of ships'. Sailors were press-ganged by royal proclamation and Charles went with Buckingham, Lord High Admiral of England, to inspect the forty ships already lying in the Thames.[76] With Parliament still delayed until Henrietta's arrival in England, there could be no proper funding for war, but Charles had high ambitions – to be 'the arbiter of the Christian world' – and he would not be held back. On the strength of a loan from the City of London, he ordered vast new expenditures – on extra provisions and armaments, and on new copper sheathing for the ships' hulls.[77]

In France the Pope's dispensation had finally been released by the papal nuncio and they were preparing for the wedding. Henrietta visited a fashionable spa resort 'to take the waters and medicines to recruit herself', while back in Paris tailors, dressmakers, embroiderers and jewellers were hard at work.[78] Outside the west door of Notre

Dame Cathedral, a specially erected wedding stage was hung with tapestries, while a huge gold awning kept off the sun. At its centre, the dais where Henrietta would be married was spread with purple velvet, embroidered with gold fleurs-de-lys. A huge wooden walkway was built to carry the royal party from their dressing rooms in the archbishop's palace, and this too was adorned with yards and yards of the same purple-and-gold material.

Henrietta spent the day before the wedding in religious retreat with the Carmelite nuns at the Convent of the Incarnation, just outside Paris's city walls. She had often come here in childhood, sharing the nuns' austere life on the orders of her mother, who had founded the convent in 1604, with the help of her religious mentor, Father Pierre de Bérulle. Henrietta had come to love the place and formed a close bond with the prioress, Mother Madeleine, who served as her spiritual guide. Now, in Mother Madeleine's company, she prepared for her coming change in life.

On Sunday 1 May it rained all morning as the wedding guests arrived in reverse social order – the least important first, to suffer the longest wait. At 11 a.m. Henrietta entered the Archbishop's palace to dress for the ceremony. Six hours later the rest of the court arrived from the Louvre, and King Louis ordered the wedding procession to set out. First along the velvet-hung walkway marched 100 royal guardsmen, flags flying and drums beating, followed by the trumpets, drums and oboes of the king's music, all playing loudly. Then came the gentlemen of the French court – chevaliers, seigneurs, marshals, counts and dukes, 'their clothes strewn with diamonds, and wearing robes of inestimable value'.[79] Next were the two English ambassadors and then the Duc de Chevreuse. A prominent French courtier and Charles's 'nearest kinsman' in France, Chevreuse was to be Charles's proxy in the marriage – to 'act the part of the bridegroom up to the point of getting into the bed', as the Venetian ambassador put it. He was dressed in black velvet with a scarf 'that dazzled all beholders, being literally covered with diamond roses'.[80]

Behind followed Henrietta Maria. Her gold crown was encrusted with huge diamonds, topped by a pear-shaped pearl 'of inestimable price'. Her velvet train was so long and so heavily embroidered with gold that it required two princesses and a countess to carry it, assisted by a page who walked beneath the train, supporting it on his head and arms. Leading Henrietta on either side were her two brothers: King Louis XIII in a velvet suit so smothered in gold embroidery that the cloth could not be seen at all, while Gaston Duc d'Orléans was permitted nothing more lavish than silk embroidery. Then came Marie de' Medici, wearing black as she had done ever since her husband's death, and then the French queen, Anne of Austria, and all the ladies of the court.

Outside the Cathedral, Louis and Gaston delivered their sister into the hands of the Duc de Chevreuse. Standing side by side, he and Henrietta made their marriage vows. With the sign of the cross, Cardinal de la Rochefoucauld pronounced them man and wife, according to the Catholic rite. Immediately the two English ambassadors approached to offer their congratulations. To the French king they bowed deeply as usual. However, when they turned to Louis's fifteen-year-old sister they knelt down on the ground, with all the respect that English etiquette required. Henrietta was now queen of a country she had never seen, whose language she did not speak. She was also married to a man she had never met.

2

First Impressions

In Paris the celebrations continued for days, with 'infinite acclamations' from the people. Every night fifty cannon were fired outside the Louvre and 'very beautiful fireworks' were let off over the river.[1] Meanwhile in London there was 'great ringing [of bells] and bonfires making'. The young King was over the moon at 'the greatest felicity which could happen to me in the world'.[2]

Just as Henrietta was due to leave Paris for London, Louis XIII fell ill. Henrietta chafed at the delay, telling the English ambassadors to relay to Charles her 'desire to cast herself into your Majesty's arms'.[3] Charles too fretted constantly, but there was more than husbandly eagerness involved. All his political plans – including funding for his long-cherished war preparations – depended on the meeting of Parliament, which he was still putting off until Henrietta's arrival. A week after news came of the marriage, finding the delay 'too insupportable to bear', he despatched the Duke of Buckingham to France 'to hasten and facilitate the journey of my dear wife'.[4]

Buckingham travelled 'in great haste'. After just three days he arrived in Paris to the astonishment of the French, announcing that 'the King was dying with impatience and love' for Henrietta, and 'he could not live long if he did not see her'.⁵ However, the Duke's best efforts produced no effect. Louis remained as ill as ever, and no one would leave without him. Instead, Paris turned itself over to pleasure once again. A week passed in a whirl of 'feastings and rejoicings', processions and fireworks.⁶ Greatest of all was the feast given by Cardinal Richelieu 'in honour of Madame's marriage'. The whole of Parisian high society gathered at the Palais du Luxembourg for a 'magnificent collation of sweetmeats', presided over by the three queens – Marie de' Medici, Anne of Austria and Henrietta Maria. 'All kinds of music' played in the 'superbly prepared' rooms, and then there were fireworks in the garden – the best and most imaginatively designed that had been seen in Paris for a long time.⁷

Throughout, Buckingham dazzled them all. The French were renowned for their expensive tastes, yet the Duke – wearing clothes as 'rich as invention can frame, or art fashion'* – managed to outshine 'all the bravery that court could dress itself in'.⁸ With his 'noble spirit' and his exquisite dancing performed 'to great applause', he captivated the ladies of the French court, filling them 'with joy (and something more than joy)'. The men, however, disliked him.⁹ Worst of all was Buckingham's dalliance with Anne of Austria, whose beauty Charles himself had admired in Paris two years ago. Soon everyone was aware of Buckingham's 'so dangerous and blameworthy desires'. Louis and Marie de' Medici were infuriated, but even they dared not offend the man known to have 'all power over the mind of the [British] king'.¹⁰ Far from it: the French royals heaped 'honours and civilities' on Buckingham and showered him in expensive gifts. Yet to all his urgings that they enter the alliance against Spain that Charles 'so anxiously desired', the French remained politely evasive; his proposals 'were very important and required mature consideration'. All they would offer was limited funding for the little army that the English had sent in December to fight for the Prince Palatine.¹¹

At last Louis XIII was well enough to travel, though he would

---

* Just one of his suits, smothered in diamonds, was said to be worth 'four score thousand pounds'.

accompany his sister only a short way on her journey. On Saturday 21 May, Henrietta spent a last day in the Carmelite Convent of the Incarnation. In the refectory she served the nuns with her own hands, and when it was time for her to leave she told them how sorry she was that she could not take any of them with her to England and give them a convent there, close to her palace.[12] Next day, 'amid shouts of applause and a countless throng of people', she left Paris. With her went the French royal family with their courts, plus the entourages of the three English ambassadors, Carlisle, Kensington and Buckingham, bound for home. There were also two new French ambassadors – the secretary of state la Ville-aux-Clercs and the Duc de Chevreuse – under orders to go to London 'to obtain the ratification of the [marriage] treaty ... and to see that the terms are carried out in every respect'.[13]

So vast was the cavalcade that carriages were reported in the French news to have smothered the roads like ants on an anthill.[14] Henrietta was taking an entire French court with her to England, from counts and countesses right down to cooks and chamberwomen. There were cupbearers and carvers to serve at her table, and valets and wardrobe-keepers to look after her clothes and jewels. A bevy of young maids of honour were to wait on the Queen through the day, while further maids waited on the maids of honour. She had her own treasurer and secretary, a physician, a surgeon and an apothecary. Her staff included a specialist *pâtissier* as well as a baker, a starcher, a laundress, a clock-maker and a jeweller. A master of horse took charge of her stables, with their esquires, grooms and coachmen, and she employed her own band of French musicians. In charge of them all was the Queen's Grand Chamberlain, Comte Tanneguy Leveneur de Tillières, accompanied by his wife the Comtesse, while the female side of the household was headed by the Queen's *dame d'honneur* – Henrietta's childhood friend Mamie, now Madame St-Georges. Also going to England were twenty-eight Catholic priests, a bishop, two abbots, various chaplains and clerks and, at the core of the mission, twelve Oratorian priests, led by the founder of their order himself, Father Pierre de Bérulle, who would be Henrietta's confessor.[15]

Zealous, articulate and enthusiastic, Bérulle and his Oratorians had long been dedicated to rebutting Protestantism and spearheading a Catholic revival in France. At court Bérulle had grown ever more influential, becoming father confessor to Marie de' Medici, while winning great reputation for his saintly life, his theological acumen and his skills as a statesman. He had also become a strong advocate for Henrietta's marriage: a 'holy' affair, which would bring 'the relief of the poor English Catholics, greatly oppressed for their religion'.[16]

However, Bérulle – and the Catholic Church in general – also hoped for much more: the conversion of Charles himself back to the faith of his ancestors, bringing all Britain with him. Such hopes did not seem unrealistic in the light of recent European history. Since the first zeal of the Reformation, many Protestant states had returned to the old faith. In the 1610s the Spanish ambassador had thought it would be easy to contrive the same in England, declaring: 'everything here depends on the King's will'; James could 'introduce the sect of the Turks and Moors if he pleases'.[17] This was the hidden Catholic agenda that British Protestants most feared from their king's marriage, and it was with precisely this mission in mind that Bérulle hand-picked the Oratorians who accompanied him. Some were learned theologians, ready to defend Church doctrine against all comers in England. Others were courtiers and men of the world, all set to charm the King and his closest advisers. Two were Scots, knowledgeable in British affairs. All were model churchmen, noted for their faith and virtue, and fired with the evangelical zeal of their order.[18]

Already the Pope had written to Henrietta, urging her to champion the Catholic cause in England. Now was her chance to join the 'most holy queens' in history: women like Esther, wife of the Persian king Xerxes, who had used her husband's love for her to save the Jews from massacre; or like her own ancestor, St Clotilda, the Frankish queen who had converted her husband Clovis to Christianity; or Bertha, who married the pagan Ethelbert, King of Kent, and paved the way for the conversion of England. So Henrietta too must attack her husband's heart 'with the sword of salvation and the arts of piety' and become 'the rebuilder of Religion in those waters where it has suffered a most wretched shipwreck'.[19] At the Pope's request, Henrietta had solemnly sworn that she would do 'everything that could be useful and advantageous to the Faith, and to the Catholics of the Kingdom of Great Britain'.[20]

Nonetheless, he remained concerned. As Henrietta's great entourage stayed at Amiens, where Marie de' Medici had fallen ill, a papal legate arrived, bearing a letter for the British queen and a most important gift. The Golden Rose was an ornament of the greatest price and the most holy significance, blessed each year by the Pope himself, and then given away only occasionally, to the greatest and most devout notables of the Church. In his letter the Pope urged Henrietta to become herself like the rose – 'a flower of the root of Jesse among the spines of Hebrew iniquity'.[21] Henrietta treated the Pope's legate with exceptional marks of respect, going out herself to greet him and conduct him into her presence chamber. When the Duke of Buckingham objected that her behaviour was improper for the Queen of Great Britain, Henrietta retorted 'that it so behoved her to treat the representative of the head of her religion'.[22] It was the first quarrel in what would become a very troubled relationship.

Meanwhile Charles was in agonies of impatience. The Lords and Commons had already gathered, ready for Parliament, but without Buckingham to manage his political business, and without Henrietta to charm the members into accepting the marriage treaty, Charles would not let the session begin. All through May the King was forced to put Parliament off from week to week.[23] Some MPs – complaining at the expense of this prolonged city living and at the 'danger of the plague', which was multiplying frighteningly even though summer had not yet begun – had already returned to their homes. Those who remained spoke openly against the marriage and expressed as much distrust of Charles as they had of James the year before.[24] Rumours circulated that the French were demanding yet more changes in the marriage treaty, and there were wild stories of Henrietta's total subjection to the Pope who, it was said, had imposed 'upon her I know not what penitential confession . . . for consenting to marry our King without the Pope's dispensation'.[25]

For weeks Charles had been in a state of instant readiness to leave London and meet his bride at the coast; at last he could bear the delay no longer. Early on Tuesday 31 May 1625 he descended Whitehall steps to the river, where he embarked in his royal barge and was rowed swiftly down to Gravesend. Charles's court and luggage had already gone on ahead of him, so now he travelled light and fast – the romantic adventurer once again, as he had been on his journey to Spain two years earlier. He reached Canterbury that evening – a journey of fifty-six miles that normally took travellers three days.[26] Here the bulk of his court was assembled, waiting to receive their queen in style. The King spent two nights with them, before driving on to Dover, 'accompanied by five or six only of his suite, of the highest rank'.[27]

At Dover Castle, expensive building repairs had recently been completed and a suite of nine rooms was lavishly fitted out with Crown furniture for Henrietta's first night in England. Anxiously Charles inspected it all, making sure it was 'answerable to the dignity of the persons whom it must pay tribute of honour to' and giving further 'directions of what was fitting for the Queen's accommodation'.[28] Then, satisfied with his labours, he mooned away an evening on the roof of Dover Castle, looking out over the harbour to the sea beyond, where his bride herself would soon appear. A group of courtiers who found him there at 9 p.m. had to remain with him for 'two very cold hours', until the light finally faded and the King was ready to come down.[29]

Next day Charles had himself rowed out through the harbour, where his great fleet lay at anchor, 'as strong for the number, and as beautiful for the equipage as possibly may be'. He ate dinner aboard the flagship, the *Prince Royal*, which would carry Henrietta herself to England. Then he visited a couple of other ships, inspecting the preparations for her courtiers before he returned to shore.[30] For three more days he remained in Dover, writing yet again to Henrietta, urging her to hurry and 'come straight to him'. Finally, as his ships set off for France, Charles returned reluctantly to Canterbury: Marie de' Medici had expressed a 'passionate desire' that he should not meet Henrietta on her first arrival, in case she was seasick and disappointed his great expectations.[31]

Meanwhile, in Amiens, the physicians had pronounced it would take a month for Marie de' Medici to recover. And so, at Buckingham's insistence, it was agreed that Henrietta would leave without her mother. On Monday 6 June she and her court rode out of the town, to loud artillery salutes. For the first league, Marie and Anne of Austria accompanied the great procession.[32] Then, at the final moment of parting, Marie gave Henrietta a letter of 'last farewell', telling her to keep it always with her, to 'speak for me when I can no longer speak to you myself'.

Here was advice to guide Henrietta through all the difficulties of her new life. There were sections on the kindness she must show her British subjects, on the orderliness she must maintain in her large royal household, and on the high standards of virtue she must observe in a nation notorious for the liberty it allowed its women. To her husband Henrietta owed a duty of love, respect, humility and patience. 'Do nothing that could displease him even a little,' Marie instructed.

The bulk of the letter, however, was devoted to religious instruction, and here the real author was Henrietta's confessor, Father Bérulle, using Marie's maternal authority to prepare Henrietta for the mission the Catholic Church saw as the true purpose of her marriage. Her first duty, before even that owed to her husband, must be to 'God and the religion he has established in the world'. Each day she must give thanks to God 'that He has made you Christian and Catholic' – a faith 'that you must maintain much more dearly even than your own life'. Again Henrietta was exhorted to 'be an Esther' to the English Catholics: 'God has sent you into this country for them, for they are his people, and his people who have suffered for so many years!' And it was God's plan too that she must labour for Charles's conversion: 'this must be your most ardent desire on earth.' If Henrietta failed in her duty, Marie warned, she would be cursed by a mother who was 'able to hold you for my daughter only so long as you remain the daughter of Jesus Christ and his Church'.[33] On her knees, Henrietta asked her mother's farewell blessing, which Marie gave, but added 'that if she changed her religion she gave her instead a thousand curses'. Both were in tears, each expecting never to see the other again.[34]

Two days later at Boulogne Henrietta's spirits revived as she saw the sea for the first time in her life. 'Very merry', she rushed down to the shore, approaching the water 'so near that it was bold to kiss her feet, so that her Majesty was over shoes'. Having reassumed her royal grandeur the next day, she gave audience to the six 'ladies of rank' despatched by Charles to greet her, including the Duke of Buckingham's mother, sister and niece.[35] Careful to please, Henrietta received these important courtiers with 'strange courtesy and favour', and they were duly impressed. Their new queen was no mere child, as hostile English rumour had reported, but already on the verge of womanhood. Conversing through the Catholic courtier Sir Toby Matthew, who accompanied the Buckingham ladies as translator, Henrietta showed herself 'full of wit', with 'a lovely manner in expressing it'. 'Upon my faith,' Sir Toby enthused, 'she is a most sweet lovely creature, and hath a countenance which opens a window into her heart, where a man may see all nobleness and goodness; . . . she will be extraordinarily beloved by our nation, and deserve to be so.'

If the new queen felt nervous she concealed it well. Sir Toby noticed just 'a little remnant of sadness' in her face, which he ascribed to 'the fresh wound' of parting from her mother. Her dress was 'very plain', he noted, such simplicity being the height of sophisticated French fashion: Henrietta was all set 'to teach our country wit in this kind'. Then the Buckingham ladies departed and Henrietta returned to girlish things once more, going out 'in a poor little boat in the company of her brother', Gaston d'Orléans, to the horror of the English courtiers. Yet even as they feared for their queen's safety, they admired her courage in venturing out 'for mere pastime'.[36]

That same day Charles's fleet of twenty ships sailed into the harbour, firing off a 100-gun salute. Three days later, with the sea calm and a fine southerly breeze blowing, Henrietta entered an English longboat and was rowed out to the flagship. Firing their cannon again in salute, the other ships followed her out to sea.[37] It was a magnificent sight – the sails bellying full with wind while the ships ploughed deeply through the strangely still water, their holds heavily laden with the palace-load of royal gear that Henrietta was taking with her to England.

There was solid-gold tableware for her dining room; basins and curling irons and a big silver mirror for her dressing room. She had a crimson-velvet bed embroidered with gold and silver and topped with white ostrich feathers, with a suite of bedroom furniture to match, plus tapestries and carpets. There were carriages – some heavily built for country travelling, others swathed in velvet for city use. There were litters for grand state processions, and six extra carriages for Henrietta's courtiers. Then there were mules to carry the litters, horses to draw the carriages, and a further forty riding horses – all with bridles, saddles, decorative coats and plumes of feathers.

Everyone was provided for, with furniture graded according to social status, from a silk-embroidered velvet bedroom suite for Mamie St-Georges right down to mere mattresses on the floor for the lowest valets. For the lodgings of Henrietta's Oratorian priests there were suitably austere provisions – pewter vessels, and a simple serge bed, a wooden table and a chair for each of their twelve cells. However, for the Queen's chapel, where the Oratorians would serve mass, no expense had been spared. The crosses for the altars, the chalices for holy wine, the pyxes and the monstrances for consecrated bread – all were of gold or silver. There were chandeliers and religious paintings, and five rich sets of vestments and altar cloths in different colours, plus a library of tomes of Catholic theology, ready to convert the English heretics. Nothing was forgotten: six shrouds were even packed, for wrapping the bodies of courtiers who might die in England.

More chests were full of Henrietta's clothes: wraps and nightgowns, handkerchiefs, stockings and linen caps by the dozen. There were perfumed gloves and embroidered shoes. Luxurious dresses and state robes were smothered with gold and silver lace, stitched with pearls, or lined with fur, each one worth a fortune by itself. And then there were her jewels: some ropes of hundreds of pearls, but mostly diamonds and more diamonds – in ear-pendants and rings, in buttons and crosses and knots, and in chains of up to 200 stones at a time.[38] The expense was vast. The total value of the trousseau stood at some £30,000 – or roughly £7 million in modern money – and Henrietta was bringing twice as much again in solid-gold coins as the first instalment of her dowry.[39]

Just six hours after leaving Boulogne, the English fleet dropped anchor beneath the White Cliffs of Dover after an exceptionally calm crossing, which the French took as a sign of 'how much this marriage is agreeable to God'. On shore, a deputation of grand courtiers received their queen with 'humble respect'. Then she entered Dover 'in most stately and magnificent manner', winding up through the streets of the town to the Castle.[40] Months later, after everything had turned sour, the Comte de Tillières would say that even on that first night the Queen had been 'badly lodged, even worse equipped, and her train treated with very little magnificence'. Yet at the time the French were delighted with the fine royal furniture and the 'magnificent supper' prepared for the Queen: 'nothing was omitted which could mark her status,' the ambassadors wrote to Paris that evening.[41]

Meanwhile news of Henrietta's arrival had reached Charles in Canterbury. Honouring his bride's wishes, the King stayed put for the night but early next morning, full of 'wondrous impatience', he left for Dover 'in the most private manner', romantically abandoning all royal ceremony 'to see and visit his Queen'.[42] He arrived at the Castle while Henrietta was still at breakfast. Abandoning her food, she rushed downstairs to meet him. It was a moment of real romance. Falling to her knees, the young Queen kissed her husband's hand. 'Sire,' she said, speaking in French, in which Charles was fluent, 'I am come to this land for Your Majesty, to be used and commanded by you.' Charles would have none of this submission. At once he lifted her up, wrapped her tightly in his arms, and kissed her over and over 'with all the tendernesses which an immaculate and unspotted affection could express'.[43] Everyone was moved by the couple's open display of affection, their 'pure and unfeigned caressments'. This was a true meeting of souls, they said; you could almost see the two young lovers' hearts flying out through 'the windows of their eyes' to fix 'themselves in each other's bosom'.[44]

Briefly, the couple talked together in front of their courtiers. Henrietta begged Charles's pardon for her delayed arrival. Seeing him now, she 'was most content', to which Charles replied with 'dear expressions of a never changing love'.[45] At the same time the King examined his new wife closely. For months he had been worried by stories of how small she was. Even the Earl of Holland (as Lord Kensington had now become in reward for his success as 'wooing ambassador') had had to admit that 'her growth is not great yet', though he reassured Charles that 'her shape is perfect'. Nonetheless Charles had continued to worry and had asked the Duke of Buckingham to get an exact measurement of his new wife's height.[46] Now, finally, he could see for himself. Henrietta was indeed rather small – 'her head reached just to his shoulder', observers noted, so she must have been around four feet ten inches tall, although this was more than rumour had reported. So was she wearing high heels? Charles peered down at his wife's feet, trying to see past her long skirts, until Henrietta noticed. 'Sir,' she reassured him, 'I stand upon mine own feet; I have no helps by art. Thus high I am, and am neither higher nor lower.'[47]

Then the couple retired to spend some time in private. Later, Charles himself recorded the request Henrietta now made to him: 'that she being young and coming to a strange country, both by her years and ignorance of the customs of the place, might commit many errors, therefore that I would not be angry with her for her faults . . . and . . . to use no third person, but to tell her myself when I found she did anything amiss.' It was a formal speech, clearly prepared in advance, but Charles was charmed. Readily he granted his bride's request, asking in return 'that she would use me as she had desired me to use her, which she willingly promised me'.[48] Henrietta's modesty and eagerness to please were delightful, and she was attractive in appearance too. 'She is nimble and quick,' the English noted, 'black eyed, brown haired, and, in a word, a brave lady.' If she seemed pale – 'perhaps a little touched with the green sickness' – there was no need to worry: anaemia was common in teenage girls and contemporary medical practitioners agreed it was easily cured by a husband's attentions.[49]

After an hour alone the couple emerged and Henrietta introduced her French household to Charles one by one, in order of their status. Then the royal pair sat down to dinner, where Charles served his wife with his own hands, carving pheasant and venison. Concerned only to please him, she ate 'heartily of both', ignoring her confessor's protests that it was a Catholic fast day and that 'she should take heed how she gave ill examples or scandal at her first arrival'.[50]

Charles and Henrietta had hit it off perfectly, and that afternoon the Queen readily agreed to her husband's request that he and some of the Buckingham ladies should travel in her carriage on the way to Canterbury. The French household, however, were furious when they heard there would now be no room for Henrietta's *dame d'honneur*, Mamie St-Georges. The two ambassadors protested vigorously to Buckingham: it was a gross violation of French etiquette; Mamie's title was one of the best in France, a true ancient, aristocratic dignity, no mere novelty, conferred recently by the King (as were all the Buckingham family's titles). Buckingham retorted that Henrietta herself had given her consent, and it was the custom of England that no lady had any right to travel in the Queen's carriage, where places were given only by her command. As the quarrel escalated, a new figure stepped in: the energetic young Bishop of Mende, the Grand Almoner in charge of Henrietta's priests, 'a man of ready wit', 'highly esteemed' by Louis XIII, and a nephew of Cardinal Richelieu.[51] Eager to advance Richelieu's policy of alliance with England, he would repeatedly pour oil on the troubled waters of Anglo-French relations. Now he advised the French ambassadors to show moderation. At last they had to agree, seeing they could not alter matters 'whatever remonstrance we made'.[52]

So disgraceful was the arrangement in French eyes – so gross the violation of their native customs, so disgraceful the English contempt for all their arguments – that when the Comte de Tillières and the ambassador la Ville-aux-Clercs later wrote their memoirs, neither would admit what had actually happened. La Ville-aux-Clercs reported with self-satisfaction how his own firmness against Buckingham had won Madame St-Georges a place in the Queen's carriage, while the Comte de Tillières embroidered the story much further. According to him, this was not a dispute between Buckingham and the French household at all, but a violent quarrel between Charles and Henrietta themselves. In his version Henrietta, not Mamie St-Georges, protested vainly against the King's command, desperate to have her friend with her in the coach, but unable to obtain her wish 'whatever supplications she could make'. In this version, Charles finally backed down and allowed Mamie into the carriage only on the 'solicitations of the French ambassadors', 'which annoyed the Queen extremely'. In fact, 'she evinced a little too lively a resentment of it, in my opinion,' Tillières added with pompous self-righteousness.[53]

Tillières's account of this episode and his portrait of Henrietta as a wilful, tantrum-prone teenager, lacking even the self-confidence to ride unaccompanied in a coach with her new husband and some English ladies whom she had mostly already met and charmed in Boulogne, has been reproduced by historians ever since. Yet both Tillières's and la Ville-aux-Clercs's narratives are disproved by the French ambassadors' letters written at the time, which survive in manuscript transcripts in the British Library. Here Chevreuse and la Ville-aux-Clercs excused their own failure to enforce French etiquette and have Mamie St-Georges ride in Henrietta's coach, explaining that it had all been agreed between Henrietta and Charles before they knew anything of it. Their letters portray a bride at one with her husband: 'she had no will but his,' Henrietta told Charles, perfectly happy to neglect her own followers to please him.[54] To English eyes it was so trifling a matter that none of the contemporary newsletters mention it. However, these were no trivia for the courtiers concerned, whose status rested on the privileges they were entitled to. The French would neither forget nor forgive the insult.

As the royal carriages drove out of Dover 'a gallant volley of shot' came from the Castle and from the fleet below, so loud that even the echo from the surrounding hills could be heard across the Channel in Calais. All along their route the roads were 'strewed with green rushes, roses and the choicest flowers that could be gotten, and the trees loaden with people of all sorts, who with shouts and acclamations gave them a continual welcome'. Village church bells rang as the gentry and militia of Kent turned out 'to attend and receive the Queen . . . in such solemn manner and equipage as beseemed . . . the quality of her person'.[55]

Five miles outside Canterbury, on the open hilltop of Barham Down, the procession was met by Charles's courtiers – dazzling in their finery 'like so many constellations'.[56] Anxious to behave correctly, Henrietta had asked the English ambassadors in France about the correct etiquette for this occasion. Now, as Charles presented all the lords and ladies in order of their rank, she performed her part perfectly. Each grand lady, 'from a fitting distance', made three low curtsies and then approached and kissed her hand. Then the Queen returned their kisses 'with such good grace that she won the esteem and good-will of everyone'. 'She hath eyes that sparkle like stars,' the English enthused; her face was 'a mirror of perfection'.[57]

At last the ceremonies were over. Even the lesser court ladies, the wives of knights and gentlemen, had been presented – curtsying to the Queen from a distance without any kisses. Charles and Henrietta now remounted into her carriage and drove on to Canterbury.[58] At a grand nobleman's house just outside the city walls 'magnificent preparations' had been made for their wedding night. In the medieval hall the King and Queen sat down to a state banquet in view of all. Again Charles offended Henrietta's courtiers – this time by arranging that he and the Queen should be 'waited on by the king's attendants only, to the disgust of the French'.[59] Afterwards Henrietta retired to her bedchamber, accompanied by the Duchesse de Chevreuse, who helped her into her nightgown and put her to bed. A little later Charles joined his bride. Unwilling to endure the bawdy high jinks commonly practised on newlyweds, the King bolted the doors of the room, allowing in just two of his gentlemen to undress him. Then he locked them out as well, and the couple were left alone.[60]

Next morning they lay late in bed. Charles, normally a rigorously early riser, did not emerge until 7 a.m., when his courtiers found him uncharacteristically light-hearted, joking about how he had cheated them of their amusements the night before. All that day he continued 'very jocund'. Meanwhile the ladies of Henrietta's court, having made the necessary inspections and enquiries, sent letters off to Paris, inform-ing the Queen Mother 'that the marriage of their British Majesties had been consummated to their common satisfaction'. All that day the honeymooning couple and their courts remained in Canterbury, which 'seemed for that little time a very Eden or Paradise, where nothing was wanting that might serve joy or delight'.[61] Next morning, with her great cavalcade, Henrietta set off for London and married life.

3

Quarrelling

On 16 June 1625 the royal couple entered London in triumph, rowed upriver in their grand state barge, attended by thousands of boats bearing 'an infinite number of lords, ladies, and other people'. Along their route 200 warships, 'decorated and beflagged', fired off their guns: a deafening thunder 'of fifteen hundred great shot' that continued for 'twelve or fifteen miles together, and the nearer the King and Queen came to London, the greater and greater still the volley increased'. Charles was elated: observers thought they had never beheld the king to look so merrily', and Henrietta's beauty and good nature were the talk of the watching crowd. As the barge approached the City itself just before 5 p.m., the Tower of London fired off all its guns; 'nothing could be heard for the terror of the noise'. Proudly Charles brought his wife out onto the deck so that 'she might see the people and the city', but at once it began to rain: a heavy downpour that forced the couple back inside. Still, eager to be seen by the crowd, they had the barge's large windows opened and stood together just inside one, braving the violent weather in their matching green suits, a picture of mingled majesty and love.

While the great flotilla swept beneath the medieval arches of London

Bridge and on past the City, the rain continued to flood down, but no one's enthusiasm was dampened. Bells rang out from the churches, and crowds in 'infinite numbers' cheered and cheered from streets and wharves, gardens and house windows, and from boats moored along the river's banks. Under the weight of 100 eager spectators, one ship actually capsized and sank: it was one of the marriage's miracles that everyone in her survived. And still the royal couple sailed on, past St Paul's Cathedral and then the Strand, where the noblemen's houses stretched down in formal gardens to the river's northern bank. At the long pier that was Whitehall's Privy Stairs the barge put in amidst more 'acclamations of joy', and Henrietta Maria saw her new home for the first time.[1]

It must have been a disappointment. Rambling roofs and chimneys, and blank walls irregularly scattered with small square windows made Whitehall seem more 'an assemblage of several houses, badly built, at different times and for different purposes' than a royal palace, noted another seventeenth-century European royal arriving there.[2] Yet this straggling Tudor tangle of some 1400 interconnected chambers was the principal seat of Britain's royal court and national government alike. The public road of King Street cut it in two. To the west lay an elaborate sports complex: tennis courts and a bowling alley, a cockpit and a jousting yard, with St James's Park beyond. To the east, reaching to the river, was a hothouse world where royals, courtiers and government officials ate, slept, worked and played. Servants laboured in kitchens, pantries and stables, while grandees entertained in their halls and withdrawing chambers. Next door to the King's bedchamber the Privy Council met to decide the nation's affairs, while secretaries hunched over their papers in scattered lodgings. Fountains played in gardens; choirboys sang in the royal chapel. And at the palace's heart, connected via their adjoining presence chambers, lay the two suites of apartments known as the King's Side and the Queen's Side. Charles's rooms extended westwards, looking out over the Privy Garden, while the Queen's spread east with views over the river. Here Henrietta retired with her French household while the church bells rang on till midnight and 'all the streets were full of bonfires'.[3]

In the following days the wedding festivites continued. In White-hall's grand Renaissance Banqueting House – purpose-built by Charles's father for such state occasions – the royal couple sat side by side on their thrones for the formal ratification of their marriage treaty. Henrietta was proclaimed queen, an Anglican bishop gave his blessing – the closest thing to a Protestant wedding ceremony the French would allow – and Charles kissed his bride.[4] A banquet followed, then dancing, at which Henrietta distinguished herself, dancing beautifully yet 'without losing any of the gravity which must be kept by persons of her rank'. Next day there was jousting, where Charles 'made himself as much admired in these exercises as the Queen his wife had been at the ball'. Then the Duke of Buckingham excelled himself, entertaining Henrietta's French courtiers 'with such magnificence and prodigal plenty . . . that the like hath not been seen in these parts'.[5]

Despite all the lavish display, the English could not match up to French expectations. The Parisian court was considered the most splendid in Europe. Louis XIII had more courtiers than any other monarch; his palaces were 'very huge and stately'; French clothes were richer, their furniture more costly and more comfortable.[6] Henrietta's courtiers complained bitterly at their reception, which lacked all the 'gallantries that are usually made on such occasions'. There should have been a state procession through London's streets, stopping to see the citizens' 'shows and pageants'. At Whitehall there should have been masques and ballets, with Londoners coming to entertain their queen.[7] Charles had in fact planned such entertainments, but all had been abandoned, for the plague was spreading in the capital. In the previous week, ninety-one had died of it, making people 'much afraid'. Nonetheless the French felt insulted. Even Henrietta's great state bed seemed to them merely a leftover from the reign of Queen Elizabeth I, its design so passé that even the oldest Frenchman present had never seen such a thing.[8]

More galling still were Charles's manifest violations of his marriage promises. The treaty stated that only Catholics should serve in Henrietta's court, yet already some English Protestants had been appointed, whom the French angrily dismissed. However, in the matter of the

Catholic chapels that Henrietta was supposed to have 'within every one of the King's houses ... kept as Madame shall appoint', they were powerless.⁹ At St James's Palace, Henrietta's official London residence, building work on a large Catholic chapel had begun two years earlier, when Charles was courting the Spanish Infanta. It remained un-finished. And at Whitehall – as Henrietta found when she emerged from her bedchamber the first morning, coming to mass 'in her petticoat, with a veil upon her head', holding the arm of the Comte de Tillières – there was no proper chapel at all, merely a room set aside 'for ecclesiastical purposes', and that 'only a very small oratory in which no privacy is possible'.¹⁰ When the French complained, Charles merely answered that if Henrietta's closet at Whitehall was inadequate, they should hold mass in her great chamber, 'and if the great chamber was not wide enough, they might use the garden; and if the garden would not serve their turn, then was the park the fittest place'.¹¹

Then too there was the active persecution being inflicted on English Catholics, despite all Charles's and James's promises when they signed the *Escrit Secret* back in December. Even some of Henrietta's own servants were arrested and brought before the justices, charged with recusancy. The French clergymen especially were utterly disheartened, seeing their co-religionists, 'in fear of prison and of the hangman', unable 'to seek God but while trembling'. All their dreams for how the marriage would 'profit the Catholic Religion' were in tatters; their promises to the Pope unfulfilled.¹² Yet Charles would do nothing: Parliament was now in session, and he could not risk offending the anti-Catholic MPs until they had voted through the war funding he needed.

Even so, the MPs were beginning 'to mutter about matters of religion', noting how Charles had promised, as Prince of Wales, 'that he would never contract a marriage with conditions derogatory' to their religion. Yet the marriage treaty was being kept secret, making them 'suspect the more'.¹³ Henrietta's priests, in particular, were an affront. For the first time since the reign of Queen Mary, nearly seventy years earlier, when Protestant martyrs had been burnt at the stake, Catholic clergymen walked openly through Whitehall, dressed 'in their clerical habits'. Every morning, at the very heart of the nation's government, they performed the hated Catholic mass, with its alien trappings of incense, holy water and images of saints: a ceremony that was otherwise illegal throughout the country. In the euphoria of Henrietta's first arrival, there had been hopes she might convert to Protestantism. But now the reality had become plain: 'we have got a good and devout Princess,' Catholics gloated, overjoyed at 'the confusion of the malignant [Protestants]'.[14]

Yet amidst all the animosities, the royal couple remained unaffected. Continuing their honeymoon from Canterbury, they treated each other with 'the greatest respect and affection', whilst avoiding talking of the Catholic persecution and Charles's disputes with the French ambassadors. 'The King shows the greatest respect and affection for the Queen,' the Florentine ambassador in London commented, 'and she, whilst sensitive to all that is going on around her, conducts herself with much prudence, and towards the King with every symptom of veneration and regard.'[15]

Their happiness was short-lived. As the plague spread relentlessly, killing hundreds every week, the couple fled from London with their courts. Again Charles ordered Mamie St-Georges's exclusion from their coach, and this time, concerned for her French household, Henrietta objected, 'showing some resentment', though in her usual witty style with 'more of gaiety than bitterness'. It was Charles's first experience of opposition from his wife and he did not like it. Special orders from him now formally deprived Mamie of any right of entry to the royal coach, leaving Henrietta's courtiers deeply angry that they had 'not met with that fair treatment which they were led to expect'.[16]

Their resentment only intensified as the Duke of Buckingham pressed them to appoint the ladies of his family to important positions at Henrietta's court. In the King's court Buckingham reigned supreme: 'nothing is done without him'.[17] It was therefore hardly surprising that he desired a similar influence over the Queen. Briefly Richelieu dithered. Was it worth abandoning the treaty terms just this once to please Charles and Buckingham? The English might do something even worse if they resisted. Perhaps the Duke's wife and mother at least should have the posts they desired. In the end Richelieu decided no compromise was possible; quite apart from breaking the promises the French had made to the Pope, having Protestants about the Queen could so easily lead to 'incalculable evils'. Only the Duke's mother, Mary Countess of Buckingham, could be appointed, for she was a Roman Catholic and so 'not contrary to the treaty'.[18]

Here Charles himself intervened. There would be no British Catholics in the Queen's household, he insisted, for fear of papist plotting and rebellions. So Buckingham's mother too was rejected. Enraged, the Duke 'spoke bitterly to the queen' and insulted the French ambassadors to the point where la Ville-aux-Clercs decided he must be challenged to a duel, which was abandoned only when Buckingham apologised abjectly next day. For the French the incident was unforgettable. 'Strongly set against the Duke', they would blame all their ills – all the rejections, insults and disappointments that were still to come – on Buckingham alone.[19]

All Henrietta's high hopes for her marriage were ruined. Still the plague pursued the court, forcing them to abandon first Hampton Court then Windsor Castle. 'We do nothing but travel,' the teenage queen complained, as the French ambassadors left England, demoralised, with none of the treaty disputes settled.[20] Father Bérulle was especially dismayed. What would become of his young charge, trapped in so terrible a land, 'which has more storms and tempests than the Ocean itself'? He had hoped to see Henrietta happy amidst the royal roses of England but instead she seemed to him now like a solitary, fragile flower among the spines of heresy. Eager to keep the young Queen's spirits and resolution up, he encouraged her to throw herself into special religious devotions and austerities. Soon she was eagerly confiding to Mother Madeleine in Paris: 'we have here a Convent of the Incarnation just as much as you do.' Here Henrietta and her ladies lived like the Carmelite nuns, though not so strictly. 'Monsieur de Bérulle who is here dispenses us from it,' Henrietta explained playfully.[21]

Gradually Bérulle began to steer the Queen towards his great end. His methods were subtle. 'In order not to startle her, one must hold a light bridle to her,' he wrote. 'It is necessary to speak to her little, with gentleness and respect, and not to burden or press her.' Soon his persuasions had their effect: en route for Oxford, where Parliament was to reconvene on Charles's orders, Henrietta spoke to her husband for the first time about the persecution of the British Catholics.[22] However, Charles could not afford to offend Parliament. He was desperate for his war funding now: massive sums had already been borrowed and spent on the fleet, but without still more money it could not set out. On 4 August he made a personal appeal to the assembled Lords and Commons, to no avail: the MPs refused any payment unless the nation's anti-Catholic penal laws were put into full execution. It fell to Buckingham to save the day. Their enforcement was quite possible, he told the Privy Council. Charles's marriage treaty had involved no real promise of toleration at all; the *Escrit Secret* signed in Cambridge had been a mere form, designed to deceive the Pope into issuing a dispensation for the marriage. To Parliament he lied again, assuring them 'that his Majesty had not entered into any engagements in favour of the Catholics'. All their religious demands, he promised, would be satisfied.[23]

Henrietta and her household were astounded. They had trusted in the *Escrit*'s promises of toleration, but now they saw that Buckingham was capable of any treachery. His persecution of the Catholics was an act of revenge, they believed, for Henrietta's refusal to appoint his womenfolk to her court.[24] Henrietta could restrain her resentment no longer. To everyone at the English court 'of whatsoever quality' she was cold and disrespectful. The Bishop of Mende tried to reason with her: she should 'treat the King and the grandees of the state with more courtesy'; her role here was to be an ambassador, persuading her husband to co-operate with French government policies. But his words had no effect. Instead Henrietta and Mamie St-Georges approached the Earl of Pembroke, Buckingham's chief rival at court, proposing that he join them to make a party dedicated to 'ruining Buckingham in parliament and elsewhere'.[25]

Their plot was soon discovered and, on Charles's insistence, there were public reconciliations all round.[26] Yet it appeared that

Buckingham had far more powerful enemies even than Henrietta and her friends. Within days of Parliament's first meeting, the MPs had turned to investigating the government's military ineptitude. The fleet was unready, the troops fruitlessly inactive, the money previously granted all misspent. 'Everything goes wrong,' they complained, and it was clear where the fault lay. 'The Duke of Buckingham is trusted,' they pointed out, 'and it must needs be either in him or his agents.' As they began to draw up a formal charge-sheet, accusing Buckingham of incompetence and abuse of power, Charles was forced to act. His 'passionate love for the Duke' left him no choice.[27] Forfeiting his long-awaited funding, the King dissolved Parliament less than two weeks after the session had begun.

The court left Oxford hurriedly, for the plague had arrived. There was no question of returning closer to London, where the disease was now killing 4000–5000 people every week. So Charles and Henrietta travelled south to the coast. Nowhere was big enough to house both courts, so the couple separated to live in houses fourteen miles apart, on opposite sides of Southampton Water.[28] The physical distance exacerbated their emotional divisions. While Charles 'went almost daily out hunting', Catholic priests flocked to Henrietta's court at Titchfield, firing her anger with tales of the horrors being inflicted on their English flocks. She wished 'she might be the first martyr' in the common cause, she exclaimed. When Charles visited, she 'treated him coldly', full of 'unkindnesses' and 'neglects'.[29]

Once again Henrietta found consolation in religious retreat, living with her ladies as nuns. Mamie St-Georges was the abbess, empowered to 'command . . . and punish'; the Comtesse de Tillières was her deputy. Below them the rest lived 'as young religieuse[s] in probation under discipline', sharing one long table at mealtimes, eating and drinking from earthenware vessels 'to show the love of poverty and mortification'. 'Lowest of all' was the Queen herself, so 'that better she might forget her queenly majesty'. Unlike Henrietta's earlier light-hearted, Carmelite-inspired convent, this was a serious matter, modelled on the extreme austerity of St Elizabeth of Hungary. Catholic priests boasted of the ladies' remarkable 'religious discipline'; 'perpetual

prayers', fasting, going barefoot, kissing the ground and even fla-
gellation were mentioned. The English were horrified at these 'vulgar
and lowly exercises', so inappropriate for a queen. The greatest affront
lay in what Charles delicately referred to as Henrietta's 'eschewing
to be in my company'. The retreat's sexual abstinence, imposed by
Henrietta's priests with 'their feigned mantles of piety', was threatening
the very succession to the British throne.[30]

On one occasion Charles complained in person to Henrietta; his
courtiers, he told her, had assured him that if she was their wife they
would exercise their marital rights much more often than he did, yet
'for the little I require from you, you make yourself difficult'. Usually
it was the Duke of Buckingham rather than the King who entered
Henrietta's quarters, even late at night, to berate the diminutive fifteen-
year-old for her misdemeanours. The King was 'very displeased', he
told her. If she did not change her ways 'the time of affliction had
come for her'; in the end 'she would no longer be treated as a queen,
but as she deserved'.[31] Under siege with her embattled court, Henrietta
found no support from France: Marie de' Medici had sent 'private
letters', ordering her to behave more diplomatically. So, reluctantly,
the English queen agreed that Father Bérulle return to France to
present her side of the story. 'I envy your happiness in seeing Monsieur
de Bérulle,' she wrote to Mother Madeleine in Paris, 'but it will only
be for a month at most,' she consoled herself.[32]

In the meantime Bérulle chose another Oratorian to replace him as
her confessor. Father Sancy was highly qualified: he had been a courtier,
soldier and statesman before taking orders, and he knew at least some
English. However, Sancy was also hot-tempered and obstinate, and
his incendiary behaviour soon brought new troubles for the royal
marriage. One incident occurred when Charles was dining with Henrietta at Titchfield. As the King's chaplain began to say grace as usual,
Sancy stepped forward and would have begun prayers of his own, 'but
that Hacket [the chaplain] shoved him away'. So Sancy went to stand
by Henrietta, where his prayer was prevented only by the King 'pulling
the dishes unto him, and the carvers falling to their business'. When
the meal was over, Sancy again tried to jump in, but Charles's Anglican

started to speak first. So Sancy began loudly on his own grace, 'with such a confusion, that the King, in a great passion, instantly rose from the table, and, taking the queen by the hand, retired into the bedchamber'.[33]

The outrages continued on Sunday 18 September, when the Anglican vicar of Titchfield arrived to preach at Henrietta's court. In the midst of his sermon Henrietta emerged from her apartments with the Comte de Tillières and all her maids of honour, making 'such a noise' that they brought the preacher to a standstill. His angry demand 'whether he might proceed or no' was ignored by the Queen's party who continued, apparently oblivious, out through the hall with as much noise as ever. Before he finished they passed back again with an even 'greater noise and disorder than before'. The shocking incident filled the news. According to some, the Queen and her ladies were merely 'talking loudly'. Others said she had brought her hunting dogs and passed through making 'the loud cries usual in chasing hares'. However, everyone agreed that it was a deliberate disruption, the result of Henrietta's 'zeal in religion'.[34] In the following days the vicar received verbal abuse and death-threats from the French. Then, while he walked in his garden, a gun was fired from an adjoining orchard, where two of the Queen's valets were shooting birds. Miraculously the clergyman was unhurt, but the shot was clearly directed at him: the hail of tiny balls landed all around him. Soon the culprit was arrested and charged with attempted murder, yet far more was involved than just 'the folly of a lackey'. The Venetian ambassador feared that the fate of nations hung in the balance; the 'evil results' of such incidents could 'disturb for ever cordial relations' between England and France.[35]

Charles, who was at Plymouth at the time with the Duke of Buckingham, waiting to see his navy sail for Spain, rushed to resolve the crisis in person. To his surprise, he found it hardly necessary. 'My wife begins to mend her manners,' he reported happily to Buckingham, though 'I know not how long it will continue, for they say it is by advice [from France]'. For the moment, at least, Henrietta was 'very gracious' to her husband and the couple sometimes spent three hours together at night. Pleasing too was Henrietta's abandonment of her religious retreat; one of her court ladies had died, begging the Queen to 'take warning', for she believed 'her indiscreet mortifications' in their nunnery had caused her death.[36] 'Best of all,' Charles told Buckingham, 'the monsieurs desire to return home.' The King seized his opportunity and paid off thirty or forty of those 'of low condition'. However, too many still remained: 'excitable French people who cannot be quiet', who continued to augment 'the bad understanding between the two nations'.[37]

As the plague eased that autumn, the royals moved back to Hampton Court, where a new French ambassador arrived. Although the Seigneur de Blainville-sur-Orne was a high-ranking courtier and a councillor of state, he received scant respect from the English. His demands for the proper execution of the marriage treaty were met with intransigent refusal. 'What had been done against the Catholics was only for the good of his state,' Charles said; besides, 'their sufferings were not as great as people made out.'[38] Blainville too had a bloody-minded streak, and he would no more back down than Charles. For weeks all court business was 'confined to disputes with the French'. By mid-November the English were furious at Blainville's 'violence and rude conduct', while the French were 'full to the throat with disgust' at the English treachery.[39] Henrietta was desperate. 'I receive every day new afflictions', she wrote to Bérulle. 'As for the poor Catholics, the persecution is greater than ever. The ambassador and all of us despair at it. He does all he can for the service of God and for my service . . . Every day they promise to satisfy him and, an hour later, they do all they can to annoy him and they laugh at him . . . I beg you very strongly to come back the soonest that you can. I have great need that you be here.'[40]

But Father Bérulle remained firmly in France. Richelieu distrusted his enthusiastic Catholicism, and blamed him for setting Charles and Henrietta against each other for his own religious ends. With the French government determined to maintain the English alliance against Spain, Bérulle's complaints about the English went unregarded. Still Marie de' Medici insisted that Henrietta tread the impossible line of pleasing everyone, giving 'honour and respect to the King, warm welcome to the nobility, protection to the Catholics, affection to all'.

All Bérulle could do was to resign himself to the will of God and offer Henrietta consolation: 'no day passes when I do not think of Your Majesty and the travails you endure,' he assured her.[41]

Soon a new battleground was opening up. With their return to Hampton Court it was time, Charles thought, to reform the laxity of his wife's court, where the French approached the Queen 'without ceremony', sharing her conversation with 'openness and freedom'.[42] For Charles, proper court etiquette was the very basis of monarchy, the best means to make 'princes to be adored'. Henrietta on the other hand was appalled by his demand that she follow the same rules that had been used in 'the Queen my mother's house'.[43] These regulations 'wounded her maids whom she loved, and distanced them from around her person'. 'She could not surrender her liberty,' she replied; she hoped her husband 'would give her leave to order her house as she list'. Charles was bitterly resentful, not so much at the refusal itself, which could be ascribed to ignorance of English court customs, but at the way his wife had given it, in public, in front of all their courtiers. He could never have imagined 'that she should affront me so'. Later he drew her aside and explained her mistakes, both in making a 'public denial' and in 'the business itself'. His reproof only infuriated Henrietta further. Far from 'acknowledging her fault', the Queen launched at once into so long a tirade of French, full of 'so ill an answer', that Charles refused to record it.[44]

Charles would stand no more. He had endured 'the unkind usages of my wife' for too long, thinking she was 'but young' and her manners might mend. Buckingham had encouraged such hopes, eager to preserve the French alliance.[45] Now, however, Buckingham was away in the Netherlands, seeking further anti-Spanish treaties, and Charles no longer trusted his assurances. He still believed in Henrietta's basic good will; all her 'disrespects' were 'not in her nature', but caused by 'the maliciousness of the monsieurs'. The worst offender was Mamie St-Georges. It seemed to Charles that ever since he had excluded her from Henrietta's coach, Mamie had been set on ruining his marriage, stirring Henrietta up into 'such an humour of distaste against me, as that from that very hour to this, no man can say that ever she used me two days together with so much respect as I deserved'.[46]

Charles came to a decision. He would 'cashier my monsieurs' and send them back to France, every last one, but he would not act without consulting his one true friend. 'Steenie,' he wrote, 'send me word with what speed you may, whether you like this course or not, for I shall put nothing of this in execution until I hear from you; . . . but I am resolute; it must be done, and that shortly.'[47]

Despite Charles's indignation, none of the French was sent packing. The Duke himself, we can presume, prevented it. Nevertheless, Buckingham's dogged diplomacy was coming to seem futile, as France abandoned its hostility towards the Spanish and turned its military might instead against the Protestant Huguenot rebels at La Rochelle. When the last remnants of the Huguenots' fleet took refuge in England, Blainville demanded they be handed over to the French authorities. Charles refused: such a betrayal of his co-religionists would upset his fiercely Protestant subjects as well as spoiling his own pretensions of leading the Protestant cause in Europe. The French were livid. Henrietta's match had been intended 'to marry England to France more than to marry individuals', Richelieu declared, 'but it has turned out the reverse'. With Richelieu threatening to ally with Spain, England now risked an international disaster: simultaneous war with all Catholic Europe.[48]

Despite the failures in his foreign policies, Buckingham received 'a most affectionate welcome' from Charles when he returned to England in December. 'Grief is eased being told to a friend,' the King confided to the Duke. And Charles needed consoling, for his relations with Henrietta grew 'worse and worse'.[49] First the couple quarrelled over her refusal to attend the ceremonies of Charles's beloved Order of the Garter. 'Scruples of conscience' prevented her presence at the Protestant ceremony, the Queen explained, but the English took it as a deliberate insult. Then Charles insisted her courtiers swear an oath of allegiance to him; if they refused, they must leave the country at once. This created such 'a great commotion' that Henrietta went down on her knees to the King and wept.[50]

Amidst the quarrels, Henrietta's sixteenth birthday passed

unremarked, but Christmas was another matter. With the plague almost gone, professional actors were summoned to perform at Hampton Court. The Queen even braved the capital herself, going Christmas shopping incognito in the Exchange, where she 'went nimbly from shop to shop, and bought some knacks, till, being discovered, she made away with all the haste she could'. In the season of goodwill, reconciliations were begun. Henrietta was trying 'to appear more wise', she assured Louis XIII; though still feeling wronged, 'I affect to do nothing by passion.'[51] Pleased, Charles responded with a lavish New Year's gift to his wife: Somerset House, which had been his mother's London home. Here at last Henrietta would have 'a noble palace' in Renaissance style, such as she had known in France. With it came 'all the ornaments and household stuff' from Charles's mother's time, including a fine art collection – making a present that was 'greatly appreciated and has led to a more intimate understanding between their Majesties'.[52]

Buckingham was keen for reconciliation too. His immense war fleet – 'the greatest that ever England sent out' – had been utterly defeated by the Spanish at Cadiz; just a third of the ships had limped home, war-torn and storm-battered, in what the English public regarded as 'a shameful return'.[53] Now he needed money for more ships, but he had no desire to call Parliament. The second half of Henrietta's dowry had still not been paid by the French, and in hopes of getting it, Buckingham set out to appease the Queen, becoming 'as intimate as possible' with her. He 'humbled himself frequently, offering his services', and promised to settle the dispute about appointing English ladies to Henrietta's court 'to her satisfaction'. He even offered Henrietta a place on the King's Privy Council. The Queen politely declined, on Blainville's advice that this was some new English trick.[54] She and her courtiers would never trust Buckingham now. Even the pacific Bishop of Mende had abandoned hope of a real rapprochement. Despatched to Paris, he delivered 'a clear account of all the disturbances that took place in the queen's household', complaining 'very highly and in often biting terms' about the Duke.[55] As the French turned away from their alliance with England, at last Henrietta's side of the story began to gain some credence. With 'her eyes ... full of tears', Marie de' Medici declared that 'she would rather have given a finger off her hand than have married her daughter in England.' There would be no dowry payment now, Louis told Charles's ambassadors, not until 'the queen enjoys the fulfilment of what was promised' in the marriage treaty.[56]

And so the English court was forced to call Parliament again. In hopes of placating the House of Commons, Catholic persecution was stepped up. The King's pursuivants searched Catholic homes, where they 'robbed ... and made good prize of their books, beads, images, and priest's vestments', as well as 'money and other things' they were not authorised to take. The magistrates' courts summoned suspected Catholics to swear the oath of allegiance to the King – an oath forbidden by the Pope. Those who refused were 'thrown into prison and their goods confiscated'. 'No one is excepted, even barons,' Blainville reported; he and Henrietta were in despair at the Catholics' sufferings. Nothing worse could be done to them now 'except banishment or death'; they had reached their 'extreme unction'.[57]

Yet still Buckingham sought Henrietta's help. As the besieged Huguenots of La Rochelle were driven closer to starvation and surrender, he and Charles were frantic to save them and so placate Parliament. 'If the town fell he would recover it in person,' Charles stated. With the English ambassadors in Paris doing all they could to broker a peace deal for the Huguenots, Buckingham asked Henrietta to write in person to her mother. She was only too ready to comply, fearing that war with France would cut her off from her family. In her own hand, 'expressing her anguish at being involved in the quarrels between her brother and her husband', Henrietta begged Marie to persuade Louis to show 'moderation towards la Rochelle'.[58]

By now Charles was preparing for his coronation, and he was determined it would be perfect. On his orders a committee of bishops and peers had drawn up an order of ceremony corresponding exactly to the crownings of the medieval kings of England, except that Charles's service would be performed in English, not Latin. The King himself 'viewed all the regalia' and tried on the Saxon vestments worn since the time of Edward the Confessor. However, his plans had a flaw: his ceremony was for 'the crowning of the King and Queen together', and the French had 'scruples' about Henrietta's participation in this Anglican ceremony.[59] It would offend the Pope, Louis feared, and the British Catholics would be disgusted to see their Queen, 'in whom they have put their hopes, on her knees in front of a protestant bishop, taking from him oaths and a diadem and the other ornaments of royalty'. Yet Louis knew there were strong arguments for Henrietta's coronation – especially 'that in rejecting this honour she is wounding the kingdom and even the dignity and birth of her children', whose right to the throne might thereby be called into question.

The French suggested compromise. Perhaps the Bishop of Mende could crown her, just outside the church, as Charles had been married outside Notre Dame. Or maybe, after Charles's Protestant rites were done, Henrietta could enter Westminster Abbey and have the crown placed on her head 'without any other ceremony'. Then she could proceed to the coronation feast and the opening of Parliament, so she would be seen 'by all the people with the crown on her head'.[60] These alternatives fell on deaf ears. Charles would not allow the slightest alteration in his meticulously planned ceremonies, with the result, the learned doctors of the Sorbonne decided, that 'the queen cannot be crowned without offending religion'. Whilst Henrietta would lose 'many prerogatives and the affection and respect of the people', at least there would be no 'prejudice to her conscience'. After all, Louis commented, 'a heavenly crown is better'.[61]

So, on Thursday 2 February 1626, Charles sat alone, enthroned on the stage in Westminster Abbey. Dressed in the ancient robes of King Edward the Confessor, with the Confessor's crown upon his head, he looked out over the crowd of 'thousands within the Church' who now at last were truly his subjects.[62] Henrietta would not enter the Abbey even as a spectator, and the curtained gallery prepared for her remained unoccupied through all the five hours of church ceremonies: from Charles's procession up the nave, bareheaded and clothed in white satin, through the anointing of his shoulders, arms, hands and head with sacramental oil, to his departure, crowned, dressed in ermine-lined robes of black velvet. Instead the Queen went with Blainville and her courtiers to a nearby house, from whose windows she watched Charles's procession to and from the Abbey, while – according to one hostile rumour – 'her ladies [were] frisking and dancing in the room' behind her.[63] English public opinion, at first antagonistic only to Henrietta's priests, was now turning against the Queen herself. 'The people ... rejoice that she is not crowned,' noted the Venetian ambassador, and for a while the Duke of Buckingham gained some popularity when rumour reported that he had personally prevented her coronation.[64]

Charles bore Henrietta's absence with apparent good grace. He even made a joke when he met her afterwards, 'putting his two hands to his crown and lifting it a little', like a gentleman doffing his hat to a lady. Even so, it must have rankled, and just four days later the couple were enmeshed in their bitterest quarrel yet. It was the opening of Parliament, and Henrietta was again taking no part in the ceremonies 'from the same religious scruples'.[65] Instead, on Charles's suggestion, she was to watch the King's procession to Parliament from the apartments of the Countess of Buckingham, whose windows at Whitehall looked out onto Charles's route. Carefully dressed and coiffured, Henrietta set off from her chambers to join the Countess. When she reached the Privy Garden, an open space some 100 yards across, she found it was raining. Could she not go back inside and watch from her own windows? she asked Charles. Perhaps it was only drizzling slightly, for Charles retorted that it was not raining at all. It was indeed raining, Henrietta contradicted her husband; the ground was wet and muddy, and her clothes would be dirtied; the rain and wind would disorder her hair; if she went out now, she would have to dress all over again for the evening. After some dispute, the King allowed his wife to return to her apartments.

However, the Duke of Buckingham's prestige was also at stake: it would be a great honour for the Queen to visit his mother. Buckingham headed for Henrietta's apartments and told her she had deeply offended her husband by refusing to go where he wished, just because of a little rain. Concerned, Henrietta consulted Blainville who persuaded her to go at once to the Countess of Buckingham's chambers, despite the rain. Yet her compliance displeased Charles more than ever: his wife was doing for the hated French ambassador what she had refused to do for her husband. And so, soon after Henrietta had joined the Countess, the Duke of Buckingham came to see her once again, saying this time that the King wished her to leave. By now Henrietta was enjoying herself in the company of a large group of ladies, so she sent the Duke back to Charles, begging to be allowed to stay. For Charles it was another affront: he had already expressed his desires. He sent Buckingham back again: Henrietta must leave at once, by his absolute command. If she refused, he would postpone his procession to Parliament rather than allow her to watch it from where she was. Henrietta was astonished at his rudeness, and was especially upset because it was done in public, in front of her own court and many English observers. Whilst she had to obey the King's direct command, she made no effort to restrain her tongue. As she left, she told Buckingham that she was most unfortunate; that obedience seemed to be a crime in England; that she was treated in a way most different from her due; and that in truth she would never have believed they would have mistreated her so in front of the English court just for having said the weather was bad, and more.[66]

That night the Queen was still fuming. When Charles joined her in bed she complained furiously about his public offence to her, 'and at the Duke acting as messenger on this occasion'. She was the most unhappy princess in the world, she said. She would rather die than offend him, but since she had done neither she begged him not to treat her in that manner in front of the whole court, making everyone think he did not love her. In return, Charles justified his anger. Henrietta had offended him in four particulars: first she had said it was raining; then that she would be dirtied; then that her hair would be spoilt; and finally that she did not want to do what she was told. Henrietta flew off the handle. She was innocent of all blame, she retorted. She would never have believed that such words as hers could be considered faults, but from now on she would take great care not to say them. And so on. Charles got out of bed, saying he would torment Henrietta no longer with his visits, and left the room.[67]

Next day the King retaliated. In his view, this disgraceful quarrel was yet another result of Blainville's pernicious influence over the Queen.[68] So Blainville was banned from the English court, while Charles wrote off to France with his grievances. When Buckingham informed Henrietta that she must no longer permit the French ambassador to enter her presence, she was up in arms. For hours Buckingham 'pressed her for a promise of acquiescence' while she continued her retorts. She was astonished at the Duke's insistence, she said. 'She would rather die than shut out her brother's ambassador.' She was sorry for Charles, who already had too many foreign enemies without offending France as well. If Blainville came to her door she would certainly let him in, and Charles should be grateful to her for it, since his own ambassadors in France would receive just the same treatment as he gave Blainville. Despite the Queen's tirades, Buckingham persisted. Finally, under his 'constant pressure and the king's commands', Henrietta declared that 'if his Majesty absolutely wished it, she would obey'. In any case, she consoled herself, she would never be put to the test, since Blainville would do nothing indiscreet.[69]

For two nights now Charles and Henrietta had not slept together. Her husband would visit her no more, Buckingham told the Queen, unless she begged his pardon with due humility. If she had not done so within two days, Charles would treat her as a person unworthy to be his wife; furthermore he would expel Madame St-Georges and all the French household. Henrietta replied with her usual spirit. She was astonished. There was only one fault that could make her unworthy to be the King's wife, and she was certainly too well bred to commit adultery. If the English expelled the French, they would wound their own honour by breaking the marriage treaty. As for asking pardon, the affair had taken place so publicly that everyone had seen it, and all the English lords and ladies had praised her obedience to the King's commands. She could hardly beg pardon for a fault she had not committed. Nevertheless if the King her husband formally commanded her to do it, she would obey. However, she would also have to say that she begged his forgiveness only out of obedience to his orders, having actually offended him neither in word, nor in deed, nor even in intention.[70]

In truth, Henrietta was eager for reconciliation. Next day she asked to see the King alone, and at last the couple talked it through. She had been very surprised by what Buckingham had said, she began, for she was sure she had never committed any offence against her husband. If Charles thought she had, she begged him to overlook it. When Charles again demanded she ask his pardon, the Queen replied she could not, since in doing so she would be wrongly accusing herself. Instead she begged her husband to tell her what he thought she had done wrong. For a moment Charles was nonplussed. Then, recovering, he answered, 'You assured me that it was raining when I had told you that it was not'. Surprised, Henrietta replied that she would never have thought that offensive, but if her husband thought it was, then she would try to think so too, and she begged him to think of it no longer. For Charles this was close enough to an apology. After embracing his wife, he graciously conducted her back to her chamber, talking to her all the while, as lively now as he had been gloomy before.[71] That night the royal couple resumed sleeping together, and court observers noted 'the complete and sincere affection which subsists between the King and Queen'.[72]

It was carnival time and, despite Blainville's continued banishment, peace reigned. On Shrove Tuesday, Henrietta and her ladies performed the pastoral play they had been rehearsing since before Christmas. *L'Artenice*, written by the French poet Racan, was a story of love among shepherds and shepherdesses. Henrietta appeared in the lead, while her ladies took the remaining parts, some even 'disguised ... with beards' for the male roles. Unlike English court masques, where the genteel performers danced and acted but never spoke, this continental-style entertainment gave the French ladies extensive lines to speak: Henrietta herself 'repeated, it is said, 600 French verses by heart'. When news got out, Puritan public opinion was scandalised, especially at 'the first part being declaimed by the queen'.[73] However, Charles and his courtiers loved the spectacle. The imaginative sets and costumes produced a 'beautiful' effect; to honour the occasion, the King's Surveyor of Works, Inigo Jones, had built the first perspective stage scenery ever seen in England. And there was 'remarkable acting' from the Queen in particular, 'surpassing all the others' with her 'youthful grace'.[74]

For four months all remained quiet in the royal marriage while Charles and his ministers focussed on their business with Parliament. The MPs were angry at the government's failures – especially the navy's defeat at Cadiz and the ruinous peace terms negotiated in Paris for the Huguenots – and they blamed 'that great man, the Duke of Buckingham'. The accusations against him came thick and fast – incompetence, nepotism, corruption, even sedition and treason.[75] Charles was incensed. It was not their part 'to question my servants, much less one that is so near me', he told the Members in person, although this merely inflamed the MPs' opposition: 'they came not thither, either to do what the King should command them, or to abstain where he forbade them,' they replied.[76] Soon the Commons was preparing to bring the Duke to trial. So once again Charles dissolved Parliament without receiving any money. In desperate straits, he and his Privy Councillors sought their war funds elsewhere: via increased customs duties, melting down the royal plate, pawning the Crown jewels, a forced loan from the unwilling English counties. Then, at last, Charles turned once more to his wife.

After a year in England, Henrietta could still speak no English and remained 'thoroughly French, both in her sentiments and her habits'. To Charles it seemed clear that her household was to blame; making 'a little republic' all by themselves, they 'wholly captivated his wife's will and affections'.[77] English personnel were needed if he was ever to draw the Queen closer to his country and himself, so now he named three great ladies to serve in Henrietta's bedchamber. Henrietta was aghast. All of them were Buckingham's creatures, and they were Protestants. Worse still: Lucy, Countess of Carlisle had an undesirable reputation. A great court beauty, she was already the Duke of Buckingham's mistress and now, it was said, she was setting her cap at the King, encouraged by both her lover and her husband. 'I hold her in great aversion,' Henrietta tried to explain to Charles; if she must take some English ladies, perhaps Buckingham's wife could be substituted, for she was a 'most upright' lady.[78] As usual, Charles would not compromise. Even Henrietta's French household urged her to comply; the King was clearly determined, they said, and it would be better to yield with good grace. At last Henrietta agreed. Charles 'was master', she told him, although 'she would never have confidence with those ladies'.[79]

Amid the tensions, a new quarrel erupted almost at once. One night, when the couple were in bed together, Henrietta gave Charles a list of officials she had chosen to manage the lands that he was giving her as part of the marriage settlement. Charles bridled: he was the one who should name her jointure officials, and he refused to allow any French. When Henrietta objected that Charles's mother, Anne of Denmark, had chosen all her own officials, Charles replied that 'his mother was a different sort of woman from her'. An exchange of insults followed, with Henrietta claiming pre-eminence as a 'daughter of France' over a mere Danish princess, while Charles dismissed her status as 'nothing very great'. 'Besides', he added 'she was the third and last' of Henri IV's daughters, 'and therefore of less account'.[80] Enraged now, Henrietta launched into one of her great tirades – 'a passionate discourse' on 'how miserable she was'. All business only went the worse for her the more she was involved, she complained. Her most ordinary actions were taken as crimes. It was disgraceful for her 'to be used so ill'. Eventually Henrietta ran out of breath, or perhaps Charles could stand no more. In any case, the King ended the matter in no uncertain terms. The French household were behind it all, he declared, but 'I shall put them to rights'. On that note, he went to sleep. For three days Charles avoided his wife's company. Only then did he revisit her bed: 'not for love of her', he told Henrietta, but only 'for the love of his people', for whom he must get an heir.[81]

At this point the very last straw came. For months the Queen's religious practices had been causing scandal. At Easter she had again retired to live with her ladies like nuns, performing 'spiritual exercises' and singing the hours of the Virgin. They even went on foot through the streets of London from her 'monastery' at Somerset House to the

Palace of St James's, where Henrietta's chapel was almost completed.[82] For Henrietta this was merely normal Catholic devotion, but English public opinion was shocked. Henrietta's priests had humiliated the nation's Queen, making her 'dabble in the dirt, in a foul morning, from Somerset House to St James's, her Luciferian confessor riding along by her in his coach'. And if they 'dare thus insult over the daughter, sister, and wife of so great kings, what slavery would they not make us, the people, to undergo[?]' Charles bitterly resented her priests too, for ruining his sex life. Almost every day seemed to bring a different saint's feast when, they told the Queen, 'you must not let the King approach'. And by these means, Charles complained, 'the happy conversation that ought to pass between him and his dear wife, which is the principal comfort of marriage, hath not only been interrupted but wholly squenched or perverted'.[83]

Now, while Charles's anger still festered after his latest quarrel with Henrietta, he heard of a new affront. Henrietta had gone into another religious retirement, to observe 'the most holy Jubilee' that the Pope had declared for 1626.[84] Amidst a welter of Catholic observances, Henrietta and some thirty of her courtiers set out one afternoon to 'walk afoot (some add barefoot)' across Hyde Park to the public gallows at Tyburn. Here London's condemned criminals were brought for torture and execution, including many Catholic priests who had 'shed their blood in defence of the Catholic cause'. Arrived at this 'holy place', the Queen and her courtiers went down on their knees in the public highway and prayed before the gallows. Henrietta asked that, if necessary, God would 'give her grace with the like constancy to die for her religion'.[85]

London opinion was scandalised. Henrietta's so-called 'martyrs' were common criminals and traitors. There were even rumours that she had prayed specially for the Jesuit priest, Henry Garnett, who 'had suffered cruel torture and death on that spot' for his involvement in the Gunpowder Plot twenty years earlier.[86] To Charles it was an abomination: Garnett was a ruthless traitor, convicted of attempting to assassinate Charles's own father and his whole Parliament. He could 'no longer bear it', Charles said. Yet still he believed it was all due to 'the ill crafty counsels' of Henrietta's servants 'for advancing of their own ends'. Now, he decided, he would 'deliver his dear wife' from these most undesirable attendants.[87]

Back in November 1625 the Duke of Buckingham had dissuaded Charles from such a course of action; but since then France had made peace with Spain, ruining the Duke's grand foreign plans. Angrily, Buckingham ranted against 'the inconstancy and faithlessness of the French'.[88] Henrietta's household were nothing but trouble. They encouraged the English Catholics and sheltered illegal priests in Whitehall itself while the government's pursuivants sought them all over London. They 'thwarted and censured' whatever the government did, and made 'cabals' against him in particular.[89]

So Charles's plan went ahead, unimpeded. On 31 July, he and his Privy Council arrived in the Queen's apartments. Finding Henrietta in her bedchamber suffering from toothache, Charles ordered everyone else to leave. Locking the door behind them, he turned to his wife and explained. 'For the good of herself and the nation', he must 'cashier all her attendants, priests and others'. In future, he promised, 'she would be better served and with more decorum'.[90] For once Henrietta was speechless, taken unawares. Then, 'seeing herself deprived at one blow of all those in whom she had any confidence, she began to weep bitterly'.[91] From the other side of the door the Comtesse de Tillières heard it all. 'Never could a similar affliction be seen,' she reported; 'she almost died, crying out, despairing, demanding us back with such prayers and tears that if it had been another [man than Charles] assuredly we would have been called back'. On her knees, Henrietta begged her husband 'with words that would have moved stones to pity' to let her keep her poor servants. They had never advised her contrary to his service, she swore. If the King had too great an aversion for Madame St-Georges, perhaps he might allow at least the Comtesse de Tillières to remain. Charles was unmoved. All must leave and at once.[92]

Meanwhile, in the ante-rooms outside, Charles's secretary of state, Lord Conway, informed the French that, 'without reply or impertinent strife', they must quit Whitehall at once for Somerset House, from there to leave the country as soon as may be.[93] As the Queen's maids peered from the window, trying to see what was happening in her bedchamber next door, she rushed to her own window to say a last farewell. In her urgency she broke the panes and, when the King followed to prevent her, she seized the iron bars on the far side of the shattered glass. As Charles pulled her away, her dress was torn and her hands bloodied.[94] The household could do nothing. When Mamie St-Georges spoke for them all, refusing to go, Lord Conway called in the guard, who 'thrust them and all their country folks out of the Queen's lodgings', while the women 'howled and lamented, as if they had been going to execution'.[95]

4

New Beginnings

Henrietta was devastated. That evening she wept without cease, refusing to eat or drink unless some of her servants were returned to her. Finally Charles summoned back one of her dressers, her cook, her baker, her pantry-keeper and her dressmaker. Two of the Oratorian priests were also allowed to return, to say mass in her chapel in accordance with the marriage treaty.[1] But the great court ladies and gentlemen, Henrietta's friends and companions from childhood, had to go. When they objected that they had no money for their journey, since their salaries had gone unpaid for months and they had lent what cash they had to the Queen, Charles flew into a fury. 'Steenie,' he wrote to Buckingham from the Palace of Nonsuch, where he had retired with his wife, 'I command you send all the French away tomorrow out of the town. If you can, by fair means (but stick not long in disputing), otherwise force them away; driving them away like so many wild beasts, until you have shipped them; and so the devil go with them.'[2] Evicted by Lord Conway and his yeomen of the guard, Henrietta's servants were carried downriver by barge to Gravesend. On 12 August they sailed from Dover.

Left alone, Henrietta felt 'a complete prisoner', surrounded by

Buckingham's relations, 'persons who had shown themselves her enemies since the moment she landed in England'. They were always with her, spying with their 'Argus eyes'. Even at night she was never alone, for 'the Duke's niece sleeps constantly in her chamber, nor does she ever quit the Queen's presence, unless her place be taken by the Duke's mother, wife or sister, who wait on her Majesty alternately.'[3] Henrietta's 'tears and displeasure' were 'continuous'; 'she hardly sleeps any more and eats very little'. Several times Henrietta protested to Charles, leading to 'angry discussions' between them.[4]

Desperately Henrietta wrote to her mother: 'Consider that I am your daughter and the most afflicted there be in the world; if you do not take pity on me, I am in despair.' She begged to be allowed to return to France: 'I cannot be happy without that.' Letters went to Louis and Cardinal Richelieu too, imploring them 'to succour me in my woes'.[5] Henrietta's former household filled Paris with vivid stories of injustices 'of the worst possible description'. The Bishop of Mende, 'having great access to Richelieu, told him at all hours the nature of the affront and incited him to vengeance'.[6] And at Richelieu's request the Comte de Tillières wrote a lengthy memoir of his year in England. Henrietta was perhaps a little too young for her role, he admitted. She might occasionally have been too passionate, too obstinate, too carried away. However, her household was blameless. Everything was the Duke of Buckingham's fault. From the beginning he had hated the French and was determined to be rid of them. All the royal couple's quarrels had been caused by his total power over the English king – a pitiful creature, according to Tillières, without a mind of his own.

Tillières's story of the triangular relationship between Charles, Henrietta and Buckingham has dominated historians' accounts ever since, yet it is a tissue of fabrications. In his eagerness to blacken the Duke's name, Tillières created a melodrama of improbably souped-up emotions and reasonless prejudices. His endless circumstantial stories of what people said in private behind closed doors, of their inner motivations and secret evil designs, are the stuff of the historical novels of Dumas and Scot – dramatic and exciting, but obviously beyond

Tillières's or anyone else's real knowledge, and completely unconfirmed by any other historical source. The memoirs are full of errors of fact and internal inconsistencies – some probably just misremembered, but others deliberately falsified to promote his own partisan position. My own account of the marriage's first year has relied upon Tillières's memoirs only when they are confirmed by other sources, resulting in a story that is substantially different from any previously told.

Nevertheless, Cardinal Richelieu was persuaded and later reproduced the essentials of Tillières's story in his own memoirs, authorising and perpetuating this version of events for the benefit of history. Certainly in Paris that summer, Louis and his court were furious with the English, and with Buckingham especially. Marie de' Medici wept, denouncing the English as hypocrites who 'habitually spoke fair and acted ill'. 'We shall be avenged,' a Parisian courtier vowed,[7] but the French were not ready for war with England. Their navy was too weak, and their troubles with the Huguenots preoccupied their attention. They therefore opted to negotiate, ready to 'yield upon some points [rather] than come to blows'.[8]

Two ambassadors were chosen for the delicate talks in London: the Comte de Tillières and his brother-in-law, the Maréchal de Bassompierre. Henrietta was delighted. The Comte had always been her champion – 'the English have great fear of him,' she told her mother – and she had known Bassompierre from childhood. A cultivated courtier and experienced international diplomat, the Maréchal had been close to her father and mother and was now a trusted counsellor of her brother's. However, Charles utterly refused to receive Tillières. Even Bassompierre was unwelcome.[9]

When he arrived in London that September, the ambassador received none of the usual honours. On Charles's orders, no house was provided for him, and Bassompierre had to pay all his own expenses. His first meeting with Buckingham descended rapidly into mutual recriminations. Four days later there was a tense audience at Hampton Court, where Charles allowed Bassompierre only 'a brief exchange of civilities', fearing that any more would push him or Henrietta into some violent outburst 'in front of the whole world'.[10] At Somerset

House two days later, Bassompierre found Henrietta in a dreadful state, 'so stirred by the outrage they have done her by the distancing of her domestics that I could not in any way compose her'. When he finally got his private meeting with Charles, it was more of the same: the King ranted about his grievances, and it took all Bassompierre's courtly tact to soothe him.[11]

The next three weeks passed in a frenetic round of meetings with courtiers, civil servants and royals. It was a wearying, discouraging process, Bassompierre reported:

> The king has spoken to me with such resolution ... that if I had had permission to go back [to France], I would have taken leave of him at that same audience. I am so scandalised and angry to see this little queen, so good and pretty, in danger of losing her religion that I despair of it. I hear nothing every day from all the ministers of state but complaints that they make of the misbehaviours of the French; I answer them back sometimes, but in the end I grow angry or tired of it and I leave them alone.[12]

Nevertheless, he still persisted in his policy of 'prudent and amicable approaches', thrashing out the possibilities for mutual compromise. He saw Henrietta almost daily, finding her exasperating as she oscillated between bouts of depression and outbursts of 'youthful passion', quarrelling furiously with both himself and her husband.[13] Her formal reconciliation with Buckingham, which Bassompierre engineered 'with a thousand pains', lasted a mere twenty-four hours, after which the quarrels began all over again.[14] At last an agreement was reached. Instead of her previous 400 or so attendants, Henrietta would now be allowed forty or fifty French courtiers and servants, including a doctor, a secretary, gentlemen ushers and waiters, and two ladies of the bed-chamber for companionship. For her chapel there would be a bishop and twelve priests who, the English insisted, must be neither Jesuits nor Oratorians. And all these personnel must be newly appointed, for Charles would allow none of her old household to return, except the physician.[15]

Next day everyone was happy. It was the Lord Mayor's procession, and Henrietta and Bassompierre took Buckingham and the Earl of Dorset with them in the Queen's coach to Cheapside, to watch. While they waited, the four of them played cards – a revolution in Henrietta's relations with Buckingham that delighted Bassompierre.[16] Yet just three days later the royal couple quarrelled once more, over Henrietta's religious devotions for All Saints' Day. Annoyed that his wife was once again 'shut up in her monastery' at Somerset House 'without decorum', Charles demanded that Bassompierre make her desist. The ambassador found Henrietta both 'obstinate and very determined'.[17] Losing patience, he threatened to return at once to Paris and tell her brother and mother that everything was her fault. It was several days before he and Henrietta were reconciled.

For two more weeks Bassompierre remained in London to celebrate the successful conclusion of his negotiations. In the whirl of dinners, balls, plays and musical soirées, all previous disagreements were forgotten. The Duke of Buckingham entertained King, Queen and ambassador with 'the most superb feast' that Bassompierre had ever seen. Each course was accompanied by a separate ballet, with its own scenery and music, and then the three guests of honour joined the rest of the company to watch a grand masque, representing the French royal family, sitting among the gods and making peace for all Europe, each figure so lifelike that Henrietta could name them. The dancing afterwards lasted until four in the morning, when the party closed with 'a splendid refection of sweetmeats'.[18] Buckingham's reconciliation with the Queen was apparently complete, and on Henrietta's birthday he joined in the 'very fine assembly' she laid on at Somerset House, performing with other prominent English courtiers in a masque for the company's entertainment.[19]

At last Bassompierre departed for France, 'very well satisfied'. However, in Paris he had a rude awakening. Henrietta's former confessor, Father Sancy, had accompanied him to London and now told tales behind his back. 'Little had been gained for the satisfaction of his sister,' Louis fumed, and Cardinal Richelieu 'found a thousand objections' to Bassompierre's treaty.[20] So the French king refused to ratify it. New negotiations must be opened, he insisted, 'to win more', both for Henrietta herself and for the poor English Catholics, whose persecution continued unabated, despite Charles's promises to Bassompierre.[21]

The English court was disgusted, as was Charles, who claimed 'he was treated contemptuously'. He had already yielded more than he really wanted to, 'out of consideration for his brother-in-law', and 'he could not go a step farther'.[22] Hostilities between the two nations escalated. When the French confiscated the entire English wine fleet in Bordeaux – 200 ships, with their sailors and guns, as well as some 16,000 tons of Gascony wine – Charles ordered his navy to sea, to embark on a campaign of organised piracy, intercepting French merchantmen and bringing them into English ports, where the ships and goods were impounded, the sailors imprisoned.[23]

Amidst the drama, Henrietta began to build a new life for herself. She bought a lute and started lessons with 'a certain Monsieur Gouttier, a Frenchman and a famous performer'. All through December she was busy 'with fourteen ladies of her court' rehearsing a new masque, to be performed on Twelfth Night.[24] Christmas Day was a religious occasion, which Henrietta and Charles celebrated apart, but the next day they were together at Whitehall to begin 'the festivities of Christmas', culminating in Henrietta's masque, which was 'very pretty'.[25] Led by 'His Majesty, with the Duke and fourteen others of the noblemen and knights', everyone danced until four in the morning. 'Doubtless it cost abundance,' a jealous Londoner commented; 'it was said one Mr Chalmer sold 1000 yards of taffeta and satin towards it.'[26]

But neither Charles nor the French royal family were content to leave Henrietta in peace. Marie de' Medici and Father Bérulle sternly warned Henrietta against her new English courtiers. 'My most dear daughter', implored Marie, 'continue your exercises of piety, and do not listen to those who wish to divert you from them, under the pretext of gaiety. Their counsel is pernicious and will bring you to terrible miseries ... I am sorry to see these people close to you. But I would be much more sorry if their words entered your heart ... Remember each day, that Jesus Christ Our Saviour died to give you life.'[27] Meanwhile Charles's aversion to Henrietta's French attendants flared up once more. All along, there had been rumours that her servants were spying. Now, suddenly, Charles had her lute teacher arrested and sent to the Tower of London. Three more servants soon followed him there, and threats were made that all her remaining French personnel would be 'got rid of like the first, their conduct being so unsatisfactory'.[28]

Still angry, Charles left to go hunting in the country. Weeks passed, and from their separate little enclaves the couple exchanged cold letters, containing nothing but 'dry, ceremonious compliment'. When Charles planned to visit his capital, he dreaded a renewal of their quarrels and asked Buckingham to see Henrietta first to 'set her in tune'.[29] Charles spent a mere couple of days in London, but his reunion with Henrietta must have been a success. Inviting her to join him at Theobalds, the royal palace near Waltham Cross in Essex, he 'bestowed a dinner upon her'. Later that day, on Henrietta's invitation, he rode back with her to London, where 'Her Majesty gave him a supper' at Somerset House. There Charles 'lay all night' with his wife, before returning to his hunting the next afternoon.[30] Although neither knew it then, it was a turning point in their relations.

Gradually Henrietta was settling down. At Somerset House the remnants of her French household provided some of the comforts and sophistication of home. In the end Charles had allowed twenty or more servants to remain, including twelve musicians to play both for her entertainment and in her chapel.[31] He had also appointed three English Catholic ladies-in-waiting, who accompanied Henrietta to chapel each morning. There, mass was performed with all possible ceremony by her two remaining Oratorian priests, Fathers Philip and Viette, who would become the Queen's lifelong companions. Henrietta was particularly devoted to Father Philip, her confessor: a Scottish priest who had joined Bérulle's Oratorians after fleeing persecution in his native land. A learned man, for five years he had headed the Oratory's theological college at Lyons, before Bérulle selected him to join the English mission. He was also notably moderate, warning Henrietta to 'live well towards the protestants' and never allowing her 'to be pressed to any passionate undertaking under pretence of doing good for Catholics'. Perhaps this was why Charles had chosen him to remain in England.[32]

With her natural warmth and lively wit, Henrietta was beginning to befriend the Buckingham ladies who were now her constant companions.[33] Highest in her favour were the Duke's mother and wife. The first was a passionate Catholic convert, whose Whitehall lodgings were a notorious safe haven for 'the most active papists in England', while her daughter-in-law, Katherine Duchess of Buckingham, was a lifelong Catholic at heart, who publicly practised Anglicanism only to bolster her husband's position. She was also a woman of 'very great wit and spirit', as well as generous to boot, who now 'presented the queen with a costly coach and six horses valued generally at 20,000 crowns'.[34]

Dearest to the Queen of all the Buckingham party was a little boy named Jeffery Hudson, whom Buckingham's mother had presented to Henrietta a few months before. Emerging from under the crust of a cold pie, Hudson had made an instant impression, for at eight years old he stood a mere eighteen inches high – 'a marvellous sight, and the most perfect imperfection of nature that ever was born'.[35] Henrietta was enchanted by 'Little Jeffery', or 'the Queen's dwarf' as he came to be called, a youngster who was fearless and full of fun, throwing himself into all the court pleasures of dancing, hunting and acting. In fact, so attached to him did she become that when he fell out of a window at Somerset House that summer, 'the Queen took it so heavily that she attired not herself that day', even though the boy was not seriously hurt.[36] All in all, Henrietta was 'very happy and cheerful' with her new English companions – so much so that in May 1627 she accepted Charles's formal regulations for her court, which she had so angrily refused at Hampton Court eighteen months previously.[37]

Already new challenges were emerging for the Queen. England and France were on the verge of war. Charles was preparing a fleet to aid the Huguenots at La Rochelle, whom Louis and Richelieu were determined to destroy. During her husband's war with Spain, Henrietta had been happy to play the part of patriotic English queen, celebrating one of his naval successes with a dinner aboard the flagship, then riding in state through London with 'a fair white feather in her hat'.[38] Now the prospect of war with her French family appalled her. She longed to mediate with all 'the tenderness of a wife and sister' but she feared her intervention would only offend her husband.[39] So, on her suggestion, one of Louis's courtiers arrived in England; once he had opened talks, she hoped, she would be able to play her part. Charles, however, had no sympathy for her predicament. Louis's messenger was suspected as a spy, and when Henrietta finally plucked up the courage to speak to her husband, offering 'to mediate for a reconciliation', he flatly 'forbade her to do so'.[40]

Instead Charles hearkened to Buckingham's eager determination for war. For the Duke it was a matter of personal revenge: the French had twice now refused to receive him as an ambassador, leading him to exchange 'some very sharp notes' with Cardinal Richelieu, his opposite number in France.[41] All through the early months of 1627, Buckingham had devoted himself to preparations, organising the fleet and army, and battling to enforce the King's unpopular fund-raising policies, which saw droves of English gentlemen imprisoned for refus-ing to contribute to the forced loan. When the royal treasury failed him, Buckingham rented out his own houses and sold his jewels to raise money 'for the use of His Majesty's Navy'.[42] He even talked of commanding the expedition in person. Even though both his mother and his wife went down 'upon their knees to dissuade him', the prospect of vengeance was too sweet, and the hope of regaining his popularity at home too appealing.[43]

Appearing in military costume – 'with an immense collar and a magnificent plume of feathers in his hat' – Buckingham posed now as a Protestant hero, the defender of the Huguenots, promising to 'spend his strength in the advancement both of religion and state'.[44] Never-theless his trip had rather the air of a pleasure jaunt. An entire 'great collier-ship' was loaded up with his personal provisions: fine food and wine, clothes, jewels, furniture, books, even his coach and litter.[45] Every day there were farewell dinners in his honour. Buckingham himself laid on two separate extravaganzas for Charles and Henrietta, with masques heroicising his great mission in Europe. Charles's ardour was thoroughly roused, and for two weeks he personally supervised the final preparations at Portsmouth, 'in continual action, visiting the soldiers, and seeing them exercised' and going 'aboard every ship, great and small'.[46] Finally, at 4 a.m. on Wednesday 27 June, the fleet set sail 'with a very favourable wind': some thirty warships and forty transports laden with 'soldiers, horses, war materials, provisions, and every kind of baggage'.[47]

Henrietta put on a brave public face, writing to Buckingham 'most heartily and cheerfully' with 'her best wishes'. Underneath she was profoundly upset. Amidst the escalating hostilities she had not heard from her mother for months, 'just as if they had entirely forgotten her in France', she complained.[48] The French diplomatic agent in London remained her last link with home, but Charles now sent him back to Paris, reducing Henrietta to tears. As Charles set off for his usual summer hunting tour of the Home Counties, she left for North-amptonshire. After more than two years of marriage, she had still failed to become pregnant, leading to widespread public comment on her 'sterility' and 'barrenness'. Now she travelled to the small country town of Wellingborough, noted for its mineral waters 'which facilitate generation'.[49]

For six weeks the royal couple were apart, during which time Charles visited his wife just once, for no more than a couple of days: hardly a recipe for successful 'generation', whatever the powers of Wellingborough's water. For all Charles's hard-won reconciliation with Henrietta, it was Buckingham who occupied first place in his affections. All that summer the King worried for his friend, 'praying for your good success in all things', he told him, and 'hoping and longing for your safe return'. Even when there was no business to discuss, Charles wrote eagerly to 'Steenie', simply 'to assure you, that upon all occasions I am glad to remember you, and that no distance of place, nor length of time, can make me slacken, much less diminish my love to you.' Charles signed himself, as always, 'your faithful, loving, constant friend'.[50]

Weeks passed without news from the Duke, leaving the whole

nation in suspense. At last word came that Buckingham's troops had captured the Ile de Ré, just off the coast of La Rochelle. It was only a qualified success – the French fort on the island still held out – but Charles was overjoyed.[51] Henrietta, still at Wellingborough, eagerly told the Buckingham ladies of 'her love and good wishes' for the Duke; she hoped his action would soon win him 'the hearts of many'. When Charles wrote to her, ponderously 'expressing his regret at having to embark in a war with his brother-in-law, solely for the honour of himself and the nation, which the French have slandered', the Queen returned a model reply, 'expressing equal regret', but adding 'that she wished him all success, being more interested for him than for anyone else'.[52] Charles was thrilled by her support, eagerly informing the Duke of Buckingham: 'my wife and I were never better together; she, upon this action of yours, showing herself so loving to me, by her discretion upon all occasions, that it makes us all wonder and esteem her.'[53] By post, at least, the couple were growing closer, although their relationship would still have to stand the test of seeing one another in person.

For a time the news from La Rochelle continued good. However, as summer turned to autumn and the fort on the Ile de Ré continued in French hands, English optimism faded. Buckingham's womenfolk especially were in despair. Her husband was risking his life for nothing, the Duchess complained, for 'by this action he is not any whit the more popular man than when he went'. And Buckingham's mother, the Catholic Countess, was more outspoken: 'The kingdom will not supply your expenses, and every man groans under the burden of the times . . . This is not the way; for you to embroil the whole Christian world in war, and then to declare it for religion, and make God a party to these woeful affairs, so far from God as light from darkness.'[54]

Even Charles's exuberance was gone. 'Grieved and ashamed', he apologised abjectly to his dear Steenie 'for our slowness here in giving you supplies'. 'For God's sake be not disheartened,' he begged, 'for, by the grace of God, it is all past.'[55] His words of comfort came too late. Early in November the Duke and his remaining troops landed at Plymouth, defeated ignominiously in their attempt to storm the fort at Ré. Buckingham insisted that his losses had been slight – just 400 or 500 men – but the hostile English news-writers reported a 'great slaughter', 'a rout without an enemy', with 'great numbers . . . crowded to death, or drowned'.[56] Never had Buckingham been so unpopular. The government, in 'fear of a rising', issued orders 'to refrain from speaking of him, and of the retreat from Ré', which only further increased popular hatred against the Duke.[57]

Yet Charles was still thoroughly enamoured. 'In this action you have had honour,' he assured his friend; 'all the shame must light upon us here remaining at home' for failing to send reinforcements in time.[58] At Whitehall he received Buckingham 'most joyfully and graciously', treating him 'more familiarly and kindly than ever'. The two men passed a whole night alone together, while the Duke made his report. Next day Charles summoned his Privy Council, determined to send out a new expedition as soon as possible.[59] Over the following weeks Buckingham sped between London and Portsmouth, attending to everything himself.

Meanwhile in Paris, Louis laughed at the English king. 'Alack,' said he, 'if I had known my brother of England had longed so much for the Isle of Ré, I would have sold it him for half the money it hath cost him.' Further degradation was heaped on the English when the French king ordered their captured guns and standards to be paraded through Paris in a public day of triumph.[60] However, Louis had not forgotten his little sister in England, and in December, 'of his own accord, without being asked', he released the numerous English prisoners from Ré and sent them home 'as a present' to Henrietta Maria, to bolster her position at the English court.[61] Henrietta seized the opportunity to communicate with her family after the long months of silence. Desperately she begged them to end 'this war between her husband and brother'. She knew that Tillières and Bérulle were fomenting the war with stories of her unhappiness in England and assured the court that they were 'most false'. 'On the contrary', she 'enjoyed 'complete liberty' in every aspect of her life and received nothing but 'good treatment' from her husband.[62] There was certainly no need for the war to continue on her behalf. For the moment her appeals fell on deaf ears.

All through the spring of 1628, Charles stayed in London to manage the Parliament he had summoned in a fresh search for war-funding, and the royal couple spent much of their time together, gradually gaining a greater intimacy. 'Hot speech' even went round London 'of the queen's being quick with child', although the unfounded rumour soon passed.[63] Despite his own shortage of funds, Charles lavished generosity on his wife: a clear sign of his new warmth. He ordered Henrietta's debts to be paid off to the tune of £30,000, and gave her some of his own lands, worth £6000 per year, to increase her income to the level of 'the late Queen Anne'. At last, in his eyes, Henrietta was coming to deserve the same status and respect as his own beloved mother. The King's gift went so far as to include Greenwich Palace, a favourite country resort of Anne's, where she had begun building a luxurious, Italianate 'Queen's House' to designs by Inigo Jones.[64]

To please his wife, Charles even turned a blind eye to the English Catholics who illegally attended Henrietta's chapel, coming in such numbers that it was commonplace to hear people ask, 'Have you been to Mass at Somerset House?' Parliament protested vigorously at such 'connivance at Popery'; through the government's toleration, the number of Catholics 'increases daily', a 'very perilous' situation. Indignant at a whole raft of government abuses, the MPs drew up a formal Remonstrance, laying the blame on 'the excessive favour, authority and power of the Duke of Buckingham'.[65] Charles responded angrily. 'He never expected that the Members . . . would have thus proceeded to intermeddle in questions of religion and state,' he told them; 'he always supposed that they knew little about them, but he now realises that they knew nothing at all.' Again he dismissed Parliament, and when Henrietta asked him not to approve the new anti-Catholic Bill the House had just passed, the King readily agreed.[66]

That July the royal couple parted to spend the summer in their own separate ways. Henrietta revisited Wellingborough, 'to facilitate child bearing', and stayed on there for weeks with her courtiers.[67] She had struck up a new special friendship, with Lucy Countess of Carlisle. It was an unlikely alliance – the devout Catholic Queen and the loose-living court beauty – but Lucy was a charming woman, vivacious, witty and intelligent. A glamorous twenty-eight-year-old, she easily assumed the position of role model to the teenage Queen, introducing her to the use of cosmetics, as the English news reported, murmuring dark fears too that Henrietta 'in time ... may by her example be led unto more debaucheries'. Lucy's influence was even more resented by Buckingham's mother, wife and sister, who 'do hate her even to death ... for that she hath the Queen's heart above them all'.[68] However, they had to resign themselves to it. Lucy would remain Henrietta's favourite for the next fourteen years, until she finally betrayed her mistress on the eve of the Civil War.

Meanwhile, at Portsmouth, Charles and Buckingham laboured to get their great army and navy out to sea. While the King lodged a few miles away in the country house of Southwick, the Duke put up at the Grey-hound Inn in Portsmouth itself, taking charge of day-to-day preparations. The business was vast and multifarious – ranging from quelling mutinous sailors, who demanded their pay and shouted 'Death to the Duke', to providing tapestries to hang in the Duke's private cabin.[69]

On Saturday 23 August 1628, Buckingham was still not ready to sail. That morning, as always, his lodgings were thronged with people: courtiers, soldiers, sailors, relations, servants, hangers-on. It was some time after 9 a.m. and the Duke was on his way out to see the King, 'very jocant and well pleased', bearing a report that the starving populace of La Rochelle had been unexpectedly relieved.[70] As he left the parlour where he had been breakfasting and crossed the crowded hall, a man stepped forward and struck a single knife-blow 'with great strength and violence' deep into his left breast. Buckingham pulled the dagger out at once. 'Villain!' he said, and made to follow his attacker, whom no one else had seen.[71] After just a couple of paces, the Duke staggered and fell to the ground. The blade of the knife had passed through his lungs into 'the very heart itself', and now the blood spouted 'with much effusion' from his mouth as well as from the wound. Almost at once, without uttering another word, 'that noble great person' the Duke of Buckingham – 'the greatest and most remark-able favourite whom the world has seen for many centuries' – was dead.[72]

5

No Other Favourites

The news reached Charles almost at once. He was at morning prayers in chapel when the messenger whispered in his ear. Reverently religious and proud in the sight of his courtiers, the King remained 'unmoved, and without the least change in his countenance' until the service was done. Then he fled to his chamber, where he fell on the bed, 'lamenting with much passion and with abundance of tears'.[1] Later he summoned his Privy Councillors for an emergency meeting lasting into the night. Charles would see no one else. All the next day he remained in his bedchamber alone, 'profoundly afflicted' not only by his friend's loss but also at 'the horrid manner' of his death. His only other thought was for the widowed Duchess. To her he sent his condolences, promising that he would 'extend the protection of a husband and father to her and to her children'.[2]

Charles and Buckingham's family were the only ones who mourned. Throughout England there was 'extraordinary joy'. In London, they drank healths to the murderer; elsewhere it was 'very difficult ... to prevent bonfires and other rejoicings'.[3] One of the first to hear was Henrietta Maria, 100 miles away at Wellingborough. A long letter reached her from Dudley, Lord Carleton, one of

Charles's most trusted councillors, who had witnessed the murder. 'Madam,' he wrote, 'you may easily guess what outcries were then made ... when we saw him thus dead in a moment, and slain by an unknown hand.' At the noise, the Duchess of Buckingham had emerged from her bedchamber with another lady and stood looking down at 'the blood of their dearest lord gushing from him'. 'Ah, poor ladies,' Carleton wrote, 'such was their screechings, tears, and distractions, that I never in my life heard the like before, and hope never to hear the like again.'

In the confusion the murderer could easily have escaped. Instead – as Buckingham's friends rushed round the inn, shouting, 'Where is the villain? Where is the butcher?' – he had drawn his sword and walked out among them. 'I am the man, here I am,' he said. 'With much trouble and difficulty,' Carleton and some others prevented the crowd from killing him. As they waited for the King's musketeers to carry him away, Carleton questioned the man. His name was John Felton, and he was a lieutenant in Buckingham's army. Eighty pounds in pay was due to him from the last campaign and he had been unfairly passed over for promotion, but this was not why he had murdered the Duke, he insisted. His only aim had been to 'do his country great good service'. Expecting to die in the attempt, he had stitched a paper into his hat, explaining his reasons.[4]

Wholeheartedly Henrietta turned to comforting the 'many distressed ladies' in her court, Buckingham connections all. Her profound sympathy at 'the fatal blow' touched everyone and was 'kindly taken by the King' when he heard. Then she rushed to see Charles himself, whose 'melancholy and discomposure of mind' were clear to everyone, though he did everything he could to behave in a manner 'both manly and princely'.[5] All his feelings – anger, frustration, bitterness, desperation – the King now poured into completing the fleet preparations begun by his dead friend. He appointed a new admiral and personally attended to the provisioning of each ship. Amidst the delays, Charles fretted and fumed, chivvied and chased, and his subjects were impressed: 'the King, they say, in fourteen days after the Duke's death, despatched more business than the Duke had done three months before.' At last the fleet sailed: more than eighty ships, heading for Plymouth to rendezvous with some seventy more.[6]

A week later the Duke of Buckingham was buried in Westminster Abbey. It was a quiet affair; lack of funds and fear of riots put a stop to Charles's plans for 'as ample and sumptuous a funeral as could be performed'. Instead hardly more than 100 mourners accompanied the coffin through the dark evening streets, while the city's militia beat their drums and the crowds behind them murmured ominously, a 'noise, more like joy than commiseration'.[7] Neither Charles nor Henrietta was present. Already they had left London, on country travels together for the first time. They were inseparable now, Henrietta doing all she could 'to comfort and console' her husband, whose attention and affection could at last be hers, alone.[8] From Hampton Court they rode out together regularly, 'enjoying the pleasures of the chase' or making flying visits to London. They visited Buckingham's widow in Chelsea. For Charles there was therapy in it; he talked constantly of his old friend – 'his martyr' – repeating how 'the world was much mistaken in him'; he had been a 'most faithful and obedient servant in all things'.[9]

Now others must be found to fill Buckingham's shoes. More and more every day, people noted, it was Henrietta who received all 'the favour and love that were previously divided between her and the duke'.[10] Basking in his wife's sympathetic attention, Charles began to draw her into his own political world. Together they orchestrated the return to favour of the aristocrats who would take over Buckingham's responsibilities at court. The Marquess of Hamilton, who had spent six years in Scotland after refusing to consummate his arranged marriage to Buckingham's niece, was now summoned back to become Master of the King's Horse. That first night of his return, when Hamilton still refused to bed his bride, Henrietta sent him a posset while Charles lent him a nightshirt of his own 'and would not be satisfied till he had seen them both in bed together'. A few weeks later the royal couple rehabilitated the Duke's old enemy, the Earl of Arundel, driving in state to his London house to view his famous art collection.[11]

That November, Charles celebrated Henrietta's birthday in style, riding himself in the joust, an icon of romance and chivalry. The royal couple seemed like young lovers: 'you would imagine him a wooer again, and her gladder to receive his caresses than he to make them,' a courtier reported. When Charles left London for a few days' hunting, Henrietta was desolate: 'her Majesty can take no rest ... but sighs for his return.' Her only consolation was Charles's portrait, 'his shadow at her bedside'.[12] By Christmas 1628, there were signs that Henrietta was pregnant: she had conceived just a few weeks after Buckingham's death. Thrilled, Charles was 'always with her' and did all he could to please his wife. First he suspended the execution of the penal laws against the English Catholics. Then, realising that Henrietta was still being pestered by 'clamorous' tradesmen, he reissued his previous year's order that her vast debts should be repaid.[13]

Eagerly the royal couple began to prepare for their 'long-desired' new arrival, appointing courtiers to the baby's royal household, and making arrangements for the birth and christening.[14] Throughout the nation, in every parish church, prayers were said 'for the safe childbearing of the Queen's Majesty': 'Lord ... keep her safe ... that there may be strength to bring forth her joy and our hope. And make her a joyful mother of many children.' Public celebrations were ordered; bonfires were lit and bells rung, and all London's foreign ambassadors came to congratulate the royal couple, 'much to their satisfaction'.[15] However, a large proportion of the population was far from pleased. What if Charles was assassinated? Then Henrietta, as a papist Queen Regent during her baby's infancy, 'might mar all'. Wild rumours circulated of her pernicious influence over her husband, even that she had taken him to mass – a story that stirred one loyal Englishman into murderous desires to strike 'another Gunpowder blow'.[16] When Charles dissolved yet another Parliament, disappointed as always in his hopes for funds, Henrietta, like Buckingham before her, got the blame. The King had been 'well inclined to the Parliament', the rumour went, 'but lying with the Queen all night, the next morning, his mind was changed', and that very day he had sent the MPs home. The government acted fast to suppress the story. One serving woman was arrested for repeating it and saying 'that she wished the Queen were ducked in the midst of the sea ... with a millstone round her neck'.[17]

Henrietta's power was growing. By her intervention with the King, a condemned Jesuit priest was 'not only reprieved, but pardoned'. Boatloads of captured French fishermen were released after she 'exerted herself with much warmth' on their behalf.[18] There was one project that mattered more to her than any other: making peace between England and France. Her great ally here was the Venetian ambassador in London, Alvise Contarini, whose government desired an Anglo-French alliance against Spain. Already, just weeks after Buckingham's death, Contarini had drafted a treaty. Having seen the King, who said he would 'think about it', Contarini went straight to Henrietta, who promised 'with great joy and readiness' to speak to Charles that night.[19] 'She did not pretend to interfere in state affairs,' she assured her husband, 'yet the reconciliation with her brother concerned her greatly' and Charles must 'excuse her if she dared to recommend to him the negotiation' begun by Contarini. To her entreaties Charles readily yielded; that same evening he sent word to Contarini that he would begin talks.[20]

Still Charles was unwilling to desert the Huguenots, but then came the 'most heavy and bitter news'. Despite the presence of the English fleet off La Rochelle, the Huguenots had been forced to surrender.[21] Many thousand Rochellese had starved to death waiting for English help that never came, and the survivors looked more 'like ghosts than men'. The French king had ordered them fed, but, too starved to eat, they died 'with the meat in their mouths'. All England was shocked and shamed, and Charles, powerless, was now 'entirely in favour of peace'.[22]

However, there was one topic on which he would never compromise: his wife's household. When the French demanded he honour Bassompierre's treaty of two years earlier, Charles refused point blank. 'The King knows that the French made trouble,' his courtiers explained, 'and for the future he means to be master here.'[23] Even Henrietta was unenthusiastic, fearing that new French courtiers would only endanger her new-found closeness to her husband. Instead, she sent word to her mother that she was 'perfectly satisfied' with her present court. She was being well treated in religious matters too, so there was no need for the French to make treaty terms on her behalf.[24] Still Louis would not back down. In the end, the peace settlement between the two nations was merely a 'cessation of arms', leaving all important matters to be settled by an exchange of ambassadors. Nonetheless, on Sunday 10 May 1629 at Greenwich Palace, peace was ceremoniously proclaimed 'by sound of trumpet and four heralds', while the royal couple watched in satisfaction, standing together 'in a window of the gallery'.[25] Henrietta was now almost seven months' pregnant.

Next day she went to Somerset House, 'where she had the Te Deum solemnly chanted' in thanksgiving for the peace.[26] As she returned in her barge to Greenwich that evening she suffered a fall. It was by this, many people thought, that 'the child was turned and dislocated in her womb'. Others blamed a fright she had suffered two days previously, when she came upon 'two great dogs' fighting in her gallery at Greenwich, one of which 'did snatch at her and pull her by the gown'. Other people spoke of the unnatural 'violence of her exercises', for Henrietta loved to go out walking, climbing the hill above Greenwich, with its magnificent views over country and river to London itself.[27] Whatever the cause, on the night of Tuesday 12 May 'about twelve of the clock', Henrietta began to be 'oppressed by the pains of childbirth'.[28] Nothing was prepared: the French court ladies who had been summoned 'to wait on her in childbed' had not yet arrived, nor had the French royal midwife, Madame Peronne, whom Marie de' Medici had promised to send. So unexpected was the labour that there were not even English court physicians or midwives at Greenwich.[29]

Instead, behind the shuttered windows and guarded doors that tradition required for royal births, it was the King himself who hovered in 'constant attendance at the bedside', defying the custom that normally excluded all men from the delivery room. On the white linen sheets, with all her rings, laces and buckles removed, according to the superstition that this would ease her labour, Henrietta was in agonies of pain, with her baby in the wrong position, 'turned overthwart in her belly'.[30] The local Greenwich midwife, summoned in to face the emergency, 'swooned with fear' when she realised she was supposed to minister to the Queen. In fact there was little she could have done, for the seventeenth-century midwife came armed with little more than sponges, poultices and ointments. Realising both his wife and child were in 'the greatest danger', the King summoned a London specialist: the fashionable surgeon, Peter Chamberlen.[31]

Normally surgeons were called in only as a last resort, for the hook they used to extract the baby killed the child if it was not already dead. But Chamberlen was known for his unusual success, obtained by using a trio of revolutionary iron instruments – the forceps, vectis and fillet – which would remain a secret of the Chamberlen medical dynasty for another 100 years.[32] Even so, 'the queen was at such an extremity' that the surgeon could offer Charles only the stark choice: 'they could save either her or her child'. For Charles the decision was clear. 'He could have other children, please God,' but Henrietta was irreplaceable.[33]

The vectis was probably the first instrument that Chamberlen used – as a lever to turn the baby's head down into the normal delivery position. Then, pulling with the forceps or the fillet – a long-handled noose looped around the baby's head – Chamberlen 'with his own hands, removed the creature from her belly' at around three in the morning.[34] Despite the surgeon's dire predictions, the baby emerged alive: a boy, the first royal heir to be born in England since Henry VIII's son, Edward VI, more than ninety years earlier. However, Charles's long-cherished christening ceremonies were abandoned. There would be no processions of richly dressed nobility, no tapestries and swathes of cloth of gold and silver, no anthems, drums, trumpets and thundering cannons. The child was failing fast. In the rush to make sure he did not die unbaptised, the tiny Prince of Wales was carried unceremoniously to the font, where Dr Webb, 'then chaplain in attendance' at court, christened him Charles, after his father. Within just an hour or so of his birth, the boy was dead.[35]

The court was devastated, and Charles 'more than anyone else showed himself most affected by it'. If only the pregnancy had lasted a little longer; just a couple more weeks, the physicians said, and this 'hopeful prince' might have lived. Now 'the fruit of their desires has been cut off'.[36] The premature delivery, it was believed, especially given Chamberlen's intervention, might easily prevent Henrietta from having more children – a thought that left Charles 'very greatly distressed'. Yet Henrietta herself 'was doing well, and was full of strength and courage'. A fleet of medical personnel attended her now – 'physicians, surgeons, midwives, and others' – and the ladies of the court paid the customary calls.[37] While she remained at Greenwich with her bedchamber windows covered and the fire burning, as tradition demanded for her lying-in, her baby was carried up to London for burial. Beneath a black-velvet canopy, six earls' sons bore the tiny coffin to Westminster Abbey. Behind the children and their little burden followed a grand procession of noblemen, bishops, judges and court gentlemen, who saw the little prince laid to rest beside the body of his grandfather, King James.[38]

For over a month the royal couple remained quietly at Greenwich. Henrietta quickly recovered her health and Charles began to hope there would soon be another pregnancy. Early in July, they left to spend the summer 'away hunting, passing from one country house to another': Nonsuch, Windsor, Theobalds, Oatlands, Woodstock.[39] They parted only briefly: once when Henrietta visited Tunbridge Wells to drink the waters for her health, and again in September when she stopped at Somerset House to celebrate the Exaltation of the Cross, 'being a great day of devotion with her'.[40] Otherwise they were together. In fact, the King spent so much time in his wife's apartments, his Privy Councillors complained, that it was impossible to speak to him except when he was out hunting. Charles, oblivious to the courtiers' disapproval, kissed Henrietta repeatedly in front of them, congratulating himself on how happy his marriage was. 'You do not see that at Turin [where Henrietta's sister, Christine, was married to the Duke of Savoy],' he boasted to the new French ambassador, 'nor at Paris either,' he added, referring to Louis XIII's notoriously loveless and childless marriage. 'I wish that we could be always together,' he told his wife, 'and that you could accompany me to the Council.'

That, he knew, was impossible, for 'what would these people say if a woman were to busy herself with matters of government?'[41]

With others Charles remained as reserved and unbending as ever, 'a prince of few words', who 'obliges no one, either in deed or word'.[42] Yet in Henrietta's company he was a different man, as full of wit and fun as she. He teased his wife for her long morning lie-ins: she should at least try to get up in time to hear mass with her priests before noon, he scolded. Her lavish extravagance, despite his court's dire financial needs, provoked nothing more than indulgent joking; 'she is a bad housekeeper,' he confided loudly to the French ambassador in Henrietta's hearing.[43]

This new ambassador, the Marquis de Chateauneuf-sur-Cher, was empowered to negotiate on all the outstanding disputes between the two nations. Henrietta must have twelve priests for her chapel, he insisted, with a bishop as grand almoner, as well as a French lady of honour and physician. Charles, still smarting from the affronts of the Bishop of Mende, was immovable. The Buckingham ladies were quite sufficient he countered; there would be no French physician, and certainly no bishop. Twelve priests he would allow, but not the Oratorians.[44] After three months of fruitless labours Chateauneuf was furious. He had expected that Henrietta's 'great influence' would make Charles 'concede everything by courtesy' to her,[45] 'but she had refused to lift a finger. Seeing nothing beyond her own present happiness, she was incapable of any sustained effort, Chateauneuf complained. She had even obstructed him, insisting that Father Philip remain with her, against the French government's wishes.[46] They had selected Capuchins to serve her now – another order much favoured by the French royal family – and wanted Fathers Philip and Viette to return to France so there would be 'no diversity of tempers and conducts' among her priests, whose rivalry might weaken their mission in England. Henrietta stood firm: the two Oratorians would stay on beside the Capuchins – an awkward mishmash of orders that pleased no one but her.[47]

She was, however, readier to aid Chateauneuf in his attempts to prolong England's hostilities against Spain. Charles, who was now desperately poor – he could 'hardly find the means to provide for the daily needs of himself and the queen', let alone fund a war[48] – decided to open formal peace talks. When Chateauneuf failed to change the King's mind, he turned to Henrietta. Even she found it difficult to influence Charles in a matter so vital to his financial and political interests. When she warned her husband 'that the Spaniards would only deceive him once again', Charles 'retorted that that was only her opinion'. In a fit of pique she snubbed the new ambassador leaving for Madrid, telling him 'she would have nothing to do with Spain, nor with any person there'.[49] 'She shed tears in anger,' but still 'she could not prevail with his majesty to cross the ambassage' – even though Charles and his courtiers were now delighted 'in practically certain hopes' that she was pregnant again. By November, Henrietta had missed two periods, and her craving for mussels – for which she 'sent all about the town' – alerted the English public to her delicate state.[50]

It was not an easy pregnancy. 'Owing to her tender age and delicate constitution she suffers some discomfort,' the Venetian ambassador reported in January 1630, when Henrietta was five months' pregnant.[51] Preparations for the new arrival continued, much as the year before. Again public prayers were offered up. Again London's ambassadors congratulated the royal couple. Further expensive purchases were made: £2000 for 'linen for the Queen's lying in', and over £600 for embroidery for her bed. And again Henrietta expected her mother's midwife, Madame Peronne, and some nurses from Paris 'for the coming confinement'.[52]

Amidst it all, a new French ambassador arrived in London. The Marquis de Fontenay-Mareuil came to replace the Marquis de Chateauneuf, bringing with him the Capuchin priests who were to serve in Henrietta's chapel. The Capuchins were one of the most successful missionary orders of the time, even more severely devoted to poverty and simplicity than the Franciscan order from which they had emerged. The twelve hand-picked friars arrived in London, fired up not only to serve the Queen but to 'promote the glory of God in the assisting of Catholics and in the conversion of Protestants'. Certainly they expected to achieve more than Henrietta's old Oratorians who, they said, had 'quitted England, without any advancement of the Catholic religion'.[53]

After four years with just two priests, Henrietta was delighted to see the full ceremonial of the Catholic mass return to her chapel. The sermon on the Capuchins' first Sunday gave her 'wonderful satisfaction', and their appearance, on her orders, in their simple habits and sandals caused a sensation. London's Catholics flocked to Henrietta's chapel 'in hundreds and thousands', seeing her priests 'as men sent by Heaven' and dreaming of a new era of religious freedom. Protestants came too, to gawp and laugh at the Capuchins, 'clothed in dresses so extraordinary and so strange', though one of the crowd at least, a convinced Puritan, stayed on, impressed, to be converted.[54]

Charles, away in the country hunting, was appalled when he heard of the flagrant appearance of the Capuchins, 'very conspicuously, preaching in their habit', causing 'a great stir among all the Puritan party'. In a bid to win back public popularity, he announced, despite the terms of the marriage treaty, that in his new baby's nursery 'there should neither be nurse, rocker, nor any other officer ... save only Protestants'. He also issued orders that 'none of his subjects shall go any more to mass in the queen's chapel'; guards would be posted there, and at all the foreign ambassadors' chapels, to arrest any of his Catholic subjects trying to get in.[55] Despite Henrietta's anger, Charles stood firm: it was against the terms of her marriage treaty 'that her chaplains should be used by any but by herself and her own servants'. In the following weeks there was bloodshed outside the houses of the French and Spanish ambassadors, whose servants issued forth 'with their naked swords' to defend their co-religionists, yet still the arrests continued.[56] For Charles it was a public relations triumph. He was a true defender of the nation's faith, the news reported; his subjects must 'live in the religion that I profess and my father before me', he had told his wife. However, behind the scenes, Charles did his best to appease Henrietta, releasing many of the arrested Catholics.[57]

In March the Queen passed the point where her last pregnancy had ended prematurely. This time she was taking things carefully. There were no strenuous country walks; instead she rode out in the sedan chair her mother had sent from Paris. It was a wonderful thing, 'handsomer than I deserve', she wrote to Marie. A little heart that Marie had also sent was even more treasured. Henrietta wore it round her neck all the time, 'for I fancy it brings me such good fortune that I am always afraid when I am without it'. Charles too sent his thanks, especially for the sedan chair, for on Henrietta's 'preservation, and on this new hope that God has given us, depends my content'.[58]

Soon the French midwife and nurses arrived in London; their tangle with Dunkirk pirates while crossing the Channel, which 'moved the queen to tears', was safely over.[59] Henrietta wanted to have her birth at Greenwich and, with the plague spreading daily, the whole court was eager to leave London. Soon Greenwich was infected too. And so, afraid to travel further with the Queen so near her time, the royal couple stayed on in St James's Palace. 'The place proves very agreeable to both their Majesties ... the king having his recreations near, and the Queen her entertainments and devotions, for which the new-built chapel is decently adorned, and the new-come Capuchins lodged commodiously beyond the austerity of their rule.'[60]

On Friday 28 May 1630, Henrietta received another 'most beautiful present' from her mother, 'of diverse linen and other things' for the new baby.[61] Around dawn next day the labour began. Again there were the shuttered windows, the guarded doors, the fire burning, the Queen lying in pain on her linen sheets. The surgeon Peter Chamberlen was in attendance, as a precaution, but this time the birth was managed by Madame Peronne, and everything went as could be wished. By noon the twenty-year-old Queen found herself '(God be thanked) ... in good estate', 'the happy mother of a Prince of Wales'.[62] Charles was overjoyed. A year after the death of his first baby he now had a healthy son: 'a fair prince' showing every indication that 'he will be very strong and vigorous'.[63] At St James's that day a handful of privileged callers were ushered in to see Britain's 'great joy and expectation' lying in his cradle, while his happy nurses told and retold the story of how 'he had never clenched his fists, but had always kept his hands open' – a sure sign 'that he will be a prince of great liberality'.[64]

Charles received the visitors' congratulations 'with much joviality and with demonstrations of great pleasure'. In his excitement he even reversed his former strictures about the baby's household: to his wife's great pleasure, he now named the Catholic Countess of Roxburghe as governess in charge of the Prince's household.[65] For the King, the whole day had to be made up only of joy. By his orders prisoners were released from gaol and public prosecutions abandoned, and that night the whole city came alive with bonfires burning, bells ringing and every possible expression 'in the language of public rejoicing'. Even the heavens themselves seemed to join in England's bliss, for the next day, as Charles and the nobility rode in state to St Paul's Cathedral for a special service of thanksgiving, a new star appeared in the sky, visible even in bright daylight, promising good fortune.[66]

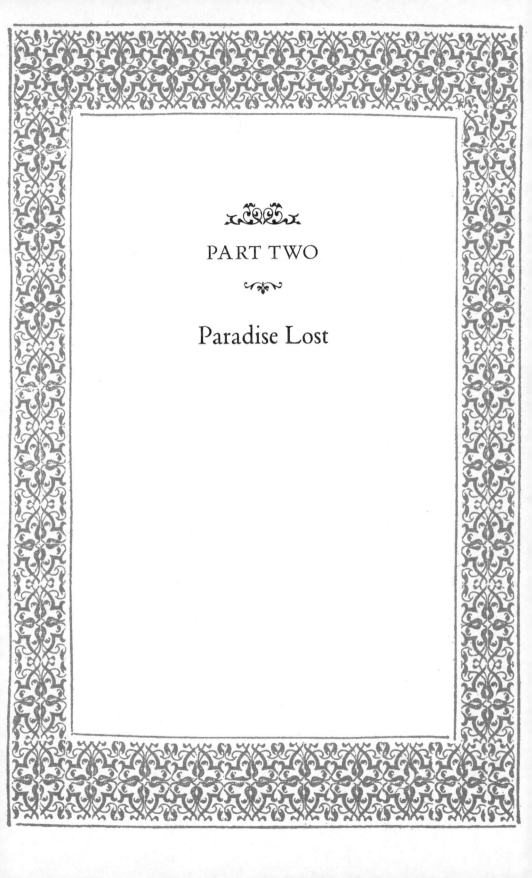

PART TWO

Paradise Lost

6

The Court of Love

Twenty-seven days after the birth of her baby boy, Henrietta Maria knelt, holding a lighted candle, just inside the door of her chapel at St James's, while one of her priests recited from the Psalms. Holding a corner of the priest's stole, she advanced to the altar, where he sprinkled her with holy water in the form of a cross. It was the Catholic 'churching' ceremony, purifying and blessing a woman after a birth, and readying her to bring up her child in a Christian manner.[1]

However, all was not as it seemed. In normal practice this ceremony was performed only after the baby's Catholic baptism. For Henrietta the rule had had to be waived. Charles insisted on an Anglican christening for his son, and two days after the Queen's churching the ceremony took place. Rich tapestries swathed the walls of the King's chapel at St James's. The Lord Mayor of London wore his velvet, the city's aldermen their scarlet gowns. Lords stood on the left, ladies on the right. Buckingham's niece, the teenaged Marchioness of Hamilton, carried the baby to the font, walking beneath a canopy borne by six barons. The nation's foremost nobility were proxies for the boy's royal godparents: the King and Queen Mother of France and Charles's brother-in-law, Frederick Elector Palatine. William Laud, Bishop of

London, took water from a great golden basin and named the boy Charles. Then heralds pronounced the Prince's full royal titles to cheers from 'the crowding multitude' outside, while drums and trumpets sounded and cannons thundered from the Tower and the ships on the river.[2]

Henrietta's priests were outraged, protesting that the bringing up of the royal children in their own faith had been promised in the marriage treaty. Historians ever since have repeated this charge, but in fact the English and French negotiators, concerned to produce an agreement that both sides could sign up to, had left the treaty deliberately vague, stipulating only that the children be brought up under their mother's care until the age of thirteen.[3] If Henrietta herself felt disappointed she showed no sign of it. Neither she nor Charles was present at the font: the Anglican liturgy of the time gave parents no role in the christening ceremony. Instead Charles watched from a window while Henrietta waited in her bedchamber. There the royal couple received the returning christening party in state, before their son was carried back to his nursery.[4]

That night bonfires again filled the city and church bells rang out. Nevertheless, many Puritans thoroughly regretted the birth. The children of Charles's sister, Elizabeth of Bohemia, were more suitable heirs to the throne, they thought, for they had been 'brought up in the Reformed religion; whereas it was uncertain what religion the King's children will follow, being to be brought up under a mother so devoted to the Church of Rome'. One Puritan was so incensed that he asserted that Henrietta had been pre-contracted to another man before she married Charles, which made the Prince a bastard – a claim so seditious that the culprit was 'like to be hanged, drawn and quartered'.[5]

As June ended, the whole nation was in terror of the plague, whose grip intensified with the summer heat. Soon Charles and Henrietta left London, first for Nonsuch near Ewell in Surrey, then moving on to the remote New Forest and Titchfield, their refuge during the plague year of 1625. However, the couple's two-month-old baby, too small and vulnerable to travel, was left behind at St James's. There the tiny Prince of Wales had a household of more than thirty people. There were eight rockers for the baby's cradle, waited on themselves by eight more maids. There were nurses, a physician and an apothecary, a laundress and her maids, and a wet-nurse whose breastfeeding would be the baby's only source of food for his first year.[6] In charge of them all was the Prince's Lady Governess: not the Catholic Countess of Roxburghe whom the elated father had named on the day of the birth, but the Anglican Countess of Dorset. The appointment forced Henrietta to break solemn oaths she had made before her marriage to 'select none but Catholics to nurse, bring up and serve the children which may be born'. Yet now, eager to keep her husband's favour and well aware of the futility of protesting, Henrietta gave way with good grace. Besides, the Countess of Dorset was well known to the Queen and had family members who were Catholics. The Countess's husband himself, now Henrietta's Grand Chamberlain, was suspected of secret Catholic sympathies.[7]

Although the plague that summer was nothing like the epidemic of five years earlier, still the city emptied, the theatres closed.[8] St James's remained in strict isolation, but from Nonsuch Charles and Henrietta made day trips to see the Prince, 'who prospereth exceedingly, to their great joy'. When the royal couple moved further away, daily letters kept them abreast of the boy's progress. 'He thrives well,' his physician reported on Sunday 15 August: 'he has neither sucked nor wakened but once all that night.' And twelve days later: 'the Prince's favour, likelihood, strength, mirth, and night's rest increase daily. The Lady Governess is most careful and diligent.'[9] By late September the King and Queen had moved closer to London. Henrietta doted on her little boy. 'He is so fat and so tall, that he is taken for a year old,' she wrote to Mamie St-Georges, 'and he is only four months: his teeth are already beginning to come.' 'I wish you could see the gentleman,' she enthused again, 'for he has no ordinary mien; he is so serious in all that he does, that I cannot help fancying him far wiser than myself.' Proudly she despatched baby pictures to her far-flung family.[10]

That autumn was a happy time, with the whole family reunited and Henrietta suspecting she was pregnant again. For Charles's birthday on

19 November there were unprecedented celebrations, all the church bells ringing 'and above a thousand bonfires kindled that night'.[11] A few days later news came that the long-desired peace treaty with Spain had been signed in Madrid. With the Spanish refusing to restore the Palatinate to his sister's family, Charles had had to rest satisfied with a mere promise that they would 'be mediators' in the matter. Even so, he was delighted. He was determined now to follow his father's precepts and stand back from the religious and political conflicts of Europe. With no expensive foreign wars, he would be able to fulfil his long-time dream of governing the nation without calling Parliament.[12]

It was the beginning of a new chapter in British history. For Puritans it would be an era of oppression, but Charles and his courtiers looked forward to a 'time of universal quiet and peace' both at home and abroad.[13] That Christmas the royal couple expressed their high expect-ations in two specially created masques: dramatic extravaganzas, one performed by the King and his gentlemen for the Queen's enter-tainment, the other by the Queen and her ladies for the King. Written by Ben Jonson, with Inigo Jones as designer of the spectacular visual effects, the two dramas shared a single theme: the nature of true love – chaste, rational, noble, aspiring – and its power to reform the world. Up on the stage, Henrietta was the goddess Chloris – 'queen of the flowers and mistress of the spring' and 'the top of paramours' – whose love and flower power banished the goblins of hatred, jealousy and fear, establishing an era of peace and happiness. In the King's masque, Charles played the Heroical Lover whose band of 'perfect lovers' – modest, courteous and valiant – drove away all the enemies of Cal-lipolis, the City of Beauty. 'Joy, joy to mortals,' the masque proclaimed, 'whilst love presents a world of chaste desires.'[14]

That winter Henrietta's hopes that she might be pregnant proved unfounded, but no one was too disappointed, for 'the youth and vigour of their Majesties affords unquenchable hopes of good fortune in the matter of the succession'. And in the New Year of 1631 the Queen conceived again. Her new baby was born in the small hours of Friday 4 November 'after a few hours' travail'.[15] The little girl, three weeks early and 'very weak', was christened at once, without ceremony, named Mary after her mother and grandmother. Despite her parents' fears, the tiny princess did well, 'so as nothing is wanting to make this joy entire'.[16]

As the years passed, the royal family grew steadily. In 1633 another boy was born, 'a goodly, lusty child', named James after Charles's father and given the title Duke of York. Two years later came another daughter, Elizabeth, and in 1637 there was another 'new princess for the kingdom', named Anne after Charles's mother.[17] Each new child was a joy, but Henrietta often found the pregnancies hard. The pregnancy with James, in particular, brought a host of ailments, including vomiting and spells of exhaustion. Then, at seven months, her right arm was almost paralysed and the physicians feared she would lose the use of that side of her body. Charles abandoned his hunting break and rushed to join her at Somerset House, to find her already 'out of danger and bettering hourly'.[18]

For each birth Henrietta retired to St James's Palace, believing that only here, where her first surviving son had been born, would all turn out well. Even in 1637, with the plague raging, the Queen insisted on coming here specially from Hampton Court for Anne's birth.[19] As Henrietta waited through the last few weeks for her labour to begin, Charles was always there, a solicitous husband, never failing 'to procure for her all suitable comforts'. Each time the birth was managed by Madame Peronne and her French nurses. Then Henrietta remained for three weeks in her bedchamber, 'recovering from the trials of her delivery', while Charles sat by her 'the greatest part of the day'.[20] Afterwards came her churching ceremony and re-emergence to public life.

Each royal child had their own establishment of servants, although none was waited on as grandly as Prince Charles, the heir to the throne, with thirty personnel. Ten or fewer became the norm for the others, including just a single nurse and a mere four rockers. As the babies grew into busy little toddlers, their rockers were in constant attendance, holding them up for a last look out of the window at bedtime, making sure they were properly dressed in hat and neckcloth against any chill evening air. For older children, the wet-nurse and rockers were replaced by a band of watchers and a dry-nurse. At the head of them all was the Lady Governess, caring for the child as well as managing the entire household and its finances. For James, as for Prince Charles, this was the Countess of Dorset, but for the girls, less politically sensitive, Charles went back to his original plan, appointing the Catholic Countess of Roxburghe.[21]

The children began early on the courtly training all-important for royal life. Even before his second birthday, Charles Prince of Wales was receiving foreign ambassadors with his parents. By the age of four he was giving audiences of his own, in company with his little sister and brother – James only just past his first birthday. The children's behaviour on these occasions was closely scrutinised. Charles reproved the six-year-old Prince of Wales, the Venetian ambassador reported, 'for having received me too stolidly when I kissed his hand'.[22] There were other grand events too. Prince Charles accompanied his father to the annual Garter ceremonies, and at eight was himself installed as a Knight of the Order – an honour the boy desired 'exceedingly'.[23] Sometimes the children dined in state with their parents in front of a watching crowd or joined them on stage to perform in court masques.

Academic education, by contrast, was a low priority. The children were tutored in French and the girls learnt to sing, but even at the age of nine Prince Charles was still struggling to use a pen, his large letters smudged and painstakingly formed on paper that had been specially ruled with guidelines. As the Prince grew older, Brian Duppa, Bishop of Chichester was made his tutor – not so much for his scholarship, but because he was a perfect gentleman, who 'hath no pedantry in him ... reads men as well as books ... and in a word strives as much discreetly to hide the scholar in him, as other men's follies study to show it.'[24]

Just as in Henrietta's childhood *troupeau*, so now all her children grew up together. St James's Palace was their London residence, with its extensive gardens and orchards, fine library and art collection, with more than 550 paintings and 300 pieces of sculpture. For the boys there was an armoury with model forts and soldiers, a riding house, and an artillery house with child-size cannons. Much of their time was spent at Richmond Palace, the traditional home for the royal children 'upon account of the unusual wholesomeness of the air'.[25] Here a jumble of stone and brick buildings towered picturesquely over the River Thames, enclosing several courtyards, which made the rooms 'very light and pleasant'. In the gardens and the various 'houses of pleasure' were facilities for bowls, tennis, archery and billiards. There were houses for pigeons and other birds, and in the 1630s King Charles created a great new deer park, covering much the same area as modern Richmond Park.[26]

Though etiquette decreed they should live in separate palaces, Charles and Henrietta loved to be in their children's company. In London they joined them at St James's for supper, and at Richmond they visited for days at a time. A Catholic priest accompanying the royal couple on one of their visits experienced at first-hand 'the happiness of those little princes [and princesses] at the arrival of their majesties'. Then, 'in the evening they all ate together, the Prince and the Duke of York at the King's side, and the Princess Mary at the Queen's, the Princess Elizabeth, being still very small, did not appear at table.' Their private family life, he noted, was full of 'reciprocal affection'. Instead of the royal ceremony and hauteur that would have been expected, there was 'a courtesy as singular as could be found in the house of any private well-bred gentleman'.[27]

Prince Charles was particularly close to his parents, and the historical record provides glimpses of the life they shared. In 1633 we see the King ready to leave for Scotland, spending his last evening walking in St James's Park with his nearly three-year-old son, and staying out 'a little too late', in the view of the boy's physicians afterwards when he fell ill. Two months later the Prince welcomed his father home 'with the prettiest innocent mirth that can be imagined'.[28] In 1636 he was performing on stage as Prince Britomart with a band of 'little cavaliers', for his mother's entertainment.[29] Two years on we see him admiring a new, beautifully bound book of his father's and asking for one himself, which the King arranged, to the boy's delight. Later again, he is an agile eleven-year-old out riding with his father. Seeing a hare, Charles Senior took a shot and wounded it, at which the Prince 'skipped off his horse, and ran after her' through a couple of water-filled ditches, caught her 'and laughing showed her to the King'.[30]

Of course there were moments of exasperation too. Three-year-old Mary embarrassed her mother by refusing to sit still to have her portrait painted. 'I shall have another done of her, which will be better,' Henrietta had to promise her sister Christine.[31] Three years later Prince Charles annoyed his mother by obstinately refusing to follow doctors' orders. 'Charles,' Henrietta wrote, 'I am sore that I must begin my first letter with chiding you, because I hear that you will not take physic. I hope it was only for this day and that tomorrow you will do it, for if you will not I must come to you and make you take it, for it is for your health.'[32]

Often Henrietta would rush to be with her ill children, excusing herself from royal business.[33] When the King was away in Scotland, Prince Charles suffered a gastric infection, with days of evil-smelling, blood-spotted diarrhoea, 'the like whereof I did never see come from a child of his age', one of his doctors commented. It was potentially fatal, and Henrietta, 'so troubled ... that I was not myself, stayed constantly with her son at St James's, consulting physicians and approving their remedies: milk enemas 'to refresh his intestines and suage his pain' followed by a gentle purge of senna and rhubarb.[34] As the boy began to recover, Henrietta had him moved to the healthier air of Greenwich, where she supervised his diet and brought him out from the sickroom into lively company. Throughout, the Queen was a marvel of solicitude: 'a more truly virtuous, noble, wise, sweet young lady did I never behold,' a courtier enthused; 'also the best wife and mother in the world'.[35]

For the royal couple – Charles was in his thirties, Henrietta her twenties – the 1630s were certainly a golden age, with the years passing in an idyllic round. Later – battered by civil war, bereaved, impoverished, exiled – the royalists looked back with the strongest nostalgia on the glorious days of spring and summer. Lovingly they painted their memories of an 'enchanted island' untouched by the ravages of war: of dappled light beneath ancient oaks, of meadow grass so lush it reached to the cattle's bellies; of hares lying in their forms all day, and stags venturing from the woods to eat the sweet marjoram on the hills. The country scents were vivid too – cows' breath, 'a field of beans when newly blown, or ... a meadow being lately mown' – and the people in the landscape with their simple pastimes: playing tabors and pipes, tying cowslips into a ball for a lover's gift, dancing. Then too there were the delights of 'most innocent convenient country houses', with their 'shady walks and close arbours', which made one exiled Catholic courtier 'sigh to be again ... in little England, where time slideth more gently away than in any part of the world'.[36]

Charles and Henrietta enjoyed this idyll to the full. Each year, as the weather warmed, they left London for 'the pleasant position and the more healthy air' of Greenwich, five miles down the Thames.[37] Up to two months were spent there, still close enough to London for government business to continue amidst the place's many rural pleasures. There was hunting, of course, and long walks up the hill above the town, where sheep grazed and huntsmen walked with their dogs. The prospect from here, across rich hedged fields to the silvery bends of the River Thames scattered with shipping and London beyond, was the most admired view in England, painted by a succession of artists. Just a short distance from the splendours of the palace the royal couple could be deep in the countryside, where they might suddenly come across 'a shepherd and his little boy reading ... the Bible to him', or the milkmaids returning home 'in pomp with their milk' and musicians playing before them. Henrietta in particular was well known for 'her taste for the country', where 'the dances of the peasantry amuse her'.[38]

And Greenwich was only the beginning of the delights of the royal year. In July began the summer progress proper, sometimes with a stay at Oatlands – Henrietta's palace in Surrey – or else a stop at Theobalds, 'one of the most charming places belonging to the crown near London and especially enjoyable for every kind of hunting'.[39] Later they went further afield, staying in royal hunting lodges – Woodstock, Newmarket and Royston were all favourites of Charles's – or in the houses of the nation's leading aristocrats. Mostly these stops were short; just a few nights spent by the court in a gentleman's house were enough to exhaust most private pockets. But at Wilton, 100 miles west of London, the wealthy Earl of Pembroke was lavishly hospitable and even rede-signed his house and grounds according to Charles's tastes: 'all *al Italian*', with a 'magnificent garden and grotto'. Charles loved Wilton 'above all places: and came thither every summer'.[40] Then, as September drew on, the court returned closer to London for extended stays at Windsor Castle and Hampton Court.

It was a huge production, two entire royal courts travelling through the English countryside. Everyone and everything went with them: Henrietta took her dwarfs, monkeys and lapdogs, even 'the billiard boards', as well as her priests and chapel choir who performed 'with most beautiful music' wherever she stopped.[41] An army of servants went before them, making everything ready. The county authorities repaired the roads, and 'extraordinary stages for posts' were arranged to make sure the King received important correspondence promptly.[42] Yet Charles paid little attention to business during these summer months. Ambassadors grew desperate, unable to fulfil their masters' 'repeated instructions', because he was 'far away hunting or else engaged in other recreations', 'grown drowsy ... in the charms of peace'. Even if they managed to catch up with him, their attempts to talk business were often skilfully diverted by Charles into talk of 'hunting, pictures and the like'. 'Immersed in the delights of banquets, in his affection for his wife and in the pleasures of the chase', the King 'would never come to any decision of consequence'.[43]

Sometimes on their progresses the royal couple took a London company of professional actors away with them, with a large tent for their performances, or else the Queen and her courtiers would appear on stage themselves in masques created for special occasions.[44] One summer night in 1634 Henrietta even 'consented to sing ... in hearing of the [Savoyard] ambassador and, after supper, danced with him and others, both French and English dances till after midnight'. The Queen's singing was a rare and special pleasure: 'never any earthly thing,' enthused a court poet,

> Sung so true, so sweet, so clear;
> I was then in Heaven, not here.'[45]

That summer the royal pair made their longest ever journey together, a six-week tour northwards as far as Nottingham and Welbeck Abbey, where they were received by the Earl of Newcastle, one of England's wealthiest aristocrats. It was a 'stupendous entertainment; which, (God be thanked) . . . no man ever after imitated'. There was also a masque, *Love's Welcome at Bolsover*, performed at another of Newcastle's nearby houses. The six nights' stay cost some £15,000: more than £3 million in modern money.[46]

In 1636, a plague year, the royal couple left London early. There was no stop at Greenwich, for the infection was already there. Instead they went to Hampton Court, Henrietta in particular feeling 'very nervous about the plague'. In July the couple parted, Henrietta staying at Oatlands while Charles hunted from Bagshot to Salisbury, and then fled in haste, even abandoning his baggage, after one of his guards died. At the end of August they were reunited in Oxford, which was still plague-free.[47] The university excelled itself. The city's streets were specially cleansed 'of dirt, filth, rubbish, and all manner of uncleanness', whilst students and dons alike were ordered 'not to wear long hair, nor any boots . . . nor to wear their gowns hanging loosely'.[48] At Christ Church the nation's rulers were welcomed with gifts: a velvet-covered Bible for Charles, and gloves for Henrietta. Two days passed in festivities. The magnificent dinners and suppers consumed seventy deer, five oxen, and seventy-four sheep, plus 'melons, grapes, fish, poultry, and so forth'. There were Latin speeches, music, a visit to the university library, and plays performed by the students. Then the royal couple parted, Charles hunting in the New Forest, while Henrietta remained at Oatlands, three months' pregnant with Anne.[49]

The couple's longest parting was in 1633, when Charles travelled north for his Scottish coronation. At first he had hoped to avoid this troublesome and costly commitment, asking that the Scottish crown be brought to London 'to save him from so long a journey', but the Scots had replied that 'he must not be so false to his country'; if he delayed too long, 'they might, perhaps be inclined to make choice of some other king'.[50] Finally Charles agreed. The preparations were immense. His entire court was going – councillors, clergymen, musicians and all – much of it by sea. A ship was even hired specially 'to transport his Majesty's buckhounds'. Fifty carts were ordered 'with necessary provisions, to attend the King in his journey'.[51] Henrietta, four months' pregnant with James, remained behind with a skeleton Privy Council to manage the affairs of England. All along the way the nobility and gentry greeted their King with honour. The hospitality was stupendous. Charles stopped frequently for hunting too, so that the 200-mile journey to York took over two weeks, an average of just fourteen miles a day. As Charles crossed the border into Scotland he began to feel a sense of urgency. Missing Henrietta, he was 'determined to make the shortest possible stay in that kingdom'.[52] Meanwhile, at Greenwich with her children, Henrietta found 'singular contentment' in her husband's frequent letters, 'whereof we had no small need considering how disconsolate she hath been'. She was 'well in health though sad for the most part', spending too much time over her needlework, 'which gives her overmuch leisure to muse'.[53]

On 15 June, Charles entered Edinburgh in triumphal manner, with pageants and music, speeches and poems, and the cheers of the populace. Three days later he was crowned with all the church ceremony he loved. Scots Presbyterians were horrified to see the bishops in their golden copes, the altar and wax candles, and especially the crucifix to which the bishops bowed, which 'bred great fear of inbringing of Popery'.[54] Charles and his courtiers, however, were 'highly delighted' by the crowd outside, whose 'affection ... surpassed all belief, and extended to all ranks', Charles reported to Henrietta. Two days later he opened the Scottish Parliament, intending 'to hasten the despatch of the remaining business'. Within ten days he was done, and full of 'extraordinary satisfaction'; the Parliament even 'offered spontaneously' to pay most of his journey expenses.[55] Henrietta was more cheerful too, with the promise of Charles's imminent return. Out on a river trip from Greenwich, she challenged Lord Goring, one of her favourite courtiers, 'to race over a long course of the Thames', watched by 'a large number of ladies and cavaliers'. The Queen won and Goring paid her 'the stakes arranged beforehand': some £30,000 in modern money.[56] Meanwhile Charles came south in a 'very hurried and almost flying journey', with coaches ready all along his route 'so that his Majesty may travel post by them'. The 360 miles from Berwick to Greenwich took him just four days, as he hoped 'to take the queen by surprise, so as to make his return more welcome to her when she was not expecting him'. Henrietta, it seems, was perfectly prepared and came out from Greenwich 'as far as Stratford Bow' to meet him. Then the normal summer pleasures recommenced.[57]

Of all pastimes, Charles's greatest passion was for hunting. He had a pack of 'harriers and beagles' for hare coursing, as well as gun dogs, or 'slug hounds', for when he went wildfowling. The Queen had her own pack of hounds under her 'Master of the Bows and String Hounds', and the King's hawks were kept in the royal mews.[58] It was deer hunting that filled Charles's time for weeks on end. Thirty-two buckhounds were kept for this, their keepers all in royal livery. Often the King would get up in the small hours, attend morning prayers in chapel, then go out 'before five in the morning', perhaps not returning until dark.[59] The day's sport was vigorous in the extreme. Charles was 'below the average height' even in an age of small people, but he was very fit, 'well proportioned and strong', and he rode with 'untiring energy'. Bad weather was no deterrent: 'this morning, his Majesty and all that hunted with him in the forest were soundly wet.' In the rush of the chase he fearlessly endured many falls from horses. Sometimes there were minor injuries: 'a blow in the face' or an injured leg during a 'grievous fall'.[60]

In September 1636 he 'came near losing his life' when, 'following a stag at full speed', his horse ran headlong into a deep bog. The beast, 'completely submerged', was left 'dead on the spot', while Charles, in so deeply that 'only his head and the top of his shoulders remained above ground', was saved by his followers only 'at the risk of their lives'. Unperturbed, he changed his clothes and mounted a new horse to continue the hunt. But if Charles had a charmed life, some of his courtiers were less fortunate. Just two weeks later one of them lost two fingers when his knife slipped at the killing of a stag.[61] Another had died after his leg, broken 'with a fall out hunting with the King', turned gangrenous. Perhaps the thrill of real danger, combined with the exhilarating outdoor exercise, was the true appeal for a man whose indoor life was so rigidly controlled by etiquette. And his contemporaries admired him for it:

> Hunting, it is the noblest exercise,
> Makes men laborious, active, wise.[62]

Certainly the King thrived on this vigorous lifestyle. Even the smallpox, that feared killer and maimer, hardly touched him. His preliminary ten days of illness he dismissed as just a passing fever 'after he had heated himself at tennis'. When the first spots appeared he refused to believe his doctors' diagnosis and would not stay in bed: 'all the day long he is . . . merry, and eats and drinks heartily, and recreates himself with some game or other'. Henrietta insisted on sleeping with her husband, despite the risk of infection, and in the daytime she would 'never be out of his company'. Just five days after the initial tell-tale lesions, Charles was already 'in a good way of recovery'.[63]

Each year in October the court returned to London. At Whitehall Palace everything proceeded 'with great pomp and splendour even to excess'. Each room of the royal apartments had its regulations about who could enter and what they should do there. Royal meals were borne in state by gentlemen wearing swords, the food served on bended knee while the assembled courtiers stood in their semicircle. Some 2000 people were employed to serve the royal couple – a similar population to that of a reasonably sized town in the period – and their maintenance cost £250,000 per year, roughly equivalent to £60 million in modern money.[64]

Despite all this, behind closed doors in Henrietta's apartments, the atmosphere was relaxed and informal, the Queen happily surrounded by her family and friends and her beloved pets: small birds and monkeys and especially lapdogs, whose clever exploits were a favourite conversational subject. Henrietta's wit was irrepressible and rather sharp, and her court was often filled with laughter, especially at the expense of outsiders, as when a luckless foreign ambassador mistook Henrietta's dwarf, Jeffery Hudson, for her eldest son. 'Becoming aware of this error too late, he apologised, which only made her Majesty and the others who were standing by laugh the more.' Two years later the court ladies laughed 'for all the rest of the day' after another ambassador held forth pompously to the Queen in Latin for over an hour; failing to understand a word, Henrietta could only give him 'a very concise and almost voiceless answer'.[65]

At Whitehall the royal couple enjoyed the many pleasures of London's winter social season. In the palace's tiltyard there was jousting and bear-baiting; a stake was set up specially for tethering the beast, and rails protected the spectators during the bouts arranged by Charles's 'Sergeant of the Bears'. There was an indoor alley for bowls, and outdoor greens next door in St James's Park. Whitehall also had three tennis courts, two roofed over and one open to the sky. Real tennis was hugely fashionable; every royal palace had at least one court, and government business was often delayed by 'the King's going to tennis'. The sport was fiercely competitive – there was certainly no question of flattering Charles by letting him win – and vast sums of money changed hands in bets. A French visitor of Henrietta's left England in 1631 with £3000 'which he had won of the king at tennis'.[66]

Since theatre was a passion for both Charles and Henrietta, actors were often summoned into Whitehall to perform: in 1632 alone, three professional companies performed at least fifty plays there. The plays of Beaumont and Fletcher were great favourites, as were those of Shakespeare, Jonson and Davenant, as well as a host of minor contemporary writers now largely forgotten. There were performances at court even during Lent and on Sundays, despite a law of 1625 forbidding it.[67] Further entertainment came from trips to see the latest rarities – manuscripts, books and artworks – brought home by England's foremost collectors from their European travels. There were feasts laid on by the couple's courtiers, and dancing in the great hall at Whitehall. The revelling rose to a particular height in 1635, when Charles's nephew, Charles Louis, the new Elector Palatine, arrived in London: 'comedies, festivities and balls are . . . indulged in every day at Court for the prince's sake'.[68]

Each year, at the end of October, all London flocked to watch the

Lord Mayor's procession: 'the greatest that is made for the reception of any municipal magistrate in the world'. Then came the two royal birthdays: Henrietta's on 15 November and Charles's four days later, celebrated with parties at court, each time a little different. One year, Charles laid on a jousting display for Henrietta. On another occasion, Henrietta arranged a feast and a play at Somerset House for Charles and a selection of favoured courtiers.[69] The Christmas holidays formed the climax of the year. After Charles and Henrietta's separate religious observances on Christmas Day, the Twelve Days of Christmas began, filled with feasting, dancing and plays in abundance, comedies especially. All London's ambassadors came to congratulate the couple on each New Year, and this, not Christmas Day, was the time for presents to be given. The culmination of it all came on 6 January, Twelfth Night, when Charles and his principal courtiers performed a masque for Henrietta and the rest of the court.

On those nights the court was always crowded, as the eager audience jostled at the door of the masquing chamber. Many came without invitations: women hoping to charm their way in with a pretty face and 'extreme brave apparel': men relying on bribery, even risking 'the danger of a broken pate' from the doorman's staff.[70] The room beyond was full to bursting, with everyone dressed in their finest, men and women alike smothered in jewels, vying for the best seats closest to the Queen. At last came the call to be seated and the wonders of the masque began: 'heavens and hells, their gods and devils, and clouds, sun, moon, and stars ... cities, castles, seas, fishes, rocks, mountains, beasts, birds, and what[ever] pleaseth the poet, painter, and surveyor'.[71] Everything here was the brainchild of the court's surveyor of works, Inigo Jones. Artist, architect and engineer, trained by years of continental travel, Jones was the ideal man to produce these masterpieces of Renaissance design. Under his direction, perspective scenery – with its ranked wings of classical ruins, palaces or forest trees framing the hazy painted backdrop beyond – was first introduced to England for royal masques. Even the use of a stage behind a curtain was his introduction. For every occasion, Jones created a new set of stage machinery, with pulleys and wheels to work the moving ships, floating clouds, growing trees and other contrivances that so provoked the audience's wonder. By 1638 his techniques were so refined that he even staged a complete aerial ballet. He also designed the costumes, consulting continental books of emblems and *commedia dell' arte* figures to create designs loaded with classical symbolism, each one a confection of opulent fabrics, gold, silver, jewels and ostrich feathers.[72]

The main body of the masque was performed by professional actors and musicians, speaking and singing the lines that a court poet had written under Jones's direction. First came the antimasque, a riot of disorder demanding to be resolved, leading up to the summoning of the heroic, godlike figures of Charles and his courtiers, whose mere approach, silent and grand in some fantastic stage machine, was sufficient to set the world to rights. The King and his lords performed a final triumphal dance, specially choreographed for the occasion, and the masque was at an end. Then everyone present danced far into the night, ending at last with a banquet.

With Christmas over, Charles and Henrietta left to hunt in the country. Sometimes the weather was just too dreadful; one winter's hunting trip to Newmarket was cut short 'on account of the cold of that place'. Henrietta, prone to catching colds and overtiring herself, grew less enthusiastic, and in 1635, as Charles left for Newmarket as usual, she remained 'doubtful because of the inconveniences of that country'.[73] In any case, these January trips never lasted long, and the royal couple always returned to London for Shrovetide in February, the traditional carnival season, when the court again abandoned business and threw itself into a whirl of 'dances, comedies and other pleasant diversions', chief of which was a masque put on by Henrietta and her ladies 'for the gratification and pleasure of the king'.[74] Henrietta was passionate about her masques. Rehearsals often began before Christmas: twice a week to start with, then every day as the great event approached. This time the King sat in the place of honour, enjoying himself immensely, and then joining the dancing afterwards 'until near daybreak'.[75]

Occasionally the season went without a masque. In January 1633, as Charles prepared to leave for Scotland, his usual Twelfth Night masque was replaced by a pastoral performed by Henrietta and her ladies. *The Shepherds' Paradise*, written by one of Henrietta's courtiers, was partly an exercise to improve the Queen's English; the performance went on for seven or eight hours, in which Henrietta alone spoke some 800 lines of English verse.[76] But usually there were the 'year's double masques', playing out the royal couple's fantasies of superhuman love and godlike power. Henrietta's roles made her the image of female perfection, pure in virtue, innocent in her love, glorious in her beauty, calming and nurturing, a softer counterpart to Charles's appearances as an all-powerful personification of manly 'heroic virtue'.[77] The result was a heady mix of romance and nationalism, as the titles of the masques themselves make clear: *Albion's Triumph, The British Heaven, The Temple of Love.*

These early months of the year were the season for fashionable society weddings – marriages made not in heaven but at Whitehall, where Charles and Henrietta were tireless matchmakers. It was no frivolous matter. With these marriages they were joining the nation's aristocratic leaders in one close-knit dynastic web, loyal to the King and each other, creating a stable and powerful government. Charles was prepared to offer prospective grooms some powerful incentives: 'a princely addition' to brides' dowries, with the promise of more favours in the future. The resulting weddings often took place at Whitehall, where Charles sometimes gave away the bride himself; afterwards 'a most sumptuous banquet was given to the flower of the nobility'.[78]

With the warmer weather of spring, the royal couple began to spend more time outdoors. Again the historical record provides us with glimpses: of Henrietta cancelling all her official audiences and going out on an impulse, 'the fairness of the day calling the Queen abroad'; of Charles at his jousting exercises in St James's Park, receiving two crimson-dressed horses from the Spanish ambassador, whom the King then took back to Whitehall, where he 'showed him his statues as he passed through the Privy Garden'.[79] There were pleasure drives into the City too, as when the couple 'spent some time at Ludgate Hill', examining a favoured shopkeeper's wares, before going on to the asylum at Bedlam, 'to see the mad folks, where they were madly entertained ... Two mad women had almost frighted the king and queen, and all their attendants, out of the house, by their foul talk.'[80]

April brought the annual ceremonies of the Order of the Garter, performed with great pomp at Whitehall or Windsor Castle, attended by Charles and sometimes Henrietta too. Then came the festivities of maying. One year Henrietta drove out at the head of a vast procession of coaches, leaping down herself to gather the season's first branch of white May blossom. Another time Charles rode with her 'on maying ... through Hyde Park to Kensington, where a collation was prepared for them by the Earl of Holland', one of Henrietta's favourite courtiers.[81] The royal couple were often to be seen at this season driving 'in Hyde Park all the day in all state',[82] where fashionable London came in their coaches to join them. Then, in the middle of May, Charles and Henrietta left for Greenwich and their summer country progress.

Wherever they went, the couple indulged their passion for all that was fine and beautiful. They redecorated their palaces at vast expense, with tapestried walls and furniture covered with pure gold leaf, or upholstered in silks and velvets and cloth of gold. Gorgeous clothes and jewels were irresistible: in fifteen years Charles spent some £20 million in modern money on his personal wardrobe.[83] They redesigned their gardens in the latest fashion, with sundials and fountains and arbours. At St James's, Henrietta laid out a French formal garden of embroidery parterres, where Charles displayed the bulk of his statuary collection: over 250 pieces, 'the rarest wonders of Italy' transported miraculously into the heart of England.[84]

Together the royal couple amassed one of the greatest art collections in Europe – more than 1700 paintings were spread through the royal palaces.[85] Their agents scoured the Continent and made vast purchases: even as he struggled to fund Buckingham's expedition to La Rochelle in 1627, Charles was arranging the largest single art purchase yet seen in Europe: the treasures of the Duke of Mantua, 'so wonderful and glorious a collection the like will never again be met with'.[86] Art arrived as gifts as well. Especially impressive was a collection of sixteenth-century Italian paintings, sent from Rome by Cardinal Barberini for the Queen. When they arrived Charles rushed to join her; 'the boxes were opened ... and the pieces viewed one by one with singular pleasure'. Charles was so delighted that Henrietta predicted, only half in joke, that 'she would not be able to keep them, as the King would steal them from her'.[87]

The royal couple were also enthusiastic commissioners of new works, and their court attracted leading continental artists. Foremost among them was Anthony Van Dyck, who arrived in 1632 and spent most of his remaining years in England, producing vast numbers of royal portraits; Henrietta sat to him at least twenty-five times. It is not hard to see why he was so favoured. In earlier paintings by Daniel Mytens, Charles had appeared stiff and coarse-featured, dwarfed by his elaborate clothes and surroundings. In contrast Van Dyck transformed the King into an individual of effortless superiority, his expression distant, his whole figure utterly elegant and poised. Somehow Van Dyck imparted not just majesty to these pictures, but something mythical. Henrietta too has metamorphosed into a figure both more mysterious than Mytens's doll-like rendition and more authoritative: unutterably beautiful but also remote like her husband, with an enigmatic Mona Lisa smile just turning up the corners of her lips. Van Dyck's portraits have become the definitive image of Charles and Henrietta, yet they were a deliberate construction. Here, as in their masques, the royals are godlike beings, monarchs by divine right, above common mortals 'as far ... as they are above beasts'.[88] We see no hint of the Queen who declared, based on her own self-appraisal, 'that women could not be beautiful beyond the age of twenty-two'. Nor do we see the vivacious young socialite, naturally 'inclined towards gaiety', who loved 'frivolous but innocent things'.[89] Van Dyck's Charles comes closer to contemporaries' descriptions of a king who was 'very majestic ... and would be approached with respect and reverence'. But in these images there is no sign that Charles was a small man who rode, admittedly with skill 'but not very gracefully'.[90]

The couple's most costly taste of all was architecture. Charles thought on the grandest scale, with plans for razing Whitehall to the ground and building in its place a vast rectangular block of buildings enclosing almost a dozen huge courtyards. There would be endless columns and classical statues, pediments, urns and balustrades, all designed by Inigo Jones and his pupil John Webb, following ancient Roman and Renaissance Italian models. The resulting construction would have filled much of St James's Park and dominated that end of London.[91] It was here that the reality of an English king ruling without the support of Parliament finally made itself felt: Charles could never fund so grand a scheme as this. Henrietta was the more effectual builder of the pair. Her Whitehall apartments were under almost continuous alteration throughout the reign. At Greenwich in 1630 she resumed work on the Italianate Queen's House left unfinished by Charles's mother. The building work alone took five years, and the interior decoration continued until 1639. There were marble floors, carved, stone fireplaces and painted ceilings – the most important being Orazio and Artemisia Gentileschi's *Allegory of Peace and the Arts under the English Crown*.[92]

The project that undoubtedly meant the most to Henrietta was at Somerset House, where she spent four years creating a new Catholic chapel and a monastery for her priests. The monastery would be simple, as required by the Capuchins' vows, but the chapel was planned on the grandest scale, paid for by Charles to the tune of some £4000, as agreed with Bassompierre back in 1626. Inigo Jones designed a stylish Renaissance building, lavishly decorated inside with arches, columns and carving. At 100 feet long and thirty wide this chapel was plainly intended to hold far more people than just the Queen and the handful of Catholic courtiers allowed, by the terms of her marriage treaty, to attend mass with her. In fact a special chamber was included at one end, behind a carved screen, to hold the Queen's court.[93] The vast space beyond, as far as the altar, was a reflection of Henrietta's rising ambitions for her faith. Here, in the heart of London, she would have 'a public church', where her priests would 'celebrate mass, preach, and hear confessions', not just for herself, but 'for the benefit of the other Catholics'.[94] Secure in her husband's love, she was ready to revive all those grand Catholic visions that had been the original *raison d'être* of her marriage.

7

Questions of Faith

By the middle of the 1630s the time was ripe for Henrietta to advance her plans. With no need now to pander to Parliament, Charles could please his wife and offer his long-persecuted Catholic subjects a lenient rule. Even before her new chapel was completed, London's Catholics flocked to the room in Somerset House where she held her religious services. On Sundays there was 'a continual ebb and flood of people from six in the morning till twelve at noon', as the Capuchins performed one mass after another, while Charles, 'looking at them from a window of the Queen's palace', made no objection, so that he seemed 'by his silence [to be] approving of their devotion'.[1]

The penal laws were now enforced only rarely, and those who did suffer under them could sue to Henrietta for assistance, which she was always ready to give. She carried individual cases to Charles, arguing their merits and winning him over. For her sake, he ordered that an imprisoned priest was 'to go freely abroad for the benefit of his health'; another time, 'merely at the queen's suit', he pardoned fourteen Catholics condemned to death at Newgate sessions. When Henrietta raised the case of four lay Catholics, 'old and simple and extremely poor', imprisoned for years in York Castle for unpaid recusancy fines, Charles ordered the release not just of them but of 'all such as were detained for matters of conscience'.[2] On each occasion Henrietta would proceed to the King's crypto-Catholic secretary of state, Sir Francis Windebank, informing him of Charles's desires, which Windebank would translate into written orders. However, the secretary was afraid: knowing the hatred these measures would stir up if they were discovered, and seeing so many orders signed on his own authority, he at last begged the King for a written warrant 'for my safety'.[3]

Under Henrietta's patronage, the royal court gained an increasingly Catholic character. It was not just the Queen's ladies who were open Catholics now; two of her favourite male courtiers – Walter Montagu and Henry Jermyn – converted in the mid-1630s. And some of Charles's closest advisers were sympathetic to Catholicism: men like Lord Treasurer Weston and the Chancellor of the Exchequer, Francis Cottington, who both publicly practised Anglicanism to advance their careers, but became Catholics before they died. In Charles's chapel at Whitehall, Anglican preachers denounced the Puritans as 'a most pernicious sect, and dangerous to a monarch', yet spoke mildly or even warmly of Catholics and much of their doctrine. Many Catholics were already beginning to hope for more: the conversion of Charles himself and ultimately of all Britain. Henrietta herself saw the Anglican Church as a mere historical aberration: the result of Henry VIII's infatuation with Anne Boleyn and his determination to have a son, perpetuated by Elizabeth I only because the Pope did not recognise her mother's marriage and thus her own right to the throne. Anglican liturgy was in essence similar to her own, Henrietta thought, with its 'altars, burning candles, priests, surplices, bishops'.[4]

Charles did much to raise Catholic hopes. In addition to his 'princely goodness' to British Catholics, there were other factors: his well-known hatred of Calvinism and Presbyterianism; his frequent description of himself as a true Catholic (though not a Roman one); his expressions of good will towards the current Pope, Urban VIII; his belief in the necessity of confessing sins to a priest; and his acceptance of 1500 years of Roman Catholic doctrine, which he felt had gone astray only at the Council of Trent, ninety years earlier. When an English

Franciscan priest at Henrietta's court published a book arguing that the English creed could be reconciled almost entirely with Roman doctrine, Charles was delighted and declared he 'would willingly have parted with one of his hands' so that the English break with Rome might never have happened.[5]

Keen to discover whether Charles and his bishops were as ripe for conversion as they seemed, the Pope despatched an envoy to England in 1634. Gregorio Panzani, an Italian priest, was soon gathering intelligence. Most of the Anglican bishops were 'moderate' men sympathetic to Catholicism, he reported hopefully; a few were even 'almost Catholic'. Panzani had been warned that Henrietta would be little help to him; she was a frivolous young woman, too much occupied with dancing and balls. However, gradually, working with her confessor, Father Philip, he began to involve the Queen in his schemes. She was the one who persuaded Charles to meet Panzani, after he at first refused. Then she was present at the 'very remote and unsuspected place' where Charles welcomed the envoy 'with a very cheerful countenance, taking off his hat, while Panzani kissed his hand' and assured him of the Pope's affection and gratitude for his kindness to his Catholic subjects.[6]

One of Panzani's most important pieces of business was to arrange a formal exchange of diplomatic agents between the papal court and Henrietta's: the first official connection between England and Rome since the death of the Catholic Queen Mary I in 1558, and an important step towards achieving the Pope's ambitions for Britain. Again it was Henrietta who approached the King. Charles was not unwilling, stipulating only that the agent must be a layman, not a priest, and that he must be officially accredited solely to the Queen and not himself – he could not afford to associate openly with the Pope. Nevertheless, Charles had great hopes from this new diplomatic contact with the papal see. He wanted the Pope's help to negotiate with the Hapsburgs and restore his sister Elizabeth's family to the Palatinate. He also wanted the Pope to remove his prohibition forbidding British Catholics to swear the oath of allegiance to their king.[7]

For Rome, the choice of agent was vital. Drawing on his intimate knowledge of the English court, Father Philip warned that the Pope's man must be a perfect courtier: 'noble, rich, handsome, and affable in conversation', charming with the ladies and especially with Henrietta, who at twenty-five took great delight in fine clothes and witty conversation. At the same time he must be 'grave and reserved . . . the king and queen being strictly virtuous, and professed enemies to immodesty'. He must also be exquisitely tactful, never reproaching Charles for his persecution of the Catholics, and he must bring rare presents of art and jewels and other 'Italian curiosities', so that everyone should be 'enticed by proper baits'. Such a man, Father Philip predicted, might bring all England back to Catholicism, in just three years.[8]

Despite the demanding brief, the Pope found the perfect man. George Con was Scottish born, like Charles himself, but he had spent the last thirteen years pursuing a successful career in Rome. Author, cardinal's secretary, diplomat: Con was a clever man, 'which may be read in his face'. Widely respected for his piety and learning, he also 'knew men and business well', and was 'graceful in his person . . . affable in conversation'.[9] Although she had never met him, Henrietta had long taken an interest in Con's career and had recently asked the Pope to make him a cardinal. The matter was important to her: the appointment of a British cardinal by her intercession would increase her prestige among Europe's Catholic monarchs, as well as winning her greater loyalty from England's Catholics. Yet Rome remained evasive. Such grants were allowed exclusively to monarchs who 'had performed some remarkable service for the church', the Pope's cousin, Cardinal Barberini, told Henrietta; but if she and Con secured 'liberty of conscience for the Catholics' it would be sufficient.[10]

Con arrived in England in 1636, fired up to make 'great impressions there'.[11] Catholic toleration, even the nation's conversion and reunion with the Roman Church were all on his agenda. Joining Panzani, who was attending Henrietta on her summer's country progress, he thought there was every reason for hope. 'In every place where the Queen goes, her chapel is set in order, which stands open and is visited by all in the neighbourhood with much reverence.' Even in Northampton, a town 'considered most puritanical', the local people were eager to see the chapel for themselves: 'once we had these beautiful things in our churches,' some sighed; others even stayed to hear mass.[12]

Con was impressed by Henrietta too. Every day or two he went to see her, finding her 'exemplary' in her religion and virtue. Her devotion at mass 'moved all those who were present', and she was 'full of incredible innocence': so much so that Father Philip told him 'she has no sins except those of omission ... as to sins of faith, or of the flesh, she is never tempted'.[13] Clearly such religious feeling could be turned to Con's purposes, but Henrietta had a long way to go before she would be the powerful political instrument he desired: 'she thinks little of the future, trusting wholly in the king. She must be more concerned to gain the ministers of state, whose mistress she could be if she wished.'[14]

In line with Father Philip's advice, Con came armed with presents. For Henrietta there was a cross of diamonds from the Pope, which she immediately fastened around her neck. She wore it all the time, showing it with pride to her visitors: 'see there ... the treasure that his holiness has sent me: ... I consider this cross the most precious thing that I have.' Con also brought her a portrait of St Catherine, which he intended to get framed, but Henrietta, too thrilled to wait, 'gave orders that the picture should be fastened to the curtains of her bed'.[15] Rosaries were handed out to her Catholic court ladies – an occasion enlivened by Jeffery Hudson, who, eager for a gift himself, called out to the Queen, 'Madam, show the father that I also am a Catholic.' There were gifts for Henrietta's Protestant courtiers too, and more still en route from Italy, including 'valuable pictures' for Charles's two secretaries of state, Windebank and Cottington.[16]

The Italian Panzani, with no English and poor French, had had only limited connections at the English court. In contrast, Con, a native Briton with all the culture of twenty-four years' residence on the Continent, was welcome everywhere. He even dined with the Bishop of London, William Juxon, to the amazement of Henrietta and London's public opinion. Gradually he was building his own party at court. Accounts of what went on in Henrietta's private apartments reached him via her Catholic ladies, especially the Duchess of Buckingham: 'Fond Kate', as Con called her affectionately. Following the Duke's death, she had publicly returned to her childhood religion: '[I] would pour out my life in defence of [Catholicism],' she protested; 'nothing can frighten me from my faith.'[17] Even Protestant ladies succumbed to Con's charms. Henrietta's favourite, Lucy Countess of Carlisle, showed him such loyalty that she was suspected of popery herself, although, Con remarked, 'the poor lady has never thought of any other religion than that of beautifying herself'. More significant was the Countess of Arundel, wife of the famous art-collecting Earl. Fluent in Italian, she had already built up close ties with Panzani. Like her husband, she was 'Catholic in all but [public] profession', Con enthused, as well as being a valuable asset, bringing him reports of the secret transactions of Charles's Privy Council. The Earl too was soon co-opted into Con's faction: 'I have made him several discourses of the disadvantages which the king has in not being a Catholic, with which he has been moved.'[18]

Francis Windebank also aided Con, as did Endymion Porter, one of Charles's grooms of the bedchamber, who gave him access to the most sensitive information. There were two other men in particular whom the agent counted as vital to his plans. One, Walter Montagu, was an enthusiastic Catholic convert whom Charles had angrily banished from court. Having been secretly ordained as a priest abroad, he now returned to England, after Con placated the King. 'The presence of Montagu, which I have earnestly desired, will be serviceable, and I hope much from it,' Con told Rome.[19] The other was the Queen's confessor, Father Philip, who had extraordinary influence over her: just a single look from him was enough to tell her what she should do, it was said. Ever present in Henrietta's chambers, Philip was intimate with all who went there: 'the king and queen do love him, and so do all the courtiers.'[20] However, beneath his mild exterior the Father was an energetic Catholic missionary, one day discussing theology with the Prince of Wales's tutor in hopes of winning him over to Rome, another talking to the King himself, urging 'that it was directly opposite to the whole design of the gospel, that there should be more churches than one; whence he inferred the necessity of a reunion'. He even hinted that, for this great end, Rome might make concessions on doctrines that Charles particularly objected to.[21]

Galvanised by Con and Father Philip, Henrietta was proud to be the leader of the newly fervent Catholic party at court, devoting herself to the job 'with enthusiasm'. She established two devotional societies – the confraternities of the Holy Rosary and of the third order of St Francis – whose rites she led in person. Every Saturday the devotees gathered in her chapel to hear the litanies 'sung with great solemnity' by her Capuchins, and on two Sundays every month they followed the Queen and her priests in 'solemn procession' to confess their sins and take communion. The ceremonies were 'so striking, and made such impressions on the heart' that both societies grew swiftly. Even Protestants came, 'some of whom ... sought conferences [with Henrietta's priests] and were converted'.[22]

Henrietta had some of the ideal qualities for a party leader. Her generosity was celebrated, and 'she was staunch in her friendship, secret and trustworthy to those who confided in her'. She was also persistent and determined in upholding her cause, as well as profoundly influential where it mattered. Once more she pressed Charles to permit a Catholic bishop to come to England. When he refused, she was unabashed and began to beg as well as argue. At last Charles relented: he would turn a blind eye to a bishop, he promised, if the Pope allowed English Catholics to take the oath of allegiance.[23]

In Henrietta's apartments, Con and Charles met almost daily and a friendship began to form. Con was precisely the kind of cultivated, well-travelled and intelligent man whose company the King most enjoyed. The two men often sat down at the same table to play cards. On one occasion, when many of the stakes were Catholic trinkets like crucifixes and relic cases, Charles refused to play, protesting that he would not know what to do with them if he won.

'Give them to my daughter,' Henrietta suggested, smiling.

'No, no,' Charles replied, 'I will give them to George here,' pointing to Con, 'and he shall give me such of the other things as he wins.'[24]

Con joined the royal couple on all sorts of occasions – eating supper in Henrietta's apartments; accompanying them to see their children at

Richmond Palace 'to my infinite comfort'; sharing their visit to the London house of the Earl and Countess of Arundel, where their famous art collection was on view.[25]

He and Charles rapidly discovered a shared passion for art. As they talked, Con brought out small items from his pockets – carved antique gems and a miniature painting – which he gave to the admiring King.[26] Charles took great delight in these conversations. When the papal agent arrived at Windsor to watch the Garter ceremonies, Charles insisted on taking him instead to the royal gallery, 'to conduct me through everything, showing me the pictures and speaking of various things'. In the chapel the Knights were already robed; but Charles merely said 'they should have patience'. Meanwhile one of the pictures prompted the King to criticise the credulity of Rome: 'the Pope ought to reform the fables that are written in the Lives of the Saints.' Con's repartee was swift. If the Pope 'were able to remedy all the disorders of Christianity, he would begin with the removal of heresy': a difficult matter, Con added pointedly, when there were still princes like Charles who lent it their support. Charles took the reproof in good part, merely telling Con such talk was more suited to Rome than England. In the meantime the waiting Knights were enraged, and Puritans among them even declared, Con heard, 'that the king had committed sacrilege on each occasion when he had taken me by the hand'.[27]

Charles had inherited his father's love of theological debate and often he would challenge Con over some central tenet of Catholic faith: the invocation of saints, purgatory, the Pope's infallibility. In Spain, he recalled one evening, he had seen a Catholic procession where the people showed more reverence to the Madonna than to the image of the Son of God himself – a clear Catholic abuse. Everyone joined the dispute. Henrietta herself corrected someone's misquotation of St Bonaventure, before Con replied that the Church should not be judged by a few ignorant Spaniards; if Charles had been to Rome he would understand Catholic practice properly – a rebuke that the King accepted. Con was often outspoken. He always referred to his Protestant opponents as 'heretics' but Charles was not offended.[28] Whatever happened in their debates, Charles was always the picture of courtesy: 'he seldom contradicted another by his authority, but by his reason.' 'By your favour, Sir, I think otherwise,' he would begin, before carefully presenting his own argument. And, at least according to Con, when the King 'saw that he was wrong he very humbly fell silent'.[29]

For Charles it was really all a game. He even laid bets with Henrietta's Catholic courtiers about the true nature of their Church's doctrine, referring to Con for the answers, which the King then refused to accept. In one case he even requested a written statement from the Pope before he would admit he had lost his wager.[30] But for Con there was always the hope of much, much more. Whenever possible he turned these sparring matches into serious discussions that might advance the Catholic cause. He urged Charles to reunite their two churches. He spent many hours discussing the disputed oath of allegiance. Charles even drafted a new version of the oath himself, which Con forwarded to Rome. It was a dangerous step. Charles's subjects denounced the idea as amounting to 'absolute liberty of conscience', 'by which one has often seen states consumed'. Finally, seeing no agreement could be reached, Rome ordered Con to close the subject.[31]

At the end of 1636 the Catholic cause received a further boost with the opening of Henrietta's new chapel at Somerset House. On Henrietta's orders, the first mass there was performed with 'all possible pomp and magnificence'. When the congregation was seated, curtains opened revealing the Holy Sacrament, which, by a careful contrivance of lamps and candles – about 400 were used in all – glowed red and appeared 'all on fire'. Around and above it was a vast painted stage set: 'a Paradise of glory' with the dove of the Holy Spirit flying above seven layers of clouds, crowded with hundreds of angelic figures. An anthem began, performed by Henrietta's choir and musicians, hidden behind the altar so that the sound seemed to come from the painted angels themselves. As mass proceeded, 'sung in eight parts so melodiously that one must have had a heart of stone not to be moved by it', everyone was lost in 'admiration, joy, and adoration'; there were even tears in Henrietta's eyes. After midday dinner there were vespers, compline and a moving sermon preached by Henrietta's grand almoner on a text from the Psalms: 'This is the Lord's doing, and it is marvellous in our eyes.' Outside, so many people thronged at the chapel doors, 'bent on forcing their way in to see the magnificence', that the congregation could barely get out. Over the following days the crush continued so great 'that it was impossible to close the doors of the church'. Charles did nothing to stop them coming. In fact, he too wanted a look; after gazing on the altarpiece for a long time, he said he had never seen anything more beautiful or more ingeniously designed.[32]

With the chapel as a base, the Capuchins set about proselytising with redoubled vigour: 'not a week passed but there were two or three conversions.' Directing it all was her grand almoner, Jacques du Perron, Bishop of Angoulême. Spurred on by Con, he openly frequented the houses of Protestants 'to dispute with them and with the women in particular, and to try and make converts'. Secretly in his own house he assembled meetings of leading Anglican clergymen, where he and Father Philip held 'almost incessant disputes and conferences'. With Con holding out the hope of cardinalships in reward for their 'labours and perils', Philip and du Perron had an even greater catch in their sights: the heir to the throne, Prince Charles.[33] For Henrietta it would be a dream come true: the conversion of her children remained a burning concern throughout her life. She had herself begun steps towards the Prince's conversion two years earlier, secretly taking him to mass, 'where he noted everything, and being asked which rites pleased him more, his own or the Queen's, he replied the Queen's'. But she had been forced to desist: 'on account of his tender age, he repeats whatever is said to him.' Still, she had resolved, she would 'instill Catholicism' in her son in due course.[34] Now Philip and du Perron set to work on the Prince's tutor, Bishop Duppa: 'as the enterprise is one of the utmost importance, it is necessary to spread the foundations widely.'[35]

That, however, was the best they could all hope to achieve, Con had realised. Despite his initial hopes, the King was clearly beyond his reach, as 'severe against the deviations of Rome ... as any gentleman in Christendom'.[36] In fact Charles was an idealist with his own vision of how Protestantism should be practised – a vision he was determined to impose on the nation's Church. His great ally in this project was his old friend William Laud, whom Charles had promoted through a series of plum appointments, culminating in the top job in the Church of England: Archbishop of Canterbury. The two men were religious soulmates: Arminians in doctrine, believing, like the Catholics, in the existence of human free will, as opposed to the Calvinist doctrine of predestination adhered to by English Puritans. They envisioned an orderly, ceremonious British church that would inspire religious awe with its 'beauty of holiness'.[37]

In 1633, when Laud was made Archbishop of Canterbury, he set to work at once to make their grand vision a reality. Intolerant, impatient and hot-tempered, Laud was a man who 'never abated anything of his severity and rigour'. His opponents feared and hated him, and that year 700 puritans fled across the ocean to New England, prompting fears that the old country would be depopulated and its trade ruined.[38] Yet still the reforms continued. By the summer of 1636, when Con arrived in England, the nation's churches had been transformed. Once more, as before the Reformation, the stone altar stood grandly at the east, separated from the congregation by a railing. Candlesticks stood on it for communion, while priests in elaborate vestments set out the wine in rich golden chalices. Images of saints adorned the walls; there was bowing at the name of Jesus. In many places the more zealous clergy had even begun to hear confessions, just like Catholic priests.

For Charles, this was 'the middle way between the pomp of superstitious tyranny [i.e. Catholicism] and the meanness of fantastic anarchy [i.e. Puritanism]'. But to many of his subjects it seemed mere 'Popish superstition and idolatry'.[39] The new ceremonies were detested 'hardly less than the [Catholic] mass itself'. Some people even said that Laud and Charles were closet papists who planned to reintroduce Catholicism to England by stealth. Opposition grew. Previously loyal Anglicans, 'from fear of falling into Catholicism', 'abandoned themselves to puritanism'. And the Puritans became ever more extreme, clinging 'to the bareness of their worship', 'performed in its purity, as they put it'. It was a 'Puritan plague', the Venetian ambassador commented, adding that the more Charles tried 'to extirpate them the stronger they become.'[40]

As 1636 came to a close, the opposition began to organise, encouraged by 'many of the leading men of the realm'. In the absence of Parliament, they had no public voice as yet. However, Charles's government knew they were holding 'secret meetings' throughout the country. They had a dual aim: to destroy Archbishop Laud and his ceremonies, and to change the nature of Charles's political rule.[41] For eight years now, there had been no Parliament. With considerable ingenuity, the King's ministers had researched ancient records to find ways of raising money on his royal authority alone. In accordance with a long-forgotten law of 1227, knighthood fines were exacted from wealthy Englishmen who had not attended Charles's coronation to be knighted. Forest fines were charged on all those who had built their houses on royal forest lands, which technically included almost all the English countryside. Most unpopular of all was 'ship money': an ancient property tax occasionally raised on coastal counties for the maintenance of the navy. 'England without a fleet was a body without a head,' Charles declared, in whose view the navy needed expanding to keep up with other European powers. In the mid-1630s he began to claim ship money annually from the entire nation, not just its maritime borders. There was a public outcry that Charles was changing the very principles of government, aiming to achieve 'absolute monarchy'.[42]

In January 1637, the Earl of Warwick spoke to Charles quite frankly. The people would not put up with ship money: a tax on which they had been given no chance to vote in Parliament, and by which they 'signed away the liberties of the realm, and ... deprived their posterity of those benefits which had been left to them uncontaminated as a sacred treasure by their ancestors'. If only Charles would summon Parliament, he would discover the true loyalty of his people. Warwick was prepared 'to stake his head that Parliament would readily consent to supply him with all that he might desire'; England's populace would give 'their substance, their blood and their children, if they saw it was done by the proper channels'.[43]

Charles, however, was immovable. After the humiliations of the early years of his reign, he abhorred the very name of Parliament. In his eyes it was a terrible monster, a 'Hydra ... as well cunning as malicious'. To call it now would destroy his years of work in establishing his own 'independent authority'. Even the needs of his nephew, the Elector Palatine, now in England to rally support, would not persuade Charles to do that.[44] His resolve was further strengthened by England's judges who unanimously pronounced ship money legal: 'His Majesty may, in times of necessity, impose what sums of money he pleaseth upon the subjects for defence of the kingdom.' And in their opinion, he alone was the one 'to determine all those times of necessity'. It was a blank cheque for Charles to take whatever he wanted from his subjects' purses, whenever he chose: 'at one stroke it roots out for ever the meeting of parliament, and renders the king absolute and sovereign ... If the people submit to this present prejudice, they are submitting to an eternal yoke and burying their past liberties, which will remain a memory only.'[45]

So the collection of ship money continued through the year, while Laud pressed ahead with depriving Puritan clergymen of their jobs. When three Puritan sympathisers came out in print, accusing Laud and his bishops 'of undermining religion in order to erect popery on its ruins', the government came down heavily. The public hangman cut off their ears, slit their noses and branded their faces with the letters 'SL' for 'seditious libeller'. The punishment caused outrage. A huge crowd gathered around the scaffold that day, crying out at the injustice and 'collecting the blood of the victims'. New libels appeared against Laud, pasted up anonymously by night all round London, claiming that 'the Arch-Wolf of Canterbury' was 'persecuting the saints and shedding the blood of the martyrs'.[46] Just a week later another anti-government agitator, John Williams, Bishop of Lincoln, was condemned to be 'shut up in the Tower without limit of time, besides a fine of £10,000'. Again there was an outcry, people accusing his judges 'of the most unjust tyranny', while more libels came out against Laud. At every act of repression the Puritan party seemed only to grow stronger, 'and prudent people ... are not a little afraid of it'. Yet

Charles remained largely oblivious, still thinking himself the happiest king in Christendom.[47]

Contemptuous of the opposition, he was determined to go even further. That summer he and Laud imposed an Anglican-style service book on the Scottish Church, to remedy what they saw as 'the disorder and indecency' of its Calvinist practices.[48] Trouble flared up immediately. In Edinburgh Cathedral the congregation rose up and interrupted the ceremony, tearing the rich vestments off the bishop and his clergy and trampling them underfoot, handling the religious men 'so savagely that they barely escaped with their lives'. Then the people in the rest of the city's churches attacked their own ministers too; 'they say even the women and children used their teeth and nails against them'. When the news reached London, Charles and his ministers were dismayed: the Scots' example could easily 'stir up revolutions among the people here, who are no less scandalised and discontented'. Briefly Charles wavered and seemed 'to incline to milder ways to pacify them', although in the end he would not back down, sending orders to Edinburgh that all his 'reforms shall be obeyed entire'.[49] The royal proclamation was read out in a heavy calm, but the next day violence erupted once more. Again the women and children 'were the special actors', attacking the Bishop of Galloway 'in such a barbarous manner, as the like has never been seen in this kingdom' so that only 'with great difficulty was he rescued'. Order was breaking down. 'The entire people there refuse to obey the ecclesiastical ceremonies introduced'. One bishop, terrified, 'confined himself to his house . . . to observe . . . the trend affairs will take'. Another was compelled by the populace to perform the usual Presbyterian service. In many places the Laudian service book was publicly burnt. Some people even talked of choosing a new, more Protestant king: 'in fact the whole kingdom is in confusion'.[50]

Meanwhile Scottish propaganda spread throughout England, depicting Laud's new prayer book as part of a court Catholic conspiracy, designed to reconquer all Britain for the Pope.[51] The notorious activity of Henrietta's party at court only added plausibility to the charge. Desperate to disprove the mounting accusations that he himself was a 'papist' in the pocket of George Con, the greatest conspirator of all, Archbishop Laud engaged in a campaign of vigorous anti-Catholic repression. Almost every day there was some new action: in Winchester a Catholic school was discovered and closed down; in London all the copies of an illegal Catholic book were seized 'and burnt by the hangman'. Prompted by Con, Henrietta complained to Charles about Laud's 'proceedings', undermining his best efforts. When Laud acted against a priest who had performed a Catholic marriage, Henrietta intervened and 'the King ... commanded him to desist'.[52] Her influence saved a popular Catholic pilgrimage site in Wales from destruction, and overturned Laud's plan 'to take away the eldest sons of all who were popishly affected, and breed them up in the [Anglican] religion established'. Meanwhile Henrietta's chapel continued as busy as ever: 'no sooner one mass is ended ... than the chapel is full for the next, though it be a goodly and spacious room'. On Sundays 'no less than 6000 persons do hear mass there'.[53]

At last Laud saw his chance to outmanoeuvre the Queen and impel Charles's government into action. On 21 October 1637 one of Charles's courtiers, the Earl of Newport, came to Laud 'in an high passion', saying that his wife had just converted to Catholicism.[54] The Countess of Newport was the most prestigious court lady that Henrietta's party had yet converted. The next day Laud complained to Charles's Privy Council. He spoke freely against 'the increasing of the Roman party', the freedom of worship at Somerset House and the behaviour of three of Henrietta's Catholic friends in particular, George Con, Walter Montagu and Sir Toby Matthew, whom the Earl of Newport blamed as the chief 'instruments in the conversion of his wife'. Down on bended knee, Laud begged Charles to punish Montagu and Matthew. As for Con, Laud 'knew not how he came hither, or what he did here', he said, 'therefore he would say nothing of him'. Everyone was in an uproar, and Charles was furious. 'He would have these things remedied,' he said, and he used 'such words' of Montagu and Matthew that the pair were in terror, knowing the law prescribed the death penalty for such a crime.[55]

'I did my duty to the King and state openly in council,' Laud stated proudly, although he too was a frightened man when he heard the news from Henrietta's apartments: 'the Queen [was] acquainted with all I said ... and highly displeased with me, and so continues'. He now had open enemies on both sides, Catholic and Puritan, 'very like corn between two millstones'.[56] Briefly he considered apologising to Henrietta, but in the end he did not dare to: only recently 'a libel' had appeared, accusing him 'of Papism, and of having continual correspondence with the Pope's nuncio [i.e. Con]'. Standing firm, Laud begged Charles 'to defend him against the violence of the queen'. At the next Privy Council meeting, with 'violent passions', he demanded the enforcement of the long-lapsed penal laws, and especially of 'the accustomed edicts against the queen's chapel'. He found many allies among the Privy Councillors – Charles himself was still 'bitterly displeased' – and so a new proclamation was drawn up, ordering 'the severest penalties' for English Catholics.[57]

'Exceedingly afflicted', Con rushed to the Queen. Complaining of 'the audacious impudence of Canterbury, the danger to the Catholic religion, and to her majesty herself', he stirred her to a frenzy of zeal; in fact, 'the queen's sentiments were so vigorous that I begged her to moderate herself, and to deal gently with the king'.[58] With Henrietta calm once more, the pair embarked on a meticulously planned campaign. Every morning they met to decide what each of them, 'partly in jest and partly seriously, ought to say to the king' that day, aiming at 'deferring the proclamation, and gaining time'. Soon Charles assured them he would 'not let it be published until it has been modified, at least to some extent'. Although he had to be seen to do something, he promised he would not proceed against the Queen's chapel.[59] However, there was still more Henrietta wanted. With Charles ill in bed, she kept him company 'almost all the time', wheedling away until he ordered the Earl of Newport to moderate his behaviour towards his wife, with whom he had been quarrelling bitterly. Walter Montagu and Toby Matthew were soon rehabilitated at court. In fact, it emerged, they had not been involved in the Countess of Newport's conversion at all; it had been an entirely female affair, the work of the Duchess of Buckingham and the Countess's sister, Olive Porter, now one of the most energetic of Henrietta's proselytising ladies.[60]

In the end Charles had no choice but to publish the proclamation. The whole Privy Council judged it necessary, he explained to Con: public indignation at Catholic activities was just too strong, and Laud had to be protected from the Scots' accusations that he was 'trying to subvert this kingdom to that faith'. It was a blow for Con, disproving all his assurances to Rome 'that through his efforts this kingdom is marching with great strides towards obedience to the Holy See'. Nevertheless, as Charles pointed out, the proclamation was far less severe than it might have been.[61] Whilst it expressly forbade new conversions, it did not prohibit British Catholics from attending mass, condemning only those 'contumacious persons' who 'give scandal by celebrating or hearing of any mass'. And there was no explicit prohibition against Catholics attending Henrietta's chapel, nor the chapels of London's foreign ambassadors, as Laud had originally demanded.[62]

If Con was dispirited, Henrietta was utterly undaunted. As the proclamation came off the presses, she was already making arrangements for the largest ever mass in her chapel. By her special command, the Countess of Newport was there, as well as other court ladies who had recently converted but not yet attended mass publicly. After leading them all to take communion, Henrietta retired to her chamber triumphant.

'Have you seen the effects of the proclamation?' she asked Con, with heavy irony.

'I have seen the effect of Your Majesty's piety,' he replied, 'and I shall not fail to represent it to our lord [the Pope], and to the lord cardinal Barberino.'[63]

All that Christmas, London's Catholic chapels were as busy as ever. 'The reformed [i.e. Protestant] church loses openly,' the Dutch ambassador reported. As the New Year of 1638 commenced, Con informed Rome with relief that not a single Catholic had been harmed over the holidays.[64] With the approach of spring, it grew ever clearer that the proclamation had been mere empty words: a government PR exercise designed to defuse Puritan agitation. To satisfy Catholic demand, there were now nine masses on festival days at Somerset House, and a further eight at Con's private chapel every day. In February, Olive Porter brought in two new ladies – her mother and her sister-in-law – for Catholic instruction. And they were not the only ones: 'our great women fall away every day', came the news from court that Easter.[65] All through Holy Week, London was filled with conspicuous displays of Catholic devotion. Representations of Christ's sepulchre were set up in all the Catholic chapels, and many worshippers made pilgrimages between them. The Countess of Arundel seized the opportunity for more good work, taking the Earl of Bath and other Protestant friends to see the sepulchre in Con's chapel, at which the Earl said he felt more devotion than in any Anglican church.[66] In the end the Newport affair had only proved the Catholic party's real power at court. At the age of twenty-seven Henrietta had become a skilful political operator, capable of outmanoeuvring even Archbishop Laud himself.

But if Henrietta was pleased by her successes, Charles's government soon saw their fearsome effect on public opinion. Libels and lampoons circulated freely. One letter went round asserting 'that the King's Majesty was a Catholic'. 'The Queen was a whore,' it was said. People spoke out against ship money 'with the utmost freedom'.[67] Everywhere its payment was refused. When even members of Charles's own Privy Council began to protest against the tax, the King angrily declared that they were not to give their view on any question unless he asked for it. The Privy Councillors were astonished, foreseeing many 'difficulties which may arise, but as he who commands wishes it, they must obey'. From Scotland came news that if Charles wanted the new prayer book enforced, he 'must send an army of 40,000 men to defend the minister who must read it'. Charles would not listen, sending back instead a declaration that anyone who persisted in anti-government meetings would be 'guilty of high treason'. [68]

For the Scots it was the last straw. On 28 February all the nobles and gentlemen in Edinburgh gathered at Grey Friars' Church where, one after another for four hours, they signed the Covenant drawn up by the leaders of the resistance. Solemnly they swore to defend their own 'true religion' against Charles's innovations, which 'do sensibly tend to the re-establishing of the popish religion and tyranny, and to the subversion and ruin of the true reformed religion and of our liberties, laws and estates'. This was not a rebellion, they asserted; merely 'an unfeigned desire to maintain the true worship of God, the majesty of our King, and the peace of the kingdom'.[69] Next day Edinburgh's church ministers came to sign the Covenant, 300 strong, and the day after the city's people, men and women alike, added their names.

Charles was 'much distressed in mind'. Henrietta begged him to back down, urging 'the fear of civil war, with danger to his royal person'. But the King told her 'not to alarm herself', claiming that 'when he wishes he can reduce those subjects to obedience'. Just a week later news came that the Scots had taken over the government. Taxes 'and every other mark of the royal authority' had been abolished; the bishops were to be expelled and their revenues distributed to the parishes. 'If the Scots decide to choose another king, as they claim to have just and legitimate cause for doing, the whole power of England would never suffice to subdue them,' the Venetian ambassador reported.[70]

At last the King began to speak of compromise, offering to withdraw the new prayer book, provided the bishops remained in place and 'the rebels ask pardon for their past offences'. It seemed the only sensible course: he had neither money nor the support of his people, so that any attempt to use force against the Scots would bring the 'manifest danger' of losing England and Ireland as well, 'which are unprovided with troops, fortresses or anything else which might secure a state'.[71] In reality, however, Charles had no thought of backing down. There was too much at stake: 'not only now my crown, but my reputation for ever ... which is irreparable'. 'I will rather die than yield to these impertinent and damnable demands ... for it is all one, as to yield to be no King in a very short time.'[72]

He began preparing an army to march into Scotland. His plans were known only to a handful of trusted advisers. Bypassing the Privy Council completely, he spent hours in 'long and secret interviews' with Archbishop Laud.[73] For some time now he had also been secretly consulting George Con about what to do with 'those countrymen of yours', as Charles jokingly called them. Using the crisis for his own benefit, Con stirred up the King's resentment against the Covenanters, insinuating that they were merely greedy, ambitious men, whose supposed religious principles were a pretext for rebellion. Enthusiastically Con talked of the assistance Charles could gain, both from his own Catholic subjects and from Catholic powers abroad. For many decades British Catholics had been forbidden to bear arms, but now, under Con's urging, Charles planned to raise Catholic forces against the Covenanters. The Scottish Catholic nobles were already arming, while the Irish Earl of Antrim offered to bring over 10,000 of his Ulster clansmen for Charles's service.[74]

At Greenwich now for the start of the summer, Charles threw himself into frenzied activity, determined to prevail. Every few days a fresh letter went off to the Marquess of Hamilton, his new chief man in Scotland. 'My train of artillery ... is in good forwardness, and I hope will be ready within six weeks,' the King wrote. 'I have sent for arms to Holland, for 14,000 foot and 2,000 horse: for my ships they are ready ... I have consulted with the Treasurer and Chancellor of the Exchequer, for money for this year's expedition; which I estimate at two hundred thousand pounds sterling, which they doubt not but to furnish me.' 'My resolution is to come myself in person,' he added five days later. Meanwhile Hamilton was instructed to draw out his negotiations with the Covenanters, 'your chief end being now to win time ... until I be ready to suppress them'.[75]

In July there was bad news: the Covenanters refused to accept the terms Hamilton had offered and had enrolled 40,000 men 'skilled in the use of arms' who could be mustered at a few hours' notice. Charles was alarmed: 'His very face clearly betrays the passions within.' He even informed his Privy Council for the first time about Scottish affairs, though the Privy Councillors made no reply, remembering they were to give no advice 'unless asked'.[76] Hoping to gain more time for his military preparations, Charles offered further concessions to the Covenanters. He agreed that the General Assembly governing the

Presbyterian Church of Scotland could meet that November, followed by the Scottish Parliament.

While the King waited anxiously, a new threat appeared. For seven years Henrietta's mother, Marie de' Medici, had been a political refugee in the Spanish Netherlands, following her failed coup against Cardinal Richelieu. All that time she had been seeking refuge with her youngest daughter in England. A 'very ardent' partisan of her mother's, Henrietta had urged her husband to do more for her. Although Charles was full of assurances, he was extremely unwilling to receive his mother-in-law. As the Venetian ambassadors put it, Marie would be an 'unspeakable annoyance': 'one of the heaviest burdens' that could fall on Charles and his government, both in terms of expense and the danger of further popular unrest.[77] Charles also recognised the risks to his own domestic happiness, given Marie's well-known influence over her youngest daughter. Furthermore, Marie's political intriguing could push Charles into greater hostilities with France than he desired, especially given that Henrietta was still 'very embittered' against Richelieu.[78]

Already Charles had reluctantly received another prominent French opponent of Richelieu's. The Duchesse de Chevreuse had fled from France, first to Spain and then to England, in April 1638, just as Charles issued his first conciliatory offer to the Covenanters. Henrietta was delighted: she had 'a special affection' for the Duchesse who had been one of her companions during her first year in England. The Spanish government was thrilled too, having 'no small hopes of the good offices that Madame de Chevreuse may do for them'.[79] In London the Duchesse lived in 'noble and well furnished' court apartments, supported by a generous stipend from Charles and Henrietta: 'All the lords pay her court and she passes the time merrily.' For Charles, however, she was nothing but trouble. She 'spends as if our treasure were infinite', Laud complained.[80] And her presence was a red rag to Puritan public opinion. Driving round London in George Con's coach, dining with the French ambassador, spending long hours at the Spanish ambassador's house in secret negotiations, she was another controversial Catholic presence at the English court, raising suspicions of who knew what? All through the summer she tempted the English royals with a Spanish proposal for marrying their eldest daughter Mary, still just seven years old, to the heir to the Spanish throne. It was an idea that 'pleases them greatly here', but Spain's enemies feared it was merely a ploy 'to lull this crown to sleep'.[81] The Duchesse even ventured to take Princess Mary to mass in Henrietta's chapel at Windsor, for which she was sternly rebuked by Charles. In sum, she was 'a cunning and practising woman', Laud complained, and 'I would ... we were rid of her'.[82]

At this point news came that Marie de' Medici was leaving Flanders for England. Driven on by Henrietta, who worked 'to coax him to undertake this most expensive entertainment', Charles ordered preparations 'to receive and entertain her properly'. 'The king yields to all the caprices of his wife,' the news-writers complained.[83] Three thousand pounds would be paid for Marie's support, and Charles stopped all court salaries to raise the money needed. Apartments were set aside for her at St James's Palace, expensively redecorated under Henrietta's personal supervision.[84] Ships were sent out to seek her storm-tossed flotilla; the King and Queen's coaches 'and twenty more' were made ready to transport her; London's mayor and aldermen were ordered to prepare the city for her grand entry. Still hoping Marie might change her mind, Charles sent off a final messenger 'under the show of compliment, in order to stop her coming'. But on 18 October, Marie's little fleet of ships was sighted off Harwich, and next day news reached London that she had landed. 'This is but a new beginning of evils,' Laud noted.[85]

Nevertheless, Marie was treated with the utmost honour. All along her route the towns turned out in welcome, and Charles himself rode out to accompany her on her state entry to London. The procession was immense: the Queen Mother had brought a suite 600 strong, not to mention Charles's own vast court. Six thousand militiamen armed with pikes and muskets lined the streets, and the shops, balconies and windows of the houses were filled with 'an infinity of people'. Cannons fired from the Tower of London, while Henrietta, six months' pregnant, waited at St James's Palace for the mother she had not seen in thirteen years. 'I look forward to seeing her every day,' she had just written to her nearest sister, Christine, Duchess of Savoy.[86] Trumpets blared amid the shouts of the crowd outside St James's, and a messenger announced Marie's approach. With her four eldest children – two princes and two princesses – Henrietta descended the palace's great staircase, followed by her ladies. In the courtyard below, her mother's state carriage came to a halt. Henrietta walked to its door and threw herself down on her knees. No sooner had Marie raised her daughter up in her arms and kissed her than Henrietta, 'filled with joy', knelt again, to be raised up and kissed once more. 'An extreme joy made mutes of everyone, as well as a great sadness.'[87]

The two had changed immeasurably. From a girl of fifteen, Henrietta had become a wife, a mother and a queen. Accompanied now by 'all the grandest and most beautiful ladies of the court', she eclipsed them all in both 'grace and ... majesty, in which she never found an equal'. But if Henrietta had grown, Marie had shrunk. Her portrait sketched by Rubens around 1625, when Henrietta had last seen her, shows a sturdy, contented matron, her authority clear in her heavy-lidded gaze and the slight smile that curls the corners of her mouth. Now, Henrietta wrote to Christine, tactfully glossing over the effects of their mother's sufferings, 'I found her a little changed.'[88]

After that first long silence, Henrietta and her mother and many others wept. 'Truly,' recalled one of Marie's courtiers, 'I have never seen so much joy nor so many tears together.' Recovering herself, Henrietta presented her children to the grandmother they had never seen; kneeling like their mother, the boys and girls received her blessing. Then Charles stepped down from the coach and, taking his mother-in-law on his arm, he led the way upstairs, followed by Henrietta, the children and all the lords and ladies. That night, looking out from their windows at St James's, Marie and her entourage saw the sky lit up with fireworks while crowds in the streets danced, sang and drank around their bonfires. At court the celebrations continued for days. Nothing was talked of but parties and balls and plays.[89]

Marie's influence at court was visible to everyone. Charles and Henrietta visited her almost daily, the King a picture of respect, taking off his hat to stand talking to his mother-in-law, while Henrietta displayed 'the most filial reverence'. As often as her health permitted, Marie returned their visits, having no greater 'pleasure than that of being with them at every moment'.[90] Her presence also brought a great strengthening to Henrietta's court Catholic party. The gift she brought her daughter from Flanders – 'a beautiful image' of the Virgin Mary, 'exquisitely carved' – provided a new focus for the devotions of Henrietta's confraternity of the Holy Rosary at Somerset House. Mother and daughter often attended mass together, sometimes at Marie's chapel at St James's, and sometimes at Somerset House, where Marie was delighted to see the crowds and experience first-hand 'the great progress of their holy religion in the kingdom where it had formerly been so persecuted'. She also met regularly with George Con, eagerly discussing his great plans for propagating their faith.[91]

On through the winter Charles continued his military preparations. Money, munitions and food were sent north to the Scottish border. Throughout England the local militias were mustered, and Charles appointed the crypto-Catholic Earl of Arundel as Lord General in overall command.[92] Amidst it all, Christmas passed without the usual court masques. On 20 January 1639, the Queen went into labour. All the signs were bad. Despite her superstitious preference for St James's, she had been forced to remain at Whitehall for the birth; her mother's court of several hundred left no room at the other palace. And soon the labour was in difficulties. In great pain and 'in evident danger of death', Henrietta Maria prayed 'with great humility and fervour' to the Virgin Mary, her patron and namesake. Almost at once the Queen's pains were eased and her baby was born. The little princess was christened Katherine, but 'after only one hour of the miseries of this world' she died. Weak and ill and in 'deep grief', Henrietta recovered only slowly.[93] Her doctors, afraid her condition might worsen, recommended she go to France 'for the better air', but she was adamant she had 'no intention of undertaking this journey'.[94] Her place was in England where, despite her infirmity, she was doing all she could to assist her husband in his political crisis.

For some months she had been involved in the plans to raise

Catholic forces in Ireland and Scotland. Now she also began to seek Catholic aid from abroad. Her miraculous survival in childbirth by the Virgin Mary's intercession provided the perfect cover for the secret missions of two Catholic priests who left England that February. One, Father Tresson, the superior of Henrietta's Capuchin priests, was ostensibly bound for the shrine of the Mother and Child at Loreto in central Italy, carrying 'a very rich votive offering of gold and jewels' in thanksgiving for her recovery. After that, he was to visit the Pope, doubtless to discuss Rome's recent offers of aid against the Covenanters.[95] The second messenger-priest, George Gage, travelled to Flanders with another thanksgiving offering – for the shrine of Our Lady of Sichem – as well as secret instructions to open talks with the Spanish court at Brussels. It was part of a plan devised by Gage and his brother Henry, a colonel in the Spanish army: the King, they suggested, could borrow an army from the Spanish, use it to defeat the Scots, and then bring it into England to 'keep the parliament in awe'. The Spanish, though willing in principle, were busy fighting their own war against the Dutch and the French, in which they had taken such heavy losses that they had to declare themselves unable to send any troops.[96]

In the meantime Henrietta was involved in a third set of negotiations. For months now the English, hoping to remove the financial burden of entertaining Marie de' Medici, had been working for a reconciliation between her and her son, Louis XIII. Marie was eager to return to France, promising to 'lay aside all her passion, and ... be entirely submissive'. However, Louis refused, whilst also rejecting the English request for her to receive her own French income in England. He insisted she must return to Florence – her childhood home – if she wanted any money from France. As Marie did not want to go, she stayed on, still costing Charles's government £3000 per month, paid promptly. Even Henrietta could see the necessity for her departure. Hoping she might succeed where Charles had failed, she now sent her own negotiator to Paris: Henry Jermyn, a Catholic convert in his early thirties, who was fast becoming one of her greatest intimates.[97]

By now the King was almost ready to leave London for the North.

Without calling an English Parliament, there was money only for a brief campaign, but Charles was optimistic, expecting his 'great army' to total 30,000 or 40,000 men. By invoking ancient feudal rights and summoning the nation's aristocracy 'to attend our royal person and standard at York', bringing their own armed retinues with them, the King planned to raise much of his cavalry at no cost to the government. Already he was talking of being 'in short time in Edinburgh to settle that disordered government'.[98] While most of his court and government went on ahead to York, Charles remained in London for one last week with his family. Then, on Wednesday 27 March 1639, leaving half his 200-strong bodyguard 'to attend the Queen and Prince', Charles departed to lead his troops 'against the Scottish covenanting rebels', Laud wrote in his diary, adding: 'God of His infinite mercy bless him with health and success.'[99]

Liberty and Religion Alike

This time there was no leisurely journey north, hunting and dining along the way. In just three days Charles was at York, where, he wrote to Henrietta, he was received with 'every sign of devotion'.[1] However, his army was a mess: poorly armed, ill-fed, undisciplined, even mutinous. For a month he remained in the city, gathering his forces, while his advisers voiced concerns about 'how unsafe it was to venture the King's person among an untaught and inexperienced army'. They made no impression. Determined to quell the 'intolerable insolency' of the Scots in person, Charles set off for Durham, New-castle, and then the border.[2]

It was a bleak march north from Newcastle in wet and windy weather, with 'no towns nor trees fit for shelter ... no fresh straw to litter a horse in all the way, nor means to lodge a Christian'.[3] The soldiers marched in water up to their ankles, then lay at night beneath the open sky. And all the time bad news kept coming in: the Scottish Catholic nobles had surrendered or fled without a fight; the Cov-enanters had taken Edinburgh Castle; their army was marching south for England, 40,000 strong. Many, at least in the officer class, kept up their spirits with their hearty detestation of the enemy: 'those scurvy, filthy, dirty, nasty, lousy, itchy, scabby, shitten, stinking, slovenly, snotty-nosed, logger-headed … villainous, barbarous, bestial, false, lying, roguish, devilish, long-eared, short-haired, damnable, atheistical, puritanical crew of the Scotch Covenant.'[4]

Just west of the border town of Berwick, they made camp on a hilltop looking out over the River Tweed to Scotland. Charles – 'the most active and vigilant prince … that I think lives' – supervised everything himself, 'riding and viewing the place and giving direction for ordering the camp'.[5] Men were set to work making trenches and ramparts, but morale was failing. The soldiers with their picks and spades 'called and complained for want of bread and drink'. Their position was perilous, they said; the river below them was 'fordable [for] 40 horse abreast' and there was 'high and commanding ground' on the far side, a perfect place for the enemy to deploy their artillery. Even the officers could not help being 'a little daunted when we look upon … our own confusion and wants'.[6]

Meanwhile, in London, Henrietta and her children were living at Whitehall under heavy guard, fearful of a predominantly Puritan populace who supported the Scottish Covenanters more than their own King. Seditious pamphlets appeared constantly and rumours ran round like wildfire: the war was part of a 'long intended devilish plot' by Charles's corrupt advisers 'to reduce these realms once more to subjection to the Roman Court', whilst the Scots were the instruments of God who alone held back Laud's 'idolatry'.[7] The archbishop went around in fear, his servants armed with swords. Con too was accused of 'perverting his Majesty's simple subjects' and spying for the Pope, while the Queen's priests, it was said, embezzled government funds to support their bastard children.[8]

Every week, on Henrietta's orders, London's Catholics came for 'solemn service and sermons' in her chapel, praying 'for the King's happy progression in his designs, and for his safe return'.[9] And she hoped for much more than their prayers. Letters went out from the Queen and two of her leading Catholic courtiers, Walter Montagu and Sir Kenelm Digby, asking the nation's Catholics to express their 'duties, and zeal to his Majesty's service … by some considerable gift', 'freely and cheerfully presented' to help the war. They owed so much to her and Charles, Henrietta urged, for by her 'extraordinary graces and protections' she had won them 'the happy moderation' they now lived under. Now was the time for them to show their gratitude and prove she had been right always to assure the King of their 'loyalty and affection'.[10]

Charles was 'exceedingly' gratified by the plan – a sum as large as £50,000 was anticipated – and soon Henrietta had a second scheme in the pipeline. She would write 'to all the great ladies' in the land, 'as well wives as widows', asking them 'to contribute ... towards the charge of the King's army'. The sum she named was £100 each. With £10,000 from the ladies, plus £10,000 of her own and the money from the Catholics, she hoped 'to surprise his Majesty'.[11] She was to be disappointed. Apart from a few 'court countesses', none of the ladies contributed, and in the end a mere £14,000 came in from the Catholics, barely enough to support the army for a week.[12] Even Rome let Henrietta down; papal aid for Charles would be given only if he converted to Catholicism, Con reported. Henrietta's sole hope now lay with the Spanish government in Brussels, where her overtures had at last brought an offer of troops for Charles, though it was too late for this campaigning season.[13]

A few days into June, the Scots army appeared suddenly across the Tweed from Charles's troops and immediately set up two batteries of guns. The English were appalled. Their force was far larger than imagined, and there was 'great ... murmuring' among the private soldiers, who blamed the scoutmaster general, a northern Catholic, for failing to gather proper intelligence. Amidst the 'hubbub', the Earl of Bristol, long an opponent of the court, spoke out publicly to the King, questioning 'the ground of this quarrel' with the Scots, and calling for an English Parliament, claiming that 'most of the lords here ... were resolved to petition his Majesty for one.'[14] At other times Bristol's outburst might have brought him a stinging put-down, such as Charles had delivered to his Privy Councillors over ship money a year earlier, but the King was too dismayed by the enemy and by his own men alike. In contrast to his earlier belligerence, he was now full of 'hopes of an approaching agreement with the Scots', Henrietta heard in London.[15] It was the first of many volte-faces that Charles would perform in the coming years; 'the facility with which the King starts on an action and his lack of firmness in sustaining it' would come to exasperate his followers. Just six days after the Scots reached the Tweed, formal peace talks began. Another six days later, it was all agreed: the armies would disband, and there would be a General Assembly and Parliament in Edinburgh in August, which Charles himself would attend.[16]

From London, Secretary Windebank begged the King to reconsider. 'I cannot without horror think upon your Majesty's going into Scotland in person, and exposing yourself ... to the mercy of a people enraged, [and] weary of monarchical government.'[17] Henrietta and the Privy Councillors added their voices to his; the latest news from Edinburgh confirmed that 'the people there are mad and mutinous'.[18] Reluctant to follow their advice, Charles stayed on at Berwick, gathering intelligence and holding talks with the Covenanting leaders, while Henrietta awaited his return 'with great impatience'. Everything Charles learnt convinced him that the situation was hopeless and so, in the end, he decided to return to London to 'take other counsels'.[19]

It had been the royal couple's longest ever separation and Charles hurried south now, 'impatient of remaining away from his wife any longer'. After just three days' journey, he joined her at Theobalds. Driving in state with Marie de' Medici, they entered London to cheering crowds, then left Marie at St James's Palace and walked together the last few hundred yards across the Park to Whitehall.[20] However, it was no happy homecoming. Charles 'was very melancholic', seeing 'he had lost reputation at home and abroad', while the Palace seethed with 'factions and animosities'.[21] Even among the couple's courtiers there were Puritans, like the Earl of Northumberland, Charles's Lord Admiral, who had consistently opposed his Scottish policy. Informed of his master's war plans only as the final preparations were made, Northumberland had joined other Privy Councillors in urging the King to summon England's Parliament, but Charles had 'sharply' rejected their advice, leaving them seething with dissatisfaction.[22] In stark opposition to this Puritan faction stood Archbishop Laud, who denounced the Scots as 'rebels and traitors', fanning the King's anger ever hotter against them. Their Covenant was 'ungodly', 'damnable', 'treasonable', Laud said, and the peace treaty made at Berwick was 'dishonourable, and meet to be broken'.[23] To men like Northumberland, who shared many of the Scots' religious principles, it seemed that Laud condemned anyone 'who spoke well of the reformed [i.e. Protestant] religion'.[24]

Henrietta and her pro-Catholic courtiers made up yet a third faction, resented and feared by Laud. 'We are undone,' the archbishop had complained, when Henrietta persuaded Charles to appoint two of her protégés to the Privy Council: 'I am so full of indignation, that I dare not let my pen go.'[25] Yet even within the Queen's camp there were divisions. The Earl of Holland, long trusted by Henrietta and used by her to 'boldly speak for the Catholics' when no others dared, in the period before Con's arrival in England, was now falling rapidly from the Queen's favour on account of his too Puritan sympathies, while Holland's wife was already joining the popular calls for a Parliament, which was needed, she said, to destroy the 'excessive power' of the Catholics.[26] Meanwhile, Henrietta's great favourite, Walter Montagu, vied with his old mentor, George Con, for the Queen's nomination to a cardinalship. And many of her courtiers were jealous of the rapid rise of Henry Jermyn. Noted for his courtly manners and 'agreeable wit', he was now 'more than ever in the favour of [the Queen] and indeed to a strange degree'.[27]

In September 1639 the balance of power between the various factions was dramatically altered when a new man arrived at court. In his late forties, Thomas Viscount Wentworth was ambitious, energetic and intelligent, 'every way qualified for [political] business'.[28]

For the past eight years he had served Charles as Lord Deputy of Ireland. There the vast challenges of government corruption, military inadequacy and a 'very insolent' Catholic majority in the population had been to him just 'means to show his abilities'.[29] Ruthlessly playing Catholics off against Protestants, he had managed Ireland's Parliament in triumphant style, gaining substantial tax grants for the King. The

Church Convocation he summoned was just as successful, reforming the Protestant Irish Church along Laudian lines. Laud and Wentworth became fast friends in these years, collaborating to advance their shared ideal of ordered, authoritarian government in church and state. Charles had been delighted with his Lord Deputy's achievements, confiding that, if he was not careful, his letters to Wentworth would become more 'panegyrics than dispatches'.[30] By 1637 he was consulting Wentworth on some of the most significant decisions facing him – how to raise money at home, whether to go to war abroad – and a year later the Lord Deputy was one of the very few whom he trusted with his secret plans for war with Scotland.

Now, with the failure of his Scottish policy, Charles wrote urgently to Wentworth 'to desire your attendance and counsel'.[31] His need was pressing. Fearful of popular resentment, Laud had withdrawn from his private discussions with Charles on Scottish affairs. George Con, long the sharer of Charles's secret military plans, left England that summer, an ill man, to die in Rome the following year. Charles ordered his Lord Deputy to join him in London as soon as possible and in the greatest secrecy: 'I will not have you take notice that I have sent for you, but pretend some other occasion of business.'[32]

Wentworth came fearfully to London: 'the nearer I come to it, the more my heart fails me; nor can I promise myself any good by this journey.'[33] The Queen and her faction, he knew, regarded him with 'great animosity', and Henrietta was now more powerful than ever. 'She was never so well with the king,' came the news from court, and her men were rising to new power. George Lord Goring, her Master of the Horse, became the King's Vice Chamberlain and a Privy Councillor, while her new favourite, Henry Jermyn, advanced to Goring's old post. Even Sir Kenelm Digby and Walter Montagu, Catholics long distrusted by Charles, were on the way up.[34] However, Wentworth found a warm welcome from Charles. The newly appointed Queen's men were primarily courtiers without real political experience, and so, in his hour of need, the King turned eagerly to Wentworth; within a few weeks he was the man who had 'most influence with his Majesty'.[35]

Already Charles had begun fresh military preparations against Scotland. Troops were sent to the frontier; the fleet was readying to sail north. When the Scottish Assembly and Parliament met in defiant mood, exiling the nations' bishops to England and threatening to expel his garrisons from all their castles, Charles's resolution for war hardened: the Scots must be crushed to prevent 'the same pernicious sentiments' of rebellion from spreading into England.[36] Money, as always, was the great stumbling block. Every day the King's ministers met to discuss the best methods for raising more, 'but all involve inextricable difficulties'. Some were too likely to raise popular resistance; others were 'rejected as illegal'. Although Charles considered cutting Marie de' Medici's allowance, he was soon dissuaded by Henrietta's 'influential offices'.[37]

Wentworth, however, was sure he had the answers: 20,000 soldiers could be sent from Ireland, funded by the Irish Parliament and commanded by officers of 'devoted loyalty', whilst in England there should be a new Parliament – the only way to gain the funds Charles needed.[38] Wentworth, an articulate and persuasive man, battled determinedly throughout November against the King's 'inveterate objection' to Parliament.[39] His own recent successes in managing the Irish Parliament were undeniable, and he was confident that the English MPs, faced with an invading Scottish army, would rally wholeheartedly behind Charles. As the news from Scotland worsened, his arguments were also supported by Charles's intimate Committee of Eight, with whom alone he discussed Scottish affairs. All agreed that war 'was visibly necessary'. Yet there was no prospect of Crown money to fund it: Parliament must be called. True, the last Parliament, twelve years before, had been 'mutinous', but since then the 'happy peace and universal plenty over the whole nation' must surely guarantee the people's good will towards Charles. Only 'sober men' would be elected to the House of Commons, who would 'provide remedies proportionable' to the King's need.[40] Recognising his 'extreme necessity', Charles could only agree. The war was 'a public business and of great weight, and not to be undertaken but upon the public charge', he announced to his Privy Council, and as a result it was 'our own desire to meet our people, and to demand their assistance in the ancient and ordinary way of a Parliament'.[41]

Everywhere people 'expressed great joy' at the news. The political opposition, afraid that Charles might change his mind, were full of assurances 'that they will arrange everything to please him.' Only the Catholics were apprehensive, seeing 'no talk of anything except against the Catholic religion'.[42] As the New Year of 1640 began, the government pressed ahead with 'huge preparations' for the campaign, mustering troops, preparing a fleet and appointing commanding officers. Money was no problem: the Privy Council had agreed that its members would lend Charles what he needed from their own private funds, to be repaid once Parliament met in April and voted proper supplies. Substantial moneys were expected too from the Irish Parliament.[43] And if the English MPs did 'prove peevish' and refuse to pay up, there were fall-back plans. Wentworth, fresh from autocratic rule in Ireland, promised to 'find a way to obtain promptly from the people [of England] a fresh levy of £300,000'. Charles himself was rumoured to have 'secret intentions' to use his northern army to terrify Parliament into submission.[44]

He and Henrietta were in high spirits, relieved to be over their seemingly interminable indecision, and full of hope that they would now leave behind the financial, political and military failures of the past. At Whitehall on 21 January the couple appeared together on stage for the first time, expressing their robust optimism in the lavish fantasy-world of a new court masque, more spectacular than any before, performed for the entertainment of Marie de' Medici.[45] Devised as usual by Inigo Jones, with the text written by Henrietta's courtier, the playwright William Davenant, *Salmacida Spolia* carried a clear message for Scotland. Amidst a fierce storm appeared the malicious, snake-haired fury, Discord, come from the wars of Europe to disturb Britain's peace. However, Discord's evil designs were short-lived, as the Good Genius of Great Britain descended from the heavens in a silver chariot, imploring Concord to 'ease the cares of wise Philogenes' – Charles himself, the Lover of his People. The masque proclaimed Charles's peaceful virtues: prudence, innocence, 'forgetfulness of injuries' and 'affection to the country'. 'Without blood, without sweat', like the ancient Greek colonists at Salmacis referred to in the title, he would reduce the 'turbulent natures' of the country's 'fierce and cruel' barbarian inhabitants 'into a sweet calm of civil concord'. Finally Henrietta and her ladies appeared from a cloud – all 'in Amazonian habits', with helmets topped with ostrich plumes and curving swords at their sides – sent down from heaven to reward Charles 'for reducing the threatening storm into the following calm'.[46]

It was a last moment of peace and happiness. Henrietta, pregnant once again, was 'in perfect health' and 'very cheerful'.[47] Despite all the military demands on the royal coffers, she was busy with building and gardening projects. At Greenwich she was completing the interior of the Queen's House, ordering twenty-two paintings of the story of Cupid and Psyche for her cabinet there, and eagerly awaiting the delivery of other mythological scenes for her bedchamber and the main hall.[48] She had a completely new project too. Back in August 1639, as Charles returned to London, she had arranged to buy the manor of Wimbledon for £16,000. Situated on top of a hill, the grand Elizabethan mansion had dramatic views over a 'great orchard with walks' to countryside beyond. Just three miles from Whitehall, it would make a perfect country villa, and Henrietta launched at once into building a new royal wing and laying out elaborate gardens. With sixty orange trees in tubs, fountains, summer houses, a maze and a huge avenue of limes, elms and cypress trees, this was the most ambitious of all her garden designs: a sign of optimism and deter-mination to continue life as normal, even as the country turned against its royal leaders.[49]

That January, in gratitude for his 'prudent counsels' and multi-farious labours, Charles made Wentworth Earl of Strafford – one of the most high-ranking aristocrats in England. Almost alone among the government ministers, the new Earl unreservedly advocated Charles's war against the Scots, as observers noted how he was 'stepping quickly towards the entire control of this monarchy'.[50] In March he left for Dublin to manage the Irish Parliament. Under his coercion they soon voted funding for a 9000-strong army to be shipped to Scotland, while the Irish Church agreed to pay further substantial sums. The people there would 'give all they possess' to support the King, Strafford enthused.[51] Then he rushed back to attempt the same in London. However, the English elections had gone against the King. Angry at being 'deceived in his hopes', Charles pushed on with his military preparations, 'ostensibly in order to subdue the rebellious Scots by force, but with the secret intention of using these arms to bridle the insolent demands of parliament and make them do their duty'. As the troops mustered, he planned 'to scrutinise the quality of the men, endeavouring to have as few puritans as possible in the companies'; Catholics, by contrast, were readily given military commands.[52]

On Monday 13 April 1640, despite his misgivings, Charles rode in state to open the new Parliament. Henrietta viewed the 'very glorious' procession from a stage in Whitehall's gardens, then moved into a private gallery in the House of Lords to watch as Charles, 'arrayed in his regal robes, ascended his royal throne'. 'There was never a King that had a more great and weighty cause to call his people together than myself,' Charles told Parliament.[53] Then the case for war was made by his new Lord Keeper, Henrietta's protégé Lord Finch. Appointed after promising to 'do every favour' for the Catholics, Finch was one of the couple's few true loyalists besides Strafford. Now he declared that the Scots had 'taken up arms against the Lord's anointed, their rightful prince and undoubted sovereign'; their actions were 'foul and horrid treasons', leaving the King no choice but to send 'a powerful army, to reduce them to ... obedience and subjection'. Parliament must 'lay aside all other debates' and vote a sum of money 'fit and convenient for so great an action'.[54]

But the MPs were unmoved, focusing instead on denouncing the government's long-running encroachments on their rights: especially the collection of ship money, the Laudian reforms in the Anglican Church, and the illegal toleration of the nation's Catholic minority, 'demons ... full of subtlety, full of malignity'. Within days a new leader emerged in the House of Commons. John Pym was neither a stylish nor an entertaining orator. He read his speeches aloud from closely written pages of densely argued points, sometimes stumbling over his own handwriting. Yet his passionate conviction stirred his hearers beyond all else. 'A good oration!' the MPs called, as he ended a two-hour, systematic and exhaustive analysis of the government's oppressions in church and state.[55]

For three weeks King and Commons continued at loggerheads, as the MPs turned a deaf ear to all Charles's demands for money and his assurances that, having received it, he would hear their grievances and 'give just satisfaction to his people'. Knowing from earlier parliaments just how little trust could be placed in his promises, they devoted their time to drawing up a complete list of their grievances to present to the King.[56] Meanwhile feelings in London ran high. Talk of Charles's plan to use military force against Parliament was widespread. Handwritten libels circulated, justifying the Scots' rebellion and complaining at the political machinations of Hamilton, Laud and Henrietta herself.[57]

At last, desperate, Charles offered to abolish ship money if Parliament would vote him his supplies. It was not enough. For eleven hours that day the MPs continued in further demands and denunciations of the government. 'It was in vain to expect longer ... for no money would be had against the Scots,' Charles's secretary of state, Sir Henry Vane, reported to Whitehall.[58] Next day, dressed in his crown and robes, the King addressed his Parliament, asserting that it was 'some few cunning and some ill-affected men that have been the cause of this mis-understanding'. As for himself, 'no king in the world shall be more careful to maintain ... the liberties of their persons, and true religion.' Then Lord Keeper Finch pronounced the concluding formality: 'My Lords, and ye knights, citizens, and burgesses of the House of Commons, the King's Majesty doth dissolve this Parliament.'[59]

It was a devastating blow. 'Tuesday, the Parliament ended, and nothing done,' Laud noted in his diary. Fear and dissatisfaction were 'in the hearts and words of every creature', Lucy Countess of Carlisle observed.[60] When they met later that day, Charles's ministers urged the insuperable difficulties of pursuing his 'great designs' against the Scots; perhaps it was best 'to do nothing and let them alone', the Puritan Earl of Northumberland suggested. Only Strafford remained confident 'that there are yet ways left to make his Majesty happy'.[61]

Charles had done all he could by constitutional means, the Earl argued; 'reduced to extreme necessity', the King was now 'absolved from all rules of government', and free to do whatever 'power will admit'. There was no need to fear opposition at home; the only necessity was to 'go vigorously on' against the Scots. 'You have an army in Ireland you may employ here to reduce this kingdom,' he pointed out. 'Scotland shall not hold out five months. One summer well employed will do it.'[62] Money seemed no problem to him, what with ship money and a £100,000 loan that Charles had demanded from the City of London. The Convocation of the Church of England had already voted to supply funds. And Strafford was also 'much interested' in Henrietta's idea of borrowing Spanish troops or money, beginning meetings now with their ambassadors to negotiate the deal.[63]

Next day Strafford's policies for despotic government began to be put into effect. John Pym and other opposition leaders were imprisoned, and all their papers seized. The King summoned London's mayor and aldermen before his Privy Council. Since they had failed to provide the £100,000 loan requested, he said, 'therefore he now required £200,000'. Furthermore, the names of rich merchants who could lend this sum must be supplied by Sunday, or else 'he would have £300,000 of the City'. When they still resisted, Strafford proposed violent measures. 'Sir,' he told Charles, 'unless you hang up some of them, you will do no good.' Four of the most outspoken aldermen were committed to prison.[64]

By now all Henrietta's past distaste for the Earl was gone. Admittedly his face was plain, even ugly, she later recalled, but his manners were 'very agreeable' and 'he had the most beautiful hands in the world'. More importantly, he was without doubt 'the most capable and faithful of the King's servants'.[65] But outside Whitehall's walls Strafford's draconian measures only further infuriated Charles's subjects. Within twenty-four hours of Parliament's dissolution, there were mutterings that the Earl was 'in danger to be torn to pieces or to have his throat cut'. Laud too was blamed for 'the breach of Parliament', and printed notices called on London's apprentices to turn out 'for the hunting of "William the Fox"'. Three days later new notices went up, summoning 'every class' to appear on Monday 11 May in St George's Fields outside Southwark and 'secure . . . the death of many leading ministers, reputed enemies of the commonweal'.[66]

The government ordered troops to occupy the Fields throughout that Monday. However, in the evening, after the soldiers had gone, crowds began to gather. By dark 'some thousands' were massed there: mainly apprentices, the city's most inflammable class, all of them armed. Shortly before midnight they set out to march, 'with drums beating . . . in a riotous manner', the half-mile to Lambeth Palace, Laud's London residence, where they arrived 'with the purpose of slaying him'.[67] The archbishop had already fled to Whitehall, having 'strengthened the house as well as I could'. Shots came from the men inside, and a woman in the crowd was wounded, but still the 'rascal routers', as Laud called them, stayed on for 'full two hours'. Only once they were certain the archbishop was not there did they leave, threatening to 'come back and visit the houses of other ministers in even greater numbers and better armed'.[68]

Outraged at this 'rabble of mean, unknown, dissolute persons' and their 'infamous, scandalous, headless insurrection', Charles acted vigorously to prevent the violence from spreading. London's usual night watches were doubled; 200 militiamen kept guard day and night over the royal children at Richmond Palace. Cavalry troops were ordered into London, four cannon were placed outside Lambeth Palace, and Strafford's house too was 'well defended'.[69] Some fifty suspected rioters were arrested and interrogated, in 'great efforts' to discover whether they had parliamentary leadership. Meanwhile, 'in great wrath', Charles pressed ahead with his efforts to force money from his subjects. He also approached the new papal agent, Carlo Rossetti, requesting aid from Rome.[70]

On 14 May the rioters gathered in greater force than ever. As Lambeth was too strongly defended now, a mob of 7000 proceeded to attack another of Laud's palaces at Croydon, while other bands assaulted the city's prisons, 'knocked down the gates, slew the keepers and released all the prisoners, especially those in custody for the riot of Monday'. Alarmed, Charles reinforced the guards at Whitehall and

ABOVE: Charles and Henrietta Maria in the early years of their marriage, ready to go out hunting together. Henrietta's dwarf, Jeffery Hudson, holds one of the dogs at their feet. Such joint expeditions were a regular part of the couple's married life.

BELOW: George Villiers, Duke of Buckingham and his family. During the 1620s the Duke was the handsomest man at court and Charles I's greatest favourite. Henrietta detested him on her arrival in England, but in later years Buckingham's wife and daughter became her close friends.

Charles and Henrietta Maria with their two eldest children. Two-year-old Prince Charles, wearing a toddler's gown and cap, stands by his father, while Henrietta holds Baby Mary in her arms. Crown, sceptre and orb rest on the table beside the King, who stares authoritatively out at the viewer. There are hints, too, of a more domestic life: a lapdog sports at the couple's feet; the Prince's hands rest gently on his father's knee, while the King extends his right arm protectively behind his little son.

One of the grandest portraits of Charles I produced by his favourite painter, Sir Anthony Van Dyck. Here Charles appears as a victorious emperor, riding under a triumphal arch bearing a general's baton, in a pose of effortless superiority. The painter has erased all traces of the King's social and physical awkwardness. Charles hung this portrait at the end of the Long Gallery at St James's Palace, dominating the Roman Emperors painted by Titian and Giulio Romano that lined the gallery's long side walls.

Henrietta Maria as painted by Van Dyck: divinely beautiful and remote, a queen indeed, the true object of Charles's 'heroic love and regal respect'. Van Dyck's numerous portraits of the Queen give no hint of the fun-loving woman in her twenties who had 'an infinity of … brilliant wit' and passed much of her time in 'frivolous but innocent things'.

ABOVE: Charles and Henrietta Maria out walking on the hill above Greenwich Palace with their eldest son, Prince Charles, and one of their courtiers. The royal couple loved their country life at Greenwich and spent a month or two there at the start of every summer.

BELOW: Charles and Henrietta Maria dining in royal state. Their greatest courtiers stand in a semicircle behind the royal pair; dinner is borne in by a procession of gentlemen, while a royal cupbearer serves wine from a separate table. Only royalty were allowed to sit down in the presence of the King and Queen.

RIGHT: Lucy, Countess of Carlisle, the most beautiful and witty of all the court ladies and Henrietta Maria's favourite. Lucy was notorious for her love affairs, and caused much suspicion when she introduced the teenage Queen to the use of make-up in 1628. In the political crisis of 1642 she betrayed the royal couple's plans to Parliament. Civil War soon followed.

BELOW: The royal family grew rapidly in the 1630s. This Van Dyck portrait of 1637 shows (from left to right) Mary, James, Charles, Elizabeth and Anne. The eldest two are now in adult clothes. Seven-year-old Charles is the little man of the family, his hand extended authoritatively over the giant dog beside him. Mary at six is a pert little miss, with curled hair, pearls and a long silk dress just like her mother's. Between them, four-year-old James is still in a toddler's gown and apron. On Prince Charles's other side are the two new arrivals: Elizabeth, not yet two, holds chubby Baby Anne, a classical putto draped in white, yearning adoringly towards her eldest brother. This painting hung over Charles's breakfast table at Whitehall, a daily reminder of family life when his children were away.

Earl of Strafford.

ABOVE, LEFT: William Laud, Archbishop of Canterbury, Charles's religious soulmate, whose zealotry in reforming the Anglican Church stirred up puritan opposition throughout the nation and sparked off war with Scotland. Henrietta disliked Laud for his anti-Catholic policies.

ABOVE, RIGHT: Thomas Wentworth, Earl of Strafford, the ambitious politician Charles called in to rescue him after his first, failed war against the Scots. Henrietta at first distrusted Strafford but came to admire him for his political loyalty as well as his courtly graces – 'he had the most beautiful hands', she remembered.

RIGHT: Henrietta Maria's mother, Marie de' Medici, a stern, authoritative figure, who arrived to live with her daughter in 1638 to the 'unspeakable annoyance' of everyone except Henrietta herself. Henrietta's and Marie's enthusiastic Catholicism only further enflamed puritan public opinion against the royal government.

ABOVE, LEFT: Charles I at his trial in 1649: aged by his misfortunes but still elegant and unbowed.

ABOVE, RIGHT: The King's trial in Westminster Hall. Charles sits alone in his box, wearing his hat in defiance of the court. To his right stand the parliamentary prosecutors. At the head of the hall are the court's commissioners: 'high-flown Parliament-men' who acted as both judge and jury.

ABOVE: The execution of King Charles I outside Whitehall Palace. Soldiers with pikes held back the crowds who filled the street. As the King's head fell, there came 'such a groan by thousands then present as I never heard before, and desire I may never hear again', an eyewitness recalled.

RIGHT: After Charles's death, Henrietta wore mourning for the remaining twenty years of her life: a small, thin woman, bitterly disillusioned by her husband's 'barbarous' fate.

ordered 6000 militia troops into London 'to prevent fresh disturbances'.[71] But his resolve was failing. Strafford had fallen suddenly and seriously ill. Lacking his bold counsels, and worn down by ten days 'full of fears ever since the Parliament brake up', Charles made moves for conciliation. The imprisoned MPs and London aldermen were set free. When the City again refused a loan, no action was taken. Charles even released three Scottish negotiators whom he had imprisoned a month before, sending one of them north to Edinburgh, to try to reopen talks.[72]

The rioters were not so fortunate. As a warning to others, one of the leaders from the first night was convicted of high treason at a hasty trial, and hanged and quartered. Another man was tortured on the rack before being executed, but still revealed nothing about the instigators of the riots.[73] What did emerge from the government's interrogations was the violent anti-Catholic feeling of the mob. Laud was a papist who 'had a crucifix on the communion table in his chapel and . . . bowed towards the altar', they ranted. After demolishing his house at Lambeth, they would destroy Marie de' Medici's residence at St James's, and Henrietta's chapel at Somerset House, 'because they were houses of Popery'. A confusion of rumours raced round the streets of London, claiming that 'the Queen went to the [Anglican] Communion with the King' and that she was even considering converting. However, Archbishop Laud had dissuaded her, and now 'the King goes to mass with the Queen'.[74]

Laud was terrified, knowing the power of such talk to stir the common people to violence. The government must act at once against Catholics, to disprove the 'most hateful' notion of his own and the King's defection, he urged. Charles could no longer refuse. After years of frustration, Laud went to work with a will. Catholic books were burnt in the streets. His agents searched suspect houses and seized Catholic devotional objects, books, papers and printing machines. He ordered the arrest of forty-seven known priests and all English Catholics attending the chapels of the Queen and the foreign ambassadors.[75] The effect was immediate. Whilst rioting against the government ceased, the mob instead turned all its fury against the Catholics.

Outside Somerset House one night a wild crowd gathered, issuing threats against Henrietta's Capuchin priests. A few days later notices appeared, summoning the defenders of the purity of the Gospel to raze the papal agent's house to the ground and kill him. Rossetti fled to St James's Palace, which was under heavy guard, like Somerset House, but the houses of London's Catholics were freely looted that night. The agitation against Henrietta even reached Whitehall, where someone scratched on the window of the King's antechamber: 'God save the King, God confound the Queen and all her faction, and God grant the Palatine to reign in this kingdom.' In a fury, Charles smashed the glass with his fist.[76]

As May ended Charles and Henrietta were together at Greenwich to begin their summer holidays, but the crisis was now sparking discord even between the two of them. Distrusting Charles's policy of appeasement, Henrietta urged him 'with all her might ... to pursue the war with spirit against the rebels until they are completely subdued'. What he needed, she said, was Catholic money; she hoped to obtain 'large contributions' from his subjects and 'some help from the Pope'.[77] On Rossetti's urgings, she spoke to Charles too about the government's new persecution of the Catholics, arguing that it would only alienate these otherwise most loyal subjects, and prevent them from aiding the King's cause. But amid continuing rumours that Laud 'was turned Papist' and that Charles himself 'commonly went to mass', the King could not afford to please his wife. The nation's penal laws remained in force.[78]

It was not for long. On 8 July, Henrietta's new baby was born after an easy labour: a boy, named Henry after his mother and French grandfather. Charles was effusive in his joy, enthusiastically granting favours to his wife. He placed Henry under the care of the Catholic Countess of Roxburghe, who was already governess to the three princesses. He also suspended the penal laws for the month of Henrietta's lying-in after the birth, and ordered the release of all imprisoned Catholics. Charles was now as resolved on war as Henrietta could wish. 'Deeply incensed' after the Scots Parliament met contrary to his wishes and approved all the decisions of the Presbyterian General

Assembly, he had lost 'all hope of settling affairs there by gentle means'.[79]

However, where were the necessities of war to come from? There was a new offer from the Pope of 6000 or 8000 troops, ready to serve Charles 'to the last breath' and carried on ships from the Spanish Netherlands, but they would be available, Rossetti warned, only 'to sustain a King who was a professed Catholic, and for the defence of our Holy Religion' – a state of affairs that Henrietta would have loved to see, but which she admitted was profoundly unlikely.[80] Charles's other requests for foreign aid were no more successful. £300,000 offered to Strafford by the Spanish ambassadors never materialised, whilst the proposal of an alliance with France in return for a loan of £400,000 was also rebuffed. So Charles returned to his old policy of forcing money from his reluctant subjects. In a surprise move his government seized all the gold and silver brought by London's merchants into the Mint for coining, amounting to some £100,000.[81] The threat of replacing some of the nation's silver coins with copper was held over the merchants too, in an attempt to pressurise them into a new loan. Even so the City corporations refused. At last Charles was reduced to cutting Marie de' Medici's monthly allowance by half. This time Henrietta made no objection. Marie was forced to dismiss many of her court 'and to arrange to live a more frugal life'.[82]

Meanwhile the English troops were desperately unready for war. Many, when they heard of Parliament's dissolution, refused to serve at all; the remainder marched north only in the greatest disorder. Hundreds mutinied against their Catholic officers and the ungodly cause they were called to fight for, or simply for lack of pay. Strafford's 10,000-strong Irish army, mostly Catholic, remained unshipped, again for lack of money. And still the northern army had no commander-in-chief on the spot. The Earl of Northumberland, appointed on Strafford's advice, refused to leave London – due to illness, he protested, although many suspected that it was no more than a 'mendacious pretext'.[83] Northumberland was not alone in his disaffection. Henrietta's former favourite, the Earl of Holland, had already in secret joined his half-brother, the Earl of Warwick, as a leader of the opposition. The Earl of Pembroke, who had entertained the King so lavishly each summer at Wilton, was also fast falling out of sympathy with his master; despite his luxurious tastes, Pembroke was at heart a godly Puritan who disliked Laud and was disliked by Henrietta Maria.[84]

Nevertheless, Charles remained optimistic. The Scots had sent their soldiers home 'to save expense', he heard; they had no significant forces on the border; divisions among the enemy leaders would bring him 'considerable advantage'.[85] Suddenly news arrived that their army was mustered and marching south in force; Newcastle, lacking both men and fortifications, could not hold out against an assault. 'Extraordinarily perturbed', the King decided to leave for the North right away, in the expectation that his presence would confirm the wavering troops in their loyalty and ensure that the Scots were stayed at the border. When his advisers objected, Charles remained adamant, determined to act to 'secure his wife and children'.[86] The next few days were crammed with preparations. As the Earl of Northumberland continued to plead illness, Charles appointed Strafford to command the northern army, despite his lack of military experience. Then, on Thursday 20 August, Charles left London. There was at least this ground for hope, Strafford noted: 'that in my life I have not seen a man begin with more life and courage'.[87]

That same day the Scots army entered England, more than 20,000 strong. Well disciplined under experienced commanders, they were fearless of Charles's army of 'debauched, bragging, southern swingers', expecting significant resistance only from a few northern Catholics, sharers in 'that whorish religion' of the 'Papist wench' whom the King had married.[88] Already they had distributed their manifesto through Northumberland, professing that their 'expedition' was 'destined solely for the support of the religion and liberty of both kingdoms', and demanding the punishment of Charles's 'evil councillors': the Anglican bishops, the Catholics, Laud and Strafford. Their army would remain, they promised, until they saw the English Parliament assembled to end the nation's 'prolonged disturbances'.[89]

Charles's commanders, marching their outnumbered troops up to

Newcastle as fast as possible, despaired; their only hope was that the King's presence would 'remedy all'. Yet when Charles reached York there was little he could do. His army was small in numbers, 'with no sort of order and by no means ready to engage the enemy'. The Yorkshire militia, whose 'vigorous support' Strafford had promised, refused to muster. The King's proclamation, declaring the Scots guilty of high treason and offering a pardon if they would 'return quietly to their homes', was merely 'labour lost' as the Scots continued their advance.[90]

On 28 August the first battle took place, on the River Tyne just outside Newcastle. Charles's commander had taken out part of the town's garrison to prevent the Scots from crossing the river but, under fire from the Scots artillery, the English infantry threw down their weapons and fled. Fording the river, the Scottish cavalry charged the English horse, which retreated, 'routed and in disorder', as far as Durham, twenty miles away. Next morning the remaining English forces abandoned Newcastle. Strafford, advancing north to meet them, still held out hopes to Charles: 'some of the troops are in very good order … In a word, I believe as many of them [i.e. the Scots] were slain as of us.' Privately, however, the Earl despaired. 'Pity me,' he wrote to a friend, 'for never came any man to so lost a business … Our horse all cowardly; the country from Berwick to York in the power of the Scots; an universal affright in all; a general disaffection to the King's service, none sensible of his dishonour … God of his goodness deliver me out of this, the greatest evil of my life.'[91]

At Windsor Castle now with her children, Henrietta was 'miserably cast down' by the news of Newcastle's fall, which she viewed as a 'wilful rout' by ill-intentioned men under evil commanders.[92] But the populace at large was delighted. Even though it was 'forbidden under severe penalties to speak in favour of the rebels', London was full of talk condemning Charles and praising the Scots: 'honest people' who 'would do us no harm but rather good'.[93] Rumours of terrifying Catholic plots spread like wildfire. The King was believed to be planning to bring over Strafford's Irish army 'to gain satisfaction from his English subjects'. Marie de' Medici too was said to be involved, with '7,000 men and more in readiness to perform her designs', while London's Catholic foreign ambassadors were all plotting with the Pope.[94] Notices again appeared in the streets, with threats to burn down Henrietta's chapel and kill Rossetti. Other papers called on the apprentices and the troops quartered around London 'to fall upon' Laud. Five regiments of infantry mutinied, refusing to embark for the North. The courtiers were 'in such distraction as if the day of judgment were hourly expected'.[95] Guards were appointed for Henrietta and her children; Laud, in fear of 'the popular wrath', withdrew to her court for safety, emerging only 'with circumspection'. And at the Tower of London there were orders to build new earthworks 'and take steps to command the city with guns', in case of a rising.[96]

Meanwhile Henrietta was deeply involved in all Charles's plans. Almost every day she received new letters from him. She also saw all his official despatches immediately after Secretary Windebank; only then was the Privy Council to be informed of 'so much [of their contents] as you shall think fit', Charles ordered Windebank. Every week the Privy Council reported to Henrietta on its business in London. Her advice to Charles, the councillors knew, was far more influential than their own.[97] Yet at last Charles sought guidance from his Privy Council, 'sad at heart', seeing the Scots fortifying Newcastle, taking Durham 'without resistance, and ... approaching swiftly to York'. 'You shall do well to think of timely remedies to be applied, lest the disease grow incurable,' he wrote, 'for I apprehend you are not much better in the South.'[98]

The Council hardly needed telling. Windebank was already panic-stricken, declaring that 'the danger is greater than any since the [Norman] Conquest.' The only policy now must be 'conciliation of the disaffected lords, and redress of grievances'; Portsmouth must be fortified 'as a place of retreat, in case of the worst'.[99] Despite their shared fears, when the Privy Councillors met, they differed profoundly on what remedy to propose. Moderates and Puritans were eager for Parliament to be called, which was anathema to Charles's chief ministers, crypto-Catholics or high Anglicans all. No decision could be reached until the Earl of Manchester proposed a new idea. Three hundred years ago, King Edward III had summoned a great Council of Peers to aid his war with Scotland, when 'they raised great sums of money without a Parliament, and assisted the King'. Now was 'a like occasion'. Although a few Privy Councillors objected, the majority supported his plan.[100]

Charles was delighted with their proposal, noting in the margin of their letter, 'it is thought most fit'.[101] He had just received a petition from twelve opposition peers in London calling for a new Parliament; a second petition from the Scots was couched in such similar language that everyone could recognise 'the secret communication' between the two parties, collaborating against the King's government. At first Charles had not known how to reply, but now he could say he would discuss the matter with his Great Council of Peers. Commanding the Scots 'not to advance further ... and to await what will be decided', as well as setting a date of 24 September for the Council of Peers' first meeting in York, gained him almost three weeks to make preparations in case of further Scottish offensives.[102]

Charles was pleased when he reviewed his army outside York: '16,000 foot, and 2,000 horse, besides the trained bands of Yorkshire', which had finally agreed to muster. 'Braver bodies of men and better clad have I not seen anywhere,' Secretary Vane reported proudly to London. However, it was only surface deep. By now most of the troops were thoroughly disaffected, seeing the Scots not as the enemy but as 'the redeemers of their religion and liberty'. It was unlikely that they would stand and fight.[103]

Meanwhile, on Charles's orders, Windebank and the Privy Council in London were attempting to raise a new army in the South, ready to defend the King and Queen 'in case of disaster'. Charles was growing ever more frustrated with them: 'I see ye are all so frighted, ye can resolve on nothing.' Increasingly now he sidelined even Windebank, so that Henrietta was the first to hear the latest news from the North, sent to her direct 'by his Majesty's special order'.[104] It was in one of her replies that Henrietta proposed a radical plan. When the King met his Council of Peers at York, she proposed, he should not simply ask their advice on calling Parliament; he must act first and declare that he had already decided to summon Parliament of his own volition. Parliament was inevitable anyway; at least this way the King might win some much needed popularity.[105] Charles's Privy Councillors, alarmed at the continuing disturbances in London, wholeheartedly seconded Henrietta's advice. Secretary Vane in York agreed: just the promise alone would be sufficient 'to put the Scots out of the kingdom ... [and] to cure all our sores'.[106]

So Charles began his Great Council by announcing that a new Parliament would meet in London on 3 November: the earliest possible date, given the need for new elections. The King spoke 'freely and graciously' for much of the morning, making a remarkable impression: in more than twenty years, Vane reported, 'I have not known his Majesty express himself better.' Charles was aiming to win popularity for Henrietta as well as for himself. She was the one, he said, who 'had by a letter advised him to it'.[107] However, any hopes of impressing the Scots were soon dashed. When Charles's negotiators arrived in Ripon, midway between the two armies, to open peace talks, they found the Scots confident 'that they are on vantage-ground'. Well aware that Charles could not fight them, the Scots insisted on their original demands, as well as the 'immediate payment' of compensation for their 'loss and expense' in the war.[108] They also required any new treaty to be approved by the English Parliament; until then, they would not leave. Although Charles was furious at the rebels' 'audacity', his negotiators could achieve nothing better. At last they returned to report that there would be no peace treaty for now; instead the Scots would send commissioners to Parliament, which would have the final word. In the meantime there would be an armistice, but only on condition that the English paid £25,000 each month 'for the maintenance of the enemy's army'.[109]

This arrangement was so disadvantageous that many courtiers suspected foul play. The English negotiators, they noted, were all Scottish sympathisers: disaffected courtiers like the Earls of Pembroke and Holland, and some of the twelve opposition peers who had just sent in their petition to Charles, all 'equally zealous for the calling of parliament'. The Scots had flattered these men with their talk of remedying 'the excess of the Queen's power' and removing Laud, Strafford and other ministers from office, to be replaced with 'persons ... of honour ... who are known to be zealous for the preservation and advancement of the Protestant religion'. In fact, the Scots had insinuated, the English negotiators themselves were the ideal men to 'be in most credit about the King'.[110] So went the story, but Charles would have none of it. It was the Scots alone, he said, by their 'cavil and delay', who had made it impossible to finalise the treaty at Ripon. 'Therefore I can in nowise blame the [English] Lords ... but must thank them for their industry and pains.'[111]

Yet as he left York to meet his new Parliament in London, the King could only be apprehensive. Despite his efforts to 'sweeten' the opposition by releasing prisoners held for 'matters that may raise disputes in the ensuing Parliament'; despite his careful nomination of royalist MPs to constituencies under his control: still the elections had gone against him. The new Parliament was expected to be 'most insolent' in demanding reforms that would amount to 'a very considerable diminution in His Majesty's authority'.[112] Charles had been desperate for the Scots army to leave England before Parliament met, fearing their presence would encourage the MPs. He had failed, and now there would be eight Scottish commissioners actually in London, ready to 'sow ideas pernicious to the public quiet'. Already the opposition was declaring that it would follow the Scots' lead and remove the bishops from the House of Lords, where they generally voted in support of the King.[113] 'Total desolation' was facing England's Catholic community, who firmly expected Parliament to demand 'fresh severity' against them. Charles's most trusted ministers went in fear of 'final ruin', with the real possibility of 'most severe punishment' at Parliament's hands.[114] And in St Paul's Cathedral, Puritan protesters, like the Presbyterian Scots before them, 'gathered in great numbers and violently ... broke down the altar, and tore to pieces the books containing the new canons'. The Anglican ministers escaped hurt only by flight. Everyone, it seemed, admired the Scots. It was to their 'bold resolution' that the English would owe 'the reestablishment of liberty and religion alike'.[115]

9

Evil Counsellors

Four days before Parliament opened, Charles and Henrietta met once more at Theobalds, just north of London. For weeks Henrietta had waited 'with great impatience' for this moment, but now she was full of bitterness. Charles's agreement with the Scots was 'full of indignity'; he had set a dangerous precedent, which would encourage his other subjects 'to rebel without fear', knowing they would win not 'merited punishment', but 'rewards and other advantages'.[1] So disappointed was she that, looking back in after years, she forgot her own role in advising the King to call Parliament; instead she laid the responsibility for the whole northern disaster on political malcontents among the lords at York, who were plotting the destruction of Strafford and ultimately the King himself.[2]

Charles, ground down by the harsh political and military realities of the North, could see no alternative to his policy of appeasement. There was no triumphal procession to the state opening of Parliament this time: money was too tight and Charles could not pretend to an enthusiasm he did not feel. Instead he went privately by barge downriver to Westminster Stairs, losing a major opportunity for pleasing the crowds that always turned out for royal pageants. Inside the House of Lords, however, the King did his best to please. Concealing his anger, he made a careful speech, asking Parliament's help in satisfying the Scots and paying the English army, as well as offering in return to redress their grievances. Just one hint of his true feelings leaked out, when he referred to the Scots as 'rebels', but his subsequent apologies were so exemplary – 'so effusive . . . showing so much submission that came ill from the mouth of a great prince' – that his real terror of offending Parliament was plain to see. His speech was greeted with 'universal acclamations', for the MPs well knew his weakness and thus their own ability to direct matters as they chose.[3]

Just as in the last Parliament seven months earlier, they ignored the King's pleas for money and eagerly turned to discussing their grievances. Once more John Pym took the lead. Painstakingly he expounded the whole sorry mess of government abuses, all due, he said, to a secret Catholic conspiracy: 'the highest of treason' and 'a design to alter the kingdom both in religion and government'. Already it was almost accomplished by an unholy alliance of foreign agents, the 'Papists' party', 'the corrupt part of our clergy', and depraved government ministers: men who were ready to 'further all bad things . . . [and] to run into Popery'. On Pym's urging a committee was appointed 'to find out authors and they to receive punishment'.[4] Yet Charles showed not a single flash of anger at this denunciation of his long years of non-parliamentary government. Instead, hoping to prove himself 'equally estranged from the Catholic faith', he promised to order 'the departing and disarming of papists from London and Westminster'. The new fortifications at the Tower too would be dismantled, and the soldiers and their commander dismissed.[5]

Such easy concessions were not remotely enough. Again Pym stood up in the House of Commons, and now he denounced the Earl of Strafford: 'a main instrument to provoke the King to make a war between us and the Scots' and so 'bring in the papist party'. Pym accused the Earl of having planned to bring his Irish army into England, 'to suppress the laws and liberties of this Kingdom'.[6] That same day the MPs voted to accuse Strafford of high treason. On their request, the Lords summoned the Earl to hear the charge against him, then sent him immediately to prison, to wait while the Commons prepared the full details of his indictment. Charles had no will to resist: 'he was resolved not to protect anyone,' he told Parliament, and would do what he could 'for expedition in that business'.[7] At a single blow, he and Henrietta had lost the most powerful prop to their regime.

Over and over again Charles conceded to Parliament's demands. When they granted him money to pay his northern army, he accepted their condition that their commissioners would control the funds – a notable violation of the King's prerogative. He agreed to dismiss all suspected Catholics from his army. He even appointed the Puritan Earl of Essex to command the army in Strafford's place.[8] Still Parliament continued, unmollified, in their course. With 'accusation and outcry' against Archbishop Laud coming in 'from every quarter' – especially from the Scots negotiators, who described him as 'an incendiary' who had 'laboured to set the two nations into a bloody war' – the Commons set up a committee to investigate. Soon Laud too was arrested on charges of high treason, for his alleged involvement 'in the great design of the subversion of the laws of the realm, and of the religion'.[9] Again Charles took it quietly.

Henrietta, however, fretted and fumed by turns, 'much troubled at all the Parliament does', seeing their 'great malignity to her'.[10] Already their investigations into Pym's supposed popish plot had cast suspicion on her. A Catholic fast – arranged the previous summer 'towards the Queen's pious intentions', which had really been nothing more than a prayer for Charles's success in the North – was now seen as part of a plan for a bloody Catholic uprising. Pym whipped up the MPs' terrors with his talk 'of the Papists intending a day to cut the protestants' throats', adding that 'there was great danger to us all'. Marie de' Medici was implicated too. According to Pym, an Irish priest of hers had said that if Charles would not accept this Catholic *coup d'état*, then he too would die with the rest of the Protestants.[11] Inflamed by Pym's anti-Catholic scaremongering, popular feeling in London was running high. At Somerset House the following Sunday, while a large congregation heard mass in Henrietta's chapel as usual, a hostile mob gathered outside. Some had brought weapons, others merely stones picked up in the street. As the service ended, they attacked the emerging Catholics with fury, until a city official 'quelled the tumult, with no little trouble'.[12]

In desperate straits, Henrietta wrote off to Cardinal Barberini in Rome. The Catholics had been banished from London, she told him; their priests were to be proceeded against under the penal laws 'which go right to death'. Her Catholic courtiers were now under investigation for attempting to convert Protestants, 'and the pity is that the affairs of the King do not permit him to oppose all this violence ... on the contrary he suffers now for his [former] bounty towards those of our religion'. The only remedy, she urged, was money, with which she planned to bribe the opposition leaders and so 'forestall a great part of their violence'. Already she was preparing to open the necessary talks, by means of old court favourites like the Earls of Northumberland and Holland, and Northumberland's sister, Lucy Countess of Carlisle, who were now intimate with those in the opposition camp. 'I have so disposed my design that only the money is lacking,' she told the Cardinal. But raising such a sum was impossible in England. Could Rome oblige? A loan of £125,000 might be sent in small quantities, by bills of exchange, to ensure the utmost secrecy. 'There is no one but His Holiness, you and me who yet know of this,' she added.[13] In the meantime she responded vigorously to her opponents. If Parliament attempted to remove her Catholic servants, she would dismiss all the Protestants too, she threatened, and appoint a new household composed entirely of 'people of her faith'.[14] From Paris, Louis XIII backed her up. 'I do not want to meddle in Parliament's affairs,' he said, 'so let them keep off my sister's marriage articles, otherwise I know well what I shall have to do.'[15]

But Parliament was not to be bullied out of its anti-Catholic crusade. As new reports came in of 'the number and danger of the papists', the Commons' newly formed Committee for Inquiry after Papists turned to examining the government's long-running policy of releasing Catholic priests from gaol. Wary of attacking the royal couple directly, they avoided any mention of Henrietta's involvement, and explicitly cleared

Charles of all guilt; he had signed 'very few' of the warrants releasing priests and he always ordered the priests to leave the country promptly, 'such is his Majesty's care'. Instead the MPs vented their fury on Secretary Windebank. Detailed evidence was presented, showing how he had issued most of the warrants without written authorisation from the King or due legal process. When the Commons summoned Windebank to appear before them, he fled to France, well aware that Charles and Henrietta could not protect him.[16] In this case, at least, Parliament had failed to bring its man to justice, but the MPs were not dissatisfied. Their primary aim was 'to remove from the king all his most confidential ministers' and their project was advancing fast.[17] A fortnight later Lord Keeper Finch also fled abroad to escape arrest on yet another treason charge. And with Parliament investigating 'the Pope's pretended Nuncio', Henrietta was forced to ask Rossetti to leave the country 'as soon as possible'; neither she nor Charles could see any other way of ensuring his safety.[18]

It was just seven weeks after the opening of Parliament and almost all Charles's closest advisers were gone. Henrietta was outraged, and not just for her own sake and the Catholics. Even Laud's arrest infuriated her, as she saw 'her husband not only deprived of his most faithful ministers, but so effectively despised by his own subjects'. Ceaselessly she urged Charles 'to throw himself into desperate courses', though so far he was not listening.[19]

Christmas 1640 was a subdued affair. Just a couple of weeks earlier, Charles and Henrietta had lost their youngest daughter, Anne. While Windebank prepared to flee from London, the round-faced three-year-old princess lay in her bed too weak to move, feverish, coughing constantly, struggling for every breath. When one of her rockers reminded her to call on God, she replied: 'I am not able to say my long Prayer,' meaning the Lord's Prayer, 'but I will say my short one, "Lighten mine eyes, O Lord, lest I sleep the sleep of death".' She died soon after. The doctors' autopsy reveals the cause as tuberculosis: 'a suffocating catarrh, with inflammatory disposition of the lungs, the roots of which ailments have been in her a long time'. Despite their best efforts 'this princess could not be long-lived,' they concluded.[20]

Stricken with 'intense grief, Henrietta retreated to Wimbledon for a few days, to see the building work progressing on her new house and 'take the air'. When she returned to Whitehall for Christmas, there were none of the usual festivities. No masques were performed, nor were there any remarkable parties, dances or feasts. Venison was eaten in quantity – 109 dead deer arrived 'for the consumption of his Majesty's household' – but this was a free commodity from the King's 'several forests, chases, and parks', making no strain on the royal finances.[21]

Meanwhile Charles and Henrietta sought what support they could against their opponents. For over two years the Dutch had been asking for an English princess to marry their Stadtholder's son and heir, William Prince of Orange. Marie de' Medici had first proposed the idea in 1638, when she stopped in the Dutch United Provinces en route to England. As the match promised no honour or gain to the English royals, the matter had been dropped. Now, as Parliament began its furious assault on the royal government in November, Charles and Henrietta reconsidered. Their blonde-haired second daughter, Elizabeth, might be suitable at nearly five years old.[22] That would leave Mary, just turning nine, free for her long-mooted and more honourable Spanish match. However, as soon as the marriage with Elizabeth was agreed, the Dutch pressed to receive the eldest daughter instead, offering Charles 'a first claim on the affections and interests' of the entire United Provinces. They would intercede with the Scots and 'do all in their power to arrange a settlement'. If negotiations failed, they would be ready to provide more material assistance to the royal cause.[23] In the New Year of 1641 three Dutch ambassadors arrived to negotiate the deal, and within a couple of weeks Mary's marriage was settled.

The alliance gave the royal couple new confidence and fighting spirit. Henrietta asked Rossetti to stay on in London after all. Charles, abandoning his former 'hesitation and reserve', announced 'that he will not permit parliament to punish his servants', and threw himself into efforts on Strafford's behalf, with 'the greatest activity'.[24] When Henrietta heard that a Catholic priest had been arrested and was condemned to die, she thought nothing of asking her husband for a reprieve, as usual, and he was happy to oblige. A priest would suffer a traitor's death, by hanging, disembowelling and quartering. Since Charles's accession to the throne in 1625 this atrocious punishment had never been inflicted.[25]

However, the MPs were astounded: John Goodman had already been caught and imprisoned three times, 'and banished this kingdom', to no effect whatever. His reprieve now, 'in this time of Parliament, when they expect a thorough reformation', was a shameless instance of the court's 'great connivance at Jesuits and priests'. There must be an investigation at once, to discover who had 'dared to intercede'. The danger to Henrietta was clear, and Charles acted at once. There had been no dangerous persons interceding on Goodman's behalf, he informed Parliament. Goodman had been convicted simply for being a priest, without any other aggravating offence, so Charles had reprieved him, just as his predecessors Elizabeth and James had often done. To satisfy the MPs, he offered to banish or imprison Goodman, and to take whatever measures they advised for expelling Catholic priests from the kingdom.[26]

Parliament was unappeased: Goodman must be executed as an example, Commons and Lords alike demanded. It was clear to all that the case involved far more than the fate of just one man. Charles had the right to pardon convicted criminals, but now Parliament was pressurising him to abandon this royal prerogative. The question had become 'whether the supreme authority lies with the King or Parliament'.[27] Pulled between fear of Parliament's anger and dread of the consequences of surrendering to their power, Charles could not decide on Goodman's fate. Meanwhile, blocked for the moment over Goodman, the MPs shifted their attack onto Henrietta.

On Wednesday 27 January 1641, a paper was produced in the Commons. Entitled 'Motives for a contribution from the Catholics to the King's Northern expedition', it contained the letters that Henrietta and her courtiers had sent out, seeking Catholic funding for Charles's war with the Scots. The MPs were profoundly alarmed. To them it seemed proof of what they had long suspected: that Henrietta was involved in a dangerous Catholic conspiracy to enable Charles to govern tyranically without Parliament. The letters themselves described the King's war as 'a Catholic cause' from which the Catholics might hope to gain 'a suspension of the penal laws against them'. Sir Kenelm Digby and Walter Montagu were alleged to have been 'Treasurers general to receive the collections', and both were summoned into the Commons for questioning. Both earnestly professed their innocence. None of the Queen's current courtiers had been deeply involved, they said; it was the papal agent, George Con – now far beyond the reach of the law – who had masterminded the whole affair. But the Commons' suspicions only intensified and soon there was new evidence brought in, of Catholic troops being raised in England and Ireland at just the same time as Henrietta had been collecting her Catholic money.[28] Her contribution, it seemed, was part of a wider and yet more dangerous Catholic plot: for an armed insurrection to destroy the nation's Protestant government.

Charles and Henrietta were shocked at the paranoia, the wildfire conspiracy theories, the witch-hunting fury of the Commons. In 'extreme necessity' now, they held 'long consultations' at Whitehall, until at last they hatched a plan for joint action to defend Henrietta from further parliamentary attack.[29] First came Charles's part. On 3 February, by his order, both Houses of Parliament assembled in Whitehall's Banqueting House, where the King delivered a speech in state. He would put the penal laws into execution once again, as they desired, and would order all Jesuits and priests 'to depart the Kingdom within one month'. As for Goodman, Charles still believed he had been right to reprieve him, and yet, to avoid 'giving so great a discontentment to his people', he would leave Goodman's case to the decision of Parliament, though still he asked them to be merciful.[30]

In his determination to defuse Parliament's anger against his wife, Charles had given away a lot; he had even set the precedent of abandoning his prerogative, and the MPs showed 'great satisfaction'.[31] Having proved their real power, they had no further interest in Goodman, who was left forgotten in prison. Now it was Henrietta's turn to approach the Commons with further pacifications, as she hoped. Always she had been 'most willing to do all good offices between the king and his people', she assured them; in fact, she had written 'expressly to persuade the king to the holding of a parliament'. Now she was ready wholeheartedly to support her husband's measures against Catholics. She would send Rossetti 'out of the kingdom' and restrict her chapel ceremonies at Somerset House, allowing in only those people 'convenient and necessary for the exercise of her religion'. In return she asked a boon. She knew Parliament was displeased at her efforts to raise money for Charles's northern campaign, but she 'was ignorant of the law' and had acted 'merely out of her dear and tender affection to the king'. So she asked Parliament to forgive and forget, 'to look forwards and pass by such mistakes and errors of her servants as may be formerly'. This kindness, she promised, would 'be repaid with all the good offices she can do to the House'.[32]

Such 'suave expressions', Charles and Henrietta hoped, would halt Parliament's 'career of licence', but the MPs were unimpressed.[33] Just a week later they renewed their attack on Henrietta's Catholic courtiers: 'dangerous instruments' who were plotting with 'Romish Priests and Jesuits here, and ... foreign States abroad' to raise a Catholic insurrection. These men must be banished from court, the MPs demanded; Strafford's Irish Catholic army must be disbanded at once, and all English Catholics disarmed.[34]

There was a new assault on Charles's government too: a Bill passing rapidly through Commons and Lords, requiring that Parliament must meet at least every three years. This 'Triennial Bill' was an outrageous violation of the King's 'ancient prerogative' of calling Parliament 'at his pleasure'. When Parliament sent it in for his approval, Charles refused to answer, 'very angry'. There was an uproar in the Commons, where the Members 'loudly threatened the most extreme designs'. Still Charles delayed 'for many hours', balancing his loss of royal power against the violent uprising he feared his continued resistance could bring.[35] Henrietta, however, was all for conceding. With pressing 'entreaty', she 'used all means' to persuade her husband to sign.[36] They had particular need to please Parliament at the moment: Strafford's trial was approaching, the House of Lords would be his judges, and Strafford must be saved. He was the most 'able and loyal' of all

Charles's ministers, Henrietta believed; while he served the King, the parliamentary opposition 'could never succeed'. Parliament's destruction of the Earl was just the first step towards the 'ruin' of the King himself.[37] Now, she urged, Charles must yield up his political rights for the Earl of Strafford's sake. Then, if only they could pull through for the present, there might soon be scope for successful resistance. Strafford's largely Catholic army was still undisbanded and available in Ireland, whilst Henrietta hoped for troops from her brother Louis and the Prince of Orange too. With their aid, the King could dissolve Parliament, free the Earl of Strafford and restore a properly authoritarian royal government.[38]

Charles needed little persuasion. He had already promised to save Strafford, even if he had 'to run the greatest risks'.[39] He therefore gave his assent to the Triennial Act. 'You have taken the Government almost to pieces,' he told the assembled Lords and Commons, 'and, I may say, it is almost off the hinges.' Like a watchmaker, they must soon think of reassembling the machinery, he warned: 'just remember if you leave out one pin the watch may be the worse and not the better.'[40] Parliament was delighted, offering the King their 'most humble and hearty thanks'. At their request that night there was 'ringing of bells, and bonfires, through the whole City', all thoroughly resented by Charles. As the Venetian ambassador reported, 'nothing is left to him but the title and the naked shows of king, and he does not know how to conceal the passions which naturally torture him'.[41]

Fighting for survival now, the royal couple made desperate attempts to weaken their enemies' power. Henrietta's plans for bribing the opposition leaders with papal money had come to naught; Rome again replied that Charles must convert before receiving aid. Instead she laid new designs: to win over their opponents with offers of career advancements. Prestigious and lucrative government jobs were now available, vacated by loyal courtiers who were in prison or exile; other courtiers could always be nudged out to make room for new men. And so she began her tactful approach to her parliamentarian enemies. Even John Pym and his closest intimates 'do attend the Queen in private', word leaked out from court.[42] Ultimately these Puritan crusaders remained true to their cause, but there were other prominent opposition members who were more amenable, offering to support the royal couple in return for a share in government. On 19 February, Charles gave out the first rewards to seven parliamentarian lords, until now 'his most obstinate persecutors', who had advanced Strafford's impeachment and the Triennial Bill, and who had spoken against 'the improvidence and evil counsels' of Charles's ministers.[43] Now, however, they were appointed to the Privy Council.

The results were immediate. When Parliament once more debated the dismissal of Henrietta's Catholic courtiers, three of these new men spoke up to defend her. Far from being a danger to the nation, the Earl of Bristol asserted, Henrietta was an eager friend to the Parliament. She had 'furthered' both the calling of Parliament, last summer, and the passing of the Triennial Bill just now in February, when the King had been undecided. The Earl of Hertford confirmed Bristol's words: in the summer, the Queen had 'told him in discourse [that] a Parliament [was] the only way'.[44] And in the House of Commons, the Earl of Bristol's son, Lord Digby, urged that, rather than suspecting and penalising the Queen, the MPs ought to send her 'thanks for her furthering the calling of the Parliament and the passing of the triennial bill'.[45] They argued in vain. Urged on by Pym, the Commons voted 'to desire the removal of all popish recusants from Court'; soon the Lords joined them.[46] Embattled on every front, Charles acceded. The royal couple's new faction had failed its first test of strength, and already a far greater challenge was approaching.

On Monday 22 March the Earl of Strafford's trial began. In Westminster Hall that morning the accused man dropped to his knees in front of his judges and then stood up to wait – frowning and gloomy-faced, as he always was when not speaking – for the King's arrival. An unusually tall figure 'but stooped much in the neck',[47] the Earl was dressed simply in black, his only ornament being the bright star of the Order of the Garter on his cloak. All round the Hall, ranks of seating ten tiers high were now crammed full. All the MPs were here, as were the Scots negotiators and crowds of the curious: 500 spectators or more, predominantly hostile to the Earl. In front of them were the

Lords, dressed in their scarlet state robes, their broad-brimmed hats firmly on their heads to show their superiority over everyone else present. The King's throne stood empty, for the Lords would allow him to attend only as a private observer, concealed in a lattice-fronted gallery. Here, around 9 a.m., Charles and Henrietta arrived with some courtiers. The legal proceedings could commence.[48]

The accusation against Strafford was named – high treason – and the charge was read in full: twenty-seven articles, ranging from embezzling government revenue and encouraging Catholics, to inciting the King to fight the Scots, breaking the English Parliament the year before, and plotting to bring his Catholic Irish army over to use against the English. Strafford's written answer was read out, rebutting each article in turn. Then the court adjourned and Strafford returned to the Tower.[49]

Next day the Commons' prosecution, led by John Pym, began to call their witnesses, whom Strafford cross-examined himself. He had the perfect qualities for a law court. 'His memory was great,' a contemporary recalled, 'his elocution was very fluent, and it was a great part of his talent readily to reply, or freely to harangue upon any subject.'[50] He showed up the weakness of the prosecution's evidence, discredited and humiliated their witnesses, switching effortlessly from impassioned self-defence to biting sarcasm that raised a laugh in the audience, remaining always calm and collected under pressure. As the days passed, he began to win over many in the audience, in spite of themselves, changing 'the universal hatred against him into compassion'.[51] Soon the prosecution were forced to shift their ground. Some charges they simply abandoned. As Strafford repeatedly argued that, even if he had done many of the things he was accused of, his actions in no way amounted to treason, the prosecutors protested that the individual charges were irrelevant; it was the overall charge in its entirety that must be considered as 'constructive treason'.

Meanwhile Charles and Henrietta, hoping to 'give their servant courage', attended the trial every day. Carefully they listened to 'all that could be alleged' against him, while Henrietta's court ladies took notes 'all day'.[52] Often they returned from the sessions with 'their hearts gripped with sadness and their eyes full of tears', she later recalled. The evenings were spent in discussions and plans. Charles, leaving 'nothing untried', sought out new witnesses to give favourable testimony on the most dangerous charges, while Henrietta intensified her secret talks with the opposition leaders.[53] Every night she went alone, carrying a torch in her hand, up the private back stairs to the apartment of one of her ladies who was away in the country, there to meet 'the most wicked' of the royals' opponents, offering them the nation's most important political offices. It was a perilous policy: 'using honours as a reward for sedition' set an 'evil example'.[54] However, there was yet another, more violent and final solution.

At Portsmouth, one of the best harbours in the country, new fortifications were going up, under the command of Henrietta's favourite, Sir George Goring – the classic dashing cavalier, a man of 'wit, and courage and understanding'.[55] Henrietta was funding the work herself; she took £1300 in cash from her own income, for an undisclosed purpose, just two days after Strafford's trial began. Once well fortified, Portsmouth would be an ideal landing place for the troops she and Charles still hoped to bring in from overseas to save Strafford and themselves.[56]

The couple also had a new military hope. Despite Parliament's efforts to raise money for the two armies in the North of England, both the Scots Covenanters and Charles's English troops remained largely unpaid. By March the local people could support them no longer, 'their cattle and victual being ... exhausted and ... their commodities ... so dear, that no sort of victual is sold but at a double rate'. Urgently both armies begged Parliament for relief, while rumours spread through London 'that the [English] army were near a mutiny'. Yet Parliament took no action, 'so busy about the trial of my Lord Strafford we think of nothing else'.[57] Henrietta and her courtiers seized their opportunity. William Davenant – her servant and most favoured playwright, author of the last triumphal royal masques of the 1630s – made contact with James Chudleigh, the captain who had come south to present the English army's grievances. Davenant insinuated that Parliament was 'so well affected' to the Covenanters that it would pay their army first. Then the captain was introduced to Henry Jermyn, who invited him to see the Queen.[58]

Over the next few days, Henrietta's inner circle met repeatedly in her 'drawing chamber' and 'the little gallery in the Q[ueen's] chamber' to discuss the possibilities.[59] What emerged was a plan to seize control of the English army in the North. The Earl of Newcastle, the Governor in charge of Prince Charles's household and one of Henrietta's favourites, would be named Lord General. George Goring would be his deputy. Then the army could be brought south to Nottinghamshire, ostensibly to be entertained on their new general's estates, but really to be ready to threaten the English Parliament should Strafford's trial go awry. In that case the Prince of Wales himself would ride at their head, with 1000 court cavaliers. Strafford would be released from the Tower, by subterfuge or violence, Parliament would be dissolved, and the royal family would retire to Portsmouth. There, with the support of 'a good part of the royal army', Charles would resume his proper political power 'and impose laws on those who wished to destroy them' – with the further 'assistance of Ireland and Holland . . . through the aforenamed port'.[60]

As the first week of Strafford's trial ended, Henrietta took the scheme to Charles, who told her he too had a group of plotters planning to approach the army, led by another of her old favourites, Henry Percy. The royal couple were excited, if anxious. While Charles advocated merging the two groups of conspirators, Henrietta feared discovery; if any one man fell, he would bring down all the others, and then 'the King and she would be left with no one in whom they could trust'. In the end Charles prevailed: 'they must risk all for so great a good'.[61]

On the King's orders, the two groups met at Whitehall, but disagreements emerged at once. Charles's men were planning a measure that was, in appearance at least, both peaceful and legal. A petition from the army would ask Parliament to grant the key concessions Charles wanted: the preservation of the bishops in the House of Lords, the continuance of Strafford's Irish army, and the restoration of the impoverished King's income. On this plan, the army's military force was merely to be an unspoken threat behind the petition. When they heard Jermyn's 'extravagant discourses' in favour of a full-scale military coup, Percy's men were appalled and afraid. Such 'sharp and high' measures, 'not having limits either of honour or law', would only bring disaster to King and country alike. To quell their protests and prevent untimely disclosure, Charles was forced to disavow all the plots: 'these ways were vain and foolish, and [he] would think of them no more,' he told Percy and Jermyn.[62] However, in secret Henrietta's plans continued.

Captain Chudleigh, carefully schooled by Jermyn, was sent back north to win the army's loyalty. Meeting secretly with some of the most dissatisfied officers, he told them of Parliament's 'dislike of their letter' of complaint. 'The Parliament was so in love with the Scots that the army was not likely to be paid,' he repeated, while in contrast 'the King would pawn [his] jewels rather than leave the army unpaid'. If they did take action for the King they would find plenty of support: 'the best gentlemen would assist the army, and the French, and 1000 horse from the clergy.'[63] Then Chudleigh produced a letter for the army officers to sign, inviting George Goring to become their lieutenant general. Next day he returned to London. There, finding that Goring had left for Portsmouth, he took his letter instead to Sir John Suckling, another of Henrietta's plotters, who brought Chudleigh 'to kiss the king and queen's hands'. Charles, despite his professions to Henry Percy, was obviously still deeply involved; it was at just this time that court observers noticed that Jermyn had gained 'a strange interest' with the King. However, Chudleigh's letter had only a handful of signatures. A few days later, another meeting of army officers refused to sign a declaration 'of their readiness to serve his Majesty' and tore it up.[64] Despite the court's best efforts, the army would not support the King to the extent that had been hoped. The army plot was therefore set aside.

For the moment, anyway, there seemed no need for armed intervention in London politics. By the beginning of April, the Earl of Strafford's defence was driving his enemies to distraction. Even the House of Commons's most damning accusation – that Strafford had planned to bring his Catholic Irish army to England 'to reduce this Kingdom' – was parried successfully by the Earl in a court session that lasted for ten hours. As the last of the charges were disputed, Charles and Henrietta were full of 'hope ... that this minister so valued and beloved by their Majesties will be saved'.[65]

Saturday 10 April was set for the final summing-up of the prosecution and defence cases. Westminster Hall was packed with eager spectators: ''tis worth a hundred mile riding to see'. But when the session opened, the prosecutors asked to bring in new witnesses to two of the earlier charges. Strafford parried with the request that he too 'might be permitted to produce witnesses' on five of the charges.[66] When the judges agreed, it seemed that the prosecution had merely played into his hands and the trial would go on indefinitely, with the Earl gaining ever more public sympathy. His opponents were aghast: the prosecution must abandon their new evidence at once, so that Strafford could not present his. 'Withdraw! Withdraw!' the Puritan MPs shouted to the prosecution, rising en masse from their seats. 'Adjourn! Adjourn!' cried the anti-Strafford Lords. Determined to ensure the end of the session, they rushed out of the Hall 'in little better than tumultuous manner'. In the pandemonium, Charles and Strafford caught each other's eye. 'The King laughed ... and the Earl of Strafford was so well pleased he could not hide his joy.'[67]

But their victory was short-lived. That same afternoon in the House of Commons an MP produced a ready-prepared Bill against the Earl. The trial in Westminster Hall was clearly failing. Instead, this Bill of Attainder would simply declare Strafford guilty of high treason and require his 'punishment by death'. As the House debated Strafford's case over the following days, Henrietta stepped up her talks with the opposition leaders. Charles himself saw Pym twice, offering him the newly vacated post of Chancellor of the Exchequer.[68] But to no avail. When the Bill was put to the vote, only Lord Digby spoke against it. Almost half the MPs were absent, too frightened of Pym's party and their supporters on the streets of London to attend that day. But the remainder voted resoundingly to pass the Bill: 204 in favour, with just 59 against.[69]

London waited with bated breath to see whether the Lords would follow suit. Charles promised that, even if they did, he would never sign the Bill into law. 'Upon the word of a king you shall not suffer in life, honour, or fortune,' he assured Strafford. However, Strafford's friends had begun to fear 'that his Majesty will be put to a very great strait, and in a manner necessitated to do that in the Earl's case which is so much against his heart'.[70] Popular agitation was titanic. In the streets of London posters went up, listing all the MPs who had voted against the Bill of Attainder, calling them 'the Straffordians, enemies of justice, betrayers of their country'. In response Strafford's friends put out their own list of those who had voted for the Bill, 'the Anabaptists, Jews, and Brownists of the House of Commons'.[71] A petition to Parliament, said to bear 20,000 signatures, demanded Strafford's death. Mobs assembled outside London's Catholic ambassadors' chapels, attempting to 'force the doors'. The City authorities notified Parliament that they could not pay for supporting the northern armies until Strafford was dead; the people were determined 'not to contribute before they obtain this satisfaction'.[72]

Once again Charles and Henrietta began to think of military action. Secretly Charles sent 'a sum of money to York to be distributed to the troops quartered there, with the idea of winning their favour'. Henrietta reopened her negotiations for a papal loan, urging Rossetti to persuade Rome to accept Charles's promise of toleration for English Catholics rather than the King's own conversion. Charles already had enough men to stand out, the Queen confided; all he needed was money.[73] Charles talked openly of going in person 'to take command of his army', ostensibly against the Scots, but everyone could see he was readying for action against 'the more seditious of the English'. At Whitehall, Henrietta was packing up, ready to join Goring at Portsmouth 'in the event of fresh disturbances'. Her gold and silver plate was loaded into crates to accompany her, perhaps even as far as France, where it could be pawned or sold to pay for military action.[74] There were also secret plans for rescuing Strafford. His secretary had a ship on the Thames, ready to take the Earl to Ireland, and Sir John Suckling had recruited 100 men, enough to seize control of the Tower and set Strafford free.[75]

Meanwhile in the House of Lords the debates on the Bill of

Attainder continued 'in long discussions and dangerous altercations'. Many peers resented the Commons' interference in their own privileges, passing judgement on one of their own – ill-feeling that Charles did 'all in his power to encourage'.[76] Amidst vicious recriminations, crucial pieces of evidence against Strafford disappeared; when one turned up again, a letter 't' had been added, so that Strafford's alleged plot to use his Irish army 'here' in England had become a perfectly innocuous plan to use it 'there' in Scotland or Ireland.[77] Charles's newly won-over opposition lords advocated leniency towards Strafford, arguing that Parliament could gain any concessions they wanted from the King in return for allowing him to live. However, the other opposition lords were sure that they could never trust Charles's assurances, nor Strafford's promise to retire from politics, if acquitted; Charles's reliance on his old minister was simply too strong. 'Stone dead hath no fellow,' the Earl of Essex argued.[78]

On Saturday 1 May, Charles himself delivered a speech to Parliament. Presenting his own evidence in Strafford's favour, he pitted his word as King against the prosecution witnesses. 'You know I must have part in the judgment,' Charles reminded his auditors: any Bill they passed would need his approval. And so, he urged, they must 'find a way to satisfy justice, and not press me against my conscience, considering what inconveniences may follow. I should do much to comply with both Houses, but I must let you know that no fear or respect whatsoever shall make me go against my conscience.' This was Charles's ultimatum: if Parliament passed this Bill they would precipitate a confrontation with unimaginable consequences. At the same time he offered a compromise. 'Although I cannot find my Lord of Strafford guilty of high treason, yet I cannot hold him clear of misdemeanours,' and to this lesser charge Charles would accede willingly: 'therefore you may proceed to condemn him'.[79]

Amidst the furore the fourteen-year-old Prince William of Orange had arrived in London. Despite the political tumult he was received with great ceremony. In Henrietta's privy chamber at Whitehall he was greeted by his soon-to-be brother-in-law, Charles, Prince of Wales.

Just approaching his eleventh birthday, Charles was still a serious
boy –

> So wise, grave, aged, he in youth appears,
> As if his age had twice out-strip his years –

but he was also a notably athletic and martial one. Taking an eager
interest in his father's wars, he had used up several barrels of gunpowder
and match in his artillery practice while the King was away in the
North. He also took fencing lessons from his Governor, the Earl of
Newcastle, one of the foremost swordsmen of his day. Dark haired
and dark eyed, the boy was, people hoped, another 'valiant Black
Prince': 'that brave man of men', who had 'made France shake'.[80]

Accompanying Prince Charles that day was his younger brother,
James Duke of York, a seven-year-old of boundless energy:

> He hates dull idleness, and loves to be
> In action, such as fits his high degree.

A portrait of this time shows the short-haired, chubby-faced James
dressed in specialist tennis kit, swinging his racket in front of a
watching crowd.[81] But now, as they conducted the Dutch prince into
Henrietta's withdrawing chamber, the two boys carried themselves
with the smooth etiquette of accomplished courtiers.

The King and Queen received William 'with great affection',
although it was noted that Henrietta did not allow him to kiss her,
on the grounds of his republican origin.[82] William, however, was
unperturbed. Eager to meet Princess Mary – 'he speaks of nothing but
of seeing his bride' – he set out that afternoon to visit her at Somerset
House. Mary too denied him a kiss: she had expected to marry the
Spanish heir himself and was as unhappy as her mother at her lover's
lowly birth.[83] Day after day William came back, bringing presents of
'rich jewels' for his fiancée and her family, coming and going at
Somerset House through a garden door, to which he had been given
a key.[84] Soon the young couple were beginning to seem more suited –

'he is as good as he is pretty, which makes him more deserve so good a princess' – and William gained his reward. Nine-year-old Mary – 'mild, modest, affable ... discreet and debonnaire' – began to show him favour, 'and with her mother's permission has sealed their affection with a kiss'.[85]

On Sunday 2 May, the day after Charles issued his ultimatum to Parliament, the couple were married at Whitehall. Standing side by side, the two children made a handsome couple: William with pink-flushed cheeks and long curling brown hair, every inch the elegant cavalier with a gold sword at his side, while Mary, half a head smaller, was all in white, with ringlets and pearls in her hair, and the huge diamond brooch William had given her clasped on her breast.[86] There had been no time to prepare the usual grand festivities. Instead, around 2 p.m., the royal family sat down to dinner in the King's withdrawing chamber 'with the greatest privacy that might be'. That evening the Dutch ambassadors joined them to 'see the married couple bedded together'. For the newly-wed children, it was a mere formality, designed to ensure that the marriage could not be annulled; in the half-hour they spent in bed together, nothing more was exchanged than a few kisses. Then William spent 'the rest of the night in the bedchamber of the King of Great Britain who looks on him most fondly'.[87]

Next day the political maelstrom recommenced. Outside the House of Lords that morning a 'tumultuous' crowd was waiting: 'many thousands of the most substantial of the citizens'. The Earl of Strafford was a traitor, they shouted, a public enemy, and he must die. 'Justice, justice!' they yelled each time a lord arrived for the day's session, jostling those suspected of opposing the Bill 'with great rudeness and insolence', and 'threatening the most violent measures against the state and against His Majesty's own person and all the royal House' if Strafford was not 'condemned to death'.[88]

Meanwhile the House of Commons, 'in great passion and fury' at Charles's speech – 'the most unparalleled breach of [parliamentary] privilege that had ever happened' – reaffirmed their belief in Strafford's guilt and in the existence of 'some great design ... by the Papists to subvert and overthrow this kingdom'. To deal with the national emergency, all must join together to sign a 'protestation', swearing, much as the Scots Covenanters had done three years earlier, 'to maintain and defend ... the true, reformed, protestant religion as also the power and privilege of Parliament, [and] the lawful rights and liberties of the subjects'.[89]

Once again, John Pym fuelled the MPs' Catholic conspiracy terrors, beginning a series of dramatic revelations. He had known of the court's plotting with the northern army for over a month now. George Goring had betrayed 'the main of the business', either from real disapproval, as he gave Parliament to understand, or from his fierce ambition, 'uncontrolled by any fear of god or man', which had been bitterly disappointed when he was not appointed lieutenant general of the northern army.[90] Pym and his inner circle had kept the knowledge to themselves, waiting for the perfect moment to reveal it. Now, as the Lords vacillated over the Bill of Attainder, it was time to step up the pressure.

There were 'secret practices' at court, Pym announced on Wednesday 5 May, 'to discontent the army with the proceedings of Parliament; and to engage them in some design of dangerous consequence to the state'. His charges were vague as yet. 'The Parliament hath not openly declared what the plot was,' reported one of the Scots commissioners in London.[91] Nevertheless, Pym had said quite enough to alarm his parliamentary colleagues. A committee should be set up at once to investigate, Lords and Commons agreed. Suspects must be apprehended. The King should be asked to ensure that 'no servant of his Majesty, the Queen, or the Prince, may depart the Kingdom, or otherwise absent himself' – a request Charles 'very willing granted'. Most importantly, a new Bill must be passed to prevent 'this present Parliament from adjourning, proroguing, or dissolving without the consent of both Houses'; in effect, the Parliament was to become 'perpetual'. Drawn up overnight, the Bill went through two of its three necessary readings the next day, such was the urgency of the MPs.[92]

Meanwhile the courtier-plotters fled, despite Charles's assurances to Parliament. Henry Percy left Whitehall at once, with a passport that Henrietta had obtained from Charles. Jermyn, who was out in London enjoying himself, received an urgent note in the Queen's own hand, warning him not to return to the Palace; he must go at once to Portsmouth, and then escape to France. By the morning of Thursday 6 May, when the Commons summoned their suspects for questioning, Davenant and Suckling had also disappeared.[93] Henrietta too intended 'to take a journey to Portsmouth', the MPs heard. On their urgings, two lords were sent to Whitehall to ask the King 'for the deferring of the Queen's journey'. They were concerned, they said, at 'what danger her person may be in, if she go there'.[94] Then the Lords began the preliminary voting on the Earl of Strafford's guilt.

At Whitehall, Charles and Henrietta were in a state of distraction. Parliament had accused Jermyn not just of political crimes but also of 'too great an intimacy with the queen'. It was much more than an attack on Henrietta's honour: a queen's adultery was treason, and two of Henry VIII's wives had been executed for just that crime. Now, 'in an unprecedented manner', parliamentary agents went rummaging through Jermyn's rooms in Henrietta's apartments at Whitehall, 'without any respect for the place', in hopes alike of seizing incriminating papers and of giving further 'offence to Her Majesty'.[95] All chance of Strafford's escape was past. Parliament had reinforced the Tower with 400 new troops; the city's gates and the banks of the Thames were strongly guarded too.

With Jermyn and the others gone, the royal couple felt truly alone, 'without servants or counsel'.[96] However, they had no thought of giving up. Henrietta was born of a father who did not know the meaning of fear, she said, and from a nation that never retreated. On her behalf Father Philip made a last great appeal to France. 'Can your good Cardinal or can your King suffer a daughter of France with her children to be affronted?' he demanded. Could they allow England and Scotland to join together in one state, 'as seems to be the present design', which would surely 'be prejudicial to France'?[97] Meanwhile Henrietta's packing continued faster than ever. By Friday 7 May, her carriages were standing ready for her departure, but the French ambassador urged her not to go. Flight would only bring on the dangers she was desperate to prevent: the destruction of the King's last vestiges of power and descent into armed conflict. Henrietta remained in London, at least for the present.[98]

That same morning new revelations came to Parliament. Troops were massing in France, doubtless 'designed for Portsmouth'. The MPs agreed that this 'design' and the courtiers' plot 'to seduce the King's army' were 'united together' in one terrible master plan.[99] Public opinion was enraged at 'the greatest treason ... since the [Gun]powder plot', with 'Jesuits and priests conspiring with ill ministers of state, to destroy our religion'. Rumours spread like wildfire. The Scots were to be paid off and sent home, it was said, while the English army marched on Parliament, and the court brought in French and Irish forces 'for their assistance'.[100] Henrietta's part was supposedly to supervise the French invasion and 'to this end apparently the Queen was going to Portsmouth'. There was even a story that Charles and Henrietta had agreed to hand over Portsmouth to Louis XIII, in return for ten French regiments.[101]

Profoundly alarmed, Parliament ordered a deputation to be sent to Portsmouth 'forthwith'. They were to question the port's governor, George Goring, and send him back to Parliament if he seemed at all suspect. Then they must raise the local militias to secure the port and prepare the ships 'for the defending of that town' under 'commanders of trust and fidelity'.[102] With this arranged, the House of Lords turned once more to the Bill of Attainder. Many peers were absent, afraid 'of having their brains beaten out' by the riotous crowds outside; of the eighty lords who had sat in Strafford's trial a month previously, no more than forty-six were present.[103] Earlier voting had already established that Strafford was guilty of the Commons' charges. Now legal counsel gave their 'unanimous' opinion that these crimes did indeed amount to high treason.[104] Then came the final vote. Charles's traditional supporters, the Anglican bishops, abstained en masse, happy to be persuaded by Laud's old enemy, the Puritan Bishop of Lincoln, that, as they had not been present at the trial, they should not vote now. And the opposition peers whom Charles and Henrietta had worked so hard to win over did nothing either. Even so, the Bill of Attainder was passed by just 26 votes to 19.[105] But it had passed. Now only the King's assent was needed.

At the Tower, Strafford was reduced to 'utter despair'.[106] Charles could not afford to save him, he was sure; the 'evils which may happen' were too great. Earlier that week, as the riotous crowds demanded his death, he had urged Charles 'to pass this Bill' and so regain 'that blessed agreement which God, I trust, shall ever establish between you and your subjects'. 'Sir,' the Earl wrote, 'to a willing man there is no injury done; and, as by God's grace, I forgive all the world, . . . so, Sir, to you I can give the life of this world with all the cheerfulness imaginable.' Secretly he had still hoped the Lords 'would perhaps not have the effrontery to put him to death'.[107] Now that hope proved vain.

At Whitehall, Henrietta was 'very angry', while Charles maintained a surface calm. 'The King eats and sleeps well still,' the news reported. When a deputation arrived from the Lords next morning, asking him to assent to the Bill of Attainder, he told them to wait. 'At four o'clock this afternoon', he said, he would address the entire Parliament.[108] Meanwhile the Lords put their time to good use, voting through the Bill prohibiting the 'adjourning, proroguing, or dissolving of this present Parliament'. That afternoon they presented Charles with this as well, 'for the royal assent'. Again Charles asked for time. He would give his answer in Parliament 'on Monday morning, at ten o'clock'.[109]

A nightmarish twenty-four hours followed for the royal family at Whitehall. Outside the Palace a mob of thousands gathered, crying 'Justice, justice' and making 'great and insolent threats and expressions what they would do if it were not speedily granted'. The courtiers were horrified, expecting 'the multitude would come the next day, and pull down Whitehall, and God knows what might become of the King himself'.[110] The whole city was in 'confusion and entirely under arms', it was said; Parliament was summoning troops from the county militias 'with all speed', ready to 'undertake any kind of audacious enterprise against the royal persons'. Amidst rumours of a popular rising to massacre papists, the court's Catholics sought out Henrietta's priests and confessed their sins; then the Capuchins went into hiding in safe houses out in the City. On Charles's orders, guards were stationed on all the staircases. Panic-stricken courtiers secreted their jewels under their clothes, ready for flight.[111] When word came that the crowd was talking of moving on to attack Marie de' Medici at St James's Palace, Charles ordered 100 musketeers from the Middlesex militia to defend her, but they refused to go.[112]

Meanwhile Charles was 'in great anguish', battling with his conscience.[113] On Sunday morning he consulted his Privy Council about how 'to suppress these traitorous riots', but, terrified of Parliament and its mob, the councillors only pressed him to pass the Bill of Attainder. 'There was no other way to preserve himself and his posterity,' they said; 'he ought to be more tender of the safety of the kingdom than of any one person, how innocent soever', adding that the violence threatening him now would be 'a just excuse for whatsoever he should do'. When Charles objected that their proposals were 'in a diameter contrary to his conscience', they suggested he consult his bishops, 'who, they made no question, would better inform his conscience'.

Accordingly, Charles summoned in several leading churchmen. His conscience prevented him from condemning an innocent man, he told them – to which John Williams, Bishop of Lincoln, responded with a long speech, full of the fine distinctions so beloved by seventeenth-century academics and churchmen. Charles's 'public conscience as a king might . . . oblige him to do that which was against his private conscience as a man', he said. 'The conscience of a king to preserve his kingdom, the conscience of a husband to preserve his wife, the conscience of a father to preserve his children': all these outweighed Charles's own private conscience. In fact, Williams concluded, Charles must pass the Bill of Attainder 'for conscience sake'.[114] Just one man spoke out against William's clever equivocation. Archbishop Laud's old friend, William Juxon, Bishop of London, told Charles he should not pass the Bill 'while his conscience scrupled at it as murdering the innocent' – a 'heroic' lone voice, Charles later acknowledged.[115]

Still the King held out. After all, it was not just a matter of his conscience. There was his word too, given to the House of Lords just eight days earlier, that he would not sign the Bill of Attainder. And

Strafford himself, having recovered from his despair, was urging Charles to approach Parliament once more with defences of the Earl and offers of compromise. He could even, Strafford suggested, bring out his last letter, releasing Charles from his promise to save his life, in hopes that that would win Parliament's sympathy.[116] But with the crowd still baying for justice outside, Charles could see no hope in that. Wavering now, he prayed and looked at Strafford's fateful letter once more. It was the Earl's final undoing. When the King's advisers saw the letter, they argued that 'this free consent of his own clearly absolved the King from any scruple that could remain with him'. Charles need not authorise Strafford's death in person, they proposed; he could simply sign a commission appointing some lords to pass the Bill of Attainder for him. This way 'his own hand was not in it' – a small sop to his precious conscience.[117] At last, around 9 p.m. on Sunday evening, Charles caved in. It was not to save himself, he said, with tears in his eyes. 'If my own person only were in danger, I would gladly venture it to save Lord Strafford's life; but seeing my wife, children, and all my kingdom are concerned in it, I am forced to give way.' Charles felt utterly worthless and defeated: his conscience was abandoned; his honour shot; his promise perjured; his power as King proved naught. 'My Lord of Strafford's condition is more happy than mine,' he said.[118]

On Monday 10 May, Charles's commission of Lords gave 'the royal assent' to both of the Bills, 'one for the continuance of the Parliament, the other for the execution of the Earl of Strafford on Wednesday following'.[119] 'Now we have done our work,' an MP shouted as he left the House. On Tuesday the angry crowds were gone and the London streets were quiet once more: 'the mouth of the people is stopped.'[120] That day Charles made one last attempt to save his friend. The Prince of Wales carried the King's message to the Lords, asking that Strafford might live out his days 'in a close imprisonment', to be executed only if he attempted to escape or 'meddle in any sort of public business'. Charles hoped his almost-eleven-year-old son would win the peers' hearts, but in vain.[121]

On Wednesday 12 May, around 11 a.m., the Earl of Strafford set out for the place of execution. At first he had been angry: 'put not your trust in princes, nor in the sons of men, for in them there is no salvation,' he is supposed to have said. Now he was resigned, forgiving his enemies and repenting his sins: 'never such a white soul returned to his maker,' reported James Ussher, Archbishop of Armagh, who had spent the last two days with him.[122] On Tower Hill people had been arriving all night, creating a seething crowd around the scaffold estimated at 200,000 strong. The Lieutenant of the Tower advised that Strafford go in his coach to the scaffold to avoid being torn apart, but the Earl would have none of it. 'I care not how I die, whether by the hand of the executioner or by the madness and fury of the people; if that may give them better content it is all one to me.'[123] So they set off on foot. Archbishop Laud, aged sixty-seven and himself a prisoner in the Tower, stood at his open window to bid farewell at a distance to his old friend. While the Earl knelt on the ground, the archbishop raised his trembling hands to give his final blessing but, overcome by emotion, he fainted before the words had passed his lips. 'Farewell, my lord,' Strafford said, 'and God protect your innocency!'[124]

Beyond the Tower's gates, the crowd parted in silence to make a narrow passage for the Earl. Dressed in black, carrying his hat in his hand, he walked erect, like a general marching to victory, it was said, accompanied by a small band of friends. From the scaffold he addressed the crowd: 'I do freely forgive all the world ... I am not the first man that has suffered in this kind, it is a common portion that befalls men in this life; righteous judgment shall be hereafter; here we are subject to error and misjudging one another.' Having said farewell to his friends, Strafford knelt and prayed. When his brother wept, he offered consolation; at last he would have rest, he said; 'no thoughts of envy, no ... cares for the King, the state, or myself shall interrupt this sleep'.[125] Refusing the cloth the executioner offered for covering his eyes, Strafford knelt by the block and spoke for one last time: 'I do solemnly protest before God I am not guilty of that great crime laid to my charge.' He prayed again, then placed his head on the block. The executioner raised his axe, Strafford stretched out his arms to show that he was ready and then, invisible to most of the crowd, his head 'was severed from his body at a blow'.[126] As the executioner lifted the dripping head, the crowd went wild in a 'universal rejoicing'. 'His head is off! His head is off!' – the news went out through London and into the country. As darkness came, bonfires were lit and candles put in every window; those without a flame were smashed by the crowd. With Strafford gone, 'all should be well', the people trusted.[127]

Meanwhile at Whitehall the royal couple mourned the passing of a hero. His last moments had displayed 'the beauty of his mind and his admirable steadfastness', according to Henrietta's earnest tribute. 'The King suffered greatly from sadness, the Queen shed many tears,' a friend of hers later related. But it was not just for Strafford that they grieved. Everyone could see now that Charles's authority was gone; he was 'a king of foolish kindness, neither loved nor feared, without esteem, without respect, without obedience'.[128] In their place Charles felt only 'the hatred of the people, which is even stronger against the queen'. As the parliamentary investigations into the army plot sought out the involvement of 'every person without exception, which means their Majesties themselves, if they appear guilty', it was clear that there were 'secret intentions to lead these princes to the last calamity'. Charles and Henrietta's names were being rendered 'utterly odious to the people', it was said, all as part of the 'ambitious designs' of the Puritans, 'whose sole profession is to sweep away every kind of superior power'. It was this, perhaps more than Strafford's death, that left the King suffering 'the tortures of the deepest affliction'. In signing the Bill of Attainder against Strafford, Henrietta later said, Charles had signed his own death warrant too.[129]

10

Shame and Fear

That summer of 1641 the last of the royal couple's confidants were wrenched from them. Rossetti fled hurriedly from England, after being summoned for questioning by the Commons. Marie de' Medici soon followed, when Parliament blamed her for having 'instilled evil counsels into her daughter' and demanded she 'leave this kingdom' at once.[1] It was a final parting for Henrietta: her mother would die the following year in Cologne, still scheming futilely against Richelieu.

Meanwhile the MPs pushed forward their 'Ten Propositions' for reforming the royal government. Parliament's men must be placed at Charles and Henrietta's courts; the Queen's Capuchins were to be 'dissolved and sent out of the kingdom'; while Prince Charles's education must be confided to 'persons of public trust, and well-affected in religion'. As the Commons began to implement their constitutional reforms, Henrietta feared Charles would 'soon lose his liberty as well as his crown'.[2]

Still the investigations into the army plot continued, now singling out Henrietta as the real mastermind behind it. 'We were sold to the French by the queen,' one MP wrote in his diary.[3] Henrietta's courtiers were interrogated; her letters to the Continent were seized and opened;

her nefarious deeds swelled by 'malignant invention'. She spent those summer months in 'the deepest affliction', with the whole court 'in a state of anxious expectation' as Parliament searched through its old records to find precedents for 'what was done with other queens in like circumstances'.[4]

By July, Henrietta was desperate to leave England. She hoped to get away to the Netherlands, ostensibly to drink the waters at Spa for her health, and to take Princess Mary to join her husband at The Hague. But her real aim, as Parliament could see, was to gain support for her husband. 'Great quantity of treasure, in jewels, plate and ready money' had been packed up, 'to be conveyed away with the Queen': far more than she would ever need to cover her own travelling expenses. Even the Crown jewels were to go, the Commons had heard.[5] They rushed to block her, alleging the risk of her being corrupted by the 'great number of English fugitives' already overseas, including army plotters and others 'who, by their late designs and practices, are known to be full of malice to this state'. Henrietta resented Parliament's interference, telling the Venetian ambassador that 'she was prepared to obey the king, but not 400 of his subjects, as this did not befit her spirit or her birth.' However, in the end, as Charles presented 'strong arguments' and Parliament stepped up the pressure, she had little choice but to comply.[6] 'I swear to you,' she wrote to her sister Christine, Duchess of Savoy,

> I am almost mad at the sudden change in my fortune ... Imagine my condition at seeing the King deprived of power, the Catholics persecuted, the priests scattered, our loyal servants removed from us and pursued for their life for having endeavoured to serve the King, and me kept here like a prisoner, forbidden even to follow the King who is leaving for Scotland, and with no one in the world to whom I can tell my afflictions, and knowing withal that I must not show any resentment at it ... The King leaves the day after tomorrow if the parliament does not restrain him by force; they threaten to. God help us: we have need of it.[7]

Charles's trip to Scotland was the couple's great new bid for power. He was going to meet the Parliament assembling in Edinburgh and ratify the peace treaty that had finally been agreed after ten months of talks: the Scottish army would withdraw and disband. Then, Charles hoped, the English Parliament would 'fall flat' without their greatest supporters. He and Henrietta had even greater visions: of Charles winning the Scots over and returning south victorious, 'accompanied by the forces of Scotland, and by the remains of the English army stationed at York'.[8]

Terrified of losing their power, the Commons strove to prevent the King's departure, talking of massed demonstrations, 20,000 strong, or even of deposing the King, perhaps to 'set up a democratic government'.[9] In the event Charles departed unmolested. As he travelled north, his hopes and Parliament's fears seemed confirmed. The Scots army at Newcastle was 'full of obedience and zeal to his person', and in Edinburgh he was welcomed 'with an incredible joy and acclamation of all this people': such a demonstration 'was never seen before', he wrote delightedly to Henrietta.[10] As the session of Parliament commenced, Charles took 'infinite pains' to please his subjects and 'fulfil absolutely the expectations of everybody'.[11]

Meanwhile Henrietta managed affairs in England, corresponding with the King, as well as issuing orders to Charles's Privy Council and his new secretary of state, Sir Edward Nicholas. She organised meetings of loyal supporters and gathered intelligence; Lucy Countess of Carlisle in particular brought her information and even written papers collected from Pym and other friends she had among the opposition leaders.[12] As popular feeling swung back against Parliament during its adjournment that autumn, with people complaining at its new taxes and its recent 'unusual' actions, Henrietta worked to win back disaffected opposition members, several of whom, she noted, 'evinced a desire to return to their duty'.[13] Among them was London's mayor who, like other wealthy citizens, was tired of Parliament's 'long continuance', which many believed was impoverishing the entire capital. With his help Henrietta now planned to put on a magnificent, crowd-pleasing pageant for her husband's return. She urged Charles to arrive in

London before Parliament met once more, but the King's Scottish business was still unfinished when Parliament reconvened 'with great ardour' on 20 October.[14]

At once the MPs resumed their anti-Catholic witch-hunt, announcing the discovery of 'a fresh conspiracy against the liberty of the state'. A committee was appointed, and Pym soon presented its report, showing that secret Catholic forces were massing for 'some wicked design ... still in hatching'. Henrietta's confessor, Father Philip, was a 'dangerous person', corresponding with English court fugitives overseas and contriving 'new and mischievous plots'. The Prince of Wales was at risk, staying with his mother at Oatlands. Parliament ordered the boy's new governor, the Marquess of Hertford, to move him back to Richmond Palace and never let him out of his sight.[15]

Just two weeks into the parliamentary session, the MPs' worst fears seemed confirmed when terrible news reached London: of a 'general rebellion of the Irish Papists ... and a design of cutting off all the Protestants in Ireland; and seizing all the King's forts there'. Ten thousand Catholics were up in arms, it was said, and as the days passed the news grew 'worse and worse'. The Catholics controlled at least nine counties and were besieging Dublin.[16] The rebels' own statement, 'that they remain obedient subjects of his Majesty and have taken action with the sole object of securing liberty of conscience and restoring the legitimate authority of their lawful sovereign,' made it seem that the uprising had been masterminded at the English court. Henrietta was again a chief suspect, and soon Parliament was seizing and opening foreign mail in search of evidence.[17] Father Philip was summoned to the House of Lords for questioning. When he said that the Bible he was given to swear his oath on 'was not a true Bible', he was sent to the Tower. Every day in London there were outcries about new Catholic plots. There was even a wild story of 108 Catholics being enrolled to assassinate 108 Puritan Lords and MPs, followed by a Catholic uprising.[18]

Despite the turmoil and with the mayor's help, Henrietta succeeded, after weeks of 'very great preparations', in staging a triumph for Charles's return to London on 25 November.[19] The streets were lined with City dignitaries. Huge crowds cheered, and Charles, on horseback beside his eldest son, thanked them 'by gesture and speech, thus causing a renewal of the shouts of welcome'. 'Long live the King!' they cried.[20] The royals and their accompanying lords and ladies were feasted at the Guildhall, where Charles promised popular measures for the City's 'honour, profit, and quiet'. Then, through the winter dark, the royal party rode by torchlight to Whitehall, 'always amid the same shouts and acclamations'. Truly it seemed that the people, 'grown tired of so much violence, are contemplating a return to their old loyalty and devotion'.[21]

Flushed with his success in Scotland and his grand re-entry into his capital, Charles was ready to confront his enemies. The very next day he dismissed the parliamentarian Earls of Essex and Holland from their command over the London militia. He also removed the guard that Parliament had appointed for its own safety during his absence. When the Commons protested, he set his own men to watch over them, who were soon threatening to fire their muskets on the crowds there.[22] For months the Commons had been preparing a 'Grand Remonstrance', demanding yet again that the King dismiss his 'evil counsellors' and abolish the 'immoderate power' wielded by the Anglican bishops 'which they have perniciously abused'. On 1 December they at last presented it to Charles, but he was not intimidated. After picking holes in their accusations and laughing at their presumption, he told them he would consider their requests at his leisure.[23] Heartened by the King's tough stance, the loyalist party at court now talked big. There would 'shortly be a great change in this kingdom', one of Henrietta's Catholic friends announced. Then everyone would see whether Charles was indeed 'a king or no king'.[24]

The Commons were infuriated. They would 'live and die together in defence of the Protestant cause', they swore. Command of the nation's armed forces must be taken out of the King's hands. Charles and Henrietta must publicly proclaim 'the rebels in Ireland to be traitors', to prove the Queen did not 'secretly . . . encourage the rebels'.[25] But Charles remained on the offensive. Ever since Parliament's recess, many loyalist MPs had stayed at home, afraid of the opposition's power. Now the King ordered the 210 absent members to take their seats in January. Then, on 22 December, to clinch his control of London, he replaced the parliamentarian Lieutenant of the Tower with a loyal army officer, recently returned from the North: Colonel Thomas Lunsford. Next day he sent the Commons a defiant answer to their 'Grand Remonstrance'. He saw no sign of the 'corruption in religion' that they alleged, for 'no Church can be found upon the Earth that professeth the true religion with more purity of doctrine than the Church of England doth'. As for evil counsellors, he declared, 'we know not any of our Council to whom the character set forth in the petition can belong', but if the Commons could bring 'a particular charge and sufficient proofs' against any man, they could have 'justice of the law'.[26]

The Commons were more alarmed than ever, protesting that Colonel Lunsford was 'a debauched quarrelsome man, very desperate, and fit to execute any dangerous design'. His appointment proved that there must be 'some dangerous design in hand against us' and they agreed to petition the King for his removal. In the meantime they asked Lunsford's superior, the parliamentarian Earl of Newport, Constable of the Tower, to take personal 'custody and guard of that place'.[27] This the King would not allow. On Christmas Eve he dismissed Newport from his post, bringing the conflict to flashpoint. Hostile mobs turned out, protesting against the continued presence of Lunsford. Order would never be restored while the colonel remained at his post, the mayor warned the King; the apprentices might even try to storm the Tower. Afraid now, Charles dismissed Lunsford. However, his new appointee, Sir John Byron, was just such another loyal officer, and 'little better accepted' by the angry citizens.[28]

Charles's aggressive actions were fast losing him the popular support that had mustered on his first return to London. When Parliament reconvened after the briefest of Christmas breaks, there was a noisy crowd at its doors once more. 'No Bishops! No Popish Lords!' they shouted.[29] It was a powerful rallying cry. For years the bishops had been the focus of popular fear and anger, hated for enforcing Laud's church reforms and widely perceived as 'Papist' – a charge not so far from the truth, in many cases. Six months earlier, news had gone around that one had secretly converted, after he refused to swear an oath of loyalty to 'the doctrine and discipline' of the Church of England.[30] And now, Pym claimed, it was these royal supporters in the House of Lords who had prevented the peers from joining the Commons' appeal for Lunsford's dismissal.[31] As the Lords arrived for that day's session, the crowd's mood was fierce. Soon there was an attack on John Williams, the former Bishop of Lincoln, whom Charles had recently made Archbishop of York in gratitude for his support for episcopacy. Then Lunsford himself joined the fray, at the head of a party of disbanded army officers. 'Chasing the citizens' round Westminster Hall with drawn swords, they wounded some of them, then beat a swift retreat to Whitehall. But still the crowds remained. Next day they moved on to Westminster Abbey, intending 'to pull down the organs and altar' and destroy the royal tombs. Here Archbishop Williams and his servants fought the rioters off; 'divers of the citizens were hurt, but none killed'.[32]

Amidst the violence, London's tradesmen shut up their shops and gentlemen walked the streets well armed, 'as in time of open hostility'. Charles called out the militia: if the people refused to go home, the soldiers were to 'kill such of them as shall persist in their tumultuary and seditious ways'.[33] Even so, the day after the assault on Westminster Abbey, the mob appeared outside Whitehall Palace, just as they had done for Strafford's attainder, seven months previously. This time Charles was prepared. His courtiers were under orders to wear their swords, and they were reinforced by numerous officers from the disbanded northern army, who had 'offered their services to his Majesty' and formed an unofficial bodyguard.[34] As the crowd approached the Palace's great gateway, carrying clubs and swords and shouting 'No Bishops, no Papist Lords', the defenders drew their swords and went over the railings towards them. To these men the yelling mob was merely 'the scum of the people' but they had no desire to kill them; it would only provoke 'more dangerous disturbances'. So they slashed with the flats or blades of their swords, rather than thrusting with the points, wounding forty or fifty, but still killing none.[35]

Whitehall was safe, but for how long? As rumours came in that the City's apprentices were mustering, 10,000 strong, 'exasperated' at the wounds received by their fellows, Charles increased his guard of army officers to 120 and ordered the local militia to watch 'night and day' under their command.[36] A guardhouse was hurriedly erected just outside Whitehall's great gatehouse, while some 400 or 500 more gentlemen gave in their names and addresses, ready to be called out at a moment's notice. Daunted, the apprentices stayed away from Whitehall, although angry crowds still ruled the rest of London. Charles's bishops were now too frightened to attend the House of Lords, having been 'violently menaced, affronted, and assaulted, by multitudes of people . . . and put in danger of their lives'. Archbishop Williams and eleven other bishops presented a 'protestation' to the King and the Lords, demanding that all legislation passed by Parliament during their 'forced and violent absence' must be declared 'null and of none effect'.[37] It was a bold bid by these King's men, not only 'to overthrow all Acts passed', but also, if order could not be restored, 'to cause a dissolution' of Parliament itself. However, Pym's party were not so easily outmanoeuvred. The bishops' protestation was 'high treason . . . endeavouring to subvert the being of Parliament', the Commons charged, and the archbishop and his eleven fellows were arrested. Far from aiding Charles's cause, their protestation had merely lost him twelve votes in the Lords, at which he was 'greatly perturbed'.[38]

Once again his enemies were seizing the initiative. Pym whipped up the MPs' alarm at the warlike preparations at Whitehall to a frenzy, alleging 'that there was a plot for the destroying of the House of Commons'. Next day the House asked the King for a guard from London's militia, commanded by the Earl of Essex: a parliamentarian military force to rival his bodyguard at Whitehall. Unwilling to provoke further popular violence, Charles played for time: the MPs' petition contained 'so many particulars', he replied, that 'he could not remember what was delivered . . . and therefore desired to have it in writing'.[39]

Even his delaying tactics could be turned to the opposition's advantage. Hurriedly submitting their written petition to the King, the

Commons appointed a committee to receive his reply next morning: New Year's Day, when Parliament would not be sitting. Yet this was no ordinary committee meeting. It would assemble in the City, where the apprentices could be relied on to protect it. All the MPs were invited to attend, 'and all that will come are to have voices at this Committee'. In effect, avoiding the constraint that Parliament must meet at Westminster, where Charles's writ had summoned it, the committee would become a secret meeting of the Commons, with none of its business recorded in the House's official journal. And the MPs were given the broadest of remits: if no reply came from Charles, they must 'consider what then shall be fit to be done for the safety of the King, the Kingdom, and this House'. And to advance this work, they were given 'power to send for parties, witnesses, papers, and records'.[40]

Early on 1 January 1642, the MPs marched 'publicly' through the City's streets to the Guildhall. Going 'supplied with arms', as if there really was 'a plot against the liberty of parliament', they won 'the affection of the ignorant people'. There is no first-hand record of what took place inside the Guildhall. Even the diarist-MP Sir Symonds D'Ewes, normally so meticulous in his recording, is silent on the business that day. But word leaked out, nonetheless. When no message arrived from Charles, the MPs' discussion ranged widely 'into the most important matters'. They considered the King's recent actions and his obvious resentment against them, although they still could not believe he was deliberately working against them; 'evil counsellors' must, therefore, be to blame. Yet every courtier of significance was already gone: executed, imprisoned or fled abroad. Only Henrietta remained. And so at last 'they persuaded themselves that the actions of the King and his resentments proceeded from the counsels of the Queen'. She was the one who must now be charged with high treason, for 'conspiring against the public liberty' and for 'secret intelligence in the rebellion in Ireland'.[41]

When word reached Charles, he resolved at once on pre-emptive action. Other ministers he had been prepared to sacrifice, but he would not lose Henrietta. On Monday 3 January, when the MPs returned to the Commons House once more, he struck. As the session opened, his Lord Keeper and Attorney General arrived in the House of Lords to charge six leading opposition members of the Parliament with high treason. One, Viscount Mandeville, was there in the Lords; the other five, including John Pym, were MPs in the Commons. All had been involved in the move to impeach Henrietta, but this was not what the King accused them of.[42]

Charles had planned this move for a long time. Returning from Scotland in November, he had brought back evidence that these same parliamentary leaders had encouraged the Scots armies to invade England. Yet back then, even as the mob took control of London's streets, Charles had hesitated, fortifying himself at Whitehall instead of, as the French ambassador put it, putting the City 'into flames and blood' as any other European monarch would have done. It was Charles's fatal flaw, many observers agreed: his 'tenderness and compassion', his excessive 'clemency', his unwillingness to resort to violence until it was too late. One commentator likened him to Julius Caesar, who had been 'merciful to such an extent that he had been forced to repent of it.[43] However, with Henrietta in danger Charles was forced to act. The Attorney General presented seven charges of treason against Pym and the others, prepared by the King himself, and asked the Lords to 'take care for the securing of the persons'. The Lords, however, though ready enough to imprison Archbishop Williams, as well as Laud and Strafford before him, on the Commons' bare accusation, were now reluctant, saying that a committee must be appointed to consider the matter, as well as to examine precedents and records. Meanwhile, when Charles's men sealed up the accused men's chambers and trunks so that they could be searched for evidence, the Commons declared the action a 'high breach of privilege of Parliament' and sent their sergeants to break them open again.[44]

Charles was furious. He knew he was in the right; he had good evidence against his enemies and needed nothing to bring them down 'save only a free and legal trial, which was all I desired'. With these agitators gone, he hoped, he could win back the rest of the Parliament and be once more 'at peace in his kingdom'. All he needed was to get them arrested. And so, in the greatest secrecy, he and Henrietta made plans for 'a bold blow', as she described it.[45]

Charles began his preparations that same night. Thirty or forty artillerymen were sent to man the cannons in the Tower, while the usual guard there remained without weapons. A message went to the Inns of Court, asking the gentlemen there to 'be ready at an hour's warning, if his Majesty should have occasion to use them'. Another message ordered the mayor to refuse the Commons' request for 'strong Guards' from the City's militia. Instead, if riots threatened, the mayor must order out troops 'to suppress all such tumults and disorders'. If the people refused 'to retire to their houses peaceably', the soldiers were to open fire and 'destroy such of them as shall persist in their tumultuous ways'.[46]

All through the following morning, on Charles's orders, armed men mustered at Whitehall until the court was 'thronged with gentlemen and officers of the army'. 'The House of Commons would not obey the King,' they were told, so now they were to go with Charles himself and 'force them to it'. A watchword was agreed. If the Commons resisted the King's demand for the delivery of the accused MPs, he would come back out to his men and give the word, and they would seize his opponents 'by force and violence'.[47] It was exactly the kind of military coup that Parliament had long dreaded.

Inside the Palace the royal couple took their midday meal as usual. Then Henrietta retired to the little cabinet behind her bedchamber, where Charles took leave of her, 'resolved to change his destiny by the destruction of his enemies'. He would be 'the master', he told her as they embraced; he hoped in just one hour to find her once again 'with more power than he had at their parting'. While Henrietta knelt at her private altar, 'making prayers for this enterprise', waiting with all 'the emotion and impatience that could be expected',[48] Charles mounted into his coach and left Whitehall at the head of 'a great multitude of men' about 400 or 500 in all, 'armed in warlike manner with halberds, swords and pistols'. His own royal guardsmen were there, and all his court servants, great and small, as well as loyal gentlemen and disbanded army officers, together with 'divers French men' associated with Henrietta's court.[49]

About 3 p.m. the party reached Westminster Hall. As the entire body of armed men thronged into the Hall, panic-stricken shopkeepers rushed to shut up their shops, 'looking for nothing but bloodshed and desolation'. The King's men encountered no opposition. Alarmed at the forces massing at Whitehall that morning, the Commons had sent to the City 'for 4,000 men to be presently sent down to them' but the mayor remained true to the King's command and none had arrived.[50] Leaving the bulk of his force in the Hall, Charles continued towards the Commons chamber with some eighty men. In the lobby just outside, he ordered this detachment 'on their lives' to go no further. Here they remained, their cloaks cast off, their hands on their swords, their pistols loaded – at least one was 'ready cocked' – cursing and threatening while they forcibly held the chamber door open against the efforts of the Commons' officers. 'A pox take the House of Commons: let them be hanged if they will,' one said. 'I am a good marksman, I will hit sure,' said another, as the King entered the Commons, accompanied only by his nephew, Charles Louis, the Elector Palatine.[51]

Charles had never been in the chamber before. His speeches to Parliament were always delivered in the House of Lords. In fact, people said, no English king had ever been inside the House except, perhaps, King Henry VIII, and he 'but once'. Straight down the middle of the chamber, bowing to the MPs on either side who 'all bowed again towards him', the King went to stand beside the Speaker's chair, followed by his nephew.[52] There Charles recited his charges and demanded that the accused MPs be handed over. All the time, Charles's eyes searched for his enemies without finding them. He asked for Mr Pym, 'whether he were present or not'. No answer came. Next he asked for Mr Holles, and again there was 'a general silence'. When Charles pressed the Speaker to answer, he fell on his knees, 'saying that he could neither see nor speak but by command of the house'.

'Well well,' the King replied, ''tis no matter; I think my eyes are as good as another's'. Then, after he had looked around 'a pretty whiles',[53] he said: 'I see all the birds are flown ... I cannot do what I came for.'[54]

Watching through the open doors, his thwarted men swore 'wicked oaths'. 'Zounds,' said one, 'they are gone and now we are never the better for our coming.' As Charles passed out through the lobby, 'discontented and angry', they called out for the watchword, but the King gave them none. Only if the five Members were present and the Commons refused to give them up would he have legal justification for ordering his troops in. Instead the cry went up to 'make a lane',[55] and, through the opening in the press, Charles and his men departed.

The 'bold blow' had failed, and ever afterwards Henrietta would blame herself. Looking back years later, she vividly remembered those agonising long minutes that extended on to a quarter of an hour, then half an hour, while she remained in her cabinet, praying and worrying. Often she looked at her watch to see whether Charles's hour had passed. Often she listened in case chance-comers brought her news. This day, she knew, 'must produce great good or great evil': 'either we shall be ruined or the King will be in absolute control.' At last, sure that it was all over by now, she could keep silent no longer. As her old favourite Lucy, Countess of Carlisle, came into her cabinet, Henrietta greeted her ebulliently: 'Rejoice, for at this time the King is, as I hope, master of his state,' adding that Pym and the others 'are without doubt arrested.'[56]

Until now Lucy's connections in the opposition camp had benefited Henrietta. Back in the autumn, the Countess had even brought her an incriminating written paper obtained from Viscount Mandeville – the peer whom Charles had just accused of treason with the five MPs.[57] Now, however, Lucy felt bound to save her friends. Concealing her surprise and anxiety, she left Henrietta's cabinet and wrote a hurried warning note to one of the five. Meanwhile Charles had been held up in the streets by petitioners bringing 'supplications of little consequence', but he had stopped to hear them and to talk, so as not to reveal his haste. A coach accompanied by hundreds of marching men could only go slowly anyway. He was only just entering Parliament when the five Members fled.

It was a 'notable fault' that Henrietta had committed, she acknowledged, but Charles, when she confessed, did not reproach her. It was not really so clear that she was the one to blame. Despite Henrietta's belief that the plan was 'an important secret between the King and the Queen, and very few people were in their confidence', the court had been leaking like a sieve.[58] Already the night before, the five MPs had heard 'of this intended design'. And that day, as Charles and Henrietta dined, the Earl of Essex, Charles's Lord Chamberlain, had sent to warn the threatened members 'that the King intended to come to the House of Commons to seize upon them there, and that they should absent themselves'. Yet still Pym and the others returned to the House after their midday dinner, having as yet 'no direct assurance that the said design should certainly be put in execution'.[59]

Around 2.30 p.m. the news broke, borne by a Frenchman, Captain Hercule Langres. Going past Whitehall as Charles and his troops were already marching towards Parliament, he met the French ambassador, who told him 'of the design of the King's going to the House of Commons ... to take out those five members by violence'.[60] Four of the five were the ambassador's friends; the divisions between King and Parliament were actively supported by the French, in order to keep Britain weak. So the ambassador asked Langres to hurry to the Commons and warn the endangered men 'to withdraw their persons'. Langres had squeezed right through the midst of Charles's troops, with their halberds, swords and pistols, and reached the Commons first.[61] Four of the accused withdrew immediately. Only William Strode remained – 'a firebrand', 'one of the fiercest men of the party' – who, 'being a young man and unmarried, could not be persuaded by his friends for a pretty while to go out'. Half an hour passed, and still Strode protested 'that knowing himself to be innocent he would stay in the House though he sealed his innocency with his blood'. At last, as the first of Charles's troops entered Westminster Hall, a friend took him by the cloak and pulled him bodily out.[62]

At Whitehall that night Charles was still determined to have his men, but it would be no easy matter. The five had gone into hiding in the City where the whole population was up in arms. 'The Cavaliers were coming to fire the city,' people shouted; 'the King himself was in the head of them.' Lord Digby, now the royal couple's most hot-blooded adviser, offered to go into the City himself, 'with a select company of gentlemen'. He knew the house where the accused MPs had taken refuge; he and his men would 'seize upon them, and bring them away alive, or leave them dead in the place'. But Charles refused, still too tender of his precious conscience to countenance such an illegal deed.[63]

Instead, next morning, he drove into the City to meet the mayor and his government. Charles laid the flattery on thick. He buttered up the aldermen with 'some familiar discourse'; he invited himself to dinner with one of the sheriffs. With 'a gracious speech' to the assem-bled worthies, he tried to win them over 'as much as in him lay', promising to redress all his subjects' grievances. Yet the strident heck-ling went on. 'Parliament! Privileges of Parliament!' many councillors called out. Charles answered mildly: 'I have and will observe all privileges of Parliament, but no privileges can protect a traitor from a legal trial.' If the five MPs could prove their innocence 'he should be glad of it', he said, but if they were guilty they were not fit to sit in Parliament, which was called 'to make good laws and to reform abuses, and not to betray their King'. Nonetheless, as Charles went out, the crowds continued to cry 'the privileges of Parliament!', following him all the way back to Whitehall, 'some of them pressing very near his own coach', so that 'the good King ... was glad when he was at home'.[64]

Meanwhile the Commons reconvened. After orders 'that the door be locked, and the key brought up', the opposition leaders stirred the MPs into a fury. Charles's coming to their House 'in a warlike manner' with 'desperate ruffians' was 'a high breach of the rights and privilege of Parliament'. And that was not all. If the five Members had been present, the entire Commons would have been forced to defend them 'for the preservation of the privileges of our house' and they would all have been massacred. Convinced they were no longer safe at West-minster, the MPs voted to adjourn for a week. In the meantime, they would meet once again as a committee, safe in the Guildhall, 'to consider and resolve of all things that may concern the good and safety of the City and Kingdom'.[65]

There, attended by 'a great number' of MPs, the Committee fell to its work with a will. The King's impeachment of the five Members was declared 'unjust and illegal'; his coming to the Commons with 'soldiers, papists, and others' was voted to have been 'a traitorous design against the King and Parliament'. The warrants Charles had since issued for the five MPs' arrest were also illegal. Any person arresting any Member of either House of Parliament without that House's consent 'should be declared a public enemy of the commonwealth', the Committee resolved.[66]

On Saturday 8 January, Pym and the other wanted men joined the Guildhall Committee in triumph, guarded by two companies of the City's militia 'and multitudes of other citizens of account', amidst 'universal acclamations'.[67] The entire city was preparing itself for war, it seemed. Six cannons had been brought in. Weapons were stockpiled in private houses – some contained as many as '20 to 40 muskets with ammunition' – while 'all the trained bands stand to arms'. Shops remained closed, 'as if an enemy were at their gates ready to enter and to plunder them'.[68] One night a rumour went round that Charles was coming with his 'soldiers and ruffians' 'to enter the City armed, to sack it'. 'Arm, arm,' the cry went up throughout London and its suburbs, and, in little over an hour, '40,000 men in complete arms' turned out, 'and near upon an hundred thousand more that had halberds, swords, clubs and the like'.[69]

The rumour soon proved false, but a steady stream of printed 'libels', full of allegations of papist plotting, kept the population in constant alarm.[70] Henrietta bore the brunt of the blame. Charles himself, the pamphlets proclaimed, was 'a good Protestant in his heart'; it was 'the persuasions of the queen's majesty, and the advice of the Catholic lords and other gentlemen' that would bring these plots to fruition. 'The Queen does all,' people said. 'She is the one who has always advised the king ill.'[71] She had refused the French ambassador's offer of mediating with the parliamentarians, the word went round. She had advised Charles to make his attempt on the five Members. And she was the one who had stirred up the revolt in Ireland 'for the advancement of Popery'.[72] Granted, people said, the King intended to use the rebels afterwards 'so as to recover his lost authority in this kingdom', but it was Henrietta who was the 'principal author' of what many now called 'the Queen's insurrection'.[73] Henrietta was fast becoming the bugbear that she would remain to Protestant English history: 'a papist, a French lady of a haughty spirit'[74] who, 'more powerful' even than Laud and Strafford, had applied 'her great wit and parts' to stir the King's 'violent purpose' against his subjects, producing 'sad desolations'. Charles 'was enslaved in his affection only to her, though she had no more passion for him than what served to promote her designs', wrote the Puritan memoirist Lucy Hutchinson. 'Nothing but the mercy of God prevented the utter subversion of protestantism in the three kingdoms.'[75]

On Sunday 9 January the most fearsome news reached Whitehall: the MPs were preparing 'to accuse Her Majesty of high treason'. Already there were charges ready to 'be put into parliament against her' when the Commons returned to Westminster in two days' time.[76] Resistance would be impossible. Determined to come with 'strong and sufficient guards', the MPs had already resolved that it was legal for the local sheriffs 'to raise the *posse comitatus* for that purpose'. In fact, the entire population was required, by 'their duty to God, the King, and their country', to turn out to defend Parliament 'from all force and violence whatsoever'.[77] On Monday the Guildhall Committee finalised the arrangements. Any citizens who chose to come, mounted and armed, would be welcome, and they accepted the offer of 1000 sailors on the Thames 'to defend the Parliament by water with muskets and other ammunition'. Viscount Mandeville and the five MPs accused of treason would go by river, surrounded by a flotilla of long boats mounted with artillery. In addition, eight companies of the militia were ordered to turn out, bringing eight cannons along with them.[78] This was no mere guard for Parliament, but the triumphal procession of a conquering army. In all some 20,000 people were expected, 'comprising countrymen, citizens and sailors', outnumbering the King's few hundred gentlemen and army officers many times over.[79]

The news threw Henrietta into 'extreme apprehension', but Charles's feelings were of 'shame more than fear'. What really weighed with him was the disgrace he would suffer from the 'barbarous rudeness' of the people, who would come with 'the boldness to demand anything, and not leave either myself, or the Members of Parliament, the liberty of our reason and conscience to deny them anything'. To him it seemed an 'intolerable oppression', reducing him to slavery.[80] He and Henrietta could afford to remain at Whitehall no longer.

It was a sorry party that rode out of the Palace gates that evening of Monday 10 January 1642. The King and Queen were accompanied by just 'thirty or forty' of their bodyguard; the rest, 'so poor that they had no horses', were forced to remain behind. Of Charles's courtiers there were only 'some few' who were truly 'devoted to him'.[81] 'Whither we go, and what we are to do, I know not,' wrote one: 'my duty and loyalty have taught me to follow my King and master, and by the grace of God nothing shall divert me from it.'[82] Charles's secretary of state, Sir Edward Nicholas, was there, as was Henrietta's new favourite, George Lord Digby; he was the one who had warned her of the Guildhall Committee's plans to impeach her for treason. Charles's nephew, the Elector Palatine, rode with them, as did three of the royal children: eleven-year-old Charles Prince of Wales, Mary aged ten, and James, now eight. The two younger children, Elizabeth and Henry, remained behind at St James's Palace.[83] Also left behind, as prisoners in the Tower, were Archbishop John Williams and his eleven loyal bishops, as well as Archbishop Laud.

Out through the suburbs of Westminster the royal party rode, past Hyde Park, where Charles and Henrietta had driven so often on happy maying expeditions, then continuing westwards and southwards towards Hampton Court. Peasants with carts carried their baggage – clothes and other necessaries, as well as valuables like gold and silver plate and jewellery, and even some of the Crown jewels – but there was no ready money to pay their drivers. It was a difficult journey. The rivers that barred their route were swollen with floodwaters after the recent rains, and crossing them was dangerous. At Hampton Court, nothing was ready, so the three royal children 'were obliged to the inconvenience of sleeping in the same bed beside their Majesties'.[84] Next day, while the MPs made their triumphant return to Westminster as planned, Charles's army officers, quartered in Kingston, just over the Thames from Hampton Court, were busy in 'warlike preparations'. Cavalry under Colonel Lunsford's command mustered some 200 strong. Cartloads of ammunition were brought in, and war saddles came by water from London. In response, the MPs ordered the local militia to be called out 'for the suppressing of these assemblies'.[85] Clearly the royal family was not safe at Hampton Court, 'an open place' with no military defences, so they moved on to Windsor Castle, where again, after 'the dangerous crossing of divers rivers', they found 'scant convenience'[86]

They were in a 'sad condition', Charles and Henrietta realised, seeing how far the King had fallen in just ten days: 'from a height and greatness that his enemies feared to such a lowness that his own servants durst hardly avow the waiting on him'. Henrietta was especially angry at the disloyalty of old friends like the Countess of Carlisle and the Earl of Holland, who were now firmly within the parliamentarian camp. Even her confidant, Lord Digby, soon fled abroad, when the Commons accused him of involvement in the mobilisations at Kingston. However, driven at last beyond all normal political niceties, neither of the royal couple was remotely disposed to compromise.[87]

Instead they threw themselves into a new round of military preparations. Utterly alone now, having 'no one in whom we could trust, everyone having betrayed us', as Henrietta wrote, she and Charles had to do everything themselves. 'I had so many affairs for the service of the King ... that I am astonished that I did not lose my mind, not having even the time to sleep.'[88] At Windsor the couple's bodyguard was reinforced with 'divers several troops of horse'. Men and ammunition were sent off to Portsmouth, where George Goring had returned to royal favour. Other wagons arrived at Windsor, laden with ammunition from the Tower of London, where Sir John Byron was under orders to blow everything up rather than surrender it to Parliament.[89]

Meanwhile Charles had already ordered the Earl of Newcastle to take command of Hull and its royal arsenal, where there were more arms even than in the Tower of London. Then, Charles hoped, he could just 'sit still' and wait for his opponents to 'come to reason'. There would be no need for open military conflict.[90]

But Parliament had spies at court. On the same day that Charles wrote to the Earl of Newcastle, they ordered their own man, Sir John Hotham, to go north, where he seized Hull for them. They also placed a guard around the Tower of London 'by land and by water': no 'ordnance, ammunition or other provisions whatsoever' were to be allowed out, nor any 'extraordinary provision of victuals, or men' to come in.[91] Every day, it seemed, there was 'some committee or other' coming out from the Commons to Windsor 'with petitions and expostulations'. Prince Charles must not be allowed to leave the country and anyone assisting his departure would be guilty of 'high treason'. Charles must make 'a public declaration and promise in parliament' that he would not receive any political or religious advice from his wife, while Henrietta must 'take a solemn oath ... that she will not ... at all intermeddle in any of these affairs'. Her Catholic servants and all her priests were to be dismissed, whilst her sons and all future royal princes were forbidden to marry Catholic brides.[92]

At first the Lords were reluctant to pass the Commons' more extreme measures, but at the beginning of February, with angry crowds mobilised again at Westminster, they caved in. They joined the Commons in petitioning the King that the nation's militia forces be entrusted to 'such hands as the Parliament may confide in'. After months of inaction, they finally passed the Bill depriving the Anglican bishops of their seats in the Lords. Through London there was 'great joy': church bells were rung and bonfires lit. Three days later, 'after four denials formerly to the same request', they voted to join the Commons in asking Charles to remove Sir John Byron from his command of the Tower.[93]

Unready to provoke an open confrontation yet and hoping still to win back popular support, Charles accepted Byron's resignation and appointed the Commons' man in his place. He also abandoned his prosecution of John Pym and the other parliamentarians accused of high treason; 'for the full contentment of all his loving subjects', he would grant them a 'free and general pardon'.[94] But on the militia he would not back down. Supreme command of the nation's armed forces was the King's absolute prerogative, the heart of his power; if he abandoned this, he would be left with 'nothing but the title of king'. He could see Parliament was bent on 'high ways of destruction': 'their purpose was by degrees to get so much power into their hands that they need not care for what was left in his.'[95] On the bishops too, he was determined not to yield. It was a matter of conscience. 'How shall I remove the bishops, having sworn at my coronation to maintain them in their privileges and pre-eminences?'

Already he had conceded too much, he confessed to the Dutch ambassador. 'At the beginning I was told that, if I would agree to the death of the Deputy [Strafford], my kingdom would be at peace; afterwards if I allowed a triennial Parliament; and then if I would permit the present Parliament to remain assembled as long as they wished; now that I must place the ports, the militia and the Tower in their hands; and ... remove the bishops. You see how far their intentions go.'[96] To Parliament itself, however, Charles made conciliatory noises. He would allow them to recommend military commanders, under certain conditions. As for the bishops, he would 'send an answer in convenient time.' Such weak replies, 'more prudent than spirited', encouraged his enemies. The Commons already believed 'themselves even possessed of the whole militia of the kingdom'.[97] Yet in fact Charles and Henrietta were almost ready to put new plans into action.

They agreed that it was not safe for Henrietta to remain in England, facing an imminent treason charge. 'Parliament's violence was so great against me that I had to flee to be sure of my own life,' Henrietta told her sister Christine: 'they said publicly that a queen was merely a subject and that she could be punished like any other. Yet it is not the fear of death that has made me leave, but of a prison separating me from the King which I avow would have been more insupportable than death, for that would have ruined all our affairs.'[98] So Henrietta would go to Holland. The Dutch had been pressing Charles to send

Mary to join her new husband ever since the marriage the previous year. Now he agreed that Henrietta would accompany her. That was the public reason for the Queen's journey, announced to Parliament.[99] In reality the royal couple had ambitious plans. Henrietta would take the couple's jewels with her: everything from Charles's pearl buttons and her own 'great chain' of pearls and 'that cross ... from the queen my mother' to important Crown jewels like Charles's 'ruby collar', and a selection of rich coronets, diadems and circlets.[100] In the great mercantile cities of the Netherlands she would pawn or sell them all, for the benefit of Charles's war effort. In personal talks with the Dutch government, she might persuade them to send military assistance, or at least to put diplomatic pressure on Parliament. Then she could always go on to France, where she had 'very extensive designs'.[101]

Meanwhile Charles would remain in England. After seeing Henrietta off at the coast, he would head north in the utmost secrecy. There lay the heartland of his party; in Yorkshire, Henrietta told the Dutch ambassador, the whole population supported the King. At York, Charles would find 'a safe place' where he could muster supporters like Lord Digby, who were currently too afraid of the 'rage and violence' of Parliament to join him. Then he would secure some sea-port, opening a safe route for correspondence with Henrietta and for receiving the supplies she would send. Newcastle and Berwick were both possibilities, but best of all would be Hull where the King's magazine still lay. Even though the Earl of Newcastle had been turned away, the royal couple hoped that Charles might be admitted to the town once he arrived in person. Then, perhaps, he might consider going to Scotland or Ireland, to gather yet more support.[102]

As the moment of parting approached, both he and Henrietta suffered greatly. Her husband, Henrietta recalled, was 'touched by a lively sadness to see himself in the state he was in, devoured by his own subjects and constrained to separate from his wife whom he loved dearly, without knowing what their fate would be'. She too grieved at their misfortunes, which 'forced me to leave the King and my children'. She would be the most 'wretched creature in this world ... separated far from the king my lord, from my children, out of my country, and without hope of returning there, except at imminent peril – abandoned by all the world, unless God assist me'.[103]

Stronger still than her sadness was her fear – not so much of Parliament itself, for she would be out of their reach now – but rather of what her husband might do without her. Henrietta was the one who truly believed in the need for war. 'To settle affairs it was necessary to unsettle them first,' she said; it would be 'impossible to re-establish her husband's authority in any other way'. 'You have already shown your goodness sufficiently,' she told Charles, which 'has been very ill repaid'; there must be no more negotiation until 'your people . . . apply themselves to their duty'. Her husband, she knew, was more inclined to a waiting game. He was going into Yorkshire 'not to take up arms', he said, but to see what his opponents would do. Once they saw his threat of force, 'he did not doubt that they would be more pliable'. An 'honourable' agreement would be reached, and then Henrietta would 'soon return'.[104]

In Henrietta's eyes, her husband seemed unrealistic, too indecisive, timid and changeable, too reluctant to insist on his unquestionable rights. He was, she feared, utterly unfitted to deal with the crisis they now faced – an assessment that many of the King's followers would come to share.[105] Henrietta hardly dared to leave him alone. Her friends at court, 'much agitated', urged against it. 'I am risking all we have left in the world to get money,' she told him; if he failed in his part, everything she did would be 'rendered ridiculous'. Their jewels would be lost, 'and we too; for we should have nothing left to help ourselves with'.[106]

'Continue your resolution, and do not change'; 'lose no time, it is too dear'; 'you have lost enough already': these would be her constant refrains in the coming months. 'If you wait . . . you will be ruined altogether.' 'To begin, and then to stop, is your ruin – experience shows it'; 'you must dare'.[107] Her desperation and frustration were palpable:

> this is no longer a mere play. You must declare yourself; you have testified your gentleness enough, you must show your justice. Go

on boldly: God will assist you. You see what you have got by not following your first resolutions, when you declared those of the Parliament traitors. Let that serve you as an example; do not delay longer now in consultations, it is action which must do the work at this hour; – it is time.

But even as she reproached her husband, she was ashamed of herself. 'My dear heart', she begged, 'pardon me if I have written a little too much on this subject ... My whole hope lies only in your firmness and constancy, and when I hear anything to the contrary, I am mad. Pardon once again my folly and weakness: I confess it.'[108] Yet still she could not help herself. Too much was at stake. Her dread was that if Charles failed in his tasks she might never see him again; it would be safe for her to return to England only when 'his original authority' was restored.[109] If he could not achieve that – if he gave up his command of the militia, as she feared he might – then he would be lost 'and I too'. At that point, when 'you are no longer capable of protecting anyone, not even yourself', she would 'retire into a convent' and bid him 'Adieu, my dear heart'.[110]

On 9 February the royal party left Windsor in great dejection. Charles and Henrietta – more divided on their plans and expectations than either cared to admit – saw their hour of parting approaching ever nearer. Charles especially suffered 'greatly': his love for his wife was 'beyond expression'. His sons too 'grieved at the going away of their mother and sister'.[111] The bodyguard of officers had been dismissed now. There was no money to pay for them or for anything else. With Charles's usual income cut off by Parliament, Henrietta had been forced to turn her gold and silver plate into coin just to pay for her 'most necessary occasions'. Only a small group of courtiers would accompany her abroad, including Father Philip and Jeffery Hudson, with the Queen's maids of honour and just three of her great ladies – all of them 'much agitated ... fearful of the object and of the results of this journey'.[112]

That night they stopped at Hampton Court where, next morning, the painful family partings began. The Princes were left behind, to allay Parliament's fears that they 'should be transported beyond the seas'.[113] The rest continued on to Greenwich. In the palace where they had passed their early summer months each year so pleasantly, the royal couple now became locked in disagreement. Charles was still refusing to pass the Bill removing the bishops from the House of Lords, yet again he had advisers who urged that this one concession would be enough to pacify his opponents. Sir John Colepeper, his new Chancellor of the Exchequer, argued this case at length with the King, but to no avail. He therefore proceeded to try Henrietta. 'Her own safety very much depended upon the King's consent to that bill,' he told her; 'if he should refuse it, her journey into Holland would be crossed by the Parliament, and possibly her person in danger.'[114]

In fact, as Henrietta realised afterwards, there was never any danger of Parliament hindering her journey. They were glad to see her go, believing 'perhaps that they would dispose of the King more easily when the Queen was not there'. At the time, however, 'terrified with the apprehension of her being hindered from pursuing her purpose', she interceded with the King, as Colepeper requested. It was no easy matter to persuade Charles against his conscience. For two days she 'gave not over her importunity with the King', and at last he yielded for her safety's sake. As he had for Strafford's attainder, he refused to pass the Bill in person, appointing a commission of Lords to do the business for him. Then, late in the evening of 12 February, the royal party set off for Dover.[115]

At Canterbury, where the younger Charles and Henrietta had spent their honeymoon in 'a very Eden or Paradise', the King and Queen now heard that the Bill had been passed into law. There was rejoicing in London: bonfires were lit, and Parliament sent a message to the King 'to express their gratification'.[116] But the royal couple were utterly disappointed in their hopes of appeasing their enemies. That same day Parliament impeached Charles's Attorney General for treason in 'falsely scandalously, and maliciously' contriving the charge against John Pym and the others. They also drew up an 'ordinance concerning the militia', naming the commanders they wanted the King to appoint. Soon Parliament's messengers were with Charles, pressing him to assent. Concerned for Henrietta's safety, he did not want to refuse directly, and so he replied that he would need some time for advisement thereupon'. He would give them 'a positive answer' when he returned to London.[117]

By now the royal party was at Dover. Out in the harbour five royal ships were hurriedly preparing for the voyage. 'Things are done in such post-haste that I never heard of the like for the voyage of persons of so great dignity,' a harassed navy official complained. Henrietta's 'goods and baggage' were being loaded aboard: linen and clothes, money and other personal valuables, her collection of Crown jewels, and 'all her vessels for her chapel', which were worth tens of thousands of pounds alone. Last of all to go aboard were the Queen's coaches, six in all, with 'about 120 horses of all sorts' and their fodder.[118]

Henrietta was now eager to be gone 'without further delay': to be done with the agonies of parting, get on with her work in Holland, and then, hopefully, return to her husband and children.[119] For some days a contrary wind prevented her from sailing, until the morning of 25 February when, down on the sea-front, the royal couple made their sad farewells. Charles, 'deeply moved ... did not know how to tear himself away'. For a long time he remained by Henrietta, 'conversing with her in sweet discourse and affectionate embraces'. Neither could 'restrain their tears', lost in 'extreme regret and grief'. Finally, 'after many kisses, many tears', they drew apart.[120] Henrietta stepped into the royal barge and was rowed out to the flotilla's flagship, the *Lion*. There she stood on the deck while the sails were hoisted, the anchors weighed, and the ships put out from the harbour. From the mast above her, the royal standard and pennants flew. Beneath her feet, safe in the hold in heavy locked chests, lay England's Crown jewels. Beside her stood her tiny court, and Princess Mary with her governess, the Countess of Roxburghe. While Henrietta looked back to England, Charles mounted his horse and followed her ship eastwards along the coast, past Dover Castle and out into the country 'for more than four leagues'. At last, when Henrietta's figure disappeared from sight, he lifted off his hat and 'waved it round several times, bidding her a very affectionate, but very sad and painful adieu'.[121]

Then, bypassing London, the King set off northwards to muster his forces. Six months later, atop the Castle Hill in Nottingham, he stood in the rain to see his standard raised. A herald proclaimed England's Parliament traitors to the Crown. Drums and trumpets sounded, and a few companies of wet, wind-battered troops shouted 'God save the King'.[122] The Civil War had begun.

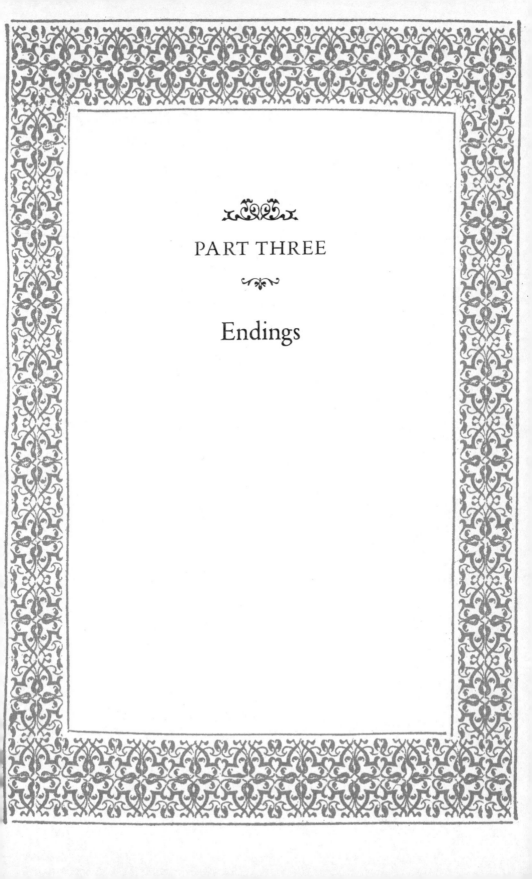

PART THREE

Endings

Newcastle, January 1647

The town of Newcastle-upon-Tyne was strongly fortified, 'in a condition to resist any army however powerful'. On its high stone walls Scottish sentries in baggy blue bonnets and red wool coats kept watch, shivering and stamping to keep out the cold. After three years' service, these men were in a 'ragged and naked condition'. Beside them their heavy muskets stood ready for use. From the leather bandoliers over their shoulders hung powder horns and pouches of shot. At their sides were swords or dirks. Beneath tall castellated towers more Scottish troops guarded the town's gates, which were locked every night. No one was allowed to enter without an official pass. On high ground cannons stood ready, and out in the nearby villages, starved and made poor by the Scottish occupation, cavalry regiments kept guard.[1] The Scots had come to Newcastle in 1644, when they joined the English Parliament's war against the King. In the winter of 1647 the town was full of Scotsmen of importance: politicians and Presbyterian churchmen, as well as the army's commander-in-chief, Alexander Leslie, Earl of Leven.

One single man was the reason for their presence. In New House, a grand Elizabethan manor just within the town walls, King Charles

I was a changed man, his hair cut short, his face 'melancholy, and . . . very grey with cares'. Outside the mullioned windows of his chamber lay extensive gardens and grounds, where the Scottish guards had recently been doubled and ordered to 'go the rounds continually'. Inside a coal fire burnt in his grate, while more Scots guards patrolled his apartments, annoying him with 'their continual smoking'. Under strict new orders, 'eight officers never let him out of their sight',[2] although the King was oblivious to them now. All his attention was focussed on what he was about to write: a letter of vital importance for saving his own life. Sitting at his desk that Saturday 2 January, he dipped his quill into the black ink and set it on the paper. 'Dear heart,' he began, as he always did when writing to Henrietta. 'I must tell thee that now I am declared what I have really been ever since I came to this army, which is a prisoner . . . the difference being only this, that heretofore my escape was easy enough, but now it is most difficult, if not impossible.'[3]

Charles had delivered himself into the hands of the Scots army eight months earlier, alone, disguised, and utterly defeated after five years of war. In those years he and Henrietta had spent just nine months together, after she returned from Holland in 1643, having raised some £2 million for her husband's cause. With her she had brought an armoury of guns, ammunition and saddles, guarded on her journey through England by a small army of royalist troops. 'Her she-majesty, generalissima', she called herself half jokingly, telling her husband that she was 'extremely diligent, with one hundred and fifty waggons of baggage to govern, in case of battle'. Charles was full of admiration and gratitude for the hazards she ran 'in which thou has expressed so much love to me, that I confess it is impossible to repay by anything I can do'.[4]

On 14 July, the Queen was welcomed into Oxford in triumphal style.[5] Church bells rang, crowds cheered, bonfires blazed. Civic authorities and university men turned out in droves to deliver speeches and poems of welcome. Oxford was Charles's headquarters throughout the war. Here he held court in the great hall at Christ Church. Here his own royalist Parliament met, the law courts heard cases, and the royal mint produced coins to fund his war effort. And here, after Henrietta's return, the delights of the couple's old court life were recreated in miniature. Plays were put on by professional actors forced out of London by Parliament's ordinances against the stage. Portraits of the royal family and their courtiers were painted by William Dobson in his studio on the High Street. Poems were composed by enthusiastic royal followers: William Davenant, Abraham Cowley and Sir John Denham. There was deer hunting and hare coursing at nearby Woodstock, walks in the college gardens, tennis in the town, and at Christmas masques were put on once more. While Anglican services were held in the Cathedral for the King, Henrietta's priests performed Catholic ceremonies in the chapel at Merton College, which was Henrietta's own base, with a private passageway leading to Charles's apartments at Christ Church. In the Queen's bedchamber one night a new royal baby was conceived.

But all the time too there was the business of war. Bitter factions divided the court. On one side were the professional soldiers, trained in the wars on the Continent. Foremost of these was Charles's nephew, Prince Rupert, just twenty-three and now general of the King's cavalry. Whilst Henrietta had no doubt of his loyalty, she distrusted his hot-headedness. 'Believe me, he is yet very young and self-willed,' she advised Charles; 'he is a person capable of doing anything that he is ordered, but he is not to be trusted to take a single step of his own head.' On the other side were men like Sir Edward Hyde, the future Earl of Clarendon: politicians who favoured negotiating with the enemy for a peaceful settlement. These too Henrietta profoundly distrusted: 'persons . . . who, at the bottom of their hearts, are not well disposed for royalty'. Former parliamentarians who had defected to the King's camp out of loyalty to the Anglican Church, Hyde's party had no wish for Charles to be an absolute monarch. In Henrietta's view, 'their counsels plainly show the contrary'.[6]

Henrietta's own faction was drawn largely from her old court favourites, and chief among them was 'Harry Jermyn', as she affectionately called him. He had laboured with her in the Netherlands, where he was trusted even with the secret cipher she and Charles used in their correspondence, then had returned to England 'as colonel of my guards', commanding her troops on their march to Oxford. Implicated in the court's plots against Parliament before the outbreak of civil war, Jermyn and the rest were adamant that it must be won and Charles re-established with all his former authority, so as to secure their own safety from parliamentary prosecution. Henrietta shared their desperate determination. Action, courage, resolution, no compromise, no delay: these were her constant watchwords to her husband.[7]

No one could fault Charles's courage in battle. 'He was very fearless in his person' and his physical strength and fitness stood him in great stead, for he was never ill 'throughout all the fatigues of the war'. However, in his decision-making, his followers lamented, he had a fatal lack of 'enterprise': the readiness to undertake difficult or dangerous ventures.[8] That summer, when Henrietta arrived in Oxford, Parliament's army was in disarray, and the Queen was determined that Charles and his forces should move against London. But, after several days of indecision, he followed more cautious advice and went in the opposite direction: to besiege Gloucester and secure his supply lines from Wales. Henrietta was left behind in Oxford in a state of 'no small dissatisfaction'. By September, Charles's siege had ended in failure and the strains of the conflict were taking their toll on Henrietta: 'I am so weary, not of being beaten, but of having heard it spoken of.'[9]

That winter her hopes were further dampened when the Scots invaded England. In the South too the King's forces were in dire straits. Henrietta was eager for peace talks with Parliament and the armistice they would bring, even if only temporarily: 'the truth is that the King's army here needs it.'[10] She herself was in great danger. Back in the spring, as her troops marched towards Oxford, winning victories and taking towns, Henrietta had at last been charged with high treason by the Commons. The MPs voted unanimously: 'The Queen hath levied war against the Parliament and Kingdom,' and must 'receive a trial and due sentence'. Clearly if she fell into Parliament's hands, Henrietta was likely to suffer the Earl of Strafford's fate. At the very least she would become a valuable pawn, allowing Parliament to 'make their own conditions' in negotiating with the King.[11]

By April 1644, parliamentarian forces were advancing towards Oxford, and the King's army – fewer than 10,000 now – was too small to face them in pitched battle. There was every likelihood that the city would be besieged, making Henrietta's escape impossible. Unhappily, the royal couple agreed to part once more. Henrietta was six months' pregnant and suffering from 'fits of the mother' – breathless panic attacks – 'and a violent consumptive cough'; modern assessment of her symptoms suggests she was in the early stages of tuberculosis.[12] It was decided that she would go to Bath to drink the spa waters, while Charles remained to command his troops. On 17 April the royal couple spent a final night together at Abingdon, five miles south of Oxford. Next day, they made their tearful farewells.[13] They did not know it, but they would never meet again.

From Bath, where rotting corpses from recent warfare lay in the streets and the plague was spreading, Henrietta hurried on westwards to Exeter: a strongly fortified city, commanded by a loyal governor, where she would find safety for the approaching birth. Here she fully expected to die. 'My dear heart,' she wrote to Charles, 'the cruel pains I have suffered since I left you ... make me believe that it is time for me to think of another world. If it be so, the will of God be done! ... Adieu, my dear heart. I hope before I leave you, to see you once again in the position in which you ought to be. God grant it!'[14] The birth on 16 June of her daughter, 'a lovely princess' named Henrietta, only brought a worsening of her condition. 'My disease ... is so insupportable,' she told Charles, 'that if it were not that we ought not to wish for death, it would be too much longed for [by me].' As she suffered paralysis and partial blindness, feeling 'as though I was so tightly squeezed in the region of the heart that I was suffocating', her misery was made 'complete' by the approach of the Earl of Essex's parliamentarian army.[15] Overcome with fears 'of being shut up' in the city, Henrietta resolved to flee, 'even at the hazard of my life', she wrote to Charles.

I shall show you by this last action, that nothing is so much in my thoughts as what concerns your preservation, and that my own life is of very little consequence compared with that; for as your affairs stand, they would be in danger if you come to help me, and I know that your affection would make you risk everything for that ... Adieu, my dear heart.

The most miserable creature in the world, who can write no more.[16]

Leaving her tiny baby with a little household of carers, Henrietta left Exeter in disguise. For over a week she was carried in a litter almost to the furthest end of Cornwall, while her physician and a small band of attendants walked or rode beside her. 'Here is the woefullest spectacle my eyes yet ever beheld,' a Cornish gentleman reported: 'the most worn and pitiful creature in the world, the poor queen, shifting for one hour's life longer.'[17] On 14 July she sailed for France, even as Charles's northern army was being destroyed in the Battle of Marston Moor.

In Paris that autumn, substantially recovered after drinking the spa waters at Bourbon l'Archambault, Henrietta threw herself into labours for her husband's cause. She wrote to Rome, Lorraine, the Netherlands, and to the French government, now headed by the Queen Regent, Anne of Austria, after the death of Louis XIII. Henrietta approached the Irish rebels too, who offered 'an army of ten thousand men' if Charles would 'condescend to the just demands of his Irish subjects'. Further communications went to Charles's military commanders in Scotland and the South-West of England, where she arranged to export tin from her Cornish dower-lands to France, in return for weapons.[18]

Most of all she wrote to Charles: letters full of love and concern for his safety in the war, but also packed with advice, instructions and exhortations. As news came that he was entering negotiations with his enemies, her anxiety increased. 'Have a care not to abandon those who have served you, as well the bishops as the poor Catholics,' she urged as 1645 began. Charles must retain his military power too, 'for if the militia and some of the fortresses are placed in the hands of some of the Parliamentarians, you will only have made war to destroy yourself and your reputation; and as for me, I should be done for, since I could not trust myself to those people.'[19]

All too soon the negotiations failed, and the following June, despite Charles's optimism that 'my affairs were never in so fair and hopeful a way', his southern army was defeated at the Battle of Naseby. 'Bodies lay slain about four miles in length, the most thick on the hill where the King stood.'[20] Almost his entire force was killed or captured, and his artillery and baggage train were taken too. Many of his commanders now talked of abandoning the cause. 'There is such a universal weariness of the war,' complained Lord Digby to Henry Jermyn in Paris, that 'I do not know four persons living . . . that have not already given clear demonstrations that they will purchase their own and, as they flatter themselves, the kingdom's quiet at any price to the King.' Even the militaristic Prince Rupert advised his uncle to capitulate, but Charles would not hear of it. 'If I had any other quarrel but the defence of my religion, crown, and friends, you had full reason for your advice', he replied;

for I confess that, speaking either as a mere soldier or statesman, I must say there is no probability but of my ruin; but as a Christian, I must tell you, that God will not suffer rebels to prosper, or this cause to be overthrown: and whatever personal punishment it shall please him to inflict upon me, must not make me repine, much less to give over this quarrel . . . whatever it cost me.[21]

However, by December 1645, Charles had little choice but to open talks. 'His Majesty hath no army at all,' wrote Sir Edward Nicholas. Only a few last strongholds still held out, their garrisons unsupplied and unpaid. Meanwhile Parliament was making preparations to besiege Oxford. Charles faced 'the certainty of being blocked up here or in any other place his Majesty can now hie unto'. He therefore sent peace proposals to Parliament again, offering terms 'as low as he can go with preserving of his conscience and honour'.[22] He also approached the parliamentarian army, hoping to exploit differences between them and Parliament. Henrietta's greatest hope lay with the Scottish

Covenanters, whose army was now besieging Newark, about 100 miles north of Oxford. Back in October, she had opened talks with the Scots envoy in Paris, and by the spring of 1646 she was pursuing this treaty 'with all diligence ... very confident it will succeed'. The French government too favoured this solution, fearing the power of an English republic if Parliament won the war.[23]

There remained one great problem: Charles himself, who adamantly rejected the Scots' demand that he establish their Presbyterian religion in England. When the French ambassador, Jean de Montreuil, pressed this point with 'many arguments' – 'without it nothing could be done in order to an agreement with the Scots' – Charles still resisted. It was a point inconsistent with 'his conscience'. Even Henrietta's desperate letters failed to move him. Imagine if their positions were reversed, he urged her: 'wouldst thou give ear to him who should persuade thee, for worldly respects, to leave the communion of the Roman church for any other? Indeed, sweetheart, this is my case.' He went on: 'For God's sake ... consider, that if I should quit my conscience, how unworthy I make myself of thy love.' Nevertheless, as Parliament's army advanced to besiege Oxford, Charles had 'neither force enough to resist, nor sufficient to escape to any secure place'. 'Mere necessity' was now his master, he told Henrietta.[24]

Desperately he asked Parliament to allow him to come to London to negotiate, and again he sent separate messages to their army commanders, but to no avail. Only the Scots remained, and to their commissioners in London Charles wrote asking for assurances 'that we shall be secure in your army both in conscience and honour'. In return, Charles offered, 'as soon as I come into the Scots army, I shall be very willing to be instructed concerning the presbyterial government: whereupon they shall see that I shall strive to content them in anything that shall not be against my conscience.' Conscience and honour were still Charles's supreme principles. 'If I cannot live as a King,' he wrote to one of his followers, 'I shall die like a gentleman, without doing that which may make honest men blush for me.'[25]

On 1 April, with the authorisation of the Scottish commissioners in London, as he thought, the French ambassador Montreuil signed a guarantee 'that if the King of Great Britain shall put himself into the Scots' army, he shall be there received as their natural Sovereign ... and that they shall employ their armies and forces to assist his Majesty ... in recovery of his Majesty's just rights'. The royalists were delighted at the 'excellent news'.[26] While Montreuil went on ahead to Newark to arrange for the King's reception there, Charles prepared to follow, 'I having resolved (by the grace of God) to begin my journey thither upon Monday or Tuesday next', he wrote to Henrietta on Thursday 2 April. There was still no formal peace treaty with the Scots, he admitted. The issues of 'the [English] militia, Ireland, and my friends' would have to be thrashed out in person when he came to the army. 'As for church business, I hope to manage it so as not to give them distaste and yet do nothing against my conscience.'

Yet on 13 April, Charles was still in Oxford. 'It much troubles me that I am not parted from hence,' he wrote to Henrietta: 'the reason is, because I have not heard one word from Montreuil since he went.' And now, 'closed upon all sides' by the parliamentarian armies, he would find escape more difficult than ever. At last a letter came from the French ambassador. It was a bombshell for the King. 'The Scots are abominable relapsed rogues,' Charles reported to Henrietta, 'for Montreuil himself is ashamed of them, they having retracted almost everything which they made him promise me.'[27] Their army refused to recognise the agreement made with their Commissioners in London. The whole idea of the Scots fighting for the King had vanished. Charles would be allowed to join the army, but only if he pretended to arrive by chance, so as not to offend the English Parliament, and he must establish Presbyterianism in England 'as promptly as possible'.[28]

His condition was 'much worse than ever', Charles wrote to Henrietta, perplexed at 'the difficulty of resolving of what to do'. He had little time to lose. If he remained where he was, he would soon be a captive. He decided to flee secretly to King's Lynn, on the Norfolk coast, where he might gather enough forces 'to procure honourable and safe conditions from the rebels'. If that failed, he could sail to Scotland, where the Marquess of Montrose was attempting to raise a new army for him. If Montrose was not ready, then he would flee abroad, to 'Ireland, France, or Denmark, but to which of these I am not yet resolved'. Still Charles dithered. Leaving England was 'in no wise counselable', his advisers agreed. It was unbecoming 'to quit his party in that faint-seeming way', and there was nothing he could gain by it, for none of these nations had the power to aid him.[29] Charles settled on a bold new plan: to go to London and negotiate with Parliament in person.

As midnight approached on Sunday 27 April 1646, he went secretly to the chamber of John Ashburnham, his groom of the bedchamber, 'the person in whom the King of Great Britain has now the greatest confidence'. Also there was Dr Michael Hudson, 'his plain dealing chaplain', as Charles called him, 'because he told him his mind, when others would or durst not'.[30] Hudson had provided horses and an old parliamentary pass, which would permit the party to travel to London. Soon after midnight, while Ashburnham used a knife to cut off the King's long flowing locks and trim his beard short, Hudson went out to fetch Sir Thomas Glemham, the military commander of Oxford, who unlocked the eastern gate of the city. As the various college clocks chimed 3 a.m., the four men – Glemham, Hudson, Ashburnham and Charles, now disguised as Ashburnham's Roundhead serving man – crossed Magdalen Bridge in pitch darkness and rode out into the fields beyond. Soon Glemham turned back, with orders not to allow any city gate to be opened, nor anybody to 'pass in or out of Oxford for five days'. 'Farewell, Harry,' he said to Charles, whose face was hidden beneath a woollen soldier's cap with flaps down over his ears, and a hat on top.[31] Then Charles and his two companions rode off to the south-east.

Hudson was the ideal man to take charge of the little expedition. During the past years of war, the clergyman had served as an army scoutmaster, in charge of reconnoitring and gathering intelligence. Round Oxford he 'understood the by-ways as well as the common, and was indeed a very skilful guide'. In one village there was a guard of parliamentarian dragoons, 'which we passed without any difficulty or examination', Hudson recorded. A few miles further on they met a party of cavalry. Observing that Hudson and Ashburnham wore pistols in their belts, the enemy troops 'asked us to whom we belonged', to which Hudson 'answered "to the House of Commons," and so passed'. At Henley-on-Thames they passed again 'without any question, only showing the pass to the corporal and giving 12d. to the guards'. At Hillingdon, twenty miles west of London, they stopped and went into a tavern 'to refresh ourselves'. It was now ten or eleven in the morning. They had not slept all night, and decisions were becoming difficult. For two or three hours they made no move while Charles, 'much perplexed', again dithered over 'what course to resolve upon – London or northward?'[32]

From Oxford, London had seemed an appealing prospect. Charles and his advisers had been sure that if he could get there safely, Parliament would show 'much more moderation' than while he remained 'at a distance'. It was an action that Parliament feared above all else, expecting that in London the King might well 'arouse the respect and affection of the people'. Now, however, so close to the City, Charles lost his nerve: the danger of being recognised and arrested en route seemed too great. So he elected to follow his original scheme and go northwards into Norfolk, 'where he was least known'. There he would wait while Hudson went to parley with the Scots at Newark in Nottinghamshire. If the news from there was bad, he would return to his former plan and 'cast himself upon his English [subjects]'.[33]

And so they rode north. When, a mile beyond St Albans, two horses came 'galloping after us very fast', they feared they had been recognised, but it turned out to be merely a gentleman 'very drunk' with his servant. Turning off the main road to avoid his company, Charles and his companions stopped for the night, then rode on at dawn. Soon they parted, Hudson bearing north-west for Newark, while Charles and Ashburnham rode into Norfolk to stay at the White Swan Inn in Downham Market. Two days later Hudson rejoined them. The Scots had agreed to all Charles's demands. They would 'secure the King in his person and in his honour' and press him 'to do nothing contrary to his conscience'. If Parliament refused to restore him, they would 'declare for the King; and take all the King's friends into their protection'. There was just one problem: the Scots absolutely refused to put anything in writing. [34]

Next morning, concerned to escape detection, Charles moved to an obscure village alehouse, disguised as a clergyman now, in a 'black coat and long cassock'. Again he considered joining Montrose in Scotland. Hudson made enquiries 'for a ship to go to the north or Newcastle, but could get none'. At last, 'destitute of any other refuge', Charles resolved to join the Scottish Covenanters, trusting himself to those who 'first began my troubles'. Perhaps, despite all, 'my rendering my person to them may engage their affections to me, who have oft professed "They fought not against me, but for me".'[35]

Under Hudson's guidance, they travelled by the most secret routes, riding south through the marshes round Ely, before turning north-wards for Newark. The King had another new identity as 'the Doctor', wearing a freshly purchased hat and a grey coat that Hudson had obtained from a friend. At 6 a.m. on Tuesday 5 May, after eight days on the run, 'having passed through fourteen guards and garrisons of the enemies', they reached Southwell, where the French ambassador had his lodgings, a few miles from the Scots army still besieging Newark.[36] Here numerous Scottish lords soon arrived, and the dis-avowals began. Whilst they were delighted to see the King there, they said, his arrival was totally unexpected. They had heard nothing of any terms settled with their commissioners in London, and so could not honour them. Charles was horrified, but all his and Montreuil's arguments had no effect. Instead, before Charles had 'either drunk, refreshed or reposed himself', the Scots issued their own demands: Charles must order his garrison in Newark to surrender to the English parliamentary army that was also besieging the town. He must sign the Presbyterian Covenant and order the Marquess of Montrose 'to lay down his arms'.[37]

That night, lodged under strict guard in the midst of the Scottish military HQ, Charles could see he was little better than a prisoner. There was nothing of 'affection or dependence' in the Scots' behaviour. General Leven never asked him for any orders, but rather forbade any army officers to see or speak to him. Meanwhile a sequence of visitors pressed the King 'ungraciously' to 'things ... most averse to his conscience and honour.'[38] Briefly Charles thought of escaping to the parliamentary army on the other side of Newark, but he had no messenger to send. So he did what he could to gratify the Scots. The very next day he sent orders to his men in Newark to surrender 'on very hard terms for those who were therein'. Then he and the entire Scottish army set out 'with much haste' for Newcastle. Fearing an attack by Parliament now that they had the King, the Scots thought they would be safer there. And Charles was willing enough to go: at Newcastle, the Scots suggested, he could meet a new set of their commissioners who might honour the conditions arranged by Montreuil.[39]

But as Charles approached the town, the omens were not good. No crowds came out to cheer. No deputation of civic dignitaries stood ready to welcome him: on Scottish orders, the mayor and aldermen remained at home. The numerous Scottish lords who had recently arrived absented themselves too. Wearing 'a sad-coloured plain suit', Charles rode between lines of silent soldiers, followed by an escort of 300 cavalry. As he crossed the River Tyne and passed under Newcastle's great stone walls, not a single ship fired its guns; there were no drums, no trumpets, no bells ringing out from the church towers. Northwards Charles continued through the streets, still without any noise or 'extraordinary concourse of people'; only more Scottish infantry lining his route. Just before reaching the town walls, he passed under a stone gateway and along an avenue of trees, leading to New House, 'one of the bravest houses in the Town'. This was now to be his home and royal court, and here at last the onlookers raised a shout. Yet it was more a sound of triumph than of welcome.[40]

That sorry scene had taken place more than seven months ago now – months that Charles had passed in disappointment and humiliation. Everything he cared for lay in ruins. In England as well as in Scotland, bishops had been abolished, and Presbyterianism established as the state religion. Amidst scenes of popular fury, stained-glass windows had been smashed, statues of saints beheaded, rood screens torn down, ancient stone churchyard crosses destroyed. His old soulmate, Archbishop Laud, had been tried for treason, and then, when his defence seemed too likely to succeed, had been condemned by a parliamentary Bill of Attainder and executed, like Strafford before him. Every last vestige of royalist military power was gone. On Charles's orders, Montrose's Scottish forces surrendered, as did the last few garrisons holding out in England. From Oxford, James Duke of York was taken to London, where he joined Elizabeth and Henry in parliamentary custody. Of all the royal children, only Prince Charles still had his freedom. After commanding the last of the King's forces in the South-West of England, he had been forced to set sail, first for the Scilly Isles and then for the Channel Islands. Repeated letters from his father urged the teenage prince to join his mother in France: 'Your going beyond sea is absolutely necessary for me.' It was the only 'real security' the King could have, and would 'make the rebels hearken, and yield to reason', but only if the boy remained constant in his religion: 'for all other things, I command you to be totally directed by your mother.'[41] By June 1646, the Prince was in Paris.

Around New House, Scottish musketeers and 'inhabitants of trust' from the local militia kept constant guard. Old men from the town sat 'at every passage', ready 'to examine and take notice what persons came in or out'.[42] The King's few servants were all appointed by the Scottish government. Hudson and Ashburnham had fled to avoid being handed over to the English Parliament. Meanwhile, far from honouring Montreuil's settlement, the Scots only intensified their pressure on the King. Incessantly their lords and Presbyterian ministers demanded his 'full concession' to the peace terms the English Parliament had offered him in their 'nineteen propositions' back in 1642, demanding, among other things, parliamentary control over both the Church and the militia.[43] On one occasion, when the King retired weeping into his bedchamber, the Scots lords followed him in to press their demands again. Every Sunday, sermons of 'wholesome doctrine' were preached before him at New House or in the churches he attended in the town, advising him 'to dispose his spirit to peace and unity'. 'Thou piece of clay, where thou sittest, think of thy death, resurrection, judgement, eternity,' one minister exhorted him, before ending 'in a most compassionate way, with offer of mercy upon repentance'. Everyone seemed to be against the King. Even the Newcastle townspeople by and large regarded him as 'not only weak but very wilful and obstinate; . . . nothing can we see in him tending to a true Christian or the power of godliness'.[44]

Charles's sole refuge lay in his correspondence with Henrietta. 'All the comfort I have is in thy love,' he wrote to her: 'let me hear often from thee', 'for seriously, without compliment, thy love preserves my life'. As long as she continued kind to him, 'I care not much for others'.[45] Somehow, in the face of his enemies, Charles managed to preserve his usual outward calm: 'never man saw him passionately angry or extraordinarily moved,' commented a Presbyterian theologian who often engaged him in debate.[46] To Henrietta alone did he reveal his true feelings at 'the false juggling of the Scots, and the base usage that I have had since I came to this army'. The only people he saw now were 'fools or knaves', he complained; every day brought 'new vexations'. 'There was never man so alone as I,' he confided; 'I never knew what it was to be barbarously baited before.'[47]

Within a fortnight of reaching Newcastle, Charles had begun to 'expect the worst'. Henrietta must not be deceived by false hopes, he told her, for the new peace proposals expected from the London Parliament were bound to be 'such as I can never yield to'. His one desire was 'to go from hence to any other part of the world'. 'And, indeed, to deal freely with thee, my condition is such, that I expect never to see thee, except . . . I find means to quit for a time this wretched country.' [48] 'If I stay any time, I am lost.' And yet, despite his certainty that escape was imperative, Charles was not prepared to take such a step without his wife's approval. He begged her to think 'seriously and speedily' about his proposal, 'for, upon my word, it will not admit of long delay'. But Jermyn and the rest of Henrietta's men opposed the idea, arguing 'the danger of the attempt, and the provocation given to the Parliament if successful'.[49]

That July the peace proposals from Parliament were extraordinarily severe, and were pressed on him mercilessly by the Scots: 'indeed, it is almost incredible ... with what impudence I have been assaulted to yield,' he told Henrietta. Yet still Charles was determined 'to make no concessions'.[50] Rather than that, he was ready to face martyrdom for his rights. 'No threatenings, no apprehensions of danger to my person', no 'misplaced pity to me' must make any of them relent 'to the dishonour or prejudice of ... that kingly authority' that was Prince Charles's birthright. 'I know my cause to be so just, that (by the Grace of God) I shall never faint in it.'[51] Nevertheless, Henrietta and her advisers urged him repeatedly to abandon his commitment to the bishops and accept Presbyterianism in their place. This might be enough to satisfy the Scottish Covenanters and the English Presbyterians. Then, allied with them, the King could defeat his irreconcilable enemies, 'the Independent and anti-monarchical party', and restore himself to the throne. It was military power, not the state of the Church, that must be Charles's supreme consideration, they argued. 'Keep the militia, and never give up, and by that everything will return,' Henrietta wrote.[52]

Charles was appalled: his wife had completely misunderstood the situation. The Presbyterians were just as anti-monarchical as the Independents. Their aim was to free the Church entirely from the authority of the Crown, which in his view would be far more destructive than if he gave up control of the militia, 'for people are governed by the pulpit more than the sword in times of peace'. 'Believe it, religion is the only firm foundation of all power: That cast loose, or depraved, no government can be stable. For where was there ever obedience where religion did not teach it?'[53] His negotiations could never gain him acceptable peace terms, he now saw; he and his enemies were irreconcilably opposed.[54] All he could do was delay them 'as long as may be' while Henrietta sought foreign troops for his service. Only with 'a strong visible force' against them would the Scots 'hear reason', he told her.[55]

However, Henrietta knew no foreign aid would come. There was one stark choice confronting Charles: 'whether you will choose to be a king of presbytery, or no king' at all.[56] To her his resistance was incomprehensible. Her own father had abandoned his Protestant faith and converted to Catholicism so as to obtain the throne of France. 'Paris is worth a mass,' was his maxim. What Henrietta now asked of Charles seemed so much less than this: just exchanging one form of Protestantism – one form of heresy in her eyes – for another. And it would only be temporary, she kept telling him. She was now so fed up with the situation, she told Charles, that she desired to retreat into a nunnery. Only her 'passion' for him prevented her, and made her willing to 'endure all, if you think it for your service'.[57]

Charles was distraught. In 'inexpressible grief and astonishment', he begged Henrietta for mercy. 'The queen will break my heart if she anymore undertake to obtain my consent for Presbyterian government.' He implored her: 'for God's sake leave off threatening me.' Henrietta must promise never to go into a nunnery, 'for I assure thee, both I and all my children are ruined, if thou shouldst retire from my business'.[58] 'There is nothing in this world I love equal to thee.' Yet even to his beloved wife, he would not yield on this one great 'matter of conscience'. He had gone against his conscience before, he told her, when he 'made that base sinful concession concerning the Earl of Strafford'. Agreeing to that Bill of Attainder had been the most unhappy event of his life. It had been wrong, he now saw, 'to wound a man's own conscience, thereby to salve state sores'.[59] And he had been 'most justly punished' for it. 'No greater calamities' could have come if he had refused to sign that fatal Bill. It was this, more than anything else, that made him absolutely determined now to resist all 'violent importunities'. 'A new relapse' now, he told Henrietta, would only 'procure God's further wrath upon me'.[60]

For days on end Charles was occupied entirely at his desk. The pastimes of his early weeks in Newcastle – golf in the surrounding countryside, rides out along the river to Tynemouth, or games of chess indoors – were a thing of the past.[61] There was a constant round of letters: to Henrietta and her men in Paris, to Parliament in London, and to his enemies as well as old friends in Scotland. In mid-November, with news from London that an agreement might yet be possible, Charles turned to drafting peace proposals. Henrietta was furious when she heard what he had conceded.

With the granting the militia [to Parliament's control], you have cut your own throat; for having given them this power, you can no longer refuse them anything, not even my life, if they demand it from you; but I shall not place myself in their hands ... Do you think that when I see you so resolute in the affair of the bishops, and so little in that which concerns yourself and your posterity, that I am not in great despair, after having so often warned you as I have done, and it avails nothing? I tell you again, for the last time, that if you grant more you are lost, and I shall never return to England, but shall go and pray to God for you.[62]

As the stresses on the couple intensified, their relationship was approaching breakdown. Driven to desperation by Henrietta's accusations that he was 'destroying by my wilfulness all that is dear unto me', Charles even threatened to abdicate; it was a final attempt to force Henrietta to back down on her proposed concessions to Presbyterianism.[63] He was right to think she would be shaken. 'I hate it,' she replied by return of post. 'If any such thing should be made public, you are undone, – your enemies will make a malicious use of it. Be sure you never own it again in any discourse.' However, the King was utterly wrong to think he could browbeat his wife into changing her mind. Still she insisted that he was the one who was mistaken about the true political situation: he must either 'satisfy the Presbyterians' or 'leave the work undone'.[64]

Charles was at his wits' end when her reply arrived. What did he have to do to make her listen? Henrietta and her advisers would apparently trust 'any other information or intelligence' rather than what he said. At last his exasperation broke out. 'Good God, what things are these to try my patience! ... I could say much more upon this subject; but I will only conjure you, as you are Christians, no more thus to torture me, assuring you that the more ye this way press me, you the more contribute ... to my ruin.'[65]

The grim reality was that any concessions Charles offered now were irrelevant. For some months the Scots and the English Parliament had been forging ahead on a peace settlement entirely independent of the

King. Money would be paid to the Scots for their services in the war, and then they would withdraw.[66] Charles would be kept by the Scots or handed over to the English, whichever his enemies should decide, but in either case 'I shall be an absolute prisoner', he wrote to Henrietta, when rumours of the business reached him. Again he urged her 'to consider well' the idea of escape. Once he was out of Britain, he thought, the Scots and the English Parliament would quarrel 'and so give me an opportunity, either to join with the weaker party, or frame one of my own'.[67] He was well placed to flee. The Prince of Orange had sent a warship to Newcastle 'to do what the King commands'; some 5000 former soldiers from the royalist army were also gathering around the town.[68]

Then at the beginning of December the reply came back from Henrietta: 'do not think of making any escape from England.' A 'general peace' was very close on the Continent now, she explained, and then the French were sure to aid him. Their ambassador was already under orders to negotiate a treaty with the Scots to fight jointly against Parliament and restore the King. If Charles fled now, 'you would destroy all our hopes'; he should leave only if the Scots declared openly 'that they will not protect you'.[69] Against his better judgement, Charles remained. She was dooming him to imprisonment, he wrote back; once the Scots declared against him, it would be impossible to escape. Perhaps, however, she was right. Perhaps 'it is less ill for my affairs that I should be a prisoner in my own dominions than at liberty anywhere else', in which case foreign governments would be shamed into declaring themselves for his restoration. Wearily he filed Henrietta's letter away with a note on the back, 'From my wife, to be kept, being the advice – not stir afore.'[70]

Henrietta was astounded when she heard her husband's reply. She had never meant him to become a prisoner. If he fell into the hands of the Independents, she would 'never be free from the greatest apprehensions'. It was 'a thing not so much as to be thought on'. Instead Charles must 'go along with the Scots into Scotland', or, if they refused to take him, he could escape, to Ireland, the Scottish Highlands or Jersey, 'according to your own wisdom, and the conjuncture of affairs'.[71]

But long before Henrietta's authorisation reached him at Newcastle, Charles had already made his first attempt to escape. It was Christmas Eve when the news came that the Scottish Parliament had passed 'very harsh resolutions'. Charles must approve 'all the proposals of peace that have been presented to him by the two kingdoms'; until then his 'royal authority will remain suspended'.[72] This was the final spur to his decision to flee. Seeing not a single place in Britain 'where he could remain in safety', he planned now to join Henrietta in France. The new French ambassador, Bellièvre, tried desperately to change the King's mind, arguing especially 'the fear I have that it may be very difficult for him to return again' and suggesting that he might 'retire to the Scottish Highlands' rather than going abroad.[73]Charles, however, was determined. The Dutch ship waiting on the river was ready, 'victualled ... and new trimmed'. That day her captain was summoned to New House, to meet 'in private' with William Murray, one of Charles's grooms of the bedchamber. Later on, £100 was carried down to the captain. On Christmas morning word came back that, if the wind was fair, the Dutchman was happy to sail on the night tide, 'notwithstanding any opposition from Tynemouth Castle'. Charles was to go in disguise, either in 'the habit of a sailor' or as William Murray's servant.[74]

Late that night Murray went out to reconnoitre, but soon turned back, possibly because his attempt to open one of the town gates had failed – 'a key was set fast and broken', one news report claimed – or because the town was too crowded with guards, who, another report suggested, regarded him 'with suspicion'. At New House, Murray gave the Scots guards the night's password yet was still suspected, being out 'at so unusual a time', and he was held in the guard chamber for three hours 'until the Governor sent for him'.[75] All Newcastle was in uproar: 'the suspicion was so great, and the stir so great upon it'. At once General Leven sent his cavalry to guard the road to Tynemouth. Next day he ordered the King's guards to 'be strictlier posed than they have been hitherto', with a squadron of the Scottish lifeguards to 'watch every night'.[76]

Through the following week the King continued his desperate

attempts to escape. The Dutch ship was no longer an option: her captain had been summoned for questioning by Newcastle's mayor, and four parliamentary warships were approaching the mouth of the Tyne. So on the last day of 1646, Tobias Peaker, one of Charles's grooms of the privy chamber, was sent off to Hartlepool, twenty-five miles south of Newcastle, to 'see what ships were there'. Just outside Newcastle he lost his nerve. Realising he would be judged an 'accessary to an action which might prove so prejudicial to the kingdom', he turned back, to tell all he knew to the mayor.[77] That day the King's guards were doubled, 'both within his residence and without, and they go the rounds continually'. Extra cavalry was brought in 'to keep guard in the neighbourhood of the town'.[78]

Aware that he was in extreme danger, Charles sat down on Saturday 2 January 1647 to write a letter to Henrietta that he hoped might yet save his life. Gone now were all the arguments, pleadings and self-justifications of his earlier letters. Instead he stated his position succinctly: he was truly a prisoner at last, his escape 'most difficult, if not impossible'. With a tone of striking authority, Charles laid down his last, great requirement from his wife. She and Prince Charles must 'declare publicly' that his offers to his enemies in matters of religion had been most reasonable, and 'that neither of you will persuade me to go further, but rather dissuade me, if I had a mind to grant more'. This statement, Charles wrote, was 'absolutely necessary for my preservation. For if there be the least imagination that Prince Charles will grant more, then I shall not live long after.' The Scots, he reckoned, would put him to death so that his son could succeed to the throne and grant them their desires. Now, Charles thought, there was 'need to say no more. For I know thy love will omit nothing that is possible for my freedom.' Facing the possibility of his own death, he ended by begging his wife 'never to despair of a good cause', nor to abandon her labours for Prince Charles, 'even as thou loves me, who am eternally thine'.[79]

Next day a train of thirty-six carts entered York, with a 'large convoy' of parliamentarian troops. The journey from London had taken seventeen days, 'the ways being very bad'. Wagons had overturned and the

200 or so boxes they carried were filthy and mud-spattered. But inside them, safe still, was £200,000 in 'good gold and silver' coins – the first instalment of the £400,000 that the English Parliament had agreed to pay the Scots in recompense for all their 'pains, hazard, and charges' during the Civil War.[80] In return the Scots would withdraw from England and deliver the King into English hands as a prisoner. For twelve days the money remained in York, while the English and Scottish treasury officials counted out the coins: several hundred thousand of them at least, and perhaps over a million, if much of the money was in silver. Carefully each £100 was packed into a bag, sealed with both English and Scottish seals, and then ten bags were placed into each wooden chest, again sealed by both parties. On 15 January the job was finished, and the carts set off northwards. Nine days later the first instalments of the money began to be paid out to the Scots soldiers in Newcastle, 'each one reaching out for his share'.[81]

In France, Henrietta was distraught. She had believed all along that the Scots would never abandon their King. Every day she wept, overcome by 'the unhappy case of the king', who 'finds himself abandoned by all and before the gates of a prison'. In desperation, she talked of going to Ireland to raise support for Charles herself, or of retiring into a monastery, but she could make up her mind to neither. Instead she went to see her sister-in-law, Anne of Austria, complaining 'with bitter tears' of 'the conditions of herself and her husband' and laying the blame on France. The French ministers had led her on with promises 'of the great things they would do' once peace came in Europe, and these 'long delayed hopes' had reduced her and Charles 'to the utmost extremity'.[82]

At Newcastle, meanwhile, Charles remained calm, at least on the surface. When a commission of three lords and six MPs arrived from Parliament he was all charm, holding out his hand 'with affability' for each of them to kiss. Carefully the commissioners told him they were there 'to receive the person of the King from the Scots army', according to the orders of Parliament, 'and to serve him during the journey' to his house of Holdenby, sixty miles north of London.[83] At this Charles 'seemed very well pleased'. They were all 'very welcome', he said, for 'none of them were strangers to him', and their business was 'no less welcome' than they. He was eager now 'to remove jealousies and distrusts, and establish a right understanding betwixt him and his Parliament'. He even managed to make some jokes with the deputation's head, the Earl of Pembroke, who had so often entertained Charles at Wilton back in the 1630s.[84]

Still it was not too late for Charles to avoid being handed over to the English. If he accepted Presbyterianism, the Scots urged, they might take him with them when they left England. Otherwise, they warned, he would have to endure the 'strictness' of the English Independents, who would not only deprive him 'of the consolation of receiving the queen's letters and of the visits of his friends', but also treat him like a criminal, they said, with a parliamentary verger deputed 'to sleep in his bedroom' at night. Still Charles replied 'that he would never give his consent'; 'what was asked of him was equally opposed to his peace of conscience and to the welfare of his people'.[85] With quiet confidence he expected all would turn out well in the end. His subjects could never manage without him. 'Without my establishing [as King], there can be no peace'; 'the two nations must needs fall out.' Once he was in English hands, the Scots would back down and 'do for him ... what they have refused to do when they had him with them'. He had great hopes too from 'the power of France'. And some of his servants assured him that, although they had failed to get him out of Newcastle, they would certainly 'deliver him from Holdenby'.[86]

Charles hurriedly prepared for his English captivity. He destroyed all his papers that 'he could not without some risk of harm carry away with him'. He wrote to the Marquess of Ormond in Ireland, the last place where the King's men still had power, ordering him 'to follow the Queen's and Prince's direction, and not to stick at anything for want of legal power from the King'. There was a last letter for Henrietta too. She must believe no future message from him, he told her, unless it came via a person of unquestionable loyalty. And she must not allow Prince Charles to go to England, whatever 'threats or entreaties' Parliament might make and whatever her fears for himself.[87]

On the morning of Saturday 30 January 1647, the Scots paraded their entire cavalry through the centre of Newcastle, then on past New House and out into the country. By the afternoon there were just 500 soldiers left in the town, ready to make the final handover to the 500 English soldiers who arrived around 2 p.m. It was a 'friendly and brotherly parting' on the Scottish side, with the troops under strict orders not 'to plunder any houses, drive away any goods, nor exact . . . any moneys or provision'.[88] Nevertheless, popular feeling in the town was running high against their former occupiers. The Scots were 'nothing but Jews', 'people who had sold their king and their honour', just as Judas had sold Christ to his enemies. The newly arrived English officers were forced to 'blows and threats, to prevent the women of this town from following the Scottish troops and throwing stones at them while they were leaving'.

Meanwhile, inside New House, the commissioners from the Scottish Parliament were taking leave of the King. Some of them had tears in their eyes as they told him 'that as he refused to sign the proposals and treaties, they were obliged to hand him over to the English'. By now Charles's patience was utterly exhausted. Their refusal to receive him in Scotland was of no importance, he replied sharply, 'as even if he had been at liberty, he would rather have gone to those who bought [him] than to those who sold him'. As the Scots withdrew, their English counterparts entered the King's presence and 'at once set their guards'.[89]

This was the moment that Charles and Henrietta had dreaded for so long. The King was to be attended now only by servants 'appointed by Parliament', with orders not 'to allow any letter or paper to be given to him that they had not previously seen'. It was the end, at last, of the regular correspondence the couple had somehow managed to maintain through five years of civil war and its aftermath. The English government was in no mood for compromise or negotiation. 'They have informed their king of what he will have to do,' the MPs said; now Charles must stay at Holdenby 'until he has granted everything'. However, knowing the King was unlikely to give in, they expected that he would remain 'always at Holdenby', a perpetual prisoner.[90]

In fact Charles would spend less than four months at Holdenby before the turmoils of English politics carried him elsewhere. Snatched out of Parliament's hands by their own army, he spent five months at Hampton Court, negotiating with Oliver Cromwell and the other commanders. From them he fled to the Isle of Wight, to find only another, stricter imprisonment. Seized once again by the angry army, he was carried to London for trial. Finally, at 2 p.m. on Tuesday 30 January 1649, two years almost to the hour after his delivery into English hands at Newcastle, the King stepped out of the Banqueting House at Whitehall to be beheaded as a traitor to his country and his people.

12

Colombes, August 1669

It was twenty years after her husband's death that Henrietta Maria reached her own last day on earth – at Colombes, the country retreat outside Paris where she now spent most of her time. In her little chateau here the Queen, now aged fifty-nine, lived once more amidst the greatest luxury. The house was laid out as a royal court, with black-liveried guardsmen standing at the entrance to a suite of sumptuous apartments. Rich wall hangings matched the finely upholstered furniture: crimson brocade patterned with gold and silver thread in the grandeur of Henrietta's privy chamber; elegant grey silk in her bedchamber. Tables and cabinets were inlaid with tortoiseshell, or decorated in Chinese lacquerwork, or painted with veins to look like marble. Gilt mirrors hung in every room. Carpets were draped over beds and tables: most of them Persian, 'of gold, silver and silk of several colours'. Innumerable objets d'art were scattered through the rooms: a pot carved from rock-crystal with a silver-gilt lid, 'an Indian teapot, garnished with gold', 'an Indian box lined with rubies'. There were fine clocks, rare books, an amber statuette of Our Lady. Henrietta ate from gilded plates with gilded cutlery; twelve gilded candlesticks lit her to bed; her chamberpot was solid silver.

Paintings lined the walls of every room. There were numerous religious pictures, and fine old masters from her 1630s collecting, confiscated by Parliament but since restored to her: works by Correggio, Tintoretto, Giulio Romano, Titian and others. However, pride of place was given to portraits of her family. Facing the Queen every day were the children she never saw now. One was of her youngest son, Henry, dressed in sky blue: the 'little cavalier' who had delighted his mother when he joined her in Paris after his release by Parliament in 1653, only to depart, estranged, eighteen months later.[1] Another was of her eldest daughter, Mary, Princess of Orange. Widowed before she was twenty, she had brought up her baby son William alone, until she died of smallpox in 1660, amidst the celebrations of King Charles II's restoration. Charles II himself stood over the fireplace in Henrietta's privy chamber, 'a tall black[-haired] man, over two yards high', in soldier's buff coat and arms.[2] He was married now to the Portuguese Infanta, Catherine of Braganza – a Catholic match that delighted his mother. For three years Henrietta had lived with them in England, until ill health forced her return to 'the much purer' air of France, leaving behind her second son too. James Duke of York was now Lord Admiral in command of his brother's navy, as his father had intended thirty years earlier. Dressed in armour, he looked down on the Queen from above the door of her bedchamber. The only child Henrietta Maria still saw regularly was her youngest, Henrietta Anne, who lived in France, the wife now of Louis XIV's younger brother, Philippe. Her portrait as a girl hung in Henrietta's dressing room, along with her baby son, the Duc de Valois, in his swaddling clothes, fourth in line to the French throne.[3]

Henrietta herself was a diminutive figure, slight and frail, in sombre widow's weeds, with the black peak-cap and veil she had worn ever since her husband's death. Chronic illness dogged her final years; her old bronchial complaints had become a lingering, wasting disease, with the Queen growing ever weaker 'in a consumption'.[4] She was 'continually subject to fainting-fits, sleeplessness, and other bodily ailments', and often passed the day in great pain, confined to the crimson brocade four-poster bed that was set up in her privy chamber, contrary to normal royal etiquette. In her bedchamber there was a caddy of gilt cutlery, for meals when she was too ill to move at all. Henrietta, however, did not repine. 'Complaints in illness were useless,' she said, 'or, if they served for anything, it was to show the great weakness and the little resolution of the persons who complained.'[5]

Every day she spent hours alone in the little cabinet that opened off her bedroom. Even more than the rest of the house, this room was crammed with luxuries: carved agates and rock crystal, statuettes, intricate pieces of gold and silver filigree-work, curiosities from India, a large collection of Chinese porcelain. All these things 'of great value' stood atop the tables and mantelpiece, or were tucked away in the little cupboards and drawers of lavishly ornate cabinets. Exquisite little boxes were crammed with jewellery and portrait miniatures; a collection of twenty-two medals 'of gold, great and small', was stored in a purse. Henrietta paid them no heed. To her this room was like a nun's cell, where she came 'to commune more quietly and more ultimately with God'. The walls were covered with religious pictures, eighty or so in all, with just a few family portraits among them. Beneath them Henrietta knelt in prayer, while her watch ticked away the passing hours, hung on a purpose-made gold filigree hook. Henrietta's life at Colombes was strictly ordered. Every hour of the day was assigned 'to some particular employment': public prayers in her chapel, private 'mental prayer, the mass, meals, company, recreations, business'.[6]

Her cabinet was a bright and airy place, with wall hangings and curtains in white damask, to match the couch where Henrietta sat to read, taking her spectacles from their gold filigree case. Always it was the same book: Thomas à Kempis's *Imitation of Christ*, a guide to leading a perfect religious life in 'contempt of all the vanities of the world'. She read a chapter every day, and when the book was finished she started again from the beginning, 'saying that it was her daily bread and that she would never tire of it'. Sometimes she sat at her table of Jamaican braziletto wood, writing in her little leather-bound notebook, or personally going through her household accounts: a self-mortification that she offered to God 'in atonement for the human pride which always attends on crowned heads'.[7] Henrietta was content in her quietness and solitude, 'for she was undeceived about the world and perfectly acquainted with the worthlessness of Earth's grandeurs'. 'For some time now she had felt entirely devoted to God,' she said. Yet, twenty years on, her love for her husband 'always occupied her mind'. Not a single portrait of Charles hung on her walls; it would be too painful to encounter his face so continually. But hidden away among the seeming infinity of treasures in her cabinet was 'a little Indian box', containing a single miniature portrait of her dead husband, along with the betrothal and wedding rings he had given her.[8]

On that February midday back in 1649, when Henrietta, in her apartments in the Louvre, first heard the news of Charles's death, she had been stunned. Despite the warning signs from England, despite Henry Jermyn's attempts to prepare her for the worst, still she had not believed it could really happen. To us today it is no surprise. In the intervening centuries, other European monarchs have met similar ends: Louis XVI condemned for high treason and guillotined; Tsar Nicholas II forced to abdicate, then shot by the Soviet revolutionaries. But to Henrietta's contemporaries Charles's fate – tried by a court of law in his own realm and condemned to die publicly 'in the face of his people' – was monstrous and unnatural, a 'barbarous' act 'without precedent': 'no age ever heard the like'.[9] A king was a sacred person, 'Gods Vicegerent upon earth', set up by divine authority to rule his people. Charles himself, on the day before his trial, continued to think his enemies merely 'aimed at his deposing and confinement in the Tower, or some suchlike place'. Even the parliamentarian commissioners who sat in judgement on him had not really foreseen the end. When it came to it, many were unwilling to sign the King's death warrant and were forced to it only by Oliver Cromwell's coercion.[10]

At the Louvre, as Jermyn finished his dreadful tale, Henrietta remained silent, lost in her own shock. The man she had loved beyond all others was gone for ever: a man she knew to have been 'good, just, wise, worthy of her affection and his subjects' love'. It was 'the most cruel and shameful death that ever king died', beheaded as a traitor to his own country 'in the presence of an innumerable concourse of people, by the hand of an executioner, that is to say, of the vilest of men'.[11] She knew the place so well, outside the Banqueting House where she and Charles had spent some of their happiest evenings in feasts and plays and masques: the formal ranks of rectangular windows with their classical pediments forming a backdrop of royal grandeur that mocked the horrific events taking place before them. In this tragic scene there was just one consolation: Charles's calm and courage. The French ambassador in London paid special attention to this in his report to St-Germain, knowing it would reach Henrietta. On the scaffold Charles 'saw the preparations for such a fatal act with tranquility, spoke always with the same freedom, undressed himself and laid himself on the ground, and suffered the greatest violence ever seen with a resignation without example.'

But what had Charles really felt? As Henrietta sat motionless, without speaking, did she try to imagine what was going through her husband's head as he spread out his arms in signal to the executioner? Had he been afraid at that last moment, or angry? Had he felt any pain as the axe struck home? Perhaps she looked back to the last time she had seen him alive, at Abingdon in 1644, when in tears they had kissed each other farewell. Now, with hindsight, did she wish she had acted differently, perhaps spent longer or said more, or even stayed on in Oxford through the war to share her husband's fate? Perhaps she still hoped, beyond all hope, that Charles was not really dead. Just a few days earlier she had heard the false report that the King had been rescued from the scaffold. Might not this latest news too be premature, exaggerated? However, she could not really keep this hope for long: the news had come from the French ambassador in London himself.

Gone for ever were those years of bliss when she had been 'the happiest princess in the world'.[12] There would be no more idyllic summers in the country, riding, hunting and partying with their friends; no more shared winter pleasures in London, with dances, masques and plays; no more spring jaunts out maying in Hyde Park; no annual move to Greenwich in May to begin their seasonal round all over again. What would become of her now: exiled, dispossessed, penniless, stateless, a Queen rejected and detested by her own subjects?

And what of her children? Her son Charles, already proclaimed King Charles II by his followers at The Hague, was a monarch without a realm. James, his younger brother, had nothing in the world but what his mother could send him from her own, long-unpaid allowance from the French government. Henrietta Anne was just four years old, sharing her mother's destitution at the Louvre. And, still in England, there were Elizabeth and Henry, whom she had not seen for almost seven years. Would they grow up never knowing their own mother? Would Henry be placed on the throne, a puppet king in the hands of his father's enemies, as the news from England suggested? One thing she knew for certain: Charles's death had made her 'the most wretched woman in the world' and 'for the rest of her life this separation would be a perpetual torment'.[13]

Amidst Henrietta's grief there was anger too, not only at the parliamentarian enemies who had brought about her husband's downfall, but also at the European powers, her native France included, who had done nothing to help during all the years of civil war. Perhaps she was angry too with Charles himself. Over and over during the years of conflict she had told him to be more resolute, more ruthless and bold, but always he had shrunk from doing what was necessary. And, imprisoned by the Scots, when the time had come for subtlety and cunning, Charles had refused to follow her advice and accept Presbyterianism to save himself and his throne. Henrietta may have been more angry with herself. She had egged Charles on to try to arrest the five leading opposition MPs in 1642, precipitating the Civil War. She had persuaded him not to escape from the Scots while he still had the chance.

Some or all of these thoughts may well have gone through Henrietta's mind as she sat at her dinner table, 'quite overwhelmed, without words, without action, without motion, like a statue'.[14] Her courtiers tried to rouse her. Her chaplain, Father Cyprien de Gamache, brought all his armoury of religious arguments to bear. He reminded her that death was followed by God's judgement, when Christ would take away our sins and lead us to salvation. She must 'resign herself to the will of God'. Clearly, Providence had overturned her power so she might outlive all worldly attachments and 'sentiments of pride'; purified by her experiences, she would be able to come nearer to God.[15] To all such urgings Henrietta seemed 'deaf and insensible', unable to stir, weep, speak, or even hear. 'Small cares speak out, greater ones are dumb,' Gamache wrote in his memoirs, quoting the ancient Roman moralist Seneca: a perfect description of the condition now known as psychological shock. At last her companions could do no more, but remained standing around her 'all in profound silence, some weeping, others sighing, all with dejected countenance, sympathising in her extreme grief'. Hours passed. Then, as it began to grow dark, the Duchess of Vendôme arrived, wife of Henrietta's illegitimate half-brother, César; Henrietta was 'much attached' to her. In tears, the Duchess took Henrietta's hand, 'kissed it very affectionately, and then talked to her', until at last she roused her from her stupor.[16]

Still Henrietta remained plunged in the bitterest grief. Next day, when Madame de Motteville came to the Louvre, she found her in bed. Weeping, the Queen held out her hand to be kissed, then talked to her friend as best she could amidst 'a thousand sobs, which often interrupted her discourse'. 'The people were a ferocious beast which could never be tamed; the King her lord had proved it,' Henrietta warned the French court, which was still locked in civil war with the Paris Parliament. She had lost 'a king, a husband and a friend, whose loss she could never sufficiently mourn'; she was surprised only that 'she had been able to survive this misfortune'. From this moment she would wear 'a perpetual mourning both on her person and in her heart'.[17]

Henrietta was only thirty-nine years old, but she had no more desire for life. The world seemed 'disgusting to her'.[18] Her one wish was to spend the rest of her days in religious retirement. However, with her young daughter, Henrietta Anne, to look after, she knew she could afford no more than a temporary withdrawal from the world. Leaving the little girl behind at the Louvre, the Queen mounted into her carriage and drove eastwards along the bank of the River Seine, then over the Pont Notre Dame and south, beyond the city walls, to the Faubourg St-Jacques: a line of houses that stretched along the road, amidst gardens, vineyards and orchards. Here, just beyond the modern Boulevard de Port-Royal, stood the Carmelite Convent of the Incarnation, where Henrietta had often retired in childhood. Mère Madeleine was still the prioress, and in the last few years Henrietta had often come here to observe the principal holy days of the Catholic calendar. Now, 'with some of her ladies and bedchamber women', she devoted herself 'to prayer, to mortification, [and] to meditation'.[19]

She was not allowed to remain for long in private mourning. Duty, in the person of Father Gamache, soon called her back to the world. In England, Parliament had appointed a Council of State to govern the country, which was now 'a republic, without King or House of Lords'. As they prepared to confiscate all the royal family's possessions to fund the navy and the army, Gamache warned Henrietta that affairs 'were in a very bad state, and required her attentions, her counsels, and her efforts'.[20] This was what her husband had wanted, she knew. 'Though the worst should come,' he had written to her from Newcastle, 'yet I conjure thee to turn thy grief into a just revenge upon mine enemies, and the repossessing of Prince Charles into his just inheritances.' So, early in March, Henrietta returned to the Louvre, where she threw herself into political work, for the sake now of her son, King Charles II.[21]

To many people Henrietta seemed her normal self once more: energetic, authoritative, full of hopes and plans for her cause, but she was a changed woman. Her wit and fun were gone, and in their place was a deep well of bitterness and anger. Her husband's fate had convinced her of the worthlessness and injustice of the world, its unpredictability, the real misery she could expect to find in it. God's determination to try her to the last extreme, 'to afflict our family' and 'to humiliate kings and princes': these were her constant refrains.[22] Disappointments flooded upon her. In England her fourteen-year-old daughter Elizabeth, whom Henrietta had not seen for eight years, died in September 1650 in parliamentary captivity, 'far from doctors and medicines'. She was fortunate 'to be out of the hands of those traitors',

Henrietta told herself, although 'I do not fail to be very touched by it'. Two months later Mary's husband, William Prince of Orange, died of smallpox, leaving Henrietta weeping for the 'wretched condition' of her children, who had 'obtained powerful support from the rich resources of that house'.[23] Ten months after this loss her eldest son became a fugitive. The Scots had invited him to come to Edinburgh as their king; from there, he hoped, he could recapture the rest of Britain. Instead his army had been destroyed by Cromwell at the Battle of Worcester. For a month Henrietta was in agonies, not knowing whether her son was a prisoner or dead, and so anxious on his account that it 'renders me unfit for anything'. 'Pray to God for the King, my son,' she begged her friends. Finally Charles made his way to Paris. With his hair cut short and his beard grown, disguised as a servant in 'a most extraordinary costume', he was so changed that Henrietta did not recognise him. 'Very melancholy', Charles remained with his mother in the French capital, lacking money or scope for action.'[24]

In these years Henrietta's religion became an obsession. 'Wearied of the world', she often withdrew for weeks or even months at a time, first to the Carmelite convent outside Paris, then to the nunnery she herself had founded in 1651 at Chaillot, 'her beloved and most delicious retiring place'.[25] Here, in rolling countryside close to River Seine just west of Paris, she had bought a grand country house, financed by the Parisian Convent of the Visitation on the rue St Antoine. An abbess and twelve nuns from that convent were soon installed and Henrietta sent her own goods and furniture for them to use. She went to Chaillot for every major Catholic festival of the year and at other times besides, sharing as much as possible of the order's strict rules of life, and finding some peace, 'shut up' from all worldly affairs among the nuns, 'her inestimable friends'.[26]

When she was back at the Louvre once more, Henrietta's religion took on a militant tone. Following Father Philip's death, her chief religious adviser was Walter Montagu, who devoted himself to his priestly calling 'with great austerity'. Under his 'very passionate' urgings, Henrietta mounted a relentless campaign against Protestantism at her court. The Anglican chapel ceremonies held for her courtiers were abolished as a 'scandal'. When Charles II's advisers objected that this would alienate the British people, Montagu merely replied that Protestant support was 'of no importance to the king's restoration'. Soon the Queen went further, announcing that her ladies would be dismissed 'unless they would come over to the Romish mass'.[27]

Her eldest son left France in 1654, forced out, as the French government formed a new alliance with Cromwellian England. Henrietta wept at their parting: 'the King is as low now as ... he can be.'[28] And still no real aid came in from foreign powers. The few small royalist rebellions in Britain were easily crushed. At Cologne, Charles merely existed as best he could, while Henrietta suffered bouts of deep, immobilising depression.[29] There was, however, one great solace in Charles's departure. His youngest brother, the fourteen-year-old Henry, was left behind with their mother. The young king ordered him to obey her 'in all things, religion only excepted', whilst Henrietta promised 'never to attempt to work a change' in his religion, but secretly she was determined 'to do some good with him, if I can'.[30] After a few months she set busily to work, and every weapon in her armoury was brought to bear. Henry was a penniless exile with no prospects, she pointed out, but through the Church he might rise to be a cardinal one day. He owed obedience not to his brother but to her, both 'by the articles of [her] marriage and by the right of a mother'. In addition, his conversion would aid his eldest brother's restoration, which was 'impossible except by Catholic help'. When Henry still proved difficult, she packed him off to the monastery at Pontoise, where Walter Montagu was the abbot.[31]

Charles was appalled when he heard. Henry's conversion 'would be the greatest misfortune that ever befell him', he wrote to his mother. She was ruining all his own chances of returning to England, for Protestants were bound to believe her attempt to convert Henry was 'done with his consent', while his own action now to prevent her would 'disoblige all Catholics' and end all hopes of aid from abroad. If she did not desist, he threatened, it would 'cause a breach between them which will never be made up'. And he warned Henry that if he converted, he would be 'not only the cause of ruining a brother who loves you so well, but also your king and country', in which case 'you must never think to see England or me again'.[32]

To ensure his own desires prevailed, Charles sent one of his most trusted counsellors, the Marquess of Ormond, to Paris. All that his interview with the Queen achieved was to open the floodgates on Henrietta's rage and frustration. She cared nothing now for the opinion of Charles who, her courtiers freely said, was a 'faint-hearted', worthless, dissolute character, living scandalously with loose women who bore him illegitimate children; a king who came far 'short ... of his predecessors'.[33] Rather, she told Ormond, she was determined 'to fulfil her first duties, which are far above the consideration of consequences'. There was too great an 'obligation that lay upon her in conscience to have her son reformed of his errors'. Her promises had extended only to 'using no violence'. Even if her husband were alive, she would not listen to him either. As for Charles's threats of 'a breach between them', she could assure him for her part 'that he can never so far displease her as to reach that point ... notwithstanding all the cause he has given her for complaint in the past, and all that he can add in the future'.[34]

So Ormond travelled to Pontoise to see Henry himself. There, after several days' assurances of 'the disloyalty and the invalidity' of Henrietta's arguments, the boy was convinced. Returning to Paris, he informed his mother that he would obey his brother's wishes, which were 'more suitable to his inclinations and his duty'. At this, Henrietta's long pent-up bitterness exploded. 'She would no more own him as her son,' she said; she 'commanded him out of her presence, [and] forbade him any more to set his foot into her lodgings'. When Henry knelt and asked her blessing as he left, she refused to give it. If he wanted to join his brother, she said, 'she would not hinder him from doing what he pleased'. Before leaving Paris, he made a last attempt to heal the rift, writing her 'a very dutiful letter'. His mother refused even to receive it.[35] She never saw the boy again.

The only child left to her now was Henrietta Anne. From the start, the little girl had received a thoroughly Catholic upbringing. Henrietta was 'passionate on the point', and Charles II had not insisted: a royal daughter did not have the political importance of her brothers. At Chaillot she was instructed by her mother's nuns, as well as by Father Gamache, who emphasised her great good fortune in being 'called to the Catholic religion'. Of all her siblings, he said, she was 'the only one ... to possess that ineffable felicity to see herself happily in the way to heaven, whither the princes and princesses of her family could not come, while heresy made them walk in other tracks'.[36] His words would fire the girl's lifelong labours for her brothers' conversion, although for the moment she saw nothing of them.

Henrietta's attempt on Henry's religion left her utterly alienated from her sons. In 1656, Charles moved to the Netherlands, where his brothers joined him, commanding 3000 English royalists fighting under Spanish command against the combined Cromwellian and French armies. Henrietta in Paris remained on the political sidelines, unregarded, frustrated and impotent. She hated Charles's advisers, especially Sir Edward Hyde, whose 'arts', she believed, were turning her son against her.[37] Hyde and his party distrusted Henrietta in return; her influence was 'pernicious and destructive'. Some even saw her as having been responsible for the Civil War and all its 'bloodshedding, with the destruction of the most Christian and orthodox church in the world'.[38] Henrietta knew she was being deliberately excluded from the King's counsels, but her pleas for 'a fairer communication' between them fell on deaf ears, and when she tried to intervene in his court politics, she merely roused Charles to new ire.[39] All she could do was send weekly assurances of her good will, praying God to make her son 'the most happy person in the world'. Sometimes, overcome by her powerlessness, Henrietta sank into dejection and gave up on the correspondence altogether; she was 'useless' to Charles, she said, and so 'I avoid importuning you with my letters'. Hardest to endure was hearing the news of battles, when weeks or even a couple of months would pass 'in the greatest possible apprehensions' without news of her sons' safety.[40]

By 1658, Henrietta was 'so wrapped up in melancholy' that even Oliver Cromwell's death left her incapable of 'any very great rejoicing'. However, at last there was a rapprochement with Charles. As France's alliance with a republican England crumbled, Charles sought aid from the French court, where Henrietta became his chief negotiator, putting 'urgent pressure' on them for her son's 'restoration ... to his dominions'.[41] At the end of 1659 mother and son met once more. After five years' separation, the King 'was joyfully received by his mother', as well as by his sister, Henrietta Anne, grown in his absence to a 'pretty princess', fifteen years old. For twelve days Charles remained at Colombes, in happy domesticity. Henrietta Maria pronounced herself 'satisfied with the King'; there would be 'no future misunderstanding' between them. For his part Charles went so far as to make Lord Jermyn Earl of St Albans 'at the Queen's entreaty'.[42] Then he rejoined James and Henry in Brussels.

Finally, after months of frantic politicking on both sides of the Channel, the long-desired news came: England's Parliament had voted to restore the monarchy, 'according to the ancient and fundamental laws of this Kingdom'. In May 1660, Charles returned to England, greeted everywhere with 'shouting and joy'.[43] To Henrietta it seemed a miracle. After 'so many enterprises and so many exertions', all of them 'useless', Charles had been restored 'without war, without battle, without drawing a sword'.[44] 'We must, amidst all this, praise God,' she wrote to him: 'all this is from His hand; you can see that it is.' At Colombes she ordered bonfires lit, then went to Chaillot 'to hear the Te Deum sung' in celebration and thanksgiving. 'You cannot imagine the joy that prevails here,' she wrote from Paris. 'I do not have a scant minute to myself, for all the visits and business that I have.'[45]

After sixteen years of exile, her way was at last clear to return to England. Charles was pressing her to come and Henrietta herself was full of hope 'to see yet before I die all my family together, who will no longer be vagabonds'. That wish was not to be granted. In London, Henry died suddenly of smallpox; he was just twenty years old. Charles wept 'bitterly', having 'loved his brother tenderly'. Henrietta, who had been looking forward to a reconciliation after six years' separation, felt the loss as 'a most painful blow'.[46] Soon there was more bad news: James had 'married a girl in England ... who was pregnant before his marriage'. Henrietta was aghast. The match was utterly 'unbecoming';

the girl was the mere daughter of an English knight. Worse still: that knight was her old opponent, Sir Edward Hyde. The birth was very near, but nevertheless, as Henrietta arrived in England, she was determined to break the marriage.[47]

On Friday 2 November, the fifty-year-old Queen entered London, 'acclaimed with the utmost affection and joy, all the city bells being rung and bonfires lighted at every corner'. Her apartments at Whitehall had been 'richly decorated to receive her', and there she and Henrietta Anne held court to London society. The diarist Samuel Pepys thought Henrietta in her widow's weeds 'a very little plain old woman', though he considered the young princess 'very pretty'.[48] At first Henrietta was delighted with Charles: 'the King, my son, has received me with all testimonies of love which could be.' However, she was soon dismayed to find him taking James's part against her. In 'a great passion' she declared that if James's new wife ever set foot in Whitehall, she would leave the Palace at once 'and never come into it again'.[49] The quarrel simmered on into Christmas, when Henrietta suffered a new blow. Just three months after Henry's death, Mary too died of smallpox, 'to the intense grief of the whole court and especially of the king, who loved her most tenderly'. Henrietta felt the loss 'severely'.[50] Just three of the nine children she had borne still remained to her. She could bear England no longer. Planning to return to France in January 1661 for Henrietta Anne's wedding, she was now 'counting the moments' until she could leave.

At last, on the day before her departure, she agreed to see James's wife. After all her fears, she found the new Duchess of York 'a woman of much spirit and worth', with 'an air of grandeur in all her actions' and 'a great deal of wit'. Henrietta said she 'heartily forgave the duke and her, and was resolved ever after to live with all the affection of a mother towards them'.[51] Then she returned to Paris, where she saw her youngest daughter married to Philippe, Duc d'Orléans, younger brother of King Louis XIV. 'I wish it much,' Henrietta wrote; the match made Henrietta Anne the second lady in France and secured close relations between the two countries. But as the new bride left her mother's palace to join her husband, both mother and daughter wept. At Colombes that summer Henrietta Maria felt profoundly alone: 'I have here much silence.'[52]

For a time she found comfort with her two remaining sons. On Charles's pressing invitation, she returned to England the following year in the grandest style. Somerset House was now thoroughly repaired and refurnished after the depredations of the Interregnum. Her chapel there was reopened and her Capuchins once more began to make conversions, which Henrietta saw 'with great joy'.[53] Once more she maintained a vast royal household, where many of her old servants held posts. She spent lavishly on building work at Somerset House, constructing a new range of royal reception rooms, 'in every respect ... magnificent and costly'.[54] Here she received London's fashionable society, regaling them with stories of her adventures 'during the rebellion and war in England'. Hers was soon the most popular of all London's royal courts. Often, in the evenings, the whole royal family gathered here: Charles with his new wife, Catherine of Braganza; James and his Duchess; and the young Duke of Monmouth, the first of Charles's many illegitimate children, 'a most pretty spark of about 15 year old'; as well as Charles's favourite mistress, Lady Castlemaine.[55]

Henrietta often went out too to join London's social whirl: dining at the Lord Mayor's house with the King and his wife, or driving in Hyde Park, 'the King, Duke and others ... a-horseback, and the two Queens in the Queen Mother's coach', or walking of an evening in Pall Mall on Henry Jermyn's arm.[56] At Christmas there were ballets at Whitehall, which Charles pressed Henrietta to see. 'I am the happiest woman in the world,' she wrote, 'the King my son showing me so much affection and confidence that I could not have wished for more.'[57] Despite all their differences over the years, Charles really was devoted to his 'Mam', as he called her: 'never any children had so good a mother as we have,' he wrote to Henrietta Anne.[58] And Henrietta adored her son's new Queen: a zealous Catholic and 'the best creature in the world, from whom I receive so much affection'. Henrietta even found she had regained some of her old political importance. As Charles began to have difficulties with Parliament, he was ready to listen to her advice, recognising her long experience of English politics.

It was in Henrietta's lodgings at Somerset House that he now held his weekly political 'secret conferences'.[59]

As before, Henrietta's high-profile Catholicism and her obvious influence roused popular resentment. As Charles acted to exclude Puritan ministers from the Church of England, all 'London was highly discontented'. People were angry too at high taxes and 'at the King's neglect of government for his mistresses'. Henrietta got the blame: 'All was carried on by the Queen [Mother] and her cabal at Somerset House.' Salacious rumours about Henrietta's relations with Henry Jermyn revived: 'for certain the Queen Mother is married to my Lord St Albans.' At first Henrietta was unconcerned,[60] but gradually her spirits sank. The damp English climate exacerbated her ill health. By 1664 she was also heavily in debt. That winter she withdrew from the glamorous social round, to spend her evenings quietly with Queen Catherine. At Christmas, papers appeared around London 'menacing the extirpation of Popery and Mass in her chapel'. When a sore throat confined her to bed, rumours reported that she was secretly pregnant. Really afraid now, Henrietta planned to retire to France. There she might recover her health, and she would also see Henrietta Anne once more. Although she promised it would be only a temporary absence, the English, noting the vast train of wagons she took, containing all the fine furniture, paintings and other possessions from Somerset House, took the view that in reality 'she did not intend ever to return into England'.[61]

Henrietta spent most of her remaining four years at Colombes. Her visitors were few. Jermyn was one of the most frequent: now Charles II's ambassador in France, wealthier, more overweight and gout-ridden than ever – 'full of soup and gold', as the poet Andrew Marvell put it. Walter Montagu came too. Most valued of all was Henrietta Anne, who visited sometimes by herself and sometimes with her husband. Henrietta Maria had little conversation to entertain them with. 'As she advanced in piety, so also she held back from speaking on almost all things,' Madame de Motteville recalled. 'The last years of her life she had become scrupulous on this, she weighed her words and appeared very detached from life.'[62]

Gradually she was preparing for death. In the past, when she had thought of it as 'far distant, still the bare idea of it made her shudder; so she did not like any one to talk of that doleful subject'. But by the end of 1668, impelled by ill health, she was facing up to it. She had already made a general confession of all her sins 'with great application and very firm designs to apply herself to the care of her salvation'. Now she often said 'that she saw clearly that it was necessary to think of leaving'.[63] March 1669 brought 'a dangerous illness': with a high fever, she was coughing up blood. Her recovery was slow, and in June she was again 'very ill' with diarrhoea, which 'made her extreme weak'.[64] Her one desire now was to move to Chaillot, 'to pass the rest of her life in this place of solitude and retirement', especially as Charles II had cut her allowance by a quarter, making it impossible for her to maintain her old court. She was sick of doctors and medicines, she said; she would think of them no more, 'but only of her salvation'.[65]

However, on Henrietta Anne's insistence, France's leading physicians descended on Colombes, before she managed to arrange her departure to Chaillot. Their examination, on Saturday 28 August, was promising. All the Queen's symptoms – the fainting fits, insomnia, recurring fevers and chest infections – were 'painful, but without danger of death', pronounced Antoine Vallot, first physician to Louis XIV. He set out a regime of opiates and purges, culminating in a grain of laudanum on Monday night. This would help Henrietta to sleep and allow 'the quieting of the humours in her body, from whence they conjectured the great disorder came'. Henrietta was reluctant. She knew from experience that laudanum 'disagreed with her'; 'the famous English physician, Monsieur de Mayerne, had warned her never to take any'. But Vallot persisted, seconded by the personal physicians of both Henrietta Anne and her husband. So, unwillingly, Henrietta agreed.[66]

All next day Henrietta was occupied with religious observances, it being Lady Day, 'the festival of the nativity of the most blessed Virgin', a time of special devotion for her. That night she took her 'usual remedy', then, on Monday morning she was purged 'with a certain opiate designed for that purpose'.[67] That day was tiring too, as the Queen received 'several visits' from friends, and spent hours in 'long spiritual conversations' with her confessor, preparing to take communion next day. By suppertime she was feeling 'something indisposed' and said: 'if she continued so ill next day she would see nobody.' Nonetheless, she 'ate heartily, [and] amused herself agreeably after her repast, laughing as if nothing ailed her'.[68] When she retired to bed she was rather feverish, and her physician, Antoine d'Aquin, decided not to give her the laudanum after all. On Henrietta's orders, the curtains were drawn around her bed and her courtiers departed. Unable to sleep, around 11 p.m. she summoned d'Aquin back and demanded the dose. Suppressing his misgivings, he gave it to her, mixed into a raw egg yolk. At once the Queen fell asleep.

D'Aquin, sitting by her bedside and observing her shallow, sighing breaths and irregular pulse, realised she was sleeping 'too profoundly'. Desperately, he 'endeavoured by all the means he could to wake her', but 'all the several remedies used in such cases' had no effect.[69] Her *valets de chambre* were sent rushing to summon more doctors and Henrietta's priests too, who begged her to confess her sins or at least 'to give some sign that she understood'. They met only 'a mortal silence'. After a while, 'seeing that there was no abatement of her malady', Father Gamache gave orders for the Queen to receive extreme unction. Through the dark night, the village curé of Colombes 'came in haste' bearing holy oil, with which he anointed the Queen's eyes, ears, nostrils, lips, hands and feet. Between three and four in the morning of Tuesday 31 August, 'without violence, without the slightest convulsion, with great serenity, and a sweet expression of countenance', the 59-year-old Queen slipped away into death.[70]

None of the earthly remains of the royal couple who had loved each other so dearly was ever reunited. On the orders of Louis XIV, Henrietta's body lay in state for five weeks in the Abbey of St Denis, just outside Paris, before being buried there, among the French royal graves dating back over 1000 years. Charles's body remained 300 miles away across the Channel, at Windsor Castle, where it had been interred 'without ceremony' after Parliament refused it a place among the kings at Westminster Abbey.[71] 'My dear heart', they had called each other so often, but after twenty years of widowhood, Henrietta's piety and world-weariness had the stronger claim. On her instructions, the heart was cut from her dead body and laid to rest in the chapel of her convent at Chaillot. The Queen's life had been, her funeral sermon that day proclaimed, 'one of those fearsome examples' that proved the world's 'utter vanity'. She had seen 'all the extremes of things human: happiness without bounds, as well as miseries'.[72]

NOTES

PROLOGUE: WINTER 1649

1. For Henrietta's apartments, see Evelyn, *Diary*, ed. Bray, II, 103 n. 1. For the date, see Petitot, (ed.), *Mémoires*, 2nd series, XXXVIII, 204. This and all other dates given in this book are in the old-style, Julian calendar that was used in England in the seventeenth century. The Gregorian calendar now in use is different by ten days.

2. Bossuet, *Oraisons*, 74.

3. Motteville, *Memoir*, 19. See also Montpensier, *Mémoires*, part 1, ch. 3; Reresby, *Memoirs*, 28. Charles too had reckoned himself the happiest king in Christendom: see Wedgwood, *King's Peace*, 19–20.

4. Petitot (ed.), *Mémoires*, 2nd series, XXXVIII, 205, 207; Motteville, *Memoir*, 19.

5. Clarendon, *History*, I, 94; Clarendon, *Life*, I, 36; Carew, *Works*, 95. See also Motteville, *Mémoires*, I, 184, 186; *CSPV 1632–1636*, 362.

6. Green, *Letters*, 248, 249.

7. Motteville, *Memoir*, 26; Bossuet, *Oraisons*, 115.

8. Motteville, *Mémoires*, I, 222. See also Montpensier, *Mémoires*, part 1, ch. 3.

9. Sophia, Electress of Hanover, *Memoirs*, 13.

10. Motteville, *Mémoires*, I, 223, 222; Sophia, Electress of Hanover, *Memoirs*, 13. See also Motteville, *Memoir*, 28.

11. Motteville, *Memoir*, 26, 27; see also Petitot (ed.), *Mémoires*, 2nd series, XXXVII, 414.

12. BL Add. MS 12, 186, ff. 8v, 10v.

13. Sources for courtly dinner etiquette are Society of Antiquaries, *Collection of Ordinances*, 341–2; Charles and Henrietta dining in public, painted by Houckgeest; *The Babees' Book*, passim; Comenius, *Orbis Pictus*, 226–7.

14. Ellis, *Original Letters*, 2nd series, vol. III: 344; Madame de Motteville, as quoted in Strickland, *Lives*, V, 351.

15. Green, *Letters*, 337–8; *CSPV 1643–1647*, 320. See also ibid., 314; Fea, *Memoirs*, 80; Green, *Letters*, 344–5.

16. *Eikon Basilike*, ch. 7.

17. *CSPV 1643–1647*, 305. See also Fea, *Memoirs*, 80, 130–1.

18. See *Eikon Basilike*, ch. 24.

19. Clarendon, *History*, I, 109.

20. Clarendon, *State Papers*, II, 274; Harrison (ed.), *Jacobean Journal*, 103; Clarendon, *State Papers*, II, 274.

21. *CSPV 1643–1647*, 306. See also ibid., 305; Montereul, *Correspondence*, I, 441; *Calendar of Clarendon State Papers*, I, 363.

22. Fea, *Memoirs*, 107.

23. Fea, *Memoirs*, 96, 80; *Eikon Basilike*, ch. 24. See also Fea, *Memoirs*, 94, 127.

24. Charles I, *Reliquiæ*, 290. See *Eikon Basilike*, passim, for many expressions of these sentiments.

25. Clarendon, *State Papers*, II, 273; Warwick, *Memoires*, 328. See also Ashley, *Charles I and Oliver Cromwell*, 178; Clarendon, *State Papers*, II, 213.

26. As quoted in Ashley, *Charles I and Oliver Cromwell*, 178. See also *ibid.*, 177.

27. Warwick, *Memoires*, 297; Fea, *Memoirs*, 97.

28. As quoted in Green, *Lives*, VI, 355.

29. Clarendon, History, IV, 251, 252–3.

30. Green, Lives, VI, 358.

31. Clarendon, *History*, IV, 281; *CSPV 1647–1652*, 39. See also Underdown, 'Parliamentary Diary', 155.

32. As quoted in Green, *Letters*, 345–6.

33. Petrie, *Letters*, 239. For Charles's offer, see Gardiner, *History of the Great Civil War*, IV, 220.

34. Warwick, *Memoires*, 326.
35. As quoted in Gardiner, *History of the Great Civil War*, IV, 119–20.
36. *CJ*, VI, 13 December 1648.
37. Clarendon, *History*, IV, 471.
38. Green, *Letters*, 349; Dauncey, *History*, 127; Green, *Letters*, 350. For Henrietta's lack of firewood, see Green, *Lives*, VI, 413.
39. BL Add. MS 12, 186, f. 12r. See *CSPV 1647–1652*, 86, for the news arriving at last.
40. *Life and Death*, 44.
41. *CSPD 1648–1649*, 346; *CSPV 1647–1652*, 86; Ellis, *Original Letters*, 2nd series, vol. 3: 344.
42. *CSPV 1647–1652*, 86. For the commissioners, see Gardiner, *History of the Great Civil War*, IV, 293.
43. Petitot (ed.), *Mémoires*, 2nd series, XXXVIII, 204.
44. BL Add. MS 12, 186, f. 3v.
45. Birch, *Court and Times of Charles*, II, 381.
46. Lockyer, *Trial*, 81; Fea, *Memoirs*, 133; Warwick, *Memoires*, 336.
47. Lockyer, *Trial*, 81. See also Fea, *Memoirs*, 132–3; Jusserand, *Recueil*, XXIV, 69–70; Warwick, *Memoires*, 336; Gardiner, *History of the Great Civil War*, IV, 297–9.
48. Petrie, *Letters*, 241–3.
49. Petrie, *Letters*, 244–6; Fea, *Memoirs*, 134; Petrie, *Letters*, 247–50.
50. Petrie, *Letters*, 249–55. For Charles's stammer, see Warwick, *Memoires*, 339.
51. Fea, *Memoirs*, 132; Lockyer, *Trial*, 102.
52. Quotes are from Lockyer, *Trial*, 101–16; Petrie, *Letters*, 255–8.
53. Warwick, *Memoires*, 94; *Oxford DNB*: William Juxon. See also Panzani, as quoted in Albion, *Charles I*, 413, for a similar character description.
54. Warwick, *Memoires*, 94; *Eikon Basilike*, ch. 2; Prideaux, *History*, 360.
55. Warwick, *Memoires*, 340; Fea, *Memoirs*, 136, 137.
56. Fea, *Memoirs*, 138. See also ibid., 141. Prince Charles's letter is printed in Charles I, *Reliquiæ*, 303.
57. Fea, *Memoirs*, 139–40.
58. Charles I, *Reliquiæ*, 300–2.
59. Fea, *Memoirs*, 140, 141–2.
60. Fea, *Memoirs*, 74.

61. Fea, *Memoirs*, 142–3, 140. See also ibid., 122–3, 129, 132; Warwick, *Memoires*, 341–2.
62. As quoted in MacGregor, *Late King's Goods*, 272. For illustrations of the clothing and jewels worn by Charles for the execution, see Fea, *Memoirs*, passim.
63. Fea, *Memoirs*, 145.
64. *CJ*, VI, 30 January 1649. See also Fea, *Memoirs*, 145; *King Charls His Speech*.
65. *True Discourse*, 35.
66. *King Charls His Speech*.
67. Pepys, *Diary*, I, 280. See also ibid., 265.
68. Ellis, *Original Letters*, 2nd series, vol. III: 346. See also ibid., 342, 345; Warwick, *Memoires*, 344.
69. Charles I, *Reliquiæ*, 304.
70. All quotes are from *King Charls His Speech*.
71. Fea, *Memoirs*, 45; Ellis, *Original Letters*, 1st series, vol. III, 323; Fea, *Memoirs*, 45. For the troops, see *King Charls His Speech*.
72. *King Charls His Speech*. See also Jusserand, *Recueil*, XXIV, 70.

CHAPTER ONE: STRANGERS

1. King James to Parliament, as quoted in Gregg, *King Charles I*, 109. James's appearance is based on portraits, and on Wilson, *History*, 289–90; W[eldon], *Court and Character*, 177–89.
2. *CSPD 1623–1625*, 521; Cabala, 292. For the court in Cambridge, see Birch, *Court and Times of James*, II, 484–6; *CSPD 1623–1625*, 405, 411, 412; *CSPV 1623–1625*, 515, 521–2; *HMC Mar and Kellie*, 216; Brienne, *Mémoires* (1824), 389–90; BL King's MS 135, ff. 167v–172v; *Hardwicke State Papers*, I, 547.
3. For the marriage treaty and other documents signed along with it, see *HMC Salisbury MSS*, 197–8; *CSPD 1623–1625*, 405; BL King's MS 135, ff. 65v–72r, 186r–188v, 204r; *Hardwicke State Papers*, I, 546; BL MS Add. 37028, ff. 8, 9; *CSPV 1623–1625*, 523–5.
4. *CSPD 1623–1625*, 166. See also Ellis, *Original Letters*, 1st series, vol. III, 181; ibid., 2nd series, vol. III, 243; Cabala, 288; Patterson, *King James VI and I and the reunion of Christendom*.
5. As quoted in Gregg, *King Charles I*, 27.

6. *CSPV 1623–1625*, 201, 405. For the history of the French and Spanish marriage proposals, see Ellis, *Original Letters*, 2nd series, vol. III, 227 (1612); Herbert of Cherbury, *Autobiography*, 199, 200; Richelieu, *Lettres*, VII, 938; Albion, *Charles I*, 1–12.

7. *CSPV 1623–1625*, 492 (for 'angry'); *CSPD 1623–1625*, 412.

8. Clarendon, *History*, I, 11.

9. As quoted in Bowle, *Charles the First*, 7; *CSPV 1621–1623*, 452.

10. *CSPD 1623–1625*, 156. For Buckingham's 'supreme influence', see also *CSPV 1623–1625*, 462; *CSPD 1623–1625*, 93, 231, 238, 413. For the French match as Buckingham's brainchild, see *Cabala*, 282, 296. Principal sources for the Duke of Buckingham are Lockyer, *Life*; Clarendon, *History*, I, 10–13, 38–43.

11. Ellis, *Original Letters*, 1st series, vol. III, 92. For Charles's character and early life, see Ellis, *Original Letters*, 1st series, vol. III, 92–6; Heylin, *Short View*, 1–34; Clarendon, *History*, III, 197–9; Warwick, *Memoires*, 64–75; *CSPV 1621–1623*, 450–4; Bowle, *Charles the First*; Carlton, *Charles I*; Gregg, *King Charles I*.

12. *CSPV 1623–1625*, 452, 500.

13. Ellis, *Original Letters*, 1st series, vol. III, 158; Fraser, *King James*, 121; Carlton, *Charles I*, 22.

14. Ellis, *Original Letters*, 1st series, vol. III, 147; Clarendon, *History*, I, 10.

15. Clarendon, *History*, I, 12. The figure of £80,000 comes from Bowle, *Charles the First*, 45.

16. As quoted in Bowle, *Charles the First*, 48.

17. *CSPV 1621–1623*, 451. See also Heylin, *Short View*, 15.

18. Carlton, *Charles I*, 22.

19. Clarendon, *State Papers*, II, Appendix, xxv; Petrie, *Letters*, 4.

20. *CSPV 1621–1623*, 451; Petrie, *Letters*, 7.

21. McClure (ed.), *Letters of Chamberlain*, II, 434. See also Birch, *Court and Times of James*, II, 313–14; *CSPV 1623–1625*, 75, 386–7; *CSPD 1623–1625*, 231; Petrie, *Letters*, 4–15, 17–30, 33–4, 40–5, 50–7; Ellis, *Original Letters*, 1st series, vol. III, 145–8; BL Harleian MS 6,988, f. 74.

22. Clarendon, *History*, I, 14. See also Wotton, *Reliquiæ*, 80–1.

23. Clarendon, *History*, I, 14–19.

24. *CSPV 1623–1625*, 37; the Spanish minister Olivares, as quoted in Bowle, *Charles the First*, 69. See also *CSPV 1623–1625*, 76, 189.

25. *CSPV 162–1625*, 136.

26. Shorney, *Protestant Nonconformity and Roman Catholicism*, 58–60.
27. As quoted in Gregg, *King Charles I*, 87.
28. *CSPV 1623–1625*, 232. See also *CSPV 1623–1625*, 269.
29. *CSPV 1623–1625*, 114, 185. Principal sources for the Spanish match and the subsequent Parliament are Albion, *Charles I*, 11–48; *CSPV 1621–1623*, passim; *CSPV 1623–1625*, passim; Bowle, *Charles the First*; Carlton, *Charles I*; Gregg, *King Charles I*.
30. *CSPD 1623–1625*, 191; *CSPV 1623–1625*, 249. See also *CSPD 1623–1625*, 169.
31. *CSPV 1623–1625*, 242; *CSPD 1623–1625*, 192. See also ibid., 191; *CSPV 1623–1625*, 254.
32. *CSPV 1623–1625*, 280. See also ibid., 295, 300–2, 303; *CSPD 1623–1625*, 196, 212.
33. *Cabala*, 281. See also ibid., 274, 279.
34. Clarendon, *History*, I, 78. See ibid., 76–9, for full characters of Kensington and Carlisle. Principal sources for the French marriage negotiations are Clarendon, *State Papers*, II, Appendix; *Cabala*, 274–97; *Hardwicke State Papers*, I, 523–72; *CSPV 1623–1625*, passim; *CSPD 1623–1625*, passim; Albion, *Charles I*, 49–77.
35. *CSPV 1623–1625*, 377; *Hardwicke State Papers*, I, 535; *CSPV 1623–1625*, 434.
36. *CSPV 1623–1625*, 365; Birch, *Court and Times of James*, II, 470.
37. *CSPV 1623–1625*, 455–6; Birch, *Court and Times of James*, II, 466.
38. Clarendon, *State Papers*, II, Appendix, x.
39. Charles to the Earl of Carlisle, 19 October 1624: as quoted in Carlton, *Charles I*, 57; *CSPV 1623–1625*, 394. See also *CSPV 1623–1625*, 478, 479.
40. *CSPV 1623–1625*, 496, 492.
41. *CSPD 1623–1625*, 383; *CSPV 1623–1625*, 503. See also ibid., 492, 497, 504; *CSPD 1623–1625*, 393, 400; Nichols, Progresses, IV, 1007.
42. *Cabala*, 292; *CSPV 1623–1625*, 496. For Charles's 'great joyfulness', see ibid., 504.
43. *Cabala*, 277.
44. Petrie, *Letters*, 8, 9. See also Bassompierre, *Mémoires*, III, 431.
45. *Life and Death*, 10. See also Clarendon, *State Papers*, II, Appendix, vi.
46. Clarendon, *State Papers*, II, Appendix, vi, iii, vi. See also ibid., xvi.
47. Ellis, *Original Letters*, 1st series, vol. III, 178; Clarendon, *State Papers*, II, Appendix, xii.

48. Ellis, *Original Letters*, 1st series, vol. III, 179; *Hardwicke State Papers*, I, 528.

49. Bodleian Library Clarendon MS 97 contains Charles's draft of this letter, printed (without indicating his amendments) in *Calendar of Clarendon State Papers*, I, Appendix II. For Charles's mode of signature, see *Calendar of Clarendon State Papers*, I, Appendix I, 5; Toynbee, 'Two Letterbooks', 358. For the date of the letter, see *CSPV 1623–1625*, 504, 510; *CSPD 1623–1625*, 400.

50. BL King's MS 135, ff. 164r–165r. For Marie de' Medici's apartments and etiquette there, see Battifol, *Vie Intime*, I, 70–5, 85–6, 102–3, 116. For Carey, see *CSPV 1623–1625*, 504, 510, 520; *CSPD 1623–1625*, 400; Clarendon, *State Papers*, II, Appendix, xiii, xvii; Clarendon, *Calendar of State Papers*, I, Appendix I, 5; BL King's MS 135, f. 159r.

51. Birch, *An Historical View*, 492.

52. My principal sources for Henrietta's parents and childhood are Battifol, *Vie Intime*, I, chapters 1–5, II, chapter 7; Strickland, *Lives*, V; Dupuy, *Henriette Marie*; Hamilton, *Henrietta Maria*; Marshall, *Henrietta Maria*; Plowden, *Henrietta Maria*. Motteville, *Mémoires*, I, 223–4 describes Henrietta's character.

53. BL MS Royal 16 E XLI is Henrietta's collection of Henri's 'reparties, rencontres, et autres dits memorables'.

54. Tillières, *Mémoires*, 57. See also *Cabala*, 276.

55. *Cabala*, 282. For Henrietta's great expectations, see ibid., 286; *CSPV 1623–1625*, 486, 559; Clarendon, *State Papers*, II, Appendix, xii, xiv. For Marie's orders, see ibid., xii.

56. *Cabala*, 280; Clarendon, *State Papers*, II, Appendix, ii, xii. See also ibid., v; *Cabala*, 276, 280.

57. *Cabala*, 280.

58. Clarendon, *State Papers*, II, Appendix, ii, iv. See also ibid, vi; *CSPD 1623–1625*, 360.

59. Clarendon, *State Papers*, II, Appendix, iii, iv.

60. Clarendon, *State Papers*, II, Appendix, ix; Ellis, *Original Letters*, 1st series, vol. III, 175. This letter is also printed in *Cabala*, 288–91.

61. *CSPV 1623–1625*, 486; Clarendon, *State Papers*, II, Appendix, xi. See also *Calendar of Clarendon State Papers*, I, Appendix I, 5.

62. BL King's MS 135, f. 165r.

63. Clarendon, *State Papers*, II, Appendix, xvii. For Henrietta's reception

of Charles's letter, see also Howell, *Epistolae*, I, 222; *Life and Death*, 9–10; Heylin, *Short View*, 35. For the date of her reply, see BL King's MS 135, ff 224r–v, 227v–228r.

64. Ellis, *Original Letters*, 1st series, vol. III, 180; *CSPV 1623–1625*, 539. See also Birch, *Court and Times of James*, II, 494.

65. Clarendon, *State Papers*, II, Appendix, xx; *Cabala*, 296.

66. *Life and Death*, 10; Clarendon, *State Papers*, II, Appendix, xxi. See also *CSPV 1623–1625*, 559.

67. Clarendon, *State Papers*, II, Appendix, xxii, xxi; *Calendar of Clarendon State Papers*, I, Appendix II, 11 *bis*.

68. *CSPV 1623–1625*, 576; *Calendar of Clarendon State Papers*, I, Appendix, II, 11.

69. *Calendar of Clarendon State Papers*, I, Appendix II, 11, Appendix I, 6; *Hardwicke State Papers*, I, 558. See also *Calendar of Clarendon State Papers*, Appendix, II, 11.

70. *CSPV 1623–1625*, 610; *Calendar of Clarendon State Papers*, I, Appendix II, 12. See also *CSPV 1623–1625*, 615; Birch, *Court and Times of James*, II, 506–7; *HMC Mar and Kellie*, 224.

71. *CSPV 1623–1625*, 625, 627; Fuller, *Church History*, book X, 113; *CSPV 1623–1625*, 627. For James's illness, see also ibid., 623; Birch, *Court and Times of James*, II, 504, 508; *CSPD 1623–1625*, 505, 507, 509; *Hardwicke State Papers*, I, 562, 565; Ellis, *Original Letters*, 1st series, vol. III, 182.

72. *CSPD 1625–1626*, 1. See also Laud, *Works*, III, 158.

73. Ellis, *Original Letters*, 2nd series, vol. III, 244; *HMC Skrine MSS*, 5, 4; Ellis, *Original Letters*, 2nd series, vol. III, 244.

74. *CSPD 1611–1618*, 273; *CSPV 1625–1626*, 26–7.

75. Warwick, *Memoires*, 65; *HMC Skrine MSS*, 6; *CSPD 1625–1626*, 10.

76. *CSPD 1625–1626*, 10; Birch, *Court and Times of Charles*, I, 5, 12. See also *HMC Skrine MSS*, 10; *CSPV 1625–1626*, 4, 11, 34; Birch, *Court and Times of Charles*, I, 17.

77. *Calendar of Clarendon State Papers*, I, Appendix I, 7. See also *HMC Skrine MSS*, 7.

78. *CSPD 1625–1626*, 25.

79. *CSPV 1625–1626*, 44.

80. *CSPV 1625–1626*, 10; BL King's MS 135, f. 123v–124r; Strickland, *Lives*, V, 205. Chevreuse was related through Charles's great-grandmother Mary of Guise, mother of Mary Queen of Scots. For the wedding, see

also BL King's MS 136, ff. 463–499v; Strickland, *Lives*, V, 203–6; *CSPV 1625–1626*, 44; *True Discourse*.

CHAPTER TWO: FIRST IMPRESSIONS

1. Clarendon, *State Papers*, II, Appendix, xxiii; BL King's MS 136, f. 499r. See also *CSPV 1625–1626*, 44.
2. Birch, *Court and Times of Charles*, I, 20; BL King's MS 136, f. 257v. See also Birch, *Court and Times of Charles*, I, 18; *CSPV 1625–1626*, 51.
3. Clarendon, *State Papers*, II, Appendix, xxiv.
4. Petrie, *Letters*, 39.
5. Laud, Works, III, 162; *CSPV 1625–1626*, 59. For Buckingham's journey, see also Birch, *Court and Times of Charles*, I, 22; *HMC Skrine MSS*, 14, 17; Laud, *Works*, III, 162; *CSPD 1625–1626*, 22; BL Add. MS 12,528, ff. 21v.
6. Rushworth, *Historical Collections*, I, 170. See also *Mercure françois*, XI, 365.
7. *CSPV 1625–1626*, 65; BL King's MS 136, f. 499v; BL King's MS 136, f. 499v.
8. *HMC Skrine MSS*, 19; Clarendon, *History*, I, 47. See also Ellis, *Original Letters*, 1st series, vol. III, 189n.
9. Motteville, *Mémoires*, I, 14; Petitot (ed.), *Mémoires*, 2nd series; XXXV, 'Memoires de P. de La Porte', in Michaud and Poujoulat (eds), *Mémoires*, VIII, 7.
10. Motteville, *Mémoires*, I, 14–15; Tillières, *Mémoires*, 61. See also ibid., 59–62; 'Memoires de La Rochefoucauld', in Michaud and Poujoulat (eds), *Mémoires*, V, 381; D'Ewes, *Autobiography*, I, 386, 389.
11. Tillières, *Mémoires*, 61; *HMC Skrine MSS*, 19; *CSPV 1625–1626*, 88. For French aid to the Prince Palatine, see Clarendon, *State Papers*, II, Appendix, xxv; *CSPV 1625–1626*, 67–8; *HMC Skrine MSS*, 17.
12. Houssaye, *Cardinal de Bérulle*, 8–9.
13. *CSPV 1625–1626*, 68, 81.
14. *Mercure françois*, XI, 373.
15. For Henrietta's domestic personnel, see Petitot (ed.), *Mémoires*, 2nd series, XXXV, 408; BL King's MS 136, ff. 416v–423; PRO SP 16/3/113–14. For her religious household, see BL King's MS 135, f. 75r; King's MS 136, f. 429v; Houssaye, *Cardinal de Bérulle*, 22.

16. BL King's MS 135, f. 40v; Richelieu, *Lettres*, II, 18–19. For Bérulle's career, see Dagens, *Bérulle et les origines de la restauration catholique*; Dagens, *Correspondance du cardinal Pierre de Bérulle*; Houssaye, *Cardinal de Bérulle*.

17. As quoted in Albion, *Charles I*, 13.

18. Houssaye, *Cardinal de Bérulle*, 9–11.

19. BL King's MS 135, 527v.

20. BL King's MS 136, f. 52r.

21. As quoted in Albion, *Charles*, 77. See also *The Catholic Encyclopedia*, Golden Rose; Isaiah xi, 1–7; Romans xv, 12.

22. *CSPV 1625–1626*, 84.

23. For Charles wanting Buckingham and Henrietta present, see *CSPV 1625–1626*, 63; *HMC Skrine MSS*, 17, 19. For Charles delaying Parliament, see *CSPV 1625–1626*, 62, 70; (Ellis, *Original Letters*, 1st series, vol. III, 192); Birch, *Court and Times of Charles*, I, 21, 22; *HMC Skrine MSS*, 17, 19; Laud, *Works*, III, 162, 163.

24. *CSPV 1625–1626*, 62. See also ibid., 63, 70, 83.

25. Birch, *Court and Times of Charles*, I, 32. See also *CSPV 1625–1626*, 69, 81.

26. See *CSPV 1625–1626*, 69–70; Birch, *Court and Times of Charles*, I, 27; Toynbee, 'Wedding Journey', 78–81.

27. *HMC Skrine MSS*, 20. See also *CSPV 1625–1626*, 69; Birch, *Court and Times of Charles*, I, 27.

28. Clarendon, *State Papers*, II, Appendix, xix; Finet, *Finetti Philoxenis*, 152. See also *CSPV 1625–1626*, 87; Brienne, *Mémoires*, 407.

29. *CSPD 1625–1626*, 37. See also Finet, *Finetti Philoxenis*, 152; *CSPV 1625–1626*, 81.

30. Clarendon, *State Papers*, II, Appendix, xix. See also Birch, *Court and Times of Charles*, I, 28; Toynbee, 'Wedding Journey', 79; *CSPV 1625–1626*, 81; *HMC Skrine MSS*, 21.

31. *CSPV 1625–1626*, 83; BL King's MS 136, ff. 316v–318r. See also ibid., ff. 315r–v; *HMC Skrine MSS*, 14, 21; Finet, *Finetti Philoxenis*, 153.

32. See Petitot (ed.), *Mémoires*, 2nd series, XXXV, 403–4; BL King's MS 136, f. 306r.

33. Tillières, *Mémoires*, 70–8; Houssaye, *Cardinal de Bérulle*, 3–8.

34. *CSPV 1625–1626*, 81.

35. *CSPD 1625–1626*, 41; *HMC Skrine MSS*, 19. See also Birch, *Court and*

Times of Charles, I, 24; Rushworth, *Historical Collections*, I, 170.

36. *Cabala*, 253.

37. See *CSPV 1625–1626*, 81; Rushworth, *Historical Collections*, I, 170; Pett, *Autobiography*, 135; Petitot (ed.), *Mémoires*, 2nd series, XXXV, 406.

38. Henrietta's trousseau is detailed in BL King's MS 136 ff. 412r–461v.

39. See *CSPV 1625–1626*, 81l; BL King's MS 136, ff. 310v, 313r; *HMC Skrine MSS*, 13; Howell, *Epistolae*, I, 238.

40. BL King's MS 136, ff. 323r–324v; *A True Discourse*, 25 *bis*. See also Toynbee, 'Wedding Journey', 83; *HMC Skrine MSS*, 21; *CSPV 1625–1626*, 70, 81; BL King's MS 136, ff. 323–4v; Petitot (ed.), *Mémoires*, 2nd series, XXXV, 407; Finet, *Finetti Philoxenis*, 153.

41. Tillières, *Mémoires*, 89–90; Petitot (ed.), *Mémoires*, 2nd series, XXXV, 407; BL King's MS 136, ff. 335v, 343v.

42. BL King's MS 136, ff. 324v–325r; *HMC Skrine MSS*, 21. See also ibid., 14; Finet, *Finetti Philoxenis*, 153; BL King's MS 136, ff. 323v–324r; *CSPV 1625–1626*, 87.

43. Birch, *Court and Times of Charles*, I, 30; *A True Discourse*, 26.

44. *A True Discourse*, 27, 26. See also BL King's MS 136, ff. 343v, 335v–336r.

45. *CSPV 1625–1626*, 87; Heylin, *Short View*, 37.

46. *Cabala*, 278; Clarendon, *State Papers*, II, Appendix, xxv.

47. Birch, *Court and Times of Charles*, I, 31, 30.

48. Ludlow, *Memoirs*, III, 306.

49. Birch, *Court and Times of Charles*, I, 30. For green sickness, see Eccles, *Obstetrics and Gynaecology in Tudor and Stuart England*, 20, 74.

50. Birch, *Court and Times of Charles*, I, 31. See also *CSPV 1625–1626*, 87.

51. *CSPV 1625–1626*, 288, 515.

52. BL King's MS 136, ff. 335v–337v, 343v–345r.

53. Petitot (ed.), *Mémoires*, 2nd series, XXXV, 407–8; Tillières, *Mémoires*, 90–1.

54. BL King's MS 136, f. 337v.

55. *A True Discourse*, 27, 28; Rushworth, *Historical Collections*, I, 170. See also Carlton, *Charles I*, 64.

56. Howell, *Epistolae*, I, 238.

57. Finet, *Finetti Philoxenis*, 153; BL King's MS 136, f. 336r; Howell, *Epistolae*, I, 238. See also *Calendar of Clarendon State Papers*, I, Appendix I, 8; BL King's MS 136, f. 344r; *CSPV 1625–1626*, 87; *A True Discourse*,

27–8; Finet, *Finetti Philoxenis*, 153; Petitot (ed.), *Mémoires*, 2nd series, XXXV, 408–9.

58. Petitot (ed.), *Mémoires*, 2nd series, XXXV, 409; BL King's MS 136, ff. 336r–v, 344r–v.

59. *HMC Skrine MSS*, 19; *CSPV 1625–1626*, 87. See also Finet, *Finetti Philoxenis*, 152; Birch, *Court and Times of Charles*, I, 31.

60. Petitot (ed.), *Mémoires*, 2nd series, XXXV, 408.

61. Birch, *Court and Times of Charles*, I, 31; Petitot (ed.), *Mémoires*, 2nd series, XXXV, 409; *True Discourse*, 28–9.

CHAPTER THREE: QUARRELLING

1. Sources for the entry to London are: Birch, *Court and Times of Charles*, I, 29–31; *CSPV 1625–1626*, 87; D'Ewes, *Autobiography*, I, 272; Finet, *Finetti Philoxenis*, 154; Heylin, *Short View*, 37; *HMC Skrine MSS*, 21–2; Laud, *Works*, III, 163; *Life and Death*, 13; *True Discourse*, 30–3.

2. Magalotti, *Travels of Cosmo the Third*, 367.

3. Birch, *Court and Times of Charles*, I, 30. For Whitehall, see Colvin, *King's Works*, IV, 301–34.

4. See Birch, *Court and Times of Charles*, I, 32; *True Discourse*, 35.

5. Petitot (ed.), *Mémoires*, 2nd series, XXXV, 410 *bis*; Birch, *Court and Times of Charles*, I, 35. See also *CSPV 1626–1626*, 99; Finet, *Finetti Philoxenis*, 155–6; *HMC Skrine MSS*, 22–3.

6. Birch, *Historical View*, 435.

7. Tillières, *Mémoires*, 91; Birch, *Court and Times of Charles*, I, 18. See also BL King's MS 136, f. 337v; *CSPV 1625–1626*, 88, 606; Clarendon, *State Papers*, II, Appendix, xix.

8. *HMC Skrine MSS*, 20; Tillières, *Mémoires*, 92. For the plague deaths, see Birch, *Court and Times of Charles*, I, 28.

9. *HMC Salisbury MSS*, 198. For the English appointments, see *CSPV 1625–1626*, 98; Birch, *Court and Times of Charles*, I, 39; *HMC Skrine MSS*, 25.

10. Birch, *Court and Times of Charles*, I, 33; *CSPV 1625–1626*, 34; *HMC Skrine MSS*, 23.

11. Birch, *Court and Times of Charles*, I, 33.

12. Clarendon, *State Papers*, I, 33; Bossuet, *Oraison*, 85; BL King's MS 136, f. 274r. See also *HMC Skrine MSS*, 24; Tillières, *Mémoires*, 92; *CSPV*

1625–1626, 98; Clarendon, *State Papers*, I, 33.

13. Birch, *Court and Times of Charles*, I, 36.

14. *HMC Skrine MSS*, 25; *CSPV 1625–1626*, 107. For hopes on Henrietta's arrival, see Birch, *Court and Times of Charles*, I, 31.

15. *HMC Skrine MSS*, 25. See also *CSPV 1625–1626*, 98.

16. Tillières, *Mémoires*, 93, 95; *HMC Skrine MSS*, 31. See also ibid., 3, 6; *CSPV 1625–1626*, 129, 144; Houssaye, *Cardinal de Bérulle*, 36, 40.

17. *HMC Skrine MSS*, 3. See also ibid., 6.

18. Letter from Richelieu to Bérulle, as quoted in Houssaye, *Cardinal de Bérulle*, 35; *CSPV 1625–1626*, 129. See also Houssaye, *Cardinal de Bérulle*, 34; Petitot (ed.), *Mémoires*, 2nd series, XXXV, 416; Tillières, *Mémoires*, 94.

19. *CSPV 1625–1626*, 129; *HMC Mar and Kellie*, 230. See also Petitot (ed.), *Mémoires*, 2nd series, XXXV, 414–20; Birch, *Court and Times of Charles*, I, 39; Tillières, *Mémoires*, 94.

20. Cousin, *Madame de Longueville*, 432.

21. Houssaye, *Cardinal de Bérulle*, 29–30; Cousin, *Madame de Longueville*, 432.

22. Houssaye, *Cardinal de Bérulle*, 33–6, 42. See also *HMC Skrine MSS*, 28.

23. *CSPV 1625–1626*, 146. For the Privy Council meeting, see ibid., 143; BL King's MS 137, ff. 37v–38r.

24. For the French belief that Buckingham was responsible for Charles's anti-Catholic policies, see Richelieu, *Lettres*, II, 137–40; Houssaye, 'L'Ambassade de Blainville', 181. For their hatred of Buckingham at this date, see *HMC Skrine MSS*, 31; *HMC Mar and Kellie*, 230; Tillières, *Mémoires*, passim.

25. BL King's MS 137, f. 23r–v; Tillières, *Mémoires*, 97. See also *HMC Mar and Kellie*, 233.

26. See *HMC Mar and Kellie*, 233; MS letter quoted in Houssaye, *Cardinal de Bérulle*, 40.

27. *CSPV 1625–1626*, 143; Gardiner, *History*, V, 429; *CSPV 1625–1626*, 6.

28. See Birch, *Court and Times of Charles*, I, 47. For the plague, see *CSPD 1625–1626*, 90; *Skrine MSS*, 28, 32; *CSPV 1625–1626*, 149.

29. Birch, *Court and Times of Charles*, I, 47; PRO SP 16/7/85, ff. 118v–119r; Tillières, *Mémoires*, 99; Ludlow, *Memoirs*, III, 305, 307.

30. PRO SP 16/7/85.

31. Tillières, *Mémoires*, 99–100.
32. As quoted in Houssaye, *Cardinal de Bérulle*, 42.
33. Birch, *Court and Times of Charles*, I, 52. For Sancy, see ibid., 34; Houssaye, *Cardinal de Bérulle*, 10, 42; *HMC Skrine MSS*, 86.
34. Birch, *Court and Times of Charles*, I, 50; Tillières, *Mémoires*, 101; *HMC Skrine MSS*, 38; Tillières, *Mémoires*, 101. See also *CSPV 1625–1626*, 177.
35. *CSPV 1625–1626*, 177, 204. See also Birch, *Court and Times of Charles*, I, 50; *HMC Skrine MSS*, 38; Tillières, *Mémoires*, 101–4.
36. Petrie, *Letters*, 41 (where this letter is wrongly dated December 1625); PRO SP 16/8/29; PRO SP 16/7/85. See also Tillières, *Mémoires*, 104.
37. Petrie, *Letters*, 41; *CSPV 1625–1626*, 177; *HMC Skrine MSS*, 52. See also ibid., 37, 38; *CSPV 1625–1626*, 607.
38. Tillières, *Mémoires*, 105. The principal work on Blainville and his embassy is Houssaye, 'L'Ambassade de Blainville'.
39. *CSPV 1625–1626*, 212; Houssaye, 'L'Ambassade de Blainville', 185; *HMC Skrine MSS*, 36. See also ibid., 34; *CSPV 1625–1626*, 198.
40. As quoted in Houssaye, *Cardinal de Bérulle*, 69.
41. As quoted in Houssaye, *Cardinal de Bérulle*, 45, 70. See also ibid., 46, n. 2.
42. Motteville, *Mémoires*, I, 223; *Life and Death*, 14.
43. *CSPV 1625–1626*, 607; Ludlow, *Memoirs*, III, 306. For the maids being excluded from Henrietta's Privy Chamber by Charles's regulations, see Society of Antiquaries, *Collection of Ordinances*, 341.
44. Tillières, *Mémoires*, 108; *CSPV 1625–1626*, 271; Ludlow, *Memoirs*, III, 306–7. This incident can be dated between 11 and 25 November, when Charles and Henrietta were both staying at Hampton Court. Tillières says it was roughly a couple of weeks after Charles left Salisbury.
45. Petrie, *Letters*, 40; Ludlow, *Memoirs*, III, 305.
46. Petrie, *Letters*, 40–1; Ludlow, *Memoirs*, III, 305–6.
47. Petrie, *Letters*, 40.
48. *CSPV 1625–1626*, 289. For Richelieu's threat, see Houssaye, 'L'Ambassade de Blainville', 184.
49. *CSPV 1625–1626*, 269; Petrie, *Letters*, 41; *CSPV 1625–1626*, 272.
50. *CSPV 1625–1626*, 271, 275. See also *CSPD 1625–1626*, 183; Tillières, *Mémoires*, 108.
51. Birch, *Court and Times of Charles*, I, 68; BL King's MS 138, f. 162v. See also PRO SP 16/12/4.

52. *CSPD 1625–1626*, 561; *CSPV 1625–1626*, 292. The gift was made early in the New Year although the official grant was not made until 14 February.

53. Rous, *Diary*, l. See also Lockyer, *Buckingham*, 281–3.

54. *CSPV 1625–1626*, 292, 299, 333. See also Houssaye, *Cardinal de Bérulle*, 108.

55. *CSPV 1625–1626*, 288; Tillières, *Mémoires*, 64. See also *HMC Skrine MSS*, 42.

56. *CSPV 1625–1626*, 272; Tillières, *Mémoires*, 129; *CSPV 1625–1626*, 318.

57. *CSPD 1625–1626*, 187; Houssaye, 'L'Ambassade de Blainville', 189–91.

58. *CSPV 1625–1626*, 276, 309. See also ibid., 300.

59. Laud, *Works*, III, 179–80; *CSPD 1625–1626*, 243; *CSPV 1625–1626*, 275.

60. BL King's MS 136, ff. 274v–275r, 276v. See also Birch, *Court and Times of Charles*, I, 72; *CSPV 1625–1626*, 311; Richelieu, *Lettres*, II, 124–36.

61. *CSPV 1625–1626*, 311, 326, 311.

62. Ellis, *Original Letters*, 1st series, vol. III, 218. Principal sources for the coronation ceremonies are: Rushworth, *Historical Collections*, I, 200–1; Ellis, *Original Letters*, 1st series, vol. III, 213–19; *CSPV 1625–1626*, 320–1; Laud, *Works*, III, 180–1; Wordsworth, *The Manner of the Coronation of King Charles the First of England*.

63. Birch, *Court and Times of Charles*, I, 78. See also ibid., 79; *CSPV 1625–1626*, 321; *CSPD 1625–1626*, 246.

64. *CSPV 1625–1626*, 326.

65. As quoted in Albion, Charles I, 83; *HMC Skrine MSS*, 44.

66. See Finet, *Finetti Philoxenis*, 171; *CSPV 1625–1626*, 327; Tillières, *Mémoires*, 118–20, 122; Houssaye, 'L'Ambassade de Blainville', 193–6.

67. *CSPV 1625–1626*, 327. See also Houssaye, 'L'Ambassade de Blainville', 195–6.

68. See *CSPV 1625–1626*, 327–8; Finet, *Finetti Philoxenis*, 171; Ludlow, *Memoirs*, III, 307.

69. Tillières, *Mémoires*, 120–1; *CSPV 1625–1626*, 329; Houssaye, 'L'Ambassade de Blainville', 199–200.

70. See Houssaye, 'L'Ambassade de Blainville', 196–7; Tillières, *Mémoires*, 121–2.

71. Tillières, *Mémoires*, 122. See also *CSPV 1625–1626*, 329.

72. *HMC Skrine MSS*, 49. See also ibid., 47; *CSPV 1625–1626*, 329.

73. McClure (ed.), *Letters of Chamberlain*, II, 630; Birch, *Court and Times of Charles*, I, 85; *CSPV 1625–1626*, 346.

74. *HMC Skrine MSS*, 47; *CSPV 1625–1626*, 346; *HMC Skrine MSS*, 47. For the performance details, see Colvin, *King's Works*, IV, 261; Orgel and Strong, *Inigo Jones* (1973), I, 383–8.

75. See *CSPV 1625–1626*, 300; BL Add. MS 22,474, f. 11; Rushworth, *Historical Collections*, I, 217.

76. Rushworth, *Historical Collections*, I, 216–17; Birch, *Court and Times of Charles*, I, 93. See also BL Add. MS 22,474, f. 19; Rushworth, *Historical Collections*, I, 220, 226–7.

77. *CSPV 1625–1626*, 605; PRO SP 16/32/91.

78. Tillières, *Mémoires*, 135. For Lucy's love life, see the *Oxford DNB* article on her.

79. *CSPV 1625–1626*, 494. See also ibid., 498; Tillières, *Mémoires*, 134; Birch, *Court and Times of Charles*, I, 122, 134.

80. *CSPV 1625–1626*, 497.

81. Ludlow, *Memoirs*, III, 308; Tillières, *Mémoires*, 137–8.

82. *CSPV 1625–1626*, 388; *HMC Skrine MSS*, 94.

83. Birch, *Court and Times of Charles*, I, 121; *CSPV 1625–1626*, 545; PRO SP 16/32/91.

84. *HMC Skrine MSS*, 77. See also Houssaye, *Cardinal de Bérulle*, 120–1. For the Pope's letters to Henrietta on the Jubilee, see BL Add. MS 15,389, ff. 150r–152v, 153r–155v; *CSPV 1625–1626*, 388.

85. BL Add. MS 39,288, f. 6; Birch, *Court and Times of Charles*, I, 121; BL Add. MS 39,288, f. 6. See also Birch, *Court and Times of Charles*, I, 132; *CSPV 1625–1626*, 531; *Life and Death*, 16. Only in France was it denied that this visit to Tyburn had been a deliberate pilgrimage: see *CSPV 1625–1626*, 517; Tillières, *Mémoires*, 148.

86. *CSPV 1625–1626*, 517. See also ibid., 531; *Life and Death*, 16.

87. PRO SP 16/32/91; Ludlow, *Memoirs*, III, 305–6; PRO SP 16/32/91. See also Ludlow, *Memoirs*, III, 308.

88. *CSPV 1625–1626*, 466. See also ibid., 482.

89. *CSPV 1625–1626*, 515; Codices Barberini, 8,616, f. 35, as quoted in Albion, *Charles I*, 85. See also BL MS Royal 18 A XXVIII; *HMC Skrine MSS*, 93.

90. *CSPV 1625–1626*, 506; Birch, *Court and Times of Charles*, I, 134. See also Tillières, *Mémoires*, 144, 251.

91. *CSPV 1625–1626*, 506. See also ibid., 495, 498; PRO SP 16/33/30; Howell, *Epistolae*, I, 242; *HMC Skrine MSS*, 82.

92. Tillières, *Mémoires*, 252, 144.

93. PRO SP 16/32/91. See also Tillières, *Mémoires*, 145, 251; Birch, *Court and Times of Charles*, I, 119–20; PRO SP 16/33/30; *HMC Skrine MSS*, 82; *CSPV 1625–1626*, 506.

94. Tillières, *Mémoires*, 144. See also Birch, *Court and Times of Charles*, I, 120; Howell, *Epistolae*, I, 242.

95. Birch, *Court and Times of Charles*, I, 120. See also Tillières, *Mémoires*, 145.

CHAPTER FOUR: NEW BEGINNINGS

1. See PRO SP 16/33/30; Tillières, *Mémoires*, 146, 249, 252; Birch, *Court and Times of Charles*, I, 137; *CSPD 1625–1626*, 396.

2. Ellis, *Original Letters*, 1st series, vol. III, 244.

3. Tillières, *Mémoires*, 253; *CSPV 1625–1626*, 542. See also *Life and Death*, 17.

4. Tillières, *Mémoires*, 253; *CSPV 1625–1626*, 520. See also ibid., 525.

5. Baillon, *Henriette-Marie*, 349–50, 348.

6. *CSPV 1625–1626*, 515; Tillières, *Mémoires*, 67. See also *CSPV 1625–1626*, 507, 515.

7. *CSPV 1625–1626*, 571, 561. See also ibid., 530; Tillières, *Mémoires*, 66–7

8. *CSPV 1625–1626*, 544. See also ibid., 566; *HMC Skrine MSS*, 84; Tillières, *Mémoires*, 67; Houssaye, *Cardinal de Bérulle*, 181–3.

9. Baillon, *Henriette-Marie*, 349. See also Birch, *Court and Times of Charles*, I, 145; *CSPV 1625–1626*, 526, 539, 546–7.

10. Bassompierre, *Journal*, III, 259–60. See also *CSPV 1625–1626*, 559–60, 565, 573; *HMC Skrine MSS*, 84–6; Birch, *Court and Times of Charles*, I, 151; Bassompierre, *Journal*, III, 257.

11. Bassompierre, *Negociation*, 283; Bassompierre, *Journal*, III, 264–5. See also ibid., 263; *CSPV 1625–1626*, 575–6, 582; *HMC Skrine MSS*, 88.

12. Tillières, *Mémoires*, 255.

13. *HMC Skrine MSS*, 86; *CSPV 1625–1626*, 547. See also Bassompierre, *Journal*, III, 264–9; Tillières, *Mémoires*, 255; Birch, *Court and Times of Charles*, I, 157–8; *HMC Skrine MSS*, 89.

14. Bassompierre, *Journal*, III, 266–7. See also *CSPV 1625–1626*, 592.

15. See Bassompierre, *Journal*, III, 269–70; *CSPV 1626–1628*, 8–9, 21, 615; Bassompierre, *Negociation*, 56, 246–7, 271; Bassompierre's letter, as

translated in Strickland, *Lives*, V, 239–42; *HMC Skrine MSS*, 91–2.

16. See Bassompierre, *Journal*, III, 271; *HMC Buccleugh*, III, 310.

17. Bassompierre, *Journal*, III, 272–3; *CSPV 1626–1628*, 9.

18. Bassompierre, *Journal*, III, 274; *HMC Skrine MSS*, 95. See also *CSPV 1626–1628*, 22; Bassompierre, *Journal*, III, 274; Birch, *Court and Times of Charles*, I, 166, 168.

19. Bassompierre, *Journal*, III, 277. See also *HMC Skrine MSS*, 91, 96; Finet, *Finetti Philoxenis*, 192.

20. *HMC Skrine MSS*, 91; *CSPV 1626–1628*, 92, 82. See also ibid., 80, 88, 92, 97, 199, 615.

21. *CSPV 1626–1628*, 62. See also ibid., 9, 63, 97.

22. *CSPV 1626–1628*, 206, 40, 97.

23. See *HMC Skrine MSS*, 100, 103, 104; Birch, *Court and Times of Charles*, I, 186.

24. *HMC Skrine MSS*, 103–4; *HMC Skrine MSS*, 101. See also *CSPD 1625–1626*, 582.

25. *HMC Skrine MSS*, 102–3; *CSPV 1626–1628*, 107. See also *HMC Skrine MSS*, 104, 105.

26. Birch, *Court and Times of Charles*, I, 185.

27. As quoted in Houssaye, *Cardinal de Bérulle*, 188–9.

28. *HMC Skrine MSS*, 104. See also ibid., 107; *CSPV 1626–1628*, 97–8; Birch, *Court and Times of Charles*, I, 186.

29. Hardwicke, *State Papers*, II, 22.

30. Birch, *Court and Times of Charles*, I, 202.

31. Birch, *Court and Times of Charles*, I, 141.

32. Clarendon, *History*, V, 167–8. For Philip, see *Oxford DNB*; Bellesheim, *History*, IV, 51; Batterel, *Mémoires*, I, 222–4; Houssaye, *Cardinal de Bérulle*, 9; McMillan, 'Robert Philip'.

33. See *CSPV 1625–1626*, 515; *HMC Skrine MSS*, 83.

34. Johnson et al. (eds.), *Proceedings in Parliament*, IV, 163; Clarendon, *History*, III, 509; *CSPV 1626–1628*, 167.

35. *CSPV 1629–1632*, 316.

36. *CSPD 1627–1628*, 222. For Hudson's life and character, see *Oxford DNB*.

37. *HMC Skrine MSS*, 84. See also Society of Antiquaries, *Collection of Ordinances*, 340–6.

38. Birch, *Court and Times of Charles*, I, 206.

39. *CSPV 1626–1628*, 177. See also Green, *Letters*, 11 (this letter is misdated there).

40. *CSPV 1626–1628*, 247–8. See also ibid., 155, 195, 202, 229; Birch, *Court and Times of Charles*, I, 224, 225.

41. *CSPV 1626–1628*, 180. See also ibid., 105, 127, 177, 239; Clarendon, *History*, I, 48.

42. As quoted in Lockyer, *Buckingham*, 367. See also Birch, *Court and Times of Charles*, I, 164; *CSPD 1627–1628*, 252.

43. Birch, *Court and Times of Charles*, I, 209. See also ibid., I, 219; *CSPV 1626–1628*, 68–9, 617.

44. *HMC Skrine MSS*, 116; Birch, *Court and Times of Charles*, I, 209. See also *HMC Skrine MSS*, 116.

45. Birch, *Court and Times of Charles*, I, 246. See also Lockyer, *Buckingham*, 373; *CSPD 1627–1628*, 209.

46. Birch, *Court and Times of Charles*, I, 241, 240. For Buckingham's entertainments, see *CSPV 1626–1628*, 239; Birch, *Court and Times of Charles*, I, 226; *HMC Skrine MSS*, 118.

47. *HMC Skrine MSS*, 121, 120. See also ibid., 119; Birch, *Court and Times of Charles*, I, 247.

48. PRO SP 16/67/105; *CSPV 1626–1628*, 298.

49. *CSPV 1626–1628*, 144; *HMC Skrine MSS*, 122; *CSPV 1626–1628*, 297.

50. Petrie, *Letters*, 53, 52.

51. See Birch, *Court and Times of Charles*, I, 223, 250; Petrie, *Letters*, 50.

52. PRO SP 16/75/83; *CSPV 1626–1628*, 342.

53. Petrie, *Letters*, 52.

54. PRO SP 16/82/42, as quoted in Gardiner, *History*, VI, 189; PRO SP 16/75/22, as quoted in Gardiner, *History*, VI, 189–90.

55. Petrie, *Letters*, 54–5.

56. Birch, *Court and Times of Charles*, I, 286; Clarendon, *History*, I, 50. See also Strafford, *Letters*, 41.

57. *CSPV 1626–1628*, 485; *Skrine MSS*, 133.

58. BL Harleian MS 6,988, f. 76, as quoted in Lockyer, *Buckingham*, 402.

59. Birch, *Court and Times of Charles*, I, 289; *CSPV 1626–1628*, 499.

60. Birch, *Court and Times of Charles*, I, 281. See also ibid., 291; *CSPV 1626–1628*, 528; *HMC Skrine MSS*, 133.

61. *CSPV 1626–1628*, 497. See also Birch, *Court and Times of Charles*, I, 303.

62. *CSPV 1626–1628*, 570, 587. For Bérulle's angry stories, see Nuncio Guidi di Bagno's letter to Barberini, 28 January 1628, as quoted in Hibbard, 'Translating Royalty', 27; *CSPV 1626–1628*, 528. For Tillières, see ibid., 558.

63. Birch, *Court and Times of Charles*, I, 328. See also *CSPV 1628–1629*, 37.

64. *CSPD 1628–1629*, 198. See also ibid., 31, 214, 215; *CSPD 1627–1628*, 573.

65. Nichols (ed.), *Discovery*, preface, 13; *CSPV 1628–1629*, 171, 173.

66. *HMC Skrine MSS*, 155–6; *CSPV 1628–1629*, 156. See also ibid., 173, 168; *HMC Skrine MSS*, 157.

67. *CSPV 1628–1629*, 242.

68. PRO SP 16/101/43. See also *CSPD 1628–1629*, 219.

69. *CSPV 1628–1629*, 261.

70. Rous, *Diary*, 28. See also *CSPD 1628–1629*, 271.

71. D'Ewes Autobiography, I, 381; Ellis, *Original Letters*, 1st series, vol. III, 256.

72. D'Ewes Autobiography, I, 381; *CSPD 1628–1629*, 271; *HMC Salisbury MSS*, 244; *CSPV 1628–1629*, 262. Other sources for the murder are: Ellis, *Original Letters*, 1st series, vol. III, 254–60; *HMC Mar and Kellie*, 244–5; Birch, *Court and Times of Charles*, I, 389, 391–3; Rous, *Diary*, 25–8; Wotton, *Reliquiæ*, 112; *HMC Skrine MSS*, 161–3; PRO SP 16/114/20.

CHAPTER FIVE: NO OTHER FAVOURITES

1. Clarendon, *History*, I, 37. See also *CSPV 1628–1629*, 262; Birch, *Court and Times of Charles*, I, 390.

2. *HMC Skrine MSS*, 162; Clarendon, *History*, I, 37; *HMC Skrine MSS*, 163. See also *CSPD 1628–1629*, 265; *CSPV 1628–1629*, 262, 283, 295; Lockyer, *Buckingham*, 461.

3. *CSPD 1628–1629*, 310, 268; *CSPV 1628–1629*, 283.

4. Ellis, *Original Letters*, 1st series, vol. III, 256–60.

5. Birch, *Court and Times of Charles*, I, 388; Clarendon, *History*, I, 37; Birch, *Court and Times of Charles*, I, 388. See also ibid., I, 394; *HMC Skrine MSS*, 162; *HMC Mar and Kellie*, 245.

6. Birch, *Court and Times of Charles*, I, 396. See also ibid., I, 389; *CSPV 1628–1629*, 283; *CSPD 1628–1629*, 277. For the fleet, see *CSPD 1628–1629*, 323–4; Birch, *Court and Times of Charles*, I, 396, 398.

7. Birch, *Court and Times of Charles*, I, 397; *CSPV 1628–1629*, 337. See also Birch, *Court and Times of Charles*, I, 389, 399.

8. *HMC Skrine MSS*, 165.

9. *HMC Skrine MSS*, 165; Birch, *Court and Times of Charles*, I, 396. See also ibid., 408.

10. *CSPV 1628–1629*, 310–11. See also *CSPD 1628–1629*, 343; *HMC Skrine MSS*, 165.

11. Birch, *Court and Times of Charles*, I, 419. See also ibid., I, 451–2.

12. PRO SP 16/121/47; *CSPD 1628–1629*, 413. See also ibid., 393.

13. *CSPV 1628–1629*, 518; *CSPD 1628–1629*, 527. For the first news of the pregnancy, see Birch, *Court and Times of Charles*, II, 4. For its dating, see *CSPD 1628–1629*, 548. For Charles's pleasure, see also *CSPV 1628–1629*, 540, 593. For the penal laws, see Albion, *Charles I*, 104.

14. Laud, *Works*, III, 102. See also *CSPV 1628–1629*, 593; *CSPD 1628–1629*, 534.

15. Laud, *Works*, III, 102; *CSPV 1628–1629*, 600. See also Birch, *Court and Times of Charles*, II, 13.

16. Rous, *Diary*, 11; *CSPD 1628–1629*, 539. For other talk against Henrietta, see ibid., 526; *HMC Mar and Kellie*, 248; Rous, *Diary*, 39.

17. *CSPD 1628–1629*, 517–8.

18. Birch, *Court and Times of Charles*, I, 448; *CSPV 1628–1629*, 379–80. For another instance of Henrietta's protection of Catholics, see *CSPD 1628–1629*, 451.

19. *CSPV 1628–1629*, 310.

20. *CSPV 1628–1629*, 311.

21. Birch, *Court and Times of Charles*, I, 422. For Charles's earlier unwillingness, see *CSPV 1628–1629*, 288, 359; *HMC Skrine MSS*, 168, 169.

22. Birch, *Court and Times of Charles*, I, 424, 425; *HMC Skrine MSS*, 171.

23. *CSPV 1628–1629*, 315. See also ibid., 340, 396.

24. *CSPV 1628–1629*, 374–7. See also ibid., 340.

25. Birch, *Court and Times of Charles*, II, 20; Finet, *Ceremonies*, 61.

26. *CSPV 1629–1632*, 69. See also BL Add. MS 27,962E, f. 282v.

27. D'Ewes Autobiography, I, 412; Birch, *Court and Times of Charles*, I, 355. See also BL Add. MS 27,962E, f. 282v.

28. D'Ewes *Autobiography*, I, 411; BL Add. MS 27,962E, f. 283r.

29. *CSPV 1629–1632*, 21. See also ibid., 65; Birch, *Court and Times of Charles*, I, 356.

30. *CSPV 1629–1632*, 70; Birch, *Court and Times of Charles*, I, 356. See also D'Ewes, *Autobiography*, I, 412.
31. Birch, *Court and Times of Charles*, I, 356; BL Add. MS 27,962E, f. 283r. For normal midwifery equipment, see Rueff, *Expert Midwife*, 44, 78, 81.
32. *Oxford DNB*.
33. BL Add. MS 27,962E, f. 284r; *CSPV 1629–1632*, 70.
34. BL Add. MS 27,962E, f. 284r.
35. *Life and Death*, 18.
36. BL Add. MS 27,962E, f. 283r; Birch, *Court and Times of Charles*, I, 355; *CSPD 1628–1629*, 548. See also *CSPV 1629–1632*, 70.
37. *CSPV 1629–1632*, 70; *CSPD 1628–1629*, 548, 585.
38. Birch, *Court and Times of Charles*, I, 356.
39. *CSPV 1629–1632*, 156. For the couple at Greenwich, see ibid., 83, 85.
40. As quoted in Hibbard, 'Translating Royalty', 27.
41. Chateauneuf's despatches, as quoted in Gardiner, *History*, VII, 106.
42. *CSPV 1629–1632*, 350, 388.
43. As quoted in Gardiner, *History*, VII, 106–7.
44. See Birch, *Court and Times of Charles*, II, 47; Gardiner, *History*, VII, 106.
45. *CSPV 1628–1629*, 287, 340. See also ibid., 293, 314, 315, 374, 396.
46. Chateauneuf's letters to Richelieu that summer, as cited in Gardiner, *History*, VII, 106–7.
47. As quoted in Houssaye, *Cardinal de Bérulle*, 483 n. See also Birch, *Court and Times of Charles*, II, 296–9; Hibbard, *Charles I*, 56, 261, n.77.
48. *CSPV 1629–1632*, 205.
49. *CSPV 1629–1632*, 136; Birch, *Court and Times of Charles*, I, 417. See also *CSPV 1629–1632*, 168.
50. Birch, *Court and Times of Charles*, II, 41; *CSPV 1629–1632*, 228; Birch, *Court and Times of Charles*, I, 417.
51. *CSPV 1629–1632*, 281.
52. *CSPD 1629–1631*, 185; *CSPV 1629–1632*, 315–16. See also Laud, *Works*, III, 103; *CSPV 1629–1632*, 272, 277, 281; Hamilton, *Henrietta Maria*, 98; Birch, *Court and Times of Charles*, II, 70.
53. Birch, *Court and Times of Charles*, II, 301, 295.
54. Birch, *Court and Times of Charles*, II, 301–2, 67, 302–3.
55. *CSPV 1629–1632*, 304; Birch, *Court and Times of Charles*, II, 63, 68.

56. Birch, *Court and Times of Charles*, II, 67, 76. See also *CSPV 1629–1632*, 315, 337.

57. Rous, *Diary*, 49. For Charles releasing Catholics, see *CSPV 1629–1632*, 315, 337; *CSPD 1629–1631*, 233.

58. Green, *Letters*, 14–15, 15–16.

59. *CSPV 1629–1632*, 316. See also *CSPD 1629–1631*, 217; Birch, *Court and Times of Charles*, II, 69.

60. Ellis, *Original Letters*, 2nd series, vol. III, 259–60.

61. BL Add. MS 27,962F, f. 110v. See also *CSPV 1629–1632*, 348.

62. Ellis, *Original Letters*, 2nd series, vol. III, 262; *CSPD 1629–1631*, 268. See also *CSPV 1629–1632*, 370.

63. BL Add. MS 27,962F, f. 107v; *CSPV 1629–1632*, 350. See also Ellis, *Original Letters*, 2nd series, vol. III, 262.

64. As quoted in Gardiner, *History*, VII, 140; *CSPV 1629–1632*, 350–1. For the callers, see also BL Add. MS 27,962F, f. 107v; Finet, *Ceremonies*, 87.

65. BL Add. MS 27,962F, f. 105r–v. See also *CSPV 1629–1632*, 373.

66. Ellis, *Original Letters*, 2nd series, vol. III, 262. For the celebrations, see also *CSPV 1629–1632*, 349; BL Add. MS 27, 962 F, f. 107v; *CSPD 1631–1633*, 218. For the procession and the new star, see BL Add. MS 27,962 F, f. 107v; *CSPD 1629–1631*, 314; *Life and Death*, 20.

CHAPTER SIX: THE COURT OF LOVE

1. For the date of Henrietta's churching, see Finet, *Ceremonies*, 88. Details of the ceremony come from *The Catholic Encyclopedia*, 'The Churching of Women'.

2. Finet, *Ceremonies*, 88. See also Birch, *Court and Times of Charles*, II, 306; *CSPD 1629–1631*, 283.

3. For the treaty article, see *HMC Salisbury MSS*, 199; BL King's MS 135, f. 70r; *CSPV 1623–1625*, 525. For the priests' protests, see Birch, *Court and Times of Charles*, II, 306; *CSPV 1628–1629*, 540–1; *CSPV 1629–1632*, 369. Recent historians include Hutton, *Charles II*, 4; Hibbard, *Charles I*, 39.

4. See Finet, *Ceremonies*, 89.

5. Heylin, *Cyprianus Anglicus*, 198; Rous, *Diary*, 54.

6. See PRO SP 16/172/81; *CSPD 1629–1631*, 548.

7. BL King's MS 136, ff. 52r, 53v. For the Dorset couple, see Hibbard, *Charles I*, 39; Smith, 'Catholic, Anglican or Puritan?'

8. See Laud, *Works*, III, 212; *CSPD 1629–1631*, 369.

9. PRO SP 16/171/42; *CSPD 1629–1631*, 329, 334. See also ibid., 330; *CSPV 1629–1632*, 388.

10. Green, *Letters*, 17, 18 (where this last letter is misdated). See also Ferrero (ed.), *Lettres*, 35.

11. Birch, *Court and Times of Charles*, II, 82. See also Green, *Letters*, 19; *CSPV 1629–1632*, 431.

12. *CSPV 1629–1632*, 431. See also *CSPV 1628–1629*, 589; *CSPV 1629–1632*, 75, 177; *CSPD 1629–1631*, 372.

13. *CSPV 1628–1629*, 593.

14. Ben Jonson, *Chloridia*; Ben Jonson, *Love's Triumph through Callipolis*.

15. *CSPV 1629–1632*, 457; as quoted in Green, *Lives of the Princesses*, VI, 101.

16. *CSPV 1629–1632*, 562; as quoted in Green, *Lives of the Princesses*, VI, 101. For the birth and christening, see also Birch, *Court and Times of Charles*, II, 140; Laud, *Works*, III, 215.

17. *CSPD 1633–1634*, 251; *CSPV 1636–1639*, 174. See also *CSPV 1632–1636*, 157.

18. *CSPD 1633–1634*, 196. See also *CSPV 1632–1636*, 144; *HMC Cowper MSS*, Appendix II, 18, 22; Green, *Letters*, 22.

19. See *CSPV 1636–1639*, 143; BL Add. MS 15,390, ff. 86v–87r; Birch, *Court and Times of Charles*, II, 265, 266; *CSPV 1636–1639*, 143; *HMC Denbigh MSS*, Part V, 47.

20. Green, *Letters*, 34; *CSPV 1632–1636*, 163; *HMC De L'Isle and Dudley MSS*, VI, 98.

21. See BL Harleian MS 7,623, f. 11v, BL Harleian MS 3,791, ff. 113v, 114v, 116r; *HMC Cowper MSS*, II, Appendix II, 12; *CSPD 1635*, 80.

22. *CSPV 1636–1639*, 128. See also Finet, *Ceremonies*, 128, 169.

23. *CSPV 1636–1639*, 288. See also ibid., 416, 418; Gregg, *King Charles I*, 251.

24. Ellis, *Original Letters*, 1st series, vol. III, 288–9. See also BL Harleian MS 6,988, ff. 97, 99.

25. Camden, *Camden's Britannia*, 155 note (e). For St James's, see Strong, *Renaissance Garden*, 188; MacGregor, *Late King's Goods*, 23; Colvin, *King's Works*, IV, 241–52.

26. Colvin, *King's Works*, IV, 225, 227. For Richmond, see also ibid., 222–34; MacGregor, *Late King's Goods*, 29.
27. BL Add. MS 15,389, f. 356r–v. See also *CSPV 1636–1639*, 128.
28. *HMC Cowper MSS*, II, Appendix II, 12, 26.
29. *The King and Queenes Entertainement at Richmond*.
30. Mayor, *Nicholas Ferrar: Two Lives*.
31. Ferrero, *Lettres*, 40.
32. BL Harleian MS 6,988, f. 95.
33. See, e.g., *CSPV 1632–1636*, 445, 447.
34. *HMC Cowper MSS*, Appendix II, 11, 12.
35. *HMC Cowper MSS*, Appendix II, 18. See also *CSPD 1633–1634*, 85.
36. Nicolson (ed.), *Conway Letters*, 27; Robert Herrick, *Poetical Works*, 223. Other memories in this paragraph come from Herrick, *Poetical Works*, I, 198–200; Cavendish, *Poems, and Fancies*, 110, 113, 116–18, 160–1.
37. *CSPV 1632–1636*, 116.
38. Pepys, *Diary*, VIII, 338; ibid., III, 221; *HMC Skrine MSS*, 161.
39. *CSPV 1632–1636*, 486.
40. Aubrey, *Aubrey's Brief Lives*, 145.
41. *CSPD 1637–1638*, 49; BL Add. MS 15,389, 173r–174v.
42. *CSPD 1631–1633*, 141. See also *CSPD 1635*, 237; *CSPD 1634–1635*, 213.
43. *CSPV 1632–1636*, 280, 287; *CSPV 1636–1639*, 46; *CSPV 1632–1636*, 486.
44. See, e.g., Hamilton, *Henrietta Maria*, 120; *CSPV 1632–1636*, 15–16; Finet, *Ceremonies*, 166.
45. Finet, *Ceremonies*, 167; Townshend, *Poems and Masques*, 13.
46. Clarendon, *History*, I, 104; Cavendish, *Life of William, Duke of Newcastle*, 103–4. For that summer's itinerary, see *CSPD 1634–1635*, 149.
47. *CSPV 1632–1636*, 570. See also *CSPV 1636–1639*, 44, 61.
48. *CSPD 1636–1637*, 91, 92.
49. *CSPD 1636–1637*, 477. See also ibid., 92; Birch, *Court and Times of Charles*, II, 266. Laud, *Works*, III, 227; ibid., V, 149–54; *CSPV 1636–1639*, 77.
50. Birch, *Court and Times of Charles*, I, 379.
51. *CSPD 1631–1633*, 590, 551.
52. *CSPV 1632–1636*, 117. See also Clarendon, *History*, I, 104

53. *CSPD 1633–1634*, 107; *HMC Cowper MSS*, II, Appendix II, 17, 22.

54. As quoted in Gardiner, *History*, VII, 285. See also *The Entertainment of . . . Charles into his ancient city of Edinburgh*.

55. *CSPV 1632–1636*, 122, 123, 125.

56. *CSPV 1632–1636*, 127.

57. *CSPV 1632–1636*, 132, 131; *HMC Cowper MSS*, Appendix II, 26. See also Laud, *Works*, III, 218; *CSPV 1632–1636*, 137.

58. *CSPD 1635*, 122, 401; Cruickshanks, *Stuart Courts*, 103. See also PRO LR5/63, Establishment List for 1629: 'master of the bowes and hounds' paid 'for keeping of hounds'.

59. *CSPD 1635*, 318. See also *CSPD 1631–1633*, 128; Clarendon, *History*, IV, 489. For the liberty, see *CSPD 1634–1635*, 505. For Charles returning late, see *CSPD 1631–1633*, 128; *CSPD 1635*, 420.

60. *CSPV 1632–1636*, 363; *CSPV 1626–1628*, 409; Laud, *Works*, III, 154. See also *CSPV 1636–1639*, 1; *CSPD 1623–1625*, 346, 349; Laud, *Works*, III, 183.

61. *CSPV 1636–1639*, 64. See also Birch, *Court and Times of Charles*, II, 249–50.

62. *CSPD 1633–1634*, 220; Jonson, *The Works*, VIII, 20.

63. Birch, *Court and Times of Charles*, II, 205, 202, 205 *bis*; *CSPD 1631–1633*, 454.

64. *CSPV 1632–1636*, 367. See also Carlton, *Charles I*, 124.

65. *CSPV 1632–1636*, 251, 572. For Henrietta's conversation and wit, see Evelyn, *Diary*, 442; Motteville, *Memoir*, 28.

66. *CSPD 1635*, 368; *CSPD 1627–1628*, 155; Birch, *Court and Times of Charles*, II, 123.

67. See *CSPD 1631–1633*, 484; Steele, *Plays and Masques at Court*; Carlton, *Charles I*, 147; Marshall, *Henrietta*, 63; Dickens, *Courts of Europe*, 198.

68. *CSPV 1632–1636*, 491. See also Birch, *Court and Times of Charles*, II, 265, 107; *CSPD 1633–1634*, 455.

69. Bassompierre, *Journal*, III, 271. For the birthdays, see Finet, *Ceremonies*, 75; BL Add. MS 15,389, ff. 355v–356r.

70. Birch, *Court and Times of Charles*, II, 214; *Deep Sigh*, A3v. See also Cavendish, *The Blazing World*, 12.

71. Cavendish, *The Blazing World*, 9.

72. See Orgel and Strong, *Inigo Jones*, passim; Strong, *Tudor and Stuart Monarchy*; Harris, Orgel and Strong, *King's Arcadia*.

73. *CSPD 1631–1633*, 482; *CSPV 1632–1636*, 334. For earlier illnesses, see *CSPV 1629–1632*, 605; *CSPD 1633–1634*, 504.

74. *CSPV 1632–1636*, 334, 28. See also ibid., 63.

75. *CSPV 1632–1636*, 86. See also Birch, *Court and Times of Charles*, II, 95; *CSPD 1629–1631*, 509; *CSPV 1629–1632*, 592.

76. See Birch, *Court and Times of Charles*, II, 176, 187, 216; Montagu, *The Shepherds' Paradise*; Sarah Poynting, ' "In the name of all the sisters": Henrietta Maria's Notorious Whores'.

77. *CSPD 1631–1633*, 270; As quoted in Strong, *Tudor and Stuart Monarchy*, 196.

78. Petrie, *Letters*, 83; *CSPV 1632–1636*, 323. See also *CSPD 1633–1634*, 64.

79. Finet, *Ceremonies*, 56, 216.

80. Birch, *Court and Times of Charles*, II, 244.

81. Finet, *Ceremonies*, 199.

82. As quoted in Ralph, *Sir Humphrey Mildmay*, 43.

83. For some of these expenses, see *CSPD 1631–1633*, 589; Smuts, 'Art and the material culture of majesty', 88–96, 103–10.

84. De la Serre, *Histoire*, sig. K. For Henrietta's gardening, see also *CSPD 1628–1629*, 16; Green, *Letters*, 19; Colvin, *King's Works*, and Strong, *Renaissance Garden*.

85. See Carlton, *Charles I*, 142.

86. As quoted in Carlton, *Charles I*, 142. See also MacGregor, *Late King's Goods*, 76.

87. Panzani, *Memoirs*, 251; Wittkower, 'Inigo Jones', 50–1.

88. As quoted in Strong, *Tudor and Stuart Monarchy*, 196.

89. Motteville, *Mémoires*, I, 223 *bis*; BL Add. MS 15,389, ff. 196r–197v.

90. Warwick, *Memoires*, 65, 66.

91. See Summerson, *Inigo Jones*, 122–31.

92. Principal sources for these royal building works are Colvin, *King's Works*, IV, and Summerson, *Inigo Jones*.

93. See Summerson, *Inigo Jones*, 68–70; Colvin, *King's Works*, IV, 263–6.

94. *CSPV 1629–1632*, 298; BL Harleian MS 3,888, f. 107; Birch, *Court and Times*, II, 307. See also ibid., 35.

CHAPTER SEVEN: QUESTIONS OF FAITH

1. Birch, *Court and Times of Charles*, II, 343. For the state of Catholics in this period, see Albion, *Charles I*; Hibbard, *Charles I*.
2. *CSPD 1633–1634*, 464; Birch, *Court and Times of Charles*, II, 211; *CSPD 1633–1634*, 349.
3. Clarendon, *State Papers*, I, 353. See also *CSPD 1631–1633*, 424; *CSPD 1633–1634*, 66.
4. Birch, *Court and Times of Charles*, I, 410; Motteville, *Mémoires*, I, 188–90. See also Panzani, *Memoirs*, 138–9.
5. Clarendon, *State Papers*, I, 355; Panzani, *Memoirs*, 135. See also Albion, *Charles I*, 168–73.
6. Albion, *Charles I*, 412–14; Panzani, *Memoirs*, 161. For Henrietta's frivolity, see Albion, *Charles I*, 148.
7. See, Panzani, *Memoirs*, 190, 206–7; Clarendon, *State Papers*, I, 354–7; II, 217, 249–50.
8. Panzani, *Memoirs*, 188. See also Albion, *Charles I*, 152.
9. *CSPV 1636–1639*, 303; Panzani, *Memoirs*, 204, 234.
10. Panzani, *Memoirs*, 206. See also ibid., 205–6, 211–14; Albion, *Charles I*, 116–43, 164, 288–98.
11. Warwick, *Memoires*, 68.
12. BL Add. MS 15,389, f. 180v; as quoted in Green, *Letters*, 31.
13. BL Add. MS 15,389, ff. 190r *bis*, 196r–v *bis*.
14. BL Add. MS 15,389, f. 197r–v.
15. As quoted in Green, *Letters*, 34, 30. See also *CSPV 1636–1639*, 69–70; MacGregor, *Late King's Goods*, 95.
16. As quoted in Green, *Letters*, 31; Panzani, *Memoirs*, 251.
17. As quoted in *Oxford DNB*. For Juxon, see Albion, *Charles I*, 160–2; Hibbard, *Charles I*, 56.
18. My translation of Con's Italian, as quoted in Albion, *Charles I*, 162; as quoted in Hibbard, *Charles I*, 54; BL Add. MS 15,390, f. 65v.
19. Green, *Letters*, 32. See also *Oxford DNB*; Hibbard, *Charles I*, 34, 53–6.
20. Batterel, *Mémoires*, I, 227; as quoted in Hibbard, *Charles I*, 52.
21. Panzani, *Memoirs*, 165. See also *CSPV 1636–1639*, 150.
22. *CSPV 1636–1639*, 97; Birch, *Court and Times of Charles*, II, 315–16, 432–3.
23. Motteville, *Memoir*, 20. See also *CSPV 1636–1639*, 69.

24. As quoted and translated in Green, *Lives of the Princesses*, VI, 104–5.

25. BL Add. MS 15,389, f. 356r.

26. See MacGregor, *Late King's Goods*, 66; Albion, *Charles I*, 395–6.

27. BL Add. MS 15,390, ff. 249r–50v.

28. As quoted in Albion, *Charles I*, 233.

29. Warwick, *Memoires*, 65; as quoted in Albion, *Charles I*, 233.

30. See BL Add. MS 15,390, f. 15r; Albion, *Charles I*, 402–5.

31. *CSPV 1636–1639*, 120. See also Hibbard, *Charles I*, 49; BL Add. MS 15,390, ff. 10v–14v; Albion, *Charles I*, 258–80, 417–19.

32. Birch, *Court and Times of Charles*, II, 314.

33. Birch, *Court and Times of Charles*, II, 343; *CSPV 1636–1639*, 149–50.

34. Panzani's letter of 24 April/4 May 1635, PRO 31/9/17B (unfoliated); BL Add. MS 15,389, f. 129v.

35. *CSPV 1636–1639*, 149–50. See also BL Add. MS 15,389, ff. 129v–30r, 190v.

36. Warwicke, *Memoires*, 73. For Con's realisation, see Albion, *Charles I*, 248.

37. Laud, *Works*, III, 407–8.

38. Clarendon, *History*, I, 132. See also Warwicke, *Memoires*, 90; Fuller, *Church History*, Book XI, 217–19; Gardiner, *History*, VII, 317. For contemporary reports of Laud's reforms, see Panzani, *Memoirs*, 138–9; *CSPV 1636–1639*, 125, 217.

39. As quoted in Dickens, *Courts of Europe*, 196; Laud, *Works*, III, 407.

40. *CSPV 1636–1639*, 300, 301, 304, 305, 242. See also ibid., 12, 217, 272; *CSPD 1634–1635*, 22.

41. *CSPV 1636–1639*, 125. See also ibid., 136; Laud, *Works*, VII, p. 319.

42. *CSPV 1636–1639*, 205, 308. See also ibid., 299, 315, 335.

43. *CSPV 1636–1639*, 124–5.

44. Petrie, *Letters*, 95; *CSPV 1636–1639*, 124. See also ibid., 309–10; *CSPV 1632–1636*, 6, 131, 140, 366–7, 491.

45. Birch, *Court and Times of Charles*, II, 278; *CSPV 1636–1639*, 154.

46. *CSPV 1636–1639*, 304, 242; Laud, *Works*, III, 228.

47. *CSPV 1636–1639*, 304 *bis*, 246. For Charles's happiness, see Wedgwood, *King's Peace*, 19.

48. Clarendon, *History*, I, 114.

49. *CSPV 1636–1639*, 259, 273; 277.

50. Hardwicke, *State Papers*, II, 95; *CSPV 1636–1639*, 350.

51. See *CSPV 1636–1639*, 272; Hibbard, *Charles I*, 90, 275 n. 1.
52. Strafford, *Letters*, II, 74; BL Add. MS 15,390, ff. 283r, 251r. See also *CSPV 1636–1639*, 273.
53. As quoted in Hibbard, *Charles I*, 58; BL Harleian MS 3,888, f. 146r. See also BL Add. MS 15,390, f. 283v; Albion, *Charles I*, 218.
54. Strafford, *Letters*, II, 128.
55. Laud, *Works*, III, 229; Strafford, *Letters*, II, 128, 125.
56. Laud, *Works*, VII, 379; ibid., III, 230; ibid., VII, 380.
57. BL Add. MS 15,390, ff. 469v–70r; *CSPV 1636–1639*, 319, 324.
58. *CSPV 1636–1639*, 324; BL Add. MS 15,390, ff. 470v–471r.
59. BL Add. MS 15,390, ff. 477r, 473v; *CSPV 1636–1639*, 324. See also BL Add. MS 15,390, f. 471r–v.
60. BL Add. MS 15,390, f. 486v; Strafford, *Letters*, II, 125. See also Albion, *Charles I*, 213; BL Add. MS 15,390, f. 472r–v; Strafford, *Letters*, II, 128; Albion, *Charles I*, 212.
61. *CSPV 1636–1639*, 359, 358; Albion, *Charles I*, 227. See also ibid., 225–6.
62. The proclamation, as printed in Albion, *Charles I*, 415–16. See also Albion, *Charles I*, 226.
63. BL Add. MS 15,391, f. 2r.
64. As quoted in Hibbard, *Charles I*, 260, n. 72. See also Harleian MS 3,888, ff. 119v, 146r–v; Albion, *Charles I*, 226.
65. Strafford, *Letters*, II, 165. See also BL Add. MS 15,390, ff. 472v–473r; Albion, *Charles I*, 163, 212.
66. See Albion, *Charles I*, 203.
67. *CSPD 1637–1638*, 14, 259; *CSPV 1636–1639*, 376.
68. *CSPV 1636–1639*, 377, 379, 387. See also Gardiner, *History*, VIII, 327–8.
69. As quoted in Gardiner, *History*, VIII, 330–2.
70. *CSPV 1636–1639*, 389, 395, 400 *bis*.
71. *CSPV 1636–1639*, 407, 436. See also ibid., 403.
72. Petrie, *Letters*, 107.
73. *CSPV 1636–1639*, 393. See also *CSPD 1637–8*, 524–5.
74. As quoted in Albion, *Charles I*, 243. See also Hibbard, *Charles I*, 90–1, 94–8; Albion, *Charles I*, 302; *CSPV 1636–1639*, 392; *CSPD 1637–1638*, 534.
75. Petrie, *Letters*, 108, 109, 107.
76. *CSPV 1636–1639*, 436, 435, 377.

77. *CSPV 1629–1632*, 544; *CSPV 1636–1639*, 275; *CSPV 1629–1632*, 580; *CSPV 1636–1639*, 460.

78. See *CSPV 1628–1629*, 539; Estrades, *Lettres*, I, 4.

79. *CSPV 1636–1639*, 278; *HMC Denbigh MSS*, Part V, 56.

80. *CSPV 1636–1639*, 385, 410; Laud, *Works*, VII, 425.

81. *CSPV 1636–1639*, 424, 410.

82. Laud, *Works*, VII, 453. See also Green, *Lives of the Princesses*, VI, 105.

83. *CSPV 1636–1639*, 460, 446, 449.

84. See *CSPD 1638–1639*, 87, 91, 103; *CSPV 1636–1639*, 463, 467; La Serre, *L'Entrée*, sigs I1r–K1r.

85. *CSPD 1638–1639*, 48; *CSPV 1636–1639*, 467; Laud, *Works*, VII, 496.

86. La Serre, *L'Entrée*, sig. F2v; Ferrero, *Lettres*, 54.

87. La Serre, *L'Entrée*, sig. L1r.

88. La Serre, *L'Entrée*, sig. K1v; Ferrero, *Lettres*, 55.

89. La Serre, *L'Entrée*, sig. L1r. See also ibid., sig. o2r; *CSPD 1638–1639*, 65; *CSPV 1636–1639*, 468; Finet, *Ceremonies*, 253–4.

90. *CSPV 1636–1639*, 471; La Serre, *L'Entrée*, sig. o2r.

91. Birch, *Court and Times*, II, 432–3, 343. See also La Serre, *L'Entrée*, sig. M2r; BL Add. MS 15,391, f. 304r.

92. See Petrie, *Letters*, 100–1; Gardiner (ed.), *Hamilton Papers*, 62; BL Add. MS 15,391, ff. 329r–330r; *CSPV 1636–1639*, 477, 479.

93. Birch, *Court and Times*, II, 330; *CSPV 1636–1639*, 495. See also Green, *Lives of the Princesses*, VI, 396; *CSPD 1638–1639*, 362.

94. *CSPV 1636–1639*, 497, 502.

95. *CSPV 1636–1639*, 507. See also Birch, *Court and Times of Charles*, II, 330–1; Hibbard, *Charles I*, 104–7.

96. Clarendon, *State Papers*, II, 20. See also ibid., 26–31; *Calendar of Clarendon State Papers*, I, 168; Hibbard, *Charles I*, 104–7, 277, n.66.

97. See *CSPV 1636–1639*, 480, 493, 497, 516; *CSPD 1638–1639*, 161.

98. *CSPD 1638–1639*, 506, 367, 506. See also ibid., 377–8; *CSPV 1636–1639*, 494, 496–7, 500–1.

99. *CSPD 1638–1639*, 575; Laud, *Works*, III, 232. For the household's departure, see *CSPD 1638–1639*, 506; *CSPV 1636–1639*, 515.

CHAPTER EIGHT: LIBERTY AND RELIGION ALIKE

1. *CSPV 1636–1639*, 533. See also *CSPD 1638–1639*, 626, 628; *CSPD 1639*, 47–8.
2. *CSPD 1639*, 248, 146. For Charles's army, see ibid., 49–50, 52, 58, 59.
3. *CSPD 1639*, 162.
4. *CSPD 1639*, 341–2. See also ibid., 72, 162.
5. *CSPD 1639*, 221, 250.
6. *CSPD 1639*, 270, 281–2, 269.
7. *CSPD 1639–1640*, 632, 536, 246. For Henrietta at Whitehall, see Green, *Lives of the Princesses*, VI, 107; *CSPD 1638–1639*, 607, 621.
8. *CSPD 1639–1640*, 246. See also ibid., 621.
9. *CSPD 1639*, 3. See also *CSPD 1638–1639*, 623; *CSPV 1636–1639*, 536.
10. *A Coppy of the Letter*, 3, 1, 3, 1. See also *CSPD 1639*, 3; *CSPV 1636–1639*, 335; Albion, *Charles I*, 335, 421; Hibbard, *Charles I*, 103.
11. *CSPV 1636–1639*, 506; *CSPD 1639*, 73–4. See also *CSPV 1636–1639*, 539.
12. *CSPD 1639*, 73. See also Gardiner, *History*, IX, 26; Hibbard, *Charles I*, 122–3; Albion, *Charles I*, 336.
13. See Hibbard, *Charles I*, 121; Albion, *Charles I*, 359; *CSPV 1636–1639*, 547.
14. As quoted in Hibbard, *Charles I*, 120; *CSPD 1639*, 294. See also *CSPD 1639*, 288.
15. *CSPV 1636–1639*, 548.
16. *CSPV 1640–1642*, 294. For the talks, see *CSPD 1639*, 330.
17. Clarendon, *State Papers*, II, 56.
18. *CSPD 1639*, 349. See also *Calendar of Clarendon State Papers*, I, 180.
19. *CSPV 1636–1639*, 559; Petrie, *Letters*, 104. For Charles at Berwick, see *CSPV 1636–1639*, 559; Finet, *Ceremonies*, 261; Hardwicke *State Papers*, II, 141.
20. *CSPV 1636–1639*, 554. See also ibid., 563; Finet, *Ceremonies*, 261; Laud, *Works*, III, 233.
21. Clarendon, *History*, I, 165, 164.
22. *CSPV 1636–1639*, 497.
23. Laud, *Works*, III, 361–2.
24. As quoted in Smuts, 'Puritan Followers', 31–2.
25. Laud, *Works*, VII, 550. See also *CSPD 1639*, 105.

26. As quoted in Smuts, 'Puritan Followers', 30; as quoted in Hibbard, *Charles I*, 146. See also Laud, *Works*, VII, 442, 570–1; *HMC De L'Isle and Dudley MSS*, VI, 158–9.

27. Motteville, *Mémoires*, I, 223; *HMC De L'Isle and Dudley MSS*, VI, 204. See also Hibbard, *Charles I*, 133.

28. Warwicke, *Memoires*, 109–10. See also Clarendon, *History*, I, 341.

29. Warwicke, *Memoires*, 109. For the state of Ireland and Wentworth's achievements there, see Wedgwood, *Thomas Wentworth; Oxford DNB*.

30. Petrie, *Letters*, 96. For Laud and Wentworth, see Laud, *Works*, VII, passim.

31. Petrie, *Letters*, 104.

32. Petrie, *Letters*, 104. For Laud and Con, see Gardiner (ed.), *Hamilton Papers*, 62; *CSPV 1636–1639*, 572; Albion, *Charles I*, 304, 312, 315.

33. As quoted in Wedgwood, *Thomas Wentworth*, 267.

34. Laud, *Works*, VII, 508; *HMC De L'Isle and Dudley MSS*, VI, 182 *bis*. See also ibid., VI, 179–180, 182, 208–9; Laud, *Works*, VII, 506, 509, 510, 537–8.

35. *CSPV 1636–1639*, 592. See also ibid., 595; Wedgwood, *Thomas Wentworth*, 267.

36. *CSPV 1636–1639*, 574. See also ibid., 567, 570, 578, 590, 599; Laud, *Works*, III, 233.

37. *CSPV 1636–1639*, 568; Laud, *Works*, III, 283; *CSPV 1636–1639*, 576.

38. *CSPV 1636–1639*, 592. See also ibid., 595; Laud, *Works*, III, 233; *CSPD 1639–1640*, 158.

39. *CSPV 1636–1639*, 601. See also Warwicke, *Memoires*, 110; Clarendon, *History*, I, 341–2.

40. Clarendon, *History*, I, 171. See also Laud, *Works*, III, 233, 282–3.

41. *CSPV 1636–1639*, 601; *CSPD 1639–1640*, 148–9. See also Laud, *Works*, III, 283.

42. Clarendon, *History*, I, 172; *CSPV 1636–1639*, 602; as quoted in Pastor, *History of the Popes*, XXIX, 323. See also *CSPD 1639–1640*, 158.

43. *CSPD 1639–1640*, 321. See also ibid., 158; Wedgwood, *Thomas Wentworth*, 273; *CSPV 1636–1639*, 602.

44. *CSPV 1640–1642*, 23; *CSPV 1636–1639*, 605. See also *CSPV 1640–1642*, 4.

45. See *CSPD 1639–1640*, 365; Finet, *Ceremonies*, 272.

46. Davenant, *Dramatic Works*, II, 310–26.

47. *CSPD 1639–1640*, 459; *HMC De L'Isle and Dudley MSS*, VI, 231.

48. See MacGregor, *Late King's Goods*, 221, 225; Albion, *Charles I*, 396–7.

49. For the purchase, see *HMC Denbigh MSS*, Part V, 68; *CSPD 1639–1640*, 157; *HMC De L'Isle and Dudley MSS*, VI, 212. For the design, see Strong, *Renaissance Garden*, 191–7.

50. *CSPV 1640–1642*, 8, 12. For the ministers opposing the war, see also ibid., 17.

51. *CSPV 1640–1642*, 35. See also ibid., 37; *CSPD 1639–1640*, 608; *CSPD 1640*, 6.

52. *CSPV 1640–1642*, 27, 30. See also *CSPV 1640–1642*, 25; Hibbard, *Charles I*, 148; Gardiner, *History*, IX, 159.

53. Evelyn, *Diary*, 14; *LJ*, IV, 13 April 1640. See also Cope, *Proceedings*, 95; *CSPD 1640*, 25.

54. As quoted in Smuts, 'Puritan Followers', 34; *LJ*, IV, 13 April 1640.

55. Cope, *Proceedings*, 138; as quoted in Gardiner, *History*, IX, 101.

56. *CSPV 1640–1642*, 40. See also *CJ*, II, 17 April 1640.

57. See Hibbard, *Charles I*, 148; *CSPD 1640*, 88, 102.

58. Laud, *Works*, III, 283. See also *CSPD 1640*, 115.

59. *LJ*, IV, 6 May 1640.

60. Laud, *Works*, III, 234; *HMC De L'Isle and Dudley MSS*, VI, 262.

61. *CSPD 1640*, 115; *HMC De L'Isle and Dudley MSS*, VI, 262.

62. *CSPD 1640*, 112–13.

63. *HMC De L'Isle and Dudley MSS*, VI, 262.

64. *CSPD 1640*, 155; as quoted in Gardiner, *History*, IX, 130.

65. Motteville, *Mémoires*, 196; as quoted in Smuts, 'Puritan Followers', 42. See also Warwicke, *Memoires*, 112; Motteville, *Mémoires*, I, 194.

66. *CSPD 1640*, 117; Laud, *Works*, III, 284; *CSPV 1640–1642*, 47. See also Gardiner, *History*, IX, 133; Laud, *Works*, III, 234.

67. Clarendon, *History*, I, 188; *CSPV 1640–1642*, 47. See also Laud, *Works*, III, 284; *CSPV 1640–1642*, 47; Gardiner, *History*, IX, 133.

68. Laud, *Works*, III, 284; *CSPV 1640–1642*, 47. See also BL Add. MS 35,331, f. 77r.

69. Clarendon, *History*, I, 188; *CSPV 1640–1642*, 47. See also *CSPD 1640*, 150, 167.

70. *CSPV 1640–1642*, 48. See also Gardiner, *History*, IX, 134–5.

71. *CSPV 1640–1642*, 48, 49. See also Gardiner, *History*, IX, 135.

72. *HMC De L'Isle and Dudley MSS*, VI, 272. See also ibid., 270; *CSPV 1640–1642*, 49; Gardiner, *History*, IX, 135–6.

73. See Laud, *Works*, III, 236; *CSPV 1640–1642*, 52; Clarendon, *History*, I, 188; Gardiner, *History*, IX, 141.

74. *CSPD 1640*, 174, 192.

75. *CSPV 1640–1642*, 49. See also Albion, *Charles I*, 339–40.

76. Pastor, *History of the Popes*, XXIX, 324. See also Gardiner, *History*, IX, 141–2; *CSPV 1640–1642*, 52; Pastor, *History of the Popes*, XXIX, 327; Albion, *Charles I*, 338.

77. *CSPV 1640–1642*, 52. See also *HMC De L'Isle and Dudley MSS*, VI, 276.

78. *CSPD 1640*, 272, 293–4. See also Albion, *Charles I*, 339; *CSPD 1640*, 528.

79. *CSPV 1640–1642*, 53. See also BL Harleian MS 3,791, f. 114v; *CSPD 1640–1641*, 172; Albion, *Charles I*, 339.

80. As quoted in Albion, *Charles I*, 359.

81. See Gardiner, *History*, IX 175; Birch, *Court and Times of Charles I*, II, 286; *CSPV 1640–1642*, 59, 66; *CSPD 1640*, 451.

82. *CSPV 1640–1642*, 60. See also *CSPD 1640*, 497, 554.

83. *CSPV 1640–1642*, 71. For mutinies, see Gardiner, *History*, IX, 186.

84. See *CSPD 1640*, 278; *Oxford DNB*.

85. *CSPV 1640–1642*, 52, 65. See also *CSPD 1640*, 516, 563, 571.

86. *CSPV 1640–1642*, 71; Hardwicke, *State Papers*, II, 147–50. See also *CSPD 1640*, 587–8, 590–1.

87. *CSPD 1640*, 601. See also *CSPV 1640–1642*, 71.

88. *CSPD 1640*, 507.

89. *CSPV 1640–1642*, 70. See also Gardiner, *History*, IX, 187.

90. *CSPD 1640*, 609; *CSPV 1640–1642*, 73.

91. *CSPD 1640*, 645, 649; as quoted in Gardiner, *History*, IX, 195.

92. *CSPD 1640–1641*, 7; Motteville, *Mémoires*, 194.

93. *CSPV 1640–1642*, 75; *CSPD 1640*, 612. See also *CSPV 1640–1642*, 70–2; *CSPD 1640*, 648; Laud, *Works*, III, 291–2.

94. As quoted in Hibbard, *Charles I*, 156; *CSPD 1640*, 602; Clarendon, *State Papers*, II, 116

95. Laud, *Works*, III, 237; *CSPD 1640*, 617. See also Albion, *Charles I*, 340; *CSPV 1640–1642*, 73.

96. *CSPV 1640–1642*, 73, 74. See also *CSPD 1640*, 633, 634.

97. Hardwicke, *State Papers*, II, 157. See also *CSPD 1640*, 652; Clarendon, *State Papers*, II, 92, 95, 96.
98. *CSPV 1640–1642*, 76; Hardwicke, *State Papers*, II, 164.
99. *Calendar of Clarendon State Papers*, I, 204. For other councillors' fears, see *CSPD 1640–1641*, 7.
100. Hardwicke, *State Papers*, II, 168–70.
101. *CSPD 1640–1641*, 8.
102. *CSPV 1640–1642*, 79.
103. *CSPD 1640–1641*, 47, 23. See also ibid., 80; *CSPV 1640–1642*, 80.
104. Clarendon, *State Papers*, II, 114, 112; *CSPD 1640–1641*, 46. See also ibid., 1.
105. See Clarendon, *History*, I, 202.
106. *CSPD 1640–1641*, 69. See also ibid., 67, 68.
107. *CSPD 1640–1641*, 92, 91; Clarendon, *History*, I, 202.
108. *Calendar of Clarendon State Papers*, I, 208; *CSPV 1640–1642*, 89.
109. *CSPV 1640–1642*, 90–2. See also *CSPD 1640–1641*, 191.
110. *CSPV 1640–1642*, 86; Clarendon, *History*, I, 203–6.
111. *CSPD 1640–1641*, 246–7.
112. *CSPD 1640–1641*, 104–5; *CSPV 1640–1642*, 97, 91. See also *CSPD 1640–1641*, 111.
113. *CSPV 1640–1642*, 93, See also ibid., 84, 87; *CSPD 1640–1641*, 246.
114. *CSPV 1640–1642*, 94, 7994.
115. *CSPV 1640–1642*, 93. See also ibid., 94.

CHAPTER NINE: EVIL COUNSELLORS

1. *CSPV 1640–1642*, 89, 92.
2. See Motteville, *Mémoires*, I, 194–5.
3. D'Ewes, *Journal*, ed. Notestein, 14; *CSPV 1640–1642*, 95, 94.
4. D'Ewes, *Journal*, ed. Notestein, 8, 11 n. 84.
5. *CSPV 1640–1642*, 95; D'Ewes, *Journal*, ed. Notestein, 14.
6. D'Ewes, *Journal*, ed. Notestein, 533.
7. *LJ*, IV, 13 November 1640. See also ibid., 11 November 1640; *CJ*, II, 11 November 1640.
8. See *CSPV 1640–1642*, 98, 112; *CJ*, II, 30 November 1640, 1 December 1640; *CSPV 1640–1642*, 102.
9. *CSPV 1640–1642*, 102; Laud, *Works*, III, 297, 279; *CJ*, II, 16 December 1640.

10. *HMC De L'Isle and Dudley MSS*, VI, 346.
11. D'Ewes, *Journal*, ed. Notestein, 24–5.
12. *CSPV 1640–1642*, 97.
13. This letter of Henrietta's, Vatican Library, Codices Barberini, 8,615, ff. 84–6, is partly printed in Bellesheim, *History of the Catholic Church*, III, 493, and Albion, *Charles I*, 360. See also PRO 31/9/19, f. 187; Gardiner, *History*, IX, 244, 251–2; *CSPV 1640–1642*, 100; *CJ*, II, 23 November 1640.
14. *CSPV 1640–1642*, 103.
15. As quoted in Albion, *Charles I*, 346.
16. D'Ewes, *Journal*, ed. Notestein, 78; *CJ*, II, 1 December 1640. See also *CSPD 1640–1641*, 312; *CSPV 1640–1642*, 105.
17. *CSPV 1640–1642*, 105.
18. *CJ*, II, 1 December 1640; *CSPV 1640–1642*, 107. See also *CSPV 1640–1642*, 111; *Oxford DNB*, article for John, Baron Finch; Albion, *Charles I*, 346–7.
19. *CSPV 1640–1642*, 111–12.
20. As quoted in Green, *Lives of the Princesses*, VI, 394. Salvetti's report of 11/21 December, BL Add. MS 27,962 I, dates Anne's death to 6 December 1640.
21. *CSPV 1640–1642*, 106; *HMC De L'Isle and Dudley MSS*, VI, 350; *CSPD 1640–1641*, 326.
22. For Elizabeth, see *True Effigies*, 12; Green, *Lives of the Princesses*, VI, 337. For the negotiations, see *CSPV 1640–1642*, 25, 52, 103; *CSPD 1640–1641*, 278, 291.
23. As quoted in Geyl, *Orange and Stuart*, 7; *CSPV 1640–1642*, 109.
24. *CSPV 1640–1642*, 107, 117.
25. See Gardiner, *History*, IX, 265; *CSPV 1640–1642*, 119.
26. *LJ*, IV, 1 January and 23 January 1641. See also ibid., 25 January 1641; D'Ewes, *Journal*, ed. Notestein, 279, 285.
27. As quoted in D'Ewes, *Journal*, ed. Notestein, 321, n. 24.
28. D'Ewes, *Journal*, ed. Notestein, 291. See also ibid., 295, 301.
29. *CSPV 1640–1642*, 123.
30. *LJ*, IV, 4 February 1641. See also D'Ewes, *Journal*, ed. Notestein, 321.
31. *HMC De L'Isle and Dudley MSS*, VI, 376. See also D'Ewes, *Journal*, ed. Notestein, 333.

32. [Henrietta Maria], *A Coppy*, 11–12. See also D'Ewes, *Journal*, ed. Notestein, 323–4.

33. *CSPV 1640–1642*, 123. See also D'Ewes, *Journal*, ed. Notestein, 324–5.

34. D'Ewes, *Journal*, ed. Notestein, 357–60.

35. *CSPV 1640–1642*, III, 126. See also *LJ*, IV, 15 February 1641; *CJ*, II, 15 February 1641.

36. D'Ewes, *Journal*, ed. Notestein, 393. See also ibid., n. 12.

37. Motteville, *Mémoires*, I, 194–6.

38. See Albion, *Charles I*, 365; Gardiner, *History*, IX, 288.

39. *CSPV 1640–1642*, 125. See Wedgwood, *Thomas Wentworth*, 306.

40. *CSPD 1640–1641*, 461. See also *LJ*, IV, 16 February 1641.

41. *CJ*, II, 16 February 1641; *CSPV 1640–1642*, 127. See also *CSPD 1640–1641*, 462.

42. *HMC Cowper MSS*, II, Appendix II, 272. See also Gardiner, *History*, IX, 259–60.

43. *CSPV 1640–1642*, 128; D'Ewes, *Journal*, ed. Notestein, 247.

44. D'Ewes, *Journal*, ed. Notestein, 393. *LJ*, IV, 23 February 1641, dates these speeches to the Lords' first debate of this issue, on 22 February.

45. D'Ewes, *Journal*, ed. Notestein, 488 and n. 10. For a similar suggestion by Digby on 4 February, see D'Ewes, *Journal*, ed. Notestein, 325.

46. D'Ewes, *Journal*, ed. Notestein, 494. See also ibid., 493; *LJ*, IV, 17 March 1641.

47. Warwick, *Memoires*, 112.

48. This scene is based on Hollar's engraving of the trial and on Wedgwood, *Thomas Wentworth*, 337–8; Motteville, *Mémoires*, I, 196.

49. Chief sources throughout the trial are *LJ* and Wedgwood, *Thomas Wentworth*.

50. Warwick, *Memoires*, 110.

51. *CSPV 1640–1642*, 138. See also Laud, *Works*, III, 440.

52. Motteville, *Mémoires*, I, 196; Clarendon, *History*, I, 289; *Life and Death*, 32. See also *CSPV 1640–1642*, 138.

53. Motteville, *Mémoires*, I, 196–7; *CSPV 1640–1642*, 136. See also *Life and Death*, 32; *CSPD 1640–1641*, 547–8.

54. Motteville, *Mémoires*, I, 196; *CSPV 1640–1642*, 128.

55. Clarendon, *History*, III, 445. For the fortifications, see *HMC Cowper MSS*, Appendix II, II, 280–1.

56. See Russell, 'First army plot', 99–100; *Calendar of Clarendon State Papers*, I, 204; Gardiner, *History*, IX, 343; Green, *Letters*, 38; *CSPV 1640–1642*, 127; Hibbard, *Charles I*, 180; D'Ewes, *Journal*, ed. Notestein, 484.
57. *LJ*, IV, 17 March 1641; *CSPD 1640–1641*, 510. See also *CSPV 1640–1642*, 140.
58. As quoted in Russell, 'First army plot', 89. See also *CSPD 1640–1641*, 507.
59. *HMC Portland MSS*, I, 22.
60. As quoted in Gardiner, *History*, IX, 343. Principal sources on the army plot are Motteville, *Mémoires*, I, 197–201; Rossetti's recollections printed in Gardiner, *History*, IX, 343; Russell, 'First army plot'. Extra details come from *CSPD 1641–1643*, 7–8; *CSPV 1640–1642*, 163–4; Verney, *Verney Papers*, 98.
61. Motteville, *Mémoires*, I, 198–9. See also ibid., 197.
62. As quoted in Russell, 'First army plot', 91. See also Verney, *Verney Papers*, 94–5, 98; *HMC Portland MSS*, I, 22–3; *CSPD 1641–1643*, 18.
63. Verney, *Verney Papers*, 87. See also Russell, 'First army plot', 93.
64. As quoted in Russell, 'First army plot', 94; *HMC De L'Isle and Dudley MSS*, VI, 397–8; as quoted in Russell, 'First army plot', 93.
65. *CSPV 1640–1642*, 138. See also Wedgwood, *Thomas Wentworth*, 346–50.
66. As quoted in Wedgwood, *Thomas Wentworth*, 353; *LJ*, IV, 10 April 1641.
67. *CSPD 1640–1641*, 540.
68. *CSPD 1640–1641*, 540. See also *CSPD 1640–1641*, 560.
69. See Rushworth, *Tryal*, 50–3; *CJ*, II, 21 April 1641; *CSPD 1640–1641*, 555.
70. Petrie, *Letters*, 115; *CSPD 1640–1641*, 555.
71. As quoted in Wedgwood, *Thomas Wentworth*, 368; *CSPD 1640–1641*, 560.
72. *CSPV 1640–1642*, 145, 141.
73. *CSPV 1640–1642*, 142. See also Albion, *Charles I*, 365.
74. *CSPV 1640–1642*, 145, 142. See also *HMC Cowper MSS*, Appendix II, 280–1; Russell, 'First army plot', 97.
75. See *LJ*, IV, 29 April 1641; Wedgwood, *Thomas Wentworth*, 370; Russell, 'First army plot', 95–6.
76. *CSPV 1640–1642*, 145, 141.

77. *CSPD 1640–1641*, 559.

78. Clarendon, *History*, I, 318–21.

79. *CSPD 1640–1641*, 567.

80. *True Effigies*, 6. See also BL Harleian MS 6,988, f. 101; Mayor, *Nicholas Ferrar: Two Lives*, 154; *CSPD 1640–1641*, 158.

81. *True Effigies*, 10–11.

82. *CSPV 1640–1642*, 142. For William's reception, see also Finet, *Ceremonies*, 309.

83. *CSPV 1640–1642*, 141. See also ibid., 139.

84. *CSPV 1640–1642*, 145. See also Green, *Lives of the Princesses*, VI, 113.

85. As quoted in Green, *Lives of the Princesses*, VI, 112; *True Effigies*, 8; *CSPV 1640–1642*, 145.

86. See Van Dyck's wedding portrait.

87. *CSPV 1640–1642*, 147; my translation of the text quoted in *CSPV 1640–1642*, 147. See also Green, *Lives of the Princesses*, VI, 117.

88. Laud, *Works*, III, 444; *CSPV 1640–1642*, 147; Clarendon, *History*, I, 337; *CSPV 1640–1642*, 148.

89. Clarendon, *History*, I, 336; as quoted in Gardiner, *History*, IX, 351–2; *CJ*, II, 3 May 1641.

90. Russell, 'First army plot', 92; Clarendon, *History*, 445. See also Verney, *Verney Papers*, 98; Motteville, *Mémoires*, I, 200. Goring's whitewashing of himself is not supported by Percy, who named Goring as a chief plotter: see *CSPD 1641–1643*, 18.

91. *CJ*, II, 5 May 1641; as quoted in Gardiner, *History*, IX, 363.

92. *CJ*, II, 5 May 1641; *LJ*, IV, 5 May 1641; *CJ*, II, 5 May 1641; *CSPV 1640–1642*, 150. See also *CJ*, II, 6 May 1641.

93. See Motteville, *Mémoires*, I, 199–200; *LJ*, IV, 6 May 1641.

94. *LJ*, IV, 6 May 1641; *CJ*, II, 6 May 1641.

95. *CSPV 1640–1642*, 150.

96. Motteville, *Mémoires*, I, 201. See also *CSPV 1640–1642*, 150.

97. *CSPD 1640–1641*, 571. See also Pastor, *History of the Popes*, XXIX, 332.

98. See Russell, 'First army plot', 97.

99. CJ, II, 7 May 1641.

100. *HMC Egmont MSS*, I, 134; as quoted in Hibbard, *Charles I*, 195. See also Gardiner, *History*, IX, 363.

101. As quoted in Gardiner, *History*, IX, 363. See also ibid., 356; *CSPV 1640–1642*, 150.

102. *CJ*, II, 7 May 1641. See also *LJ*, IV, 7 May 1641.

103. Clarendon, *History*, I, 337. See also *Oxford DNB*; Wedgwood, *Thomas Wentworth*, 377, 379, n. 45; Clarendon, *History*, I, 337; *CSPD 1640–1641*, 571.

104. *LJ*, IV, 7 May 1641.

105. See *CSPV 1640–1642*, 142; *Oxford DNB* entries for the Earls of Holland, Bristol and Hertford; Wedgwood, *Thomas Wentworth*, 377, 379, n. 45; *CSPD 1640–1641*, 571.

106. *HMC Egmont MSS*, I, 134.

107. As quoted in Gardiner, *History*, IX, 362; Motteville, *Mémoires*, I, 202.

108. *HMC Egmont MSS*, I, 134; *LJ*, IV, 8 May 1641.

109. *LJ*, IV, 7 May 1641; *LJ*, IV, 8 May 1641. See also *CSPV 1640–1642*, 151.

110. Clarendon, *History*, I, 337–8; Laud, *Works*, III, 441.

111. *CSPV 1640–1642*, 150. See also PRO 31/9/20, ff. 193–5.

112. *CJ*, II, 11 May 1641.

113. *CSPV 1640–1642*, 150.

114. Clarendon, *History*, I, 338–9.

115. Prideaux, *History*, 360.

116. See *CSPD 1640–1641*, 567; Wedgwood, *Thomas Wentworth*, 376–7.

117. Clarendon, *History*, I, 339.

118. As quoted in Gardiner, *History*, IX, 366–7; Strafford, *Letters*, II, 432.

119. *LJ*, IV, 10 May 1641; *CSPD 1640–1641*, 573.

120. As quoted in Wedgwood, *Thomas Wentworth*, 380; *CSPD 1640–1641*, 574.

121. *LJ*, IV, 11 May 1641.

122. As quoted in Gardiner, *History*, IX, 368; as quoted in Wedgwood, *Thomas Wentworth*, 383. See also Laud, *Works*, III, 442.

123. As quoted in Wedgwood, *Thomas Wentworth*, 386. See also *CSPV 1640–1642*, 151.

124. As quoted in Gardiner, *History*, IX, 369.

125. As quoted in Wedgwood, *Thomas Wentworth*, 386–8.

126. As quoted in Wedgwood, *Thomas Wentworth*, 388; Clarendon, *History*, I, 341.

127. *CSPV 1640–1642*, 151; as quoted in Wedgwood, *Thomas Wentworth*, 389.

128. Motteville, *Mémoires*, I, 202; my translation of the Italian quoted in Pastor, *History of the Popes*, XXIX, 328.
129. *CSPV 1640–1642*, 151, 153, 152. See also Motteville, *Mémoires*, I, 202–3.

CHAPTER TEN: SHAME AND FEAR

1. *CSPV 1640–1642*, 152. See also ibid., 175.
2. Gardiner, *Constitutional Documents*, 163–6; *CSPV 1640–1642*, 174.
3. As quoted in Hibbard, *Charles I*, 206. See also *CSPV 1640–1642*, 163.
4. *CSPV 1640–1642*, 152, 174, 166. See also ibid., 153, 160, 163, 166.
5. *LJ*, IV, 14 July 1641. See also *CSPD 1641–1643*, 47, 48; *CSPV 1640–1642*, 179; Verney, *Verney Papers*, 106.
6. *CSPV 1640–1642*, 183, 187. See also *CJ*, II, 21 July 1641.
7. Ferrero, *Lettres de Henriette Marie*, 57–9.
8. As quoted in Russell, *Fall*, 304; *CSPV 1640–1642*, 194.
9. *CSPV 1640–1642*, 200.
10. *CSPD 1641–1643*, 101; Evelyn, *Diary and Correspondence*, IV, 50. See also *CSPV 1640–1642*, 205.
11. *Nicholas Papers*, I, 25; *CSPV 1640–1642*, 208.
12. See *Nicholas Papers*, I, 7; Evelyn, *Diary and Correspondence*, IV, 75.
13. Evelyn, *Diary and Correspondence*, IV, 75; Motteville, *Mémoires*, I, 205. See also *CSPV 1640–1642*, 213, 225.
14. *CSPV 1640–1642*, 250–1, 236. See also Motteville, *Mémoires*, I, 205; Evelyn, *Diary and Correspondence*, IV, 77.
15. *CSPV 1640–1642*, 236–7; *CSPD 1641–1643*, 148.
16. *CJ*, II, 1 November 1641; *CSPD 1641–1643*, 168.
17. *CSPV 1640–1642*, 250. See also *Oxford DNB*: Joh Pym; *CSPV 1640–1642*, 243–5.
18. *LJ*, IV, 2 November 1641. See also ibid., 15 November 1641.
19. *CSPD 1641–1643*, 171.
20. *CSPV 1640–1642*, 254; Motteville, *Mémoires*, I, 205.
21. *CSPD 1641–1643*, 177; *CSPV 1640–1642*, 254, 250–1. See also Gardiner, *Constitutional Documents*, 201; *Ovatio Carolina*; Motteville, *Mémoires*, I, 205.
22. See D'Ewes, *Journal*, ed. Coates, 200, n. 6, 202–3, 213.
23. Gardiner, *Constitutional Documents*, 202 ff. See also *CJ*, II, 2 December 1641.

24. D'Ewes, *Journal*, ed. Coates, 261.

25. *CSPD 1641–1643*, 194; *LJ*, IV, 14 December 1641. See also D'Ewes, *Journal*, ed. Coates, 244.

26. Gardiner, *Constitutional Documents*, 233. See also *CSPV 1640–1642*, 263.

27. D'Ewes, *Journal*, ed. Coates, 345, 344; *CJ*, II, 24 December 1641.

28. *CSPD 1641–1643*, 217. See also *CSPD 1641–1643*, 215, 216, 218; *CSPV 1640–1642*, 271; Gardiner, *History*, X, 112.

29. As quoted in Gardiner, *History*, X, 117.

30. For Godfrey Goodman's conversion, see Hibbard, *Charles I*, 150.

31. See D'Ewes, *Journal*, ed. Coates, 347.

32. *CSPD 1641–1643*, 217. See also Gardiner, *History*, X, 117; *CSPV 1640–1642*, 272.

33. *CSPD 1641–1643*, 218, 214–15.

34. *CSPV 1640–1642*, 272. See also *CSPD 1641–1643*, 217.

35. *CSPD 1641–1643*, 215; *CSPV 1640–1642*, 272. See also *CSPD 1641–1643*, 216, 217.

36. *CSPD 1641–1643*, 216, 241.

37. *LJ*, IV, 30 December 1641. See also *CSPD 1641–1643*, 216, 217, 241, 242; D'Ewes, *Journal*, ed. Coates, 376; *CSPV 1640–1642*, 275.

38. *CSPD 1641–1643*, 216; *LJ*, IV, 30 December 1641; *CSPV 1640–1642*, 273.

39. D'Ewes, *Journal*, ed. Coates, 366–7; *CJ*, II, 31 December 1641.

40. *CJ*, II, 31 December 1641. See also D'Ewes, *Journal*, ed. Coates, 366–7.

41. My translation of the Italian quoted in Gardiner, *History*, X, 128, n. 1; *CSPV 1640–1642*, 275–6. See also D'Ewes, *Journal*, ed. Coates, 373, n. 18.

42. See Gardiner, *History*, X, 128, n. 1.

43. As quoted in D'Ewes, *Journal*, ed. Coates, 395; Clarendon, *History*, IV, 489; Bossuet, *Oraison*, 96. See also Clarendon, *History*, IV, 492.

44. *LJ*, IV, 3 January, 1642; *CJ*, 3 January 1642. See also *CSPD 1641–1643*, 239.

45. *Eikon Basilike*, ch. 3; Motteville, *Mémoires*, I, 205. See also *CSPD 1641–1643*, 239.

46. D'Ewes, *Journal*, ed. Coates, 379; *CJ*, II, 3 January 1642; *CSPD 1641–1643*, 236.

47. *CSPD 1641–1643*, 242; D'Ewes, *Journal*, ed. Coates, 394, 382–3. See also ibid., 379, 393–4.
48. Motteville, *Mémoires*, I, 205–6.
49. Gardiner, *Constitutional Documents*, 237ff.; D'Ewes, *Journal*, ed. Coates, 395. See also ibid., 378, 382n.; *CSPD 1641–1643*, 242.
50. D'Ewes, *Journal*, ed. Coates, 393; *CSPD 1641–1643*, 242.
51. D'Ewes, *Journal*, ed. Coates, 382n., 393, 394.
52. *CSPD 1641–1643*, 242; D'Ewes, *Journal*, ed. Coates, 381. See also *CSPD 1641–1643*, 239.
53. D'Ewes, *Journal*, ed. Coates, 381.
54. As quoted in Gardiner, *History* of England, X, 138.
55. Gardiner, *Constitutional Documents*, 237ff.; D'Ewes, *Journal*, ed. Coates, 383, 382, 393.
56. Motteville, *Mémoires*, I, 205; as quoted in Gardiner, *History*, X, 134, n. 3; Motteville, *Mémoires*, I, 205.
57. See Evelyn, *Diary and Correspondence*, IV, 75.
58. Motteville, *Mémoires*, I, 206, 205.
59. D'Ewes, *Journal*, ed. Coates, 383–4.
60. D'Ewes, *Journal*, ed. Coates, 395.
61. As quoted in D'Ewes, *Journal*, ed. Coates, 383, n. 19. See also ibid., 384.
62. D'Ewes, as quoted in Forster, *Arrest of the Five Members*, 220; as quoted in *Oxford DNB*; D'Ewes, *Journal*, ed. Coates, 384.
63. Clarendon, *History*, I, 485. See also *CSPD 1641–1643*, 244.
64. Sources for this incident are: *CSPD 1641–1643*, 240–4; *CSPV 1640–1642*, 277; Clarendon, *History*, I, 485–6.
65. For this Commons debate, see D'Ewes, *Journal*, ed. Coates, 382–7; *CJ*, II, 5 January 1642.
66. Principal sources for the committee's work are: *CSPD 1641–1643*, 243; D'Ewes, *Journal*, ed. Coates, 386–96; Verney, *Verney Papers*, 140.
67. D'Ewes, *Journal*, ed. Coates, 399, n. 9; *CSPV 1640–1642*, 280.
68. *CSPD 1641–1643*, 237; *CSPV 1640–1642*, 277; Clarendon, *History*, I, 505. See also *CSPD 1641–1643*, 242.
69. D'Ewes, *Journal*, ed. Coates, 392; *CSPV 1640–1642*, 279; D'Ewes, *Journal*, ed. Coates, 392. See also *CSPD 1641–1643*, 245, 249.
70. *CSPD 1641–1643*, 243. See also D'Ewes, *Journal*, ed. Coates, 392; *CSPV 1640–1642*, 280.
71. As quoted in Hibbard, *Charles I*, 222; *CSPD 1641–1643*, 276; BL Add.

MS 27,962 I, f. 345r. See also ibid., f. 345r; *CSPV 1640–1642*, 277.

72. Clarendon, *History*, I, 399. See also *CSPV 1640–1642*, 277; BL Add. MS 27,962 I, f. 342r.

73. BL Add. MS 27,962 I, f. 338v.

74. Hutchinson, *Memoirs*, 85.

75. Hutchinson, *Memoirs*, 88–9.

76. *LJ*, IV, 20 January 1642; Coates, *Private Journals*, I, 117.

77. As quoted in D'Ewes, *Journal*, ed. Coates, 397n.; *CSPD 1641–1643*, 248.

78. D'Ewes, *Journal*, ed. Coates, 398. See also ibid., 400–1; *CJ*, II, 11 January 1642; Verney, *Verney Papers*, 141–3.

79. *CSPV 1640–1642*, 280. See also *CSPD 1641–1643*, 252.

80. Clarendon, *History*, I, 555; *Eikon Basilike*, ch. 6.

81. Clarendon, *History*, I, 507, 519, 507; *CSPV 1640–1642*, 281. See also *CSPD 1641–1643*, 254.

82. *CSPD 1641–1643*, 256.

83. See *CSPV 1640–1642*, 285; BL Add. MS 27,962 I, f. 343r.

84. *CSPV 1640–1642*, 281. See also BL Add. MS 27,962 I, f. 343r–345r.

85. Verney, *Verney Papers*, 144; *CJ*, II, 12 January 1642. See also Clarendon, *History*, I, 515.

86. *CSPV 1640–1642*, 282; BL Add. MS 27,962 I, f. 343r. See also Clarendon, *History*, I, 520; *CSPD 1641–1643*, 252.

87. Clarendon, *History*, I, 524. See also Prinsterer, *Archives*, 2nd series, vol. IV, 6–7; *CSPV 1640–1642*, 283.

88. Ferrero, *Lettres de Henriette Marie*, 59.

89. *CJ*, II, 14 January 1642. See also *CJ*, II, 12 January 1642.

90. Clarendon, *History*, I, 554–5. See also ibid., 523; Rossetti's letter quoted in Gardiner, *History*, X, 157, n. 1.

91. *CJ*, II, 12 January 1642. See also *CJ*, II, 11 January 1642; Clarendon, *History*, I, 523–4; *CSPD 1641–1643*, 253, 256; *CSPV 1640–1642*, 284.

92. Clarendon, *History*, I, 515; Coates, *Private Journals*, I, 130. See also *CSPV 1640–1642*, 288; *CJ*, II, 19 February 1642.

93. *LJ*, IV, 1 February 1642; Laud, *Works*, III, 457; *CSPD 1641–1643*, 277.

94. *LJ*, IV, 7 February 1642.

95. *CSPV 1640–1642*, 285; Clarendon, *History*, I, 529, 554.

96. Prinsterer, *Archives*, 2nd series, vol. IV, 22.

97. *LJ*, IV, 7 February 1642; ibid., 8 February 1642; *CSPV 1640–1642*, 293; Clarendon, *History*, I, 558.

98. Ferrero, *Lettres*, 59–60.

99. Coates, *Private Journals*, I, 305, 306, 307; *CJ*, II, 7 February 1642; *LJ*, IV, 7 February 1642.

100. Green, *Letters*, 64. See also Ferard, *The Law of Fixtures*, 158n.

101. *CSPV 1640–1642*, 294. See also ibid., 13, 21.

102. Clarendon, *History*, I, 572. See also Prinsterer, *Archives*, 2nd series, vol. IV, 7; Motteville, *Mémoires*, I, 207–8; Green, *Letters*, 52–70, *passim*; *CSPD 1641–1643*, 306, 310–11.

103. Motteville, *Mémoires*, I, 208; Ferrero, *Lettres de Henriette Marie*, 59; Green, *Letters*, 72.

104. *CSPV 1640–1642*, 295; Green, *Letters*, 75; Prinsterer, *Archives*, 2nd series, vol. IV, 23.

105. See Gardiner, *History*, IX, 403–4; Clarendon, *History*, IV, 490, 492; Laud, *Works*, III, 440–1.

106. *CSPV 1640–1642*, 295; Green, *Letters*, 65, 68–9, 65.

107. Green, *Letters*, 57, 58, 65, 60, 65. See also ibid., 52, 55, 59, 61, 68, 80, 85.

108. Green, *Letters*, 70, 61.

109. *CSPV 1640–1642*, 294. See also ibid., 295; Gardiner, *History*, X, 163.

110. Green, *Letters*, 56, 69, 56, 61, 69. See also ibid., 55–6.

111. *CSPV 1640–1642*, 296.

112. Clarendon, *History*, I, 556; *CSPV 1640–1642*, 295. See also *CSPD 1641–1643*, 282; Green, *Letters*, 50.

113. Clarendon, *Life*, I, 53.

114. Clarendon, *History*, I, 567. See also ibid., 565–6; Clarendon, *Life*, I, 51.

115. Motteville, *Mémoires*, I, 207; Clarendon, *Life*, I, 51. See also *LJ*, IV, 14 February 1642; *CSPV 1640–1642*, 296; Clarendon, *History*, I, 567; *CSPD 1641–1643*, 282.

116. *A True Discourse*, 28–9; *CSPV 1640–1642*, 297.

117. *LJ*, IV, 14 February 1642; ibid., 21 February 1642. See also Clarendon, *Life*, I, 52.

118. *CSPD 1641–1643*, 283, 288, 294, 286. See also ibid., 286, 293; *CSPV 1642–1643*, 13; Birch, *Court and Times of Charles*, II, 349.

119. *CSPV 1640–1642*, 296.

120. *CSPV 1642–1643*, 5; Birch, *Court and Times of Charles*, II, 349. For the

date, see *CSPV 1642–1643*, 4, 5, 13; Laud, *Works*, III, 244; *HMC Cowper MSS*, II, Appendix II, 308; Clarendon, *Life*, I, 52; Coates, *Private Journals*, I, 449, 450, 455, 461 463, 470.

121. Motteville, *Mémoires*, I, 208; Birch, *Court and Times of Charles*, II, 349. See also *CSPD 1641–1643*, 284, 285.

122. *True and Exact Relation*.

CHAPTER ELEVEN: NEWCASTLE, JANUARY 1647

1. *CSPV 1640–1642*, 96; as quoted in Terry, 'Visits', 122. See also ibid., passim. Information on the equipment of the troops comes from Reid, *Scots Armies*.

2. As quoted in Terry, 'Visits', III, 140, n. 310, 140; *CSPV 1643–1647*, 301. See also Ellis, *Original Letters*, 2nd series, vol. III, 328.

3. Bruce (ed.), *Charles I*, 99.

4. Green, *Letters*, 222; *King's Cabinet Opened*, 38. For the money Henrietta raised, see Strickland, *Lives*, V, 290.

5. For wartime Oxford, see Roy and Reinhart, 'Oxford and the civil wars'; Roy, 'The city of Oxford'; Varley, *The Siege of Oxford*; Wood, *Life and Times*, I, 67–103.

6. Green, *Letters*, 97, 144.

7. Green, *Letters*, 222. See also Clarendon, *Life*, I, 185.

8. Clarendon, *History*, IV, 490; Warwick, *Mémoires*, 64; Clarendon, *History*, IV, 490.

9. Green, *Letters*, 225, 227–8. For Henrietta's advice for London, see Hamilton, *Henrietta Maria*, 203; *Life and Death*, 37–8.

10. Green, *Letters*, 235.

11. *CJ*, III, 23 May 1643; *LJ*, VI, 23 May 1643; as quoted in Green, *Letters*, 165–6. See also *HMC Cowper MSS*, II, Appendix II, 334.

12. Ellis, *Original Letters*, 3rd series, vol. IV, 303. See also Marshall, *Henrietta*, 114; *Oxford DNB*.

13. See Dugdale, *Life*, 65.

14. Green, *Letters*, 244–5.

15. Green, *Letters*, 246, 247.

16. *CSPD 1644*, 318; Green, *Letters*, 248–9.

17. Polwhele, *Traditions and Recollections*, I, 17. See also Ellis, *Original Letters*, 3rd series, vol. IV, 303.

18. Green, *Letters*, 271. See also BL Add. MS 12,184, f. 318r; *Life and Death*, 40; Strickland, *Lives*, V, 332–3.

19. Green, *Letters*, 283, 287–8. See also ibid., 279.

20. *King's Cabinet Opened*, 14; as quoted in Warburton, *Memoirs of Prince Rupert*, III, 111, n. 1.

21. As quoted in Kenyon, *Civil Wars*, 150; as printed in Clarendon, *History*, IV, 74.

22. Evelyn, *Diary and Correspondence*, IV, 179–81; Clarendon, *State Papers*, II, 196–7.

23. *HMC Portland MSS*, I, 327. See also *CSPV 1643–1647*, 196.

24. Clarendon, *State Papers*, II, 209; Bruce (ed.), *Charles I*, 19, 21, 28.

25. Evelyn, *Diary and Correspondence*, IV, 175; Petrie, *Letters*, 176.

26. Clarendon, *State Papers*, II, 220; *Calendar of Clarendon State Papers*, I, 310.

27. Bruce (ed.), *Charles I*, 31, 33, 34, 36.

28. Montereul, *Correspondence*, I, 180–1.

29. Bruce (ed.), *Charles I*, 37–8; Fea, *Memoirs*, 201.

30. Montereul, *Correspondence*, I, 195; as quoted in *Oxford DNB* article on Michael Hudson.

31. Fea, *Memoirs*, 70, n.1. For cutting Charles's hair and beard, see also Terry, 'Visits', 111.

32. Clarendon, *History*, IV, 192; Fea, *Memoirs*, 70.

33. Fea, *Memoirs*, 205; *CSPV 1643–1647*, 254; Fea, *Memoirs*, 70–1.

34. Fea, *Memoirs*, 72. See also Montereul, *Correspondence*, 192–3.

35. Fea, *Memoirs*, 72, n. 1; Clarendon, *History*, IV, 191; *Eikon Basilike*, section 22.

36. Fea, *Memoirs*, 72, n. 1, 206.

37. As quoted in Kaplan, 'Charles I's flight', 217. See also Clarendon, *History*, IV, 190, 193; Fea, *Memoirs*, 206.

38. Clarendon, *History*, IV, 193–4; Montereul, *Correspondence*, I, 194; Fea, *Memoirs*, 207.

39. Montereul, *Correspondence*, I, 193–4; Fea, *Memoirs*, 75. See also ibid., 208, 209.

40. Terry, 'Visits', 109–11.

41. Clarendon, *History*, IV, 110; Petrie, *Letters*, 175. See also ibid., 180; Clarendon, *History*, IV, 78, 97.

42. As quoted in Terry, 'Visits', 113.

43. Fea, *Memoirs*, 209–10. See also Montereul, *Correspondence*, I, 194; Bruce, *Charles I*, 40.

44. As quoted in Terry, 'Visits', 122, 116, 118; as quoted in Howell, *Newcastle-upon-Tyne*, 204. See also ibid., 224, n. 8; Terry, 'Visits', 117.

45. Bruce (ed.), *Charles I*, 46, 47, 50; 46.

46. As quoted in Ashley, *Charles I and Oliver Cromwell*, 177.

47. Bruce (ed.), *Charles I*, 41, 44, 46, 45.

48. Bruce (ed.), *Charles I*, 44, 50, 44, 42.

49. Bruce (ed.), *Charles I*, 51, 42; *Calendar of Clarendon State Papers*, I, 326.

50. Petrie, *Letters*, 199; Bruce (ed.), *Charles I*, 54.

51. Petrie, *Letters*, 200; Clarendon, *State Papers*, II, 247. For Charles's willingness to suffer martyrdom, see also *Calendar of Clarendon State Papers*, I, 268, 322.

52. *Calendar of Clarendon State Papers*, I, 333; Green, *Letters*, 326. See also Clarendon, *State Papers*, II, 246–8, 261–4, 268–9, 273–5, 301–2; Green, *Letters*, 325–7; Bruce (ed.), *Charles I*, 57–62; Petrie, *Letters*, 203–7.

53. Petrie, *Letters*, 200, 204. See also ibid., 205–6.

54. Clarendon, *State Papers*, II, 246.

55. Bruce (ed.), *Charles I*, 51, Clarendon, *State Papers*, II, 246; Bruce (ed.), *Charles I*, 57. See also ibid., 55, 62.

56. Clarendon, *State Papers*, II, 263.

57. Bruce (ed.), *Charles I*, 69. See also Clarendon, *State Papers*, II, 270.

58. Petrie, *Letters*, 206; Bruce (ed.), *Charles I*, 62, 76–7, 69.

59. Bruce (ed.), *Charles I*, 70, 80; *Eikon Basilike*, section 2.

60. Bruce (ed.), *Charles I*, 80–1; *Eikon Basilike*, section 2.

61. See Gardiner, *Hamilton Papers*, 113–14; Terry, 'Visits', 126.

62. Green, *Letters*, 335–6. See also Bruce (ed.), *Charles I*, 76.

63. Bruce (ed.), *Charles I*, 81.

64. Green, *Letters*, 334, 333.

65. Clarendon, *State Papers*, II, 314.

66. See *CJ*, IV, 19 May 1646, for the first suggestion.

67. Bruce (ed.), *Charles I*, 64; Petrie, *Letters*, 210. See also Bruce (ed.), *Charles I*, 66; *CSPV 1643–1647*, 292; Clarendon, *History*, IV, 211–12.

68. As quoted in Terry, 'Visits', 132. See also ibid., 133.

69. Green, *Letters*, 331. See also *Calendar of Clarendon State Papers*, I, 346.

70. Bruce (ed.), *Charles I*, 83; Green, *Letters*, 331. See also Bruce (ed.), *Charles I*, 84.

71. Clarendon, *State Papers*, II, 312–13.

72. Montereul, *Correspondence*, I, 374, 365. See also Gardiner, *History of the Great Civil War*, III, 181–2.

73. Montereul, *Correspondence*, I, 401, 375, 366. See also ibid., 387, 393.

74. As quoted in Terry, 'Visits', 134; *LJ*, VIII, 11 January 1647; Ellis, *Original Letters*, 2nd series, vol. III, 327. See also ibid., 328.

75. As quoted in Terry, 'Visits', 137; Ellis, *Original Letters*, 2nd series, vol. III, 328.

76. Gardiner, *Hamilton Papers*, 140; Ellis, *Original Letters*, 2nd series, vol. III, 328. See also ibid., 327; Terry, 'Visits', 139.

77. *LJ*, VIII, 11 January 1647. See also *LJ*, VIII, 11 January 1647; *CSPV 1643–1647*, 299, 302; Montereul, *Correspondence*, I, 402.

78. Montereul, *Correspondence*, I, 390.

79. Bruce (ed.), *Charles I*, 99–100. See also Montereul, *Correspondence*, I, 387–8.

80. *CSPV 1643–1647*, 296; as quoted in Terry, 'Visits', 140; *CJ*, V, 15 December 1646.

81. As quoted in Terry, 'Visits', 144.

82. *CSPV 1643–1647*, 299, 301, 299, 301. See also Clarendon, *State Papers*, II, 332.

83. Fea, *Memoirs*, 77; Montereul, *Correspondence*, I, 440–1.

84. Fea, *Memoirs*, 77, 78.

85. Montereul, *Correspondence*, I, 425–6, 401.

86. Petrie, *Letters*, 210; Montereul, *Correspondence*, I, 442, 426, 423.

87. Montereul, *Correspondence*, I, 443; *Calendar of Clarendon State Papers*, I, 358.

88. *CSPD 1645–1647*, 517. See also Montereul, *Correspondence*, I, 444; *CJ*, V, 15 December 1646.

89. Montereul, *Correspondence*, I, 445; *CSPV 1643–1647*, 304.

90. *CSPV 1643–1647*, 305; Montereul, *Correspondence*, I, 411–12.

CHAPTER TWELVE: COLOMBES, AUGUST 1669

1. Ferrero, *Lettres*, 104. This portrait may now be in the Royal Collection: RCIN 400962.

2. As quoted in *Oxford DNB*: Charles II.

3. Birch, *Court and Times of Charles*, II, 453. For Henrietta's possessions

at Colombes, see PRO SP 78/128, ff. 190r–202v.

4. Pepys, *Diary*, VI, 142.
5. Birch, *Court and Times of Charles*, II, 465. See also PRO SP 78/128, ff. 191r, 194r.
6. Birch, *Court and Times of Charles*, II, 470, 467. The cabinet's contents are detailed in PRO SP 78/128, ff. 200r–202r.
7. Motteville, *Memoir*, 27–8.
8. Motteville, *Memoir*, 29, 30; PRO SP 78/128, f. 201v.
9. Fea, *Memoirs*, 131; *Nicholas Papers*, I, 113, 109. See also *CSPV 1647–1652*, 87.
10. As quoted in *OED* under 'vicegerent'; Fea, *Memoirs*, 131. See also Gardiner, *History of the Great Civil War*, IV; Fraser, *Cromwell*, 286–7.
11. Petitot (ed.), *Mémoires*, 2nd series, XXXVIII, 205; *Responce de la reine d'Angleterre*, 4; Birch, *Court and Times of Charles*, II, 380.
12. Motteville, *Memoir*, 19.
13. Petitot (ed.), *Mémoires*, 2nd series, XXXVIII, 205–7. For news of Henry, see ibid., LVIII, 162.
14. Birch, *Court and Times of Charles*, II, 382.
15. *Les sanglots pitoyables de l'affliqée reyne*, 6; Bossuet, *Oraison*, 115.
16. Seneca, *Hippolytus*, ii. 3, 607; Birch, *Court and Times of Charles*, II, 382.
17. Petitot (ed.), *Mémoires*, 2nd series, XXXVIII, 207, 205–6.
18. Birch, *Court and Times of Charles*, II, 382.
19. Birch, *Court and Times of Charles*, II, 382. See also Cousin, *Madame de Longueville*, 433; Ellis, *Original Letters*, 2nd series vol. III: 344; Hurtaut and Magny, *Dictionnaire historique de la ville de Paris*, II, 45–6, 51.
20. Gardiner, *Constitutional Documents*, ch. 87; Birch, *Court and Times of Charles*, II, 383.
21. Bruce (ed.), *Charles I*, 56. See also ibid., 38–9; Green, *Letters*, 358–9; *Nicholas Papers*, I, 116–18.
22. Ferrero, *Lettres*, 99, 100. See also ibid., 106, 112, 115; Montpensier, *Mémoires*, part 1, ch. 6; Motteville, *Memoir*, 29.
23. Ellis, *Original Letters*, 2nd series, vol. III, 330; Ferrero, *Lettres*, 89–90; *CSPV 1647–1652*, 159.
24. Green, *Letters*, 372–3; Montpensier, *Mémoires*, part 1, ch. 11; Thurloe, *State Papers*, June 1653: I, 311–24. See also *CSPV 1647–1652*, 202; Green, *Letters*, 373.

25. *CSPV 1647–1652*, 145; Green, *Letters*, 371. See also Ferrero, *Lettres*, 70–1.

26. *Calendar of Clarendon State Papers*, IV, 169; Strickland, *Lives*, 471. See also Green, *Letters*, 371–2; Chaillot engraved after Lantara; Bordes, 'Personnages', 78–9; PRO SP 78/122, f. 181r.

27. Clarendon, *Life*, II, 120–1; Evelyn, *Diary*, 308: 1 October 1651.

28. *Oxford DNB*: Edward Hyde Earl of Clarendon, citing Clarendon, *State Papers*, II, 381. See also *CSPV 1653–1654*, 190, 235.

29. Thurloe, *State Papers*, I, 676–93.

30. *Calendar of Clarendon State Papers*, II, 383; Ferrero, *Lettres*, 110.

31. *Calendar of Clarendon State Papers*, II, 429. See also *Calendar of Clarendon State Papers*, II, 414; *Nicholas Papers*, II, 113.

32. *Calendar of Clarendon State Papers*, II, 425, 419, 425; Thurloe, *State Papers*, I, 661–75.

33. *Nicholas Papers*, II, 110–11, 113.

34. *Calendar of Clarendon State Papers*, II, 424, 428, 425.

35. *Calendar of Clarendon State Papers*, II, 429, 434, 436.

36. As quoted in Green, *Lives of the Princesses*, VI, 417; Birch, *Court and Times of Charles*, II, 411.

37. Thurloe, *State Papers*, I, 676–93. See also *Calendar of Clarendon State Papers*, III, 45.

38. *Nicholas Papers*, I, 116; *Calendar of Clarendon State Papers*, II, 183.

39. *Calendar of Clarendon State Papers*, IV, 53. See also ibid., 54; II, 348.

40. Thurloe, *State Papers*, I, 676–93; Green, *Letters*, 385, 388.

41. Green, *Letters*, 388–9; *CSPV 1659–1661*, 23.

42. *Calendar of Clarendon State Papers*, IV, 459, 474.

43. *CJ*, VIII, 1 May 1660; Pepys, *Diary*, I, 158.

44. Bossuet, *Oraison*, 123; Birch, *Court and Times of Charles*, II, 415.

45. Green, *Letters*, 399, 398; Ferrero, *Lettres*, 121–2.

46. Ferrero, *Lettres*, 121; *CSPV 1659–1661*, 198; Ferrero, *Lettres*, 123.

47. Ferrero, *Lettres*, 124; *CSPV 1659–1661*, 217. See also *CSPV 1659–1661*, 269.

48. *CSPV 1659–1661*, 215, 214; Pepys, *Diary*, I, 299.

49. Green, *Letters*, 407; Clarendon, *Life*, II, 36.

50. *CSPV 1659–1661*, 235.

51. Montpensier, *Mémoires*, part 2, ch. 4; as quoted in *Oxford DNB*: Anne Hyde; Clarendon, *Life*, II, 40.

52. Green, *Letters*, 403, 409. See also *Calendar of Clarendon State Papers*, V, 51; Birch, *Court and Times of Charles*, II, 423.

53. Birch, *Court and Times of Charles*, II, 437. See also ibid., 400, 431, 459; Pepys, *Diary*, V, 63.

54. Pepys, *Diary*, V, 63. See also ibid., VI, 17. See also *Life and Death*, 61–7; *Calendar of Clarendon State Papers*, V, 291.

55. Evelyn, *Diary*, 446: 21 October 1662; Pepys, *Diary*, III, 191. See also ibid., III, 299, 303; IV, 48.

56. Pepys, *Diary*, IV, 216. See also ibid., 193–4, 229–30.

57. Ferrero, *Lettres*, 126. See also ibid., 127, 128.

58. Norrington, *My Dearest Minette*, 151, 174, 57.

59. Ferrero, *Lettres*, 126; *CSPV 1661–1664*, 217. See also ibid., 212, 217; Ferrero, *Lettres*, 128.

60. *Calendar of Clarendon State Papers*, V, 278–9; Pepys, *Diary*, III, 263. See also Ferrero, *Lettres*, 127; Reresby, *Memoirs*, 29.

61. Clarendon, *Life*, II, 263. See also *HMC Hastings MSS*, II, 146; Birch, *Court and Times of Charles*, II, 453; *CSPV 1664–1666*, 125; Pepys, *Diary*, VI, 142.

62. As quoted in *Oxford DNB*: Jermyn; Motteville, *Memoir*, 29.

63. Birch, *Court and Times of Charles*, II, 467; Motteville, *Memoir*, 28, 29.

64. *CSPV 1669–1670*, 39; PRO SP 78/126, f. 233r. See also Green, *Letters*, 415; *CSPV 1669–1670*, 42.

65. Birch, *Court and Times of Charles*, II, 470; Motteville, *Memoir*, 31.

66. Birch, *Court and Times of Charles*, II, 465–6; Green, *Letters*, 416; Birch, *Court and Times of Charles*, II, 466.

67. Green, *Letters*, 416.

68. PRO SP 78/127, f. 95r; Birch, *Court and Times of Charles*, II, 466; PRO SP 78/127, f. 95r; Birch, *Court and Times of Charles*, II, 466.

69. Green, *Letters*, 417. See also *OED*: entries for palpitation, oppression.

70. Birch, *Court and Times of Charles*, II, 468. See also Green, *Letters*, 417.

71. Jusserand, Recueil, XXIV, 70. See also *HMC Buccleuch MSS*, I, 439; *Life and Death*, 66; *CSPD 1668–1669*, 469; Fea, *Memoirs*, 49, 147–51.

72. Bossuet, *Oraison*, 73–4. See also Birch, *Court and Times of Charles*, II, 470–1; Green, *Letters*, 418; *Life and Death*, 91; Motteville, *Memoir*, 9.

BIBLIOGRAPHY

MANUSCRIPTS

BODLEIAN LIBRARY, OXFORD

Clarendon MS 97. State papers collected by Edward Hyde, Earl of Clarendon.

BRITISH LIBRARY, LONDON

BL Additional MSS 12,184–12,186. Despatches of Sir Richard Browne, English Resident at Paris, from August 1641 to November 1651.

BL Additional MS 12,528. Sir Sackville Crowe's Book of Accompts, containing the receipts and disbursements on behalf of the Duke of Buckingham from January 1622 to June 1628.

BL Additional MSS 15,389–15,391. Transcripts from the Papal Registers: correspondence of Gregorio Panzani and George Con.

BL Additional MS 22,474. 'Speaches, Passages, and other Obseruations at the Parliament begun and holden at Westminster vjo Febr. 1625[6]'.

BL Additional MS 24,023. Original letters of royal and other personages, principally English; 1596–1844.

BL Additional MS 27,962E-27,962I. Transcripts from the public archives at Florence of the correspondence of the Florentine ambassadors to England.

BL Additional MS 35,331. Autograph Diary of Walter Yonge, of Colyton, Co. Devon, MP for Honiton in the Long Parliament from 1627 to April 1642.

BL Additional MS 39,288. Transcripts of state letters and papers, 1521–1631.

BL Harleian MS 3,791.

BL Harleian MS 3,888. 'Evangelicall Fruict of the Seraphicall Franciscan Order . . . Elucubravit P N Archibold, Capuccinus'.

BL Harleian MS 6,424. Parliamentary diary of John Warner, Bishop of Rochester.

BL Harleian MS 6,988. Royal letters.

BL Harleian MS 7,623. 'A Copie of the Booke (assigned by his Majestie) of Diet, Wages, &c. for Prince Charles his Highness, & the rest of his Majesties Royal Children. Anno xiiii. Rs. Caroli'.

BL King's MSS 135–136. 'Recueil de Lettres, de Mémoires, d'Actes, d'instructions et de Contracts, faits pour parvenir all Traité de Mariage d'entre Madame Honriette Marie soeur du Roy, et Charles Premier Roy de la Grande Bretagne', 1624–1625.

BL King's MSS 137–138. Negociation de Monsieur de Blainville, Ambassadeur en Angleterre en l'année 1626.

BL MS Royal 16 E XLI. 'Recueil des reparties, rencontres et autres dits memorables du roy Henry le Grand': a collection of sayings, &c. of Henry IV of France, addressed to his daughter [Henrietta Maria], Queen of Great Britain, by Gaultier Quinne, i.e. Walter Quin, formerly tutor to Charles I as prince'.

BL MS Royal 18 A XXVIII. Political tract, in form of a letter addressed to Charles I, by Henry Cock on the fortunate dismissal of Queen Henrietta Maria's French attendants and of 'those who are communely called the fathers of the Oratory, who lately were chapleins to the Queenes Majesty' and on the machinations of 'Fisher the Jesuite' [John Fisher, al. Percy, d. 1641] and [William Smith] 'Bishop of Chalcedon, superior of the English Romane clergy', who were concealed 'in the very palace', and of 'Father Phillips, the Queenes Majestyes Confessor' [Robert Philips, d. 1650?] and others.

BL Sloane MS 1,679. Sir Thomas Mayerne's Receipt Book.

PUBLIC RECORD OFFICE, LONDON

PRO 31/9/17B. Transcripts of Gregorio Panzani's Letters from England, 1634–1637.

PRO 31/9/19–20. Transcripts of Carlo Rossetti's Letters from England, 1639–1641.

PRO E 403. Exchequer of Receipt: Issue Rolls and Registers.

PRO LR 5/63. Documents subsidiary to the accounts of the Treasurer and Receiver General, 1629–1639.

PRO SP 16. State Papers Domestic, Charles I.

PRO SP 78/122. SP Foreign, France, 1666.

PRO SP 78/126. SP Foreign, France, 1669 January–June.

PRO SP 78/127. SP Foreign, France, 1669 July–October.

PRO SP 78/128. SP Foreign, France, 1669 November–December.

PUBLICATIONS

Albion, Gordon, *Charles I and the Court of Rome: A Study in 17th Century Diplomacy* (London, 1935)

Ashley, Maurice, *Charles I and Oliver Cromwell: A Study in Contrasts and Comparisons* (London, 1987)

Ashmole, Elias, *The Institution, Laws and Ceremonies of the Most Noble Order of the Garter* (London, 1672)

Aubrey, John, *Aubrey's Brief Lives*, ed. Oliver Lawson Dick (London, 1968)

The Babees' Book: Medieval Manners for the Young, trans. Edith Rickert and L. J. Naylor (Cambridge, Ontario, 2000)

Baillon, Charles, Comte de, *Henriette-Marie de France, Reine d' Angleterre: Etude Historique par le Comte de Baillon, Suivie de ses Lettres Inédites* (Paris, 1877)

Bassompierre, François de, *Journal de ma Vie: Mémoires du Maréchal de Bassompierre*, ed. Marie Joseph Audoin de La Cropte, Marquis de Chantérac, 3 vols, Societé de l'Histoire de France Publications, 153, 162, 173 (Paris, 1870–5)

——, *Negociation du Mareschal de Bassompierre, Envoyé Ambassadeur Extraordinaire, en Angleterre ... l'an 1626* (Cologne, 1668)

Batiffol, Louis, *La Vie Intime d'une Reine de France au XVIIe Siècle: Marie de Médicis*, 2 vols (Paris, n.d.)

Batterel, Louis, *Mémoires Domestiques pour Servir à l'Histoire de l'Oratoire*, 5 vols (Paris, 1902–11)

Beddard, Robert A., 'Six Unpublished Letters of Queen Henrietta Maria', *British Library Journal*, 25 (1999), 129–43.

Bellesheim, A., *History of the Catholic Church in Scotland*, trans. David Hunter-Blair, 4 vols (Edinburgh, 1887–90)

Birch, Thomas, *The Court and Times of Charles the First*, 2 vols (London, 1848)

———— *The Court and Times of James the First*, 2 vols (London, 1849)

———— *An Historical View of the Negotiations between the Courts of England, France, and Brussels: from the year 1592 to 1617* (London, 1749)

Bordes, Hélène, 'Les Perronnages de la Famille Royale Britannique d'après l'Année Sainte' in C. Smith and E. Dubois (eds), *France et Grande-Bretagne de la Chute de Charles 1er à celle de Jacques II (1649–1688)*, (Norwich, 1990), 77–89

Bossuet, Jacques-Bénigne, *Oraisons funèbres*, ed. Alfred Rébelliau (Paris, Hachette, 1906)

Bowie, John, *Charles the First* (London, 1975)

Brienne, Henri Auguste de Loménie de, *Mémoires . . . contenant les évenements les plus remarquables du Règne de Louis XIII et de celui de Louis XIV jusqu'à la mort du Cardinal Mazarin*, ed. J. F. Bernard 1824)

Britland, Karen, *Drama at the Courts of Queen Henrietta Maria* (Cambridge, 2006)

————, 'Fairy-tale Marriage: Charles and Henrietta Maria's Romance' in Alexander Samson (ed.), *The Spanish Match: Prince Charles's Journey to Madrid, 1623* (Aldershot, 2006), 123–38

Bruce, John (ed)., *Charles I in 1646: Letters of King Charles the First to Queen Henrietta Maria*, Camden Society, 1st series, 63 (1856)

Cabala: sive Scrinia Sacra: Mysteries of State & Government: in Letters of Illustrious Persons, and Great Agents; in the Reigns of Henry the Eighth, Queen Elizabeth, K: James, and the late King Charls (London, 1654)

Calendar of Clarendon State Papers Preserved in the Bodleian Library, ed. H. O. Coxe *et al.*, 5 vols (Oxford, 1869–1970)

Camden, William, *Camden's Britannia: Newly Translated into English, with Large Additions and Improvements*, ed. Edmund Gibson (London, 1695)

Carew, Thomas, *The Works of Thomas Carew* (Edinburgh, 1824)

Carlton, Charles, *Charles I: The Personal Monarch* (London, 1995)

The Catholic Encyclopedia: An International Work of Reference, ed. Charles G. Herbermann *et al.*, 16 vols (New York, 1907)

Cavendish, Margaret, Duchess of Newcastle, *The Blazing World and Other Writings* (Harmondsworth, 1994)

———, *The Life of William Cavendish, Duke of Newcastle*, ed. C. H. Firth (London, 1886)

———, *Poems, and Fancies* (London, 1653)

Charles I, *The Papers which Passed at New-castle bewixt His Sacred Majestie and Mr Al: Henderson: concerning the Change of Church-Government, Anno Dom. 1646* (London, 1649)

———, *Reliquiæ Sacræ Carolinæ: Or the Works of that Great Monarch and Glorious Martyr King Charles the I* (The Hague [i.e. London], 1651)

CJ: Journal of the House of Commons. URL: http://www.british-history.ac.uk/subject.aspx?subject=6&gid=43

Clarendon, Edward Hyde, Earl of, *History of the Rebellion and Civil Wars in England*, ed. W. D. Macray, 6 vols (Oxford, 1888)

———, *The Life of Edward, Earl of Clarendon, Written by Himself*, 2 vols (Oxford, 1827)

———, *State Papers collected by Edward, Earl of Clarendon: Commencing from the year MDCXXI*, 3 vols (Oxford, 1767–86)

Coates, Willson H., Anne Steele Young, and Vernon F. Snow (eds), *The Private Journals of the Long Parliament*, 3 vols (New Haven, 1982)

Colvin, H. M., *The History of the King's Works*, 6 vols (London, 1963–82)

Comenius, Johann Amos, *Orbis Sensualium Pictus: English and Latin* (London, 1659)

Cope, Esther S., and Willson H. Coates (eds), *Proceedings of the Short Parliament of 1640*, Camden Society, 4th series, 19 (London, 1977)

A Coppy of 1. The Letter sent by the Queenes Majestie concerning the Collection of the Recusants Mony for the Scottish Warre, Apr. 17 1639 ... (London, 1641)

Cousin, M. Victor, *Madame de Longueville: Etudes sur les Femmes Illustres et la Société du XVIIe siècle: La Jeunesse de Madame de Longueville* (Paris, 1859)

Cruickshanks, Eveline (ed.), *The Stuart Courts* (Stroud, 2000)

CSPD: Calendar of State Papers, Domestic Series, of the Reign of James I, ed. Mary Anne Everett Green, 5 vols (London, 1857–1872); *Calendar of State Papers, Domestic Series, of the Reign of Charles I*, ed. John Bruce, 23 vols (London, 1858–97)

Calendar of State Papers, Domestic Series, of the Reign of Charles II, ed. Mary Anne Everett Green *et al.*, 28 vols (London, 1860–1938). URL: http://www.british-history.ac.uk/period.aspx?period=7&gid=103

CSPV: Calendar of State Papers and Manuscripts, relating to English Affairs, existing in the Archives and Collections of Venice, ed. Rawdon Brown, 38 vols (London, 1864–1947). URL: http://www.british-history.ac.uk/ catalogue.aspx?type=3&gid=140

Cust, Richard, *Charles I* (London, 2007)

Dagens, J., *Bérulle et les Origines de la Restauration Catholique* (Paris, 1952)

———, *Correspondance du Cardinal Pierre de Bérulle*, 3 vols (Paris, 1936–39)

Dauncey, John, *The History of the Thrice Illustrious Princess Henrietta Maria de Bourbon, Queen of England* (London, 1660)

Davenant, Sir William, *Dramatic Works*, ed. J. Maidment and W. H. Logan, 5 vols (London, 1872–4)

A Deep Sigh Breath'd through the Lodgings at White-hall, Deploring the Absence of the Court, and the Miseries of the Pallace (London, 1642)

D'Ewes, Sir Simonds, *The Autobiography and Correspondence of Sir Simonds D'Ewes, Bart: during the Reigns of James I and Charles I*, ed. James Orchard Halliwell, 2 vols (London, 1845)

———, *The Journal of Sir Simonds D'Ewes from the Beginning of the Long Parliament to the Opening of the Trial of the Earl of Strafford*, ed. Wallace Notestein (London, 1923)

———, *The Journal of Sir Simonds D'Ewes: from the First Recess of the Long Parliament to the Withdrawal of King Charles from London*, ed. Willson Havelock Coates (London, 1942)

Dickens, A. G. (ed.), *The Courts of Europe: Politics, Patronage and Royalty, 1400–1800* (London, 1977)

Dugdale, William, *The Life, Diary and Correspondence of Sir William Dugdale* (London, 1827)

———, *Monasticon Anglicanum*, 6 vols (London, 1846)

Dupuy, Micheline, *Henriette Marie, Reine d'Angleterre* (Paris, 1994)

Eccles, A., *Obstetrics and Gynaecology in Tudor and Stuart England* (London, 1982)

Eikon Basilike, or the King's Book, ed. E. Almack (London, 1904). URL: http://anglicanhistory.org/charles/eikon/3.html

Ellis, Henry, *Original Letters, Illustrative of English History; including numerous royal letters: from autographs in the British Museum and one or two other collections*, 3 series, 11 vols (London, 1824–1846)

The Entertainment of . . . Charles into his ancient city of Edinburgh (London, 1633)

Estrades, Godefroi Louis, Comte d', *Lettres, Mémoires et Négociations de Monsieur le Comte d'Estrades*, 9 vols (Londres [i.e. La Haye], 1743)

Evelyn, John, *The Diary of John Evelyn*, ed. E. S. de Beer (London, 1959)

———, *Diary and Correspondence of John Evelyn . . . To which is subjoined The Private Correspondence between King Charles I and Sir Edward Nicholas, and between Sir Edward Hyde, afterwards Earl of Clarendon, and Sir Richard Browne*, ed. William Bray, 4 vols (London, 1859)

Fea, Allan, *Memoirs of the Martyr King (Being a Detailed Record of the Last Two Years of the Reign of His Most Sacred Majesty, King Charles the First, 1646–9)* (London, 1904)

Ferard, Joseph, *The Law of Fixtures, and Other Property: Partaking Both of a Real and Personal Nature*, ed. William Hogan (New York, 1855)

Ferrero, Hermann (ed.), *Lettres de Henriette-Marie de France, Reine d'Angleterre, à sa sœur Christine, Duchesse de Savoie*, Estratto dalla Miscellanea di Storia Italiana, 2nd series, vol. V (Turin, 1881)

Finet, Sir John, Ceremonies of Charles I: the Notebooks of John Finet 1628–1641, ed. Albert J. Loomie (New York, 1987)

———, *Finetti Philoxenis: Som Choice Observations of Sir J. F., . . . touching the Reception and Precedence, the Treatment and Audience, the Puntillios and Contests of Forren Ambassadors in England* (London, 1656)

Forster, John, *Arrest of the Five Members by Charles the First* (1860)

Fraser, Antonia, *King James VI of Scotland and I of England* (London, 1977)

Fuller, Thomas, *The Church-History of Britain: from the Birth of Jesus Christ, untill the year MDCXLVIII* (London, 1655)

Gardiner, Samuel Rawson, *Constitutional Documents of the Puritan Revolution, 1628–1660* (Oxford, 1899). URL: http://www.constitution.org /eng/conpur_.htm

———, (ed.) The Hamilton Papers, being Selections from Original Letters in the Possession of His Grace the Duke of Hamilton and Brandon relating to the Years 1638–1650, Camden Society, new series 27 (London, 1880)

———, *History of England 1603–1642*, 10 vols (London, 1884)

———, *History of the Great Civil War, 1642–1649*, 4 vols (London, 1897–8)

Geyl, Pieter, *Orange and Stuart 1641–1672* (London, 2001)

Gower, Lord Ronald Sutherland, The Tower of London, 2 vols (London, 1902)

Green, Mary Anne Everett, Letters of Queen Henrietta Maria: Including her Private Correspondence with Charles the First (London, 1857)

———, Lives of the Princesses of England, 6 vols (London, 1849–55)

Gregg, Pauline, King Charles I (London, 1981)

Hamilton, Elizabeth, Henrietta Maria (London, 1976)

Hardwicke, Philip Yorke, 2nd Earl of, Miscellaneous state papers from 1501 to 1726, 2 vols (London, 1778)

Harris, John, Stephen Orgel and Roy Strong, The King's Arcadia: Inigo Jones and the Stuart Court: a Quatercentenary Exhibition held at the Banqueting House, Whitehall, from July 12th to September 2nd, 1973 ([London], 1973)

Harrison, G. B. (ed.), A Jacobean Journal (London, 1941)

Herbert of Cherbury, Edward Lord, The Autobiography of Edward, Lord Herbert of Cherbury, ed. Sidney Lee (London, [1906])

Herrick, Robert, Works, ed. Alfred Pollard, 2 vols (London, 1891)

Heylin, Peter, Cyprianus Anglicus: or, the History of the Life and Death, of the Most Reverend and Renowned Prelate William, by Divine Providence, Lord Archbishop of Canterbury (London, 1671)

———, A Short View of the Life and Reign of King Charles (The second monarch of Great Britain) from his Birth to his Burial (London, 1658)

Hibbard, Caroline, Charles I and the Popish Plot (Chapel Hill, Carolina, 1983)

———, 'Henrietta Maria in the 1630s: perspectives on the role of consort queens in ancient regime courts', in Ian Atherton and Julie Sanders (eds), The 1630s: Interdisciplinary Essays on Culture and Politics in the Caroline Era (Manchester, 2006), 92–110

———, 'Translating royalty: Henrietta Maria and the transition from princess to queen', Court Historian, 5 (2000), 15–28

HMC Buccleuch MSS: Royal Commission on Historical Manuscripts, Report on the manuscripts of the Duke of Buccleuch and Queensberry, K.G., K.T., preserved at Montagu House, Whitehall, 3 vols in 4 (London, 1899–1926)

HMC Cowper MSS: Royal Commission on Historical Manuscripts, The manuscripts of the Earl Cowper, K.G. preserved at Melbourne hall, Derbyshire, 3 vols (London, 1888–9)

HMC Denbigh MSS: Royal Commission on Historical Manuscripts, Report on the Manuscripts of the Earl of Denbigh preserved at Newnham Paddox, Warwickshire, Part V (London, 1911)

343

HMC De L'Isle and Dudley MSS: Royal Commission on Historical Manuscripts, *Report on the Manuscripts of Lord de l'Isle and Dudley preserved at Penshurst Place*, 6 vols (London, 1925–66)

HMC Egmont MSS: Royal Commission on Historical Manuscripts, Report on the Manuscripts of the Earl of Egmont, 2 vols in 3 (London, 1905–9)

HMC Hastings MSS: Royal Commission on Historical Manuscripts, *Report on the manuscripts of the late Reginald Rawdon Hastings, Esq., of the Manor House, Ashby de la Zouche*, 4 vols (London, 1928–47)

HMC Mar and Kellie: Royal Commission on Historical Manuscripts, *Report on the Manuscripts of the Earl of Mar and Kellie preserved at Alloa House*, vol. II (London, 1930)

HMC Ninth Report, House of Lords MSS: Royal Commission on Historical Manuscripts, *Calendar of House of Lords Manuscripts* (London, 1884)

HMC Portland MSS: Royal Commission on Historical Manuscripts, *Report on the Manuscripts of His Grace the Duke of Portland*, 10 vols (London, 1891–1931)

HMC Salisbury MSS: Royal Commission on Historical Manuscripts, *Calendar of the manuscripts of the Most Hon. the Marquis of Salisbury: preserved at Hatfield House, Hertfordshire*, vol. XX (London, 1971)

HMC 16 Skrine MSS: Royal Commission on Historical Manuscripts, *The Manuscripts of Henry Duncan Skrine, Esq: Salvetti Correspondence* (London, 1887)

Houssaye, M., 'L'Ambassade de M. de Blainville à la Cour de Charles 1er, Roi d'Angleterre', *Revue des Questions Historiques*, 23 (1878), 176–204

———, *Le Cardinal de Bérulle et le Cardinal de Richelieu, 1625–1629* (Paris, 1875)

Howell, James, *Epistolae Ho-Elianae: The Familiar Letters of James Howell*, ed. Joseph Jacobs, 2 vols (London, 1892)

Howell, Roger, *Newcastle-upon-Tyne and the Puritan Revolution: A Study of the Civil War in North England* (Oxford, 1967)

Hurtaut, Pierre Thomas Nicolas and Magny, *Dictionnaire Historique de la Ville de Paris et de ses Environs*, 4 vols (Paris, 1779)

Hutchinson, Lucy, *Memoirs of the Life of Colonel Hutchinson, Governor of Nottingham Castle and Town* (London, 1899)

Hutton, Ronald, *Charles II: King of England, Scotland and Ireland* (Oxford, 1991)

Johnson, Robert C. *et al.* (eds), *Proceedings in Parliament, 1628*, 6 vols (New Haven, 1977–83)

Jonson, Ben, *Chloridia. Rites to Chloris and Her Nymphs, Personated in a Masque at Court. By the Queenes Majesty and her Ladies* (London, 1631)

———, *Love's Triumph through Callipolis. Performed in a Masque at Court 1630. By his Majestie with the Lords, and Gentlemen assisting* (London, 1630 [i.e. 1631])

———, *The Works of Ben Jonson*, ed. W. Gifford, 9 vols (London, 1816)

Jusserand, J. J., *Recueil des Instructions Données aux Ambassadeurs et Ministres de France depuis les Traités de Westphalie jusqu'à la Revolution Française: Angleterre*, vols 24, 25 (Paris, 1929–65)

Kaplan, Lawrence, 'Charles I's Flight to the Scots', *Albion*, 11 (1979), 207–223

Kenyon, John, *The Civil Wars of England* (London, 1988)

The King and Queenes Entertainement at Richmond. After their departure from Oxford: in a Masque, Presented by the Most Illustrious Prince Charles. Sept. 12 1636 (Oxford, 1636)

King Charls His Speech, Made upon the Scaffold at Whitehall-Gate, Immediately before his Execution, On Tuesday the 30 of Jan. 1648 (London, 1649). URL: http://anglicanhistory.org/charles/charles1.html

The King's Cabinet Opened: or, Certain packets of secret letters & papers, written with the King's own hand, and taken in his cabinet at Nasby-field, June 14 1645, by victorious Sr. Thomas Fairfax ... published by speciall order of the Parliament (London, 1645)

La Fayette, Madame de, *Fatal gallantry: or, The Secret History of Henrietta Princess of England*, trans. Ann Floyd (London, 1722)

La Serre, M. de Jean-Puget, *Histoire de l'Entrée de la Reyne Mere du Roy très Chrestien, dans la Grande-Bretaigne* (London, 1639)

Lacey, Andrew, *The Cult of King Charles the Martyr* (Woodbridge, 2003)

Laud, William, *The Works of the Most Reverend Father in God, William Laud, D.D. sometime Lord Archbishop of Canterbury*, ed. William Scott and James Bliss, 7 vols (Oxford, 1847–60)

The Life and Death of Henrietta Maria de Bourbon, Queen to that Blessed King & Martyr, Charles I (London, 1685)

LJ: Journal of the House of Lords. URL: http://www.british-history.ac.uk/subjectaspx?subject=6&gid=44

Lockyer, Roger, *Buckingham: The Life and Political Career of George Villiers, First Duke of Buckingham, 1592–1628* (London, 1981)

———, (ed.), *The Trial of Charles I: A Contemporary Account Taken from the Memoirs of Sir Thomas Herbert and John Rushworth* (1959)

Ludlow, Edmund, *Memoirs of Lieutenant General Ludlow*, 3 vols (Veyey, Switzerland, 1699)

McClure, Norman Egbert (ed.), *The Letters of John Chamberlain*, 2 vols (Philadelphia, 1939)

MacGregor, Arthur (ed.), *The Late King's Goods: Collections, Possessions and Patronage of Charles I in the Light of the Commonwealth Sale Inventories* (London, 1989)

McMillan, W., 'Robert Philip, Father Confessor to Henrietta Maria', *Records of the Scottish Church History Society* 9:2 (1946), 83–96; 9:3 (1947), 142–54

Madan, Francis Falconer, *A New Bibliography of the Eikon Basilike of King Charles the First* (London, 1950)

Magalotti, Lorenzo, *Lorenzo Magalotti at the Court of Charles II: His Relazione d'Inghilterra of 1668*, ed. and trans. William Edgar Knowles Middleton (Waterloo, 1980)

———, *Travels of Cosmo the Third, Grand Duke of Tuscany, through England, during the Reign of King Charles the Second (1669)* (London, 1821)

Marshall, Rosalind K., *Henrietta Maria: The Intrepid Queen* (London, 1990)

Mayor, J. E. B., *Nicholas Ferrar: Two Lives, by his Brother John and by Doctor Jebb* (Cambridge, 1855)

Le Mercure François (Paris, 1609–)

Michaud, Joseph François and Jean Joseph François Poujoulat (eds), *Nouvelle Collection des Mémoires pour Servir à l'Histoire de France depuis le XIIIe siècle jusqu'à la fin du XVIIIe*, 34 vols (Paris, 1850)

Millar, Oliver, *The Age of Charles I: Painting in England 1620–1649* (London, 1972)

Montagu, Walter, *The Shepherds' Paradise*, ed. Sarah Poynting (Oxford, 1997)

Montereul, Jean de, *The Diplomatic Correspondence of Jean de Montereul and the Brothers de Bellièvre, French Ambassadors in England and Scotland 1645–48*, ed. J. G. Fotheringham, 2 vols, Publications of the Scottish History Society, 29–30 (Edinburgh, 1898–1899)

Montpensier, Anne Marie Louise d'Orléans, Duchesse de, *Mémoires de Mademoiselle de Montpensier: petite-fille de Henri IV*, ed. A. Chéruel, 4 vols (Paris, 1858–68). URL: http://penelope.uchicago.edu/mlle

Motteville, Françoise de, *Memoir by Madame de Motteville of the Life of Henrietta Maria*, ed. M. G. Hanotaux, Camden Miscellany 8, Camden Society, new series 31 (1863)

——, *Mémoires de Madame de Motteville sur Anne d'Autriche et Sa Cour*, 4 vols (Paris, 1904–1911)

Nelson, Karen L, 'Negotiating exile: Henrietta Maria, Elizabeth of Bohemia, and the Court of Charles I', in Carole Levin, Jo Eldridge Carney, and Debra Barrett-Graves (eds), *'High and Mighty Queens' of Early Modern England: Realities and Representations* (Basingstoke, 2003), 61–76

The Nicholas Papers: Correspondence of Sir Edward Nicholas, Secretary of State, ed. George F. Warner, 4 vols, Camden Society, new series, 40, 50, 57, third series, 31 (1886–1920)

Nichols, John Gough (ed.), *The Discovery of the Jesuits' College at Clerkenwell in March 1627–8*, Camden Miscellany II (1854)

Nichols, J. (ed.), *The Progresses, Processions, and Magnificent Festivities of King James the First*, 4 vols (London, 1828)

Nicolson, Marjorie Hope (ed.), *Conway Letters: The Correspondence of Anne, Viscountess Conway, Henry More, and their Friends, 1642–1684* (London, 1930)

Norrington, Ruth, *My Dearest Minette: The Letters between Charles II and his Sister Henrietta, Duchesse d'Orléans* (London, 1996)

Orgel, Stephen and Roy Strong, *Inigo Jones: The Theatre of the Stuart Court; Including the Complete Designs for Productions at Court for the Most Part in the Collection of the Duke of Devonshire*, 2 vols (London, 1973)

Ovatio Carolina: The Triumph of King Charles, or the Triumphant Manner and Order, of receiving His Maiesty into his City of London, on Thursday the 25th day of November, Anno Dom. 1641 (London, 1641)

Oxford DNB: Oxford Dictionary of National Biography. URL: http://www.oxforddnb.com *Oxford English Dictionary.* URL: http://dictionary.oed.com

Panzani, Gregorio, *The Memoirs of Gregorio Panzani, giving an Account of his Agency in England, in the years 1634, 1635, 1636. Translated from the Italian original, and now first published*, ed. Joseph Berington (Birmingham, 1793)

Pastor, Ludwig, *The History of the Popes from the Close of the Middle Ages: Drawn from the Secret Archives of the Vatican and other Original Sources*, ed. Frederick Ignatius Antrobus, 40 vols (London, 1891–1953).

Patterson, William Brown, *King James VI and I and the Reunion of Chris-tendom* (Cambridge, 1997)

Pepys, Samuel, *The Diary of Samuel Pepys*, ed. Robert Latham and William Matthews, 11 vols (London, 1995)

Petitot, Claude Bernard *et al.*, (eds) *Collection des Mémoires Relatifs a l'Histoire de France, depuis l'Avenement de Henri IV jusqu'a la Paix de Paris Conclue en 1763; avec des notices sure chaque auteur, et des observations sur chaque ouvrage*, 1st series, 52 vols; 2nd series, 78 vols (Paris, 1819–29). URL: http://visualiseur.bnf.fr/CadresFenetre?O=NUMM-36334

Petrie, Sir Charles (ed.), *The Letters, Speeches and Proclamations of King Charles I* (London, 1935)

Pett, Phineas, *Autobiography*, ed. W. G. Perrin, Publications of the Navy Records Society, 51 (1918)

Plowden, Alison, *Henrietta Maria: Charles I's Indomitable Queen* (Stroud, 2001)

Polwhele, Richard, *Traditions and Recollections, Domestic, Clerical and Lit-erary; in which are included letters of Charles II, Cromwell, Fairfax, Edge-cumbe, Macaulay, Wolcot, Opie . . . and other Distinguished Characters*, 2 vols (London, 1826)

Poynting, Sarah, '"In the name of all the sisters": Henrietta Maria's Notorious Whores' in *Women and Culture at the Courts of the Stuart Queens*, ed. Clare McManus (Basingstoke, 2003)

Prideaux, Mathias, *An Easy and Compendious Introduction for Reading all sorts of Histories, Contrived in a more Facile Way then Heretofore hath been Published* (Oxford, 1682)

Prinsterer, Gulielmus Groen van, *Archives ou Correspondance Inédite de la Maison d'Orange, Nassau*, 1st series, 9 vols; 2nd series, 6 vols (Leiden, 1835–96)

Ralph, Philip Lee, *Sir Humphrey Mildmay: Royalist Gentleman: Glimpses of the English Scene, 1633–1652* (New Brunswick, 1947)

Reid, Stuart, *Scots Armies of the Civil War, 1639–1651* (Leigh-on-Sea, 1982)

Reresby, Sir John, *Memoirs of Sir John Reresby*, ed. Andrew Browning (London, 1991)

Responce de la Reine d'Angleterre au Prince de Galles son fils (Paris, 1649)

Richelieu, Armand Jean du Plessis, duc de, *Lettres, Instructions Diplomatiques et Papiers d'Etat du Cardinal de Richelieu*, ed. Denis Louis Martial Avenel, 8 vols (1853–77)

Rous, John, *Diary of John Rous: Incumbent of Santon Downham, Suffolk, from 1625 to 1642*, ed. Mary Anne Everett Green, Camden Society, 1st series, 66 ([London], 1856)

Roy, Ian, 'The city of Oxford 1640–1660' in R. C. Richardson (ed.) *Town and Countryside in the English Revolution* (Manchester, 1992), 130–68

——— and Dietrich Reinhart, 'Oxford and the civil wars' in Nicholas Tyacke (ed.), *The History of the University of Oxford, IV: Seventeenth-Century Oxford* (Oxford, 1997), 687–731

Les Royales Cérémonies faites en l'édification d'une chapelle de Capucins à Londres en Angleterre (Paris, 1632)

Rueff, Jakob, *The Expert Midwife, or An Excellent and Most Necessary Treatise of the Generation and Birth of Man* (London, 1637)

Rushworth, John, *Historical Collections of Private Passages of State, Weighty Matters in Law, Remarkable Proceedings in Five Parliaments. Beginning the Sixteenth Year of King James, Anno 1618. And Ending the Fifth Year of King Charles, Anno 1629*, 3 vols (London, 1659–1701)

———, *The Tryal of Thomas, Earl of Strafford* (London, 1630)

Russell, Conrad, *The Fall of the British Monarchies, 1637–1642* (Oxford, 1991)

———, 'The first army plot of 1641', *Transactions of the Royal Historical Society*, 38 (1988), 85–106

Les Sanglots Pitoyables de l'Affligée Reyne d'Angleterre du Trepas de son Mary (Paris, 1649)

Shorney, David, *Protestant Nonconformity and Roman Catholicism: A Guide to Sources in the Public Record Office* (London, 1906)

Smith, D. L., 'Catholic, Anglican or Puritan? Edward Sackville, fourth earl of Dorset, and the ambiguities of religion in early Stuart England', *Transactions of the Royal Historical Society*, 6th series, II (1992)

Smuts, R. Malcolm, 'Art and the material culture of majesty in early Stuart England', in R. Malcolm Smuts (ed.), *The Stuart Court and Europe: Essays in Politics and Political Culture* (Cambridge, 1996)

———, 'The Puritan followers of Henrietta Maria in the 1630s', *English Historical Review*, 93 (1978), 26–45

Society of Antiquaries, *A Collection of Ordinances and Regulations for the Government of the Royal Household, made in divers Reigns From King Edward III to King William and Queen Mary* (London, 1790)

Sophia, Electress of Hanover, *Memoirs of Sophia, Electress of Hanover, 1630–1680*, trans. H. Forester [i.e. Mary Leighton] (London, 1888)

Steele, Mary Susan, *Plays and Masques at Court during the Reigns of Elizabeth, James and Charles* (New Haven, 1926)

Strafford, Thomas Wentworth, Earl of, *The Earl of Strafforde's Letters and Dispatches: with an Essay towards his Life, by Sir George Radcliffe*, ed. William Knowler, 2 vols (Dublin, 1740)

Strickland, Agnes, *Lives of the Queens of England from the Norman Conquest*, 8 vols (London, 1851)

Strong, Roy, *The Renaissance Garden in England* (London, 1998)

——, *The Tudor and Stuart Monarchy: Pageantry, Painting, Iconography:* vol. III: *Jacobean and Caroline* (Woodbridge, 1998)

Summerson, John, *Inigo Jones* (New Haven, 2000)

Terry, C. S., 'The visits of Charles I to Newcastle in 1633, 1639, 1641, 1646–7, with some notes on contemporary local history', *Archaeologia Aeliana*, 2nd series, 21 (1899), 83–145

Thurloe, John, *A Collection of the State Papers of John Thurloe, Esq.; Secretary, first, to the Council of State, and afterwards to the two Protectors, Oliver and Richard Cromwell*, ed. Thomas Birch (London, 1742). URL: http://www.british-history.ac.uk/subject.aspx?subject=6&gid=101

Tillières, Comte Tanneguy Leveneur de, *Mémoires Inédits du comte Leveneur de Tillières: Ambassadeur en Angleterre, sur la Cour de Charles 1er, et son Mariage avec Henriette de France*, ed. M. C. Hippeau (Paris, 1863)

Todd, Henry John, *Letter to His Grace the Archbishop of Canterbury, concerning the Authorship of Eikon Basilike* (London, 1825)

Townshend, Aurelian, *The Poems and Masques of Aurelian Townshend: with Music by Henry Lawes and William Webb*, ed. Cedric C. Brown (Reading, 1983)

Toynbee, Margaret Ruth, 'Two letterbooks of Charles I in the Bodleian Library', *Notes and Queries*, 193 (1948), 358–62

——, 'The wedding journey of King Charles I', *Archaeologia Cantiana*, 69 (1956 for 1955), 75–89

A True and Exact Relation of the Manner of his Maiesties Setting up of His Standard at Nottingham, on Munday the 22 of August 1642 (London, 1642)

A True Discourse of all the Royal Passages, Tryumphs and Ceremonies, obserued at the Contract and Mariage of the High and Mighty Charles, King of Great Britaine, and the most excellentest of ladies, the Lady Henrietta Maria of Burbon (London, 1625)

The True Effigies of our most Illustrious Soveraigne Lord, King Charles Queene Mary, with the Rest of the Royall Progenie (London, 1641)

Underdown, David, 'The Parliamentary diary of John Boys, 1647–8', *Bulletin of the Institute of Historical Research*, 39 (1966), 141–64

Varley, Frederick John, *The Siege of Oxford: An Account of Oxford during the Civil War, 1642–1646* (Oxford, 1932)

Veevers, Erica, *Images of Love and Religion: Queen Henrietta Maria and Court Entertainments* (Cambridge, 1989)

Verney, Sir Ralph, *Verney Papers: Notes of Proceedings in the Long Parliament, Temp. Charles I,* ed. John Bruce, Camden Society, 1st series, 31 (London, 1845)

Warburton, Eliot, *Memoirs of Prince Rupert, and the Cavaliers: including their Private Correspondence,* 3 vols (London, 1849)

Warwick, Sir Philip, *Memoires of the Reign of King Charles I. Containing the Most Remarkable Occurrences of that Reign* (London, 1701)

Wood, Anthony à, *The Life and Times of Anthony Wood: antiquary, of Oxford, 1632–1695, Described by Himself,* ed. Andrew Clark, 5 vols (Oxford, 1891–1900)

Wordsworth, Christopher (ed.), *The Manner of the Coronation of King Charles the First of England, at Westminster, 2 Feb., 1626,* Henry Bradshaw Society, 2 (London, 1892)

Wedgwood, C. V., *The King's Peace, 1637–1641* (London, 1966)

———, Thomas Wentworth, First Earl of Strafford, 1593–1641: A Revaluation (London, 1988)

W[eldon], Sir A[rthur], *The Court and Character of King James* (2nd edn, London, 1651)

White, Michelle Anne, *Henrietta Maria and the English Civil Wars* (Aldershot, 2006)

Wilson, Arthur, *The History of Great Britain, Being the Life and Reign of King James the First* (London, 1653)

Wittkower, Rudolf, 'Inigo Jones – Puritanissimo fiero', *Burlington Magazine,* 90 (1948), 50–1

Wotton, Sir Henry, *Reliquiæ Wottonianæ. Or, A Collection of Lives, Letters, Poems; with Characters of Sundry Personages* (London, 1651)

INDEX

148–51; and Scottish crisis, 152,
157–8, 161–2, 163, 174, 177, 182;
Catholic contribution, 161–2, 174,
188–90; and Short Parliament, 167,
169; and London unrest, 173–4,
177–8, 184–5, 225–6; proposes
calling Long Parliament, 179–80,
182; conflict with Parliament, 184,
185–6, 187–92, 203, 209, 210–11, 214,
218; negotiations with
parliamentary leaders, 194, 197; and
Strafford's fall, 184, 187, 192–4, 196,
197, 203, 205, 209; and Army Plot,
194–6, 198, 203–4, 209–10; prepares
to leave England, 198, 203–4, 211;
accused of treason, 218, 219, 226–7,
230, 242; and attempt to arrest
parliamentary members, 219–20,
222–3, 225–6; flees London, 7,
227–8; at Windsor, 228–33; goes to
Holland, 230–1, 233–5; in England
during the Civil War, 2–3, 240–4;
in France during the Civil War, 3–4,
244–6; during Charles's captivity,
1–2, 4, 5–6, 8–9, 253–8, 259, 260;
and Charles's trial, 5, 9–11, 267; and
Charles's death, 11, 267–71; during
the Interregnum, 271–6; at the
Restoration, 264–7, 276–9; last
illness and death, 264, 280–1; burial,
281
APPEARANCE AND DRESS: in 1620s, 1,
34, 35, 51, 52, 54, 57, 59; in 1630s, 3,
132; in later years, 3, 265
HEALTH: taking spa waters, 41, 93, 96,
105, 211, 243, 244; anaemia, 54;
toothache, 82; early childlessness,
93, 96; pregnancies and childbirths,
96, 101, 103–5, 108–10, 115, 116–7,
155, 157, 168, 174, 243; tuberculosis,
2, 243, 265; chronic ill health after
Charles I's death, 265–6, 279, 280;
depression, 271, 273, 275
CHARACTER: love of England, 1;
charm, 3–4; wit and frivolity, 3, 34,

36, 51, 63, 126–7, 132, 136, 137; lack
of ceremony, 3, 36, 70, 119, 126;
poise and grace, 36, 39, 51, 57, 61,
79, 156; love of the countryside, 36,
120–1; happiness during the 1630s,
1–2; courage, 3, 51, 203; sadness in
exile, 1, 3, 5; political skills, 140, 151
INTERESTS AND TASTES: architecture
and gardens, 37, 131, 133, 168; art,
37, 127, 131–2; country life and
progresses, 103, 105, 120–3, 131, 137;
hunting and riding, 38, 125, 129;
jewels and clothes, 37, 52, 131;
music, 37, 89; dancing and singing,
34, 61, 122; matchmaking, 100, 130;
plays and masques, 36, 37, 78–9, 88,
89, 116, 122, 127, 128, 129–30, 167–8;
1630s cult of love and power, 116,
129–30, 132
RELIGION: religious retreats, 42, 46,
64, 66–7, 68–9, 80–1, 88, 270–1, 272;
other observances, 81, 105; religious
feeling and devotion, 63, 68, 108,
138, 140, 142, 149, 266–7, 272, 280;
protection of British Catholics,
47–8, 50, 64–5, 66, 69, 96, 102,
134–5, 140, 148, 149–51, 162: and
attempts to convert husband and
children, 47–8, 50, 143; her chapel,
52, 61–2, 137, 149, 150, 161, 178;
chapel at St James's, 81; chapel at
Somerset House, 96, 108, 133, 134,
142–3, 148, 150–1, 173, 184–5, 190,
278; prozelytising, 133–4, 147,
272–4; attitude to Anglicanism, 135;
founds devotional societies, 140, 157
COURT: her French court, 46, 52, 54,
79, 84, 87, 90, 102–3, 106; British
Protestants at her court, 61, 64, 79;
British Catholics at her court, 64,
66, 90; Catholic priests in her
household, 46, 52, 81, 84, 87, 106;
Court regulations and ceremonies,
4–5, 70, 91, 126; Finances, 52–3, 72,
80, 84, 96, 101, 106, 126, 279, 280